Society
and Natural
Resources

Society & Natural Resources Book Series

Jill Belsky, Mallika Bose, Ken Caine, Anna Haines,
Rick Krannich, and Marianne Penker

Series Editors

This series examines the complexity of interrelationships among human societies, biophysical and built environments, and natural resources and engages emergent issues and informs transformations between society and natural resources toward greater social and environmental justice, health, and sustainability and resilience.

A Community Guide to Social Impact Assessment: 2015 Fourth Edition,
    Rabel J. Burdge

The Community in Rural America, Kenneth P. Wilkinson

The Concepts, Process and Methods of Social Impact Assessment,
    Rabel J. Burdge and Colleagues

Daydreams and Nightmares: A Sociological Essay on the American
    Environment, William R. Burch Jr.

Diffusion Research in Rural Sociology: The Record and Prospects for the Future,
    Frederick C. Fliegel with Peter F. Korsching

Energy Impacts: A Multidisciplinary Exploration of North American Energy
    Development, Jeffrey B. Jacquet, Julia H. Haggerty, and Gene L. Theodori

Man, Mind and Land: A Theory of Resource Use, Walter Firey

Rural Sociology and the Environment, Donald R. Field and William R. Burch Jr.

Society and Natural Resources: A Summary of Knowledge, Michael J. Manfredo,
    Jerry J. Vaske, Brett L. Bruyere, Donald R. Field, and Perry J. Brown

Social Assessment: Theory, Process and Techniques, 3rd ed., C. Nicholas Taylor,
    C. Hobson Bryan, and Colin G. Goodrich

Three Iron Mining Towns: A Study in Cultural Change, Paul H. Landis

Society and Natural Resources

A Summary of Knowledge

Prepared for the 10th International
Symposium on Society and
Resource Management

Edited by

Michael J. Manfredo

Jerry J. Vaske

Brett L. Bruyere

Donald R. Field

Perry J. Brown

University Press of Colorado
Denver, Colorado

Society and Natural Resources Press
Logan, Utah

Published by University Press of Colorado
1624 Market Street, Suite 226
PMB 39883
Denver, Colorado 80202

The University Press of Colorado is a proud member of
Association of University Presses.

The University Press of Colorado is a cooperative publishing enterprise
supported, in part, by Adams State University, Colorado State University,
Fort Lewis College, Metropolitan State University of Denver, University of
Alaska Fairbanks, University of Colorado, University of Denver, University
of Northern Colorado, University of Wyoming, Utah State University, and
Western Colorado University.

ISBN: 978-1-64642-414-6 (paperback)
ISBN: 978-1-64642-415-3 (ebook)
https://doi.org/10.5876/9781646424153

Cataloging-in-Publication data for this title is available online at the
Library of Congress.

Cover images © LoBoCo/iStockphoto

This book was published in part to commem-
orate the 10th International Symposium on
Society and Resource Management (ISSRM)
in Keystone, Colorado. ISSRM has brought
together natural resource professionals, social
science researchers, non-government agencies,
private sector organizations, and students on an
annual basis since 1996.

Contents

**Preface to
This Edition**

**IASNR Executive
Director and the
Editorial Board of
the SNR Book Series**

Knowledge represents the fundamental roots that support our understanding of the complex relationship between society and natural resources and contributes to the sharing of ideas and wisdom that makes up a well-branched and healthy tree of social-ecological interdisciplinarity. As historians and social scientists tell us, however, we need to trace and understand our changing knowledge over time in order to improve our social-environmental world.

To explore the state of this knowledge, editors Michael J. Manfredo, Jerry J. Vaske, Brett L. Bruyere, Donald R. Field, and Perry J. Brown in 2004 published *Society and Natural Resources: A Summary of Knowledge*, which was prepared for the 10th International Symposium on Society and Resource Management (ISSRM) in Keystone, Colorado. Since 1986 the ISSRM has brought together natural resource professionals, social science researchers, non-government agencies, private sector organizations and students. (The ISSRM was re-named the International Association of Society and Natural Resources [IASNR] Conference in August 2020.) In this original volume of thirty-one chapters, an exciting period of interdisciplinary and multi-scaled approach to society and natural resource scholarship is documented. Unbeknownst to these editors, they initiated a decennial series of state-of-knowledge volumes.

Ten years later in 2014, original editors Michael Manfredo and Jerry Vaske, along with co-editors Andreas Rechkemmer and Esther Duke, expanded our state of knowledge in their edited volume *Understanding Society and Natural Resources: Forging New Strands of Integration across the Social Sciences*. In the third volume of the decennial state-of-knowledge series, our understanding of this field is further explored by editors Kate Sherren, Glad Thondhlana, and Doug Jackson-Smith on emerging perspectives, practices, and opportunities in Natural Resource Social Sciences.

This re-issue of the 2004 original first volume is an opportunity to look back at the field, while at the same time provides a deeper examination of the organization from which it grew. The IASNR, founded in 2001, is an interdisciplinary professional association that joins individuals who bring a diversity of social science and natural science backgrounds and concerns to bear on research and application strategies pertaining to natural resource issues. The IASNR was preceded by its ISSRM conference, started in 1986 at Oregon State University in Corvallis, Oregon, and its journal, *Society & Natural Resources*, first published by Taylor and Francis in 1988.

The IASNR today works with the University Press of Colorado for distribution of previous Social Ecology Press books and co-publishing of new books in the Society and Natural Resources Book Series. The SNR Book Series publishes works that examine the complexity of interrelationships among human societies, biophysical and built environments, and natural resources. We are especially interested in works that engage emergent issues and inform transformations between society and natural resources across the globe and that seek solutions that enhance social and environmental justice, health, and sustainability. The series does not privilege any particular research method, theory, or discipline; it seeks submissions that build from any—or combinations—of the environmental/natural resource social sciences. We encourage works that contribute to our understandings and actions on how global processes intersect with localities in the South or North or through comparative case studies.

We are excited by the re-issue of the first state of knowledge series volume and look forward to future editions in the decennial series.

Acknowledgments

ISSRM thanks the USDA Forest Service North Central Research Station for its financial support of this book. In particular, we thank Pamela J. Jakes, project leader for *People Forest Interactions*, and John F. Dwyer, project leader for *Natural Environments for Urban Populations*.

Many thanks are also extended to the USDA Forest Service Southern Research Station, Pacific Southwest Research Station, and USDI Bureau of Land Management for their generous contributions to this publication and to ISSRM.

A Retrospective Introduction to *Society and Natural Resources: A* *Summary of* *Knowledge*

Michael J. Manfredo

Jerry J. Vaske

Brett Bruyere

Perry Brown

The introduction of the International Symposium on Society and Resource Management (ISSRM) signified an important milestone in a broad-based transformation regarding how we think about natural resource management. To see that, it is important to reflect on how our philosophy of natural management resource evolved in the U.S. The prevailing management philosophies were borne from a rapid rise of the deleterious effects of overharvest, wildland fires, and poor land practices from the 1700s and 1800s. The need to deal with these growing problems led to the introduction of a proud professional tradition that provided protection and restoration of natural resources and allowed for "sustained yield" in serving utilitarian purposes. This tradition was forged through powerful political and legislative authority, organization structures and funded agencies, institutional arrangements, social networks, cultural beliefs and identities, and a large body of biological science. Critical to this tradition was the doctrine that decisions about natural resources would not be political but rather based on sound biological science. The decision makers, with biological expertise, became what Putnam (1977) referred to as the "technological elite" who would know what is best for the environment and consequentially be best suited to make the decisions. As Field et al. (2004) noted, "most land managers and government scientists considered people, human behavior and public use outside of their purview, or at best, intruders who brought with them problems for which they were not trained to solve. . . . The very notion of studying people, their culture, and behavior in public places did not resonate with park or forest professionals with natural science backgrounds" (p. 2). While this tradition was, in many ways, remarkably effective and made significant strides toward the ideals of the utilitarian conservation philosophy, as 20th-century America's social context and values changed, the desired outcomes from our natural resources became diversified, oppositional, and divisive. As time passed, it became increasingly obvious that problems of conservation are borne from human behavior, social institutions, and society more generally. And biology must be joined with social science information for more effective conservation planning and management. In contrast to the traditional view that biology would dictate the "right" natural resource decisions, the social sciences addressed the many voices relevant to the decision arena. They asked how we can better comprehend the social implications of decision alternatives and introduced approaches for bringing stakeholders together to seek collaborative decisions that would be more effective and enduring. They also increased the realization of how intractable social conflict can be and why this is the case.

To put the introduction of ISSRM in a chronological context, it was not until the early 1960s that social science work started to appear in professional natural resource and biological journals and agency reports. While these investigations were sometimes seen as answering mere matters of curiosity, they opened our eyes to more critical questions. The early studies were largely descriptive and focused primarily on recreation. They asked basic questions such as what segments of society use the outdoors, what do visitors do there, how much money do recreationists spend, and what would they like. These studies emerged in disciplines like parks and recreation, rural sociology, and agricultural economics. By the early 1980s, there was a recognition of the need to convene these different interests and provide a broader focus on natural resource management. This resulted in the first ISSRM that was organized by two co-authors of the original 1986 edition of this book, Don Field and Perry Brown at Oregon State University. From its inception, ISSRM coalesced social scientists working on natural resource issues and provided a focus on the importance of interdisciplinary social sciences in natural resources. Since that introduction, the presence of the social sciences in journals and conferences previously the domain of the natural sciences has increased significantly. Moreover, participation in natural resource issues has emerged from a far greater array of social science disciplinary perspectives, natural resource agencies have increased staffing of people with social science expertise, and natural resource academic programs have increased the integration of social science topics in their curricula. In many ways, ISSRM was at the inception of the "golden age of the social sciences," at least as applied to natural resource management (Buyalskaya et al., 2021).

This book was produced in association with the 2004 ISSRM conference at Colorado State University. At that time, 12 ISSRM conferences had been held, including three at international destinations. When planning the 2004 conference, we felt that it was time to ask, after almost two decades, what are the boundaries of this interdisciplinary area, what is the body of knowledge that we have assembled, what applications have we addressed, and which theories and concepts have guided the work? A review of prior conferences guided us in contacting past attendees who contributed chapters in a volume that overviewed our state of the knowledge. This book is the result of that effort. Our attempt was largely descriptive, providing a snapshot of where we were at that time relative to where we started. The idea was to provide a digest for the array of topics that had been introduced at the conferences. Authors provided a definition of topic areas including elements of the history of investigation, a synthesis and integration of main research findings, identified managerial or social significance of their area of investigation, and addressed issues for the future. As such, the book described a critical time during which social scientists were "coming in from the dark" (Field et al., 2004, p. 1).

Looking back at this document as we write this introduction, we have the benefit of reflecting on change since that time and several things are readily noticeable. In 2004, for example, there was a strong focus on outdoor recreation and human dimensions of fish and wildlife both in the book and in the 2004 ISSRM program. While these topics are still present in the ISSRM, they do not dominate the agenda. The past 20 years have witnessed a remarkable growth in attention to new areas of focus such as governance and the growth of an integrative social-ecological paradigm. There is also a less parochial involvement with specific resource issues and a greater global representation. Still, as we look at the topics covered, many concepts are as relevant and used today as they were in the past and can readily inform contemporary research efforts. Notably, Myron Floyd commented that "organizational change is a prerequisite for fostering cultural diversity in natural resource management" (2004, p. 78), which is just as relevant, if not more relevant, today as it was when it was written.

What was initiated at ISSRM in the 1980s will only become more important over time. Recent events have highlighted the seriousness of a looming, interconnected set of problems as biodiversity declines, climate change threaten livelihoods, food systems are stretched, social justice imparities lead to inequality, and zoonosis threaten our very survival. This is a time when unity of purpose is essential, but in fact, ideologies have become fractured and acrimonious worldwide. We need social science in natural resources now more than ever. It is our hope that, when future scholars look back, they will see our point-in-time state of knowledge described as a critical step in a trajectory of the social sciences rising to the fundamental challenges of social and ecological sustainability.

References

Buyalskaya, A., Gallo, M., & Camerer, C. F. (2021). The golden age of social science. *Proceedings of the National Academy of Sciences, 118*(5, e2002923118).

Field, D. R., Brown, P. J., & Burdge, R. J. (2004). Coming in from the dark. In M. J. Manfredo, J. J. Vaske, B. Bruyere, & P. J. Brown (Eds.), *Society and Natural Resources: A Summary of Knowledge* (pp. 1–8).

Floyd, M. F. (2004). Cultural diversity and natural resource management. In M. J. Manfredo, J. J. Vaske, B. Bruyere, & P. J. Brown (Eds.), *Society and Natural Resources: A Summary of Knowledge* (pp. 71–82).

Manfredo, M. J., Vaske, J. J., Bruyere, B. L., Field, D. R., & Brown, P. J. (2004). *Society and Natural Resources: A Summary of Knowledge.* Prepared for the 10th International Symposium on Society and Resource Management. St. Louis: Modern Litho.

Putnam, R. D. (1977). Elite transformation in advanced industrial societies: An empirical assessment of the theory of technocracy. *Comparative Political Studies, 10*(3), 383–412.

Society
and Natural
Resources

1

Coming in from the Dark

The Evolution of ISSRM and Social Science Research in Resource Management

Donald R. Field

Perry J. Brown

Rabel J. Burdge

The International Symposium on Society and Resource Management (ISSRM) has provided a forum for sharing social science research on natural resources and public lands. The first conference at Oregon State University in June of 1986 was the culmination of three decades of organization, legislation and individual efforts to focus social science research on problems in the use and management of public lands and natural resources.

This introductory chapter provides the background and context for the specific chapters to follow on the contributions of ISSRM to natural resource management. We describe the maturing process for our understanding of people, parks, forests and land management in general. First, we describe the events that lead up to the growth of a systematic interdisciplinary social science and management research program devoted to natural resources and the environment. Second, we outline the institutional developments that facilitated research on public lands. Third, we review the contributions of ISSRM as a venue for the comprehensive discussion of humans and natural resource systems. Lastly, we suggest a roadmap for the future of ISSRM and the International Association for Society and Natural Resources (IASNR), and on the relationship between human communities and natural resources.

Setting the Stage: Public Interest in Land Management Issues

Prior to 1960 the study of the environment and natural resources by the academic community was tangential, and if mentioned, assumed that humans were dominant and controlling of their natural environment. Prescriptions for resource management to better understand human behavior on federal and state lands were isolated events. In 1971, Klausner (1971) reviewed the content of the American Sociological Association annual meeting program from 1950 to 1970. He found one session in 1959 and another in 1967 devoted to the discussion of the environment. In the decade to follow, however, a few pioneers championed the cause of human behavior research as it related to natural resources. Walter Firey's (1977) classic volume *Man, Mind and Land* illustrated the importance of social structure and cultural linkages with natural resource systems. William Burch's (1971) essay *Daydreams and Nightmares* highlighted the interrelationship between human communities and their natural surroundings. And Beverly Driver and S. Ross Tocher (1970) began to think beyond recreational counts and reformulated recreation as a behavioral phenomenon.

In the 1950s and 1960s, most land managers and government scientists considered people, human behavior and public use outside of their purview, or at best, intruders who brought with them problems for which they were not trained to solve. People as part of nature or an integral part of the ecosystem was largely an alien idea. The very notion of studying people, their culture, and behavior in public places often did not resonate with park or forest professionals with natural science backgrounds. It was the emergence of serious social science targeted at humans and recreation issues that changed scientific practice and management protocols about human behavior and the environment.

Institutional Support for Social Science in Natural Resource Management

The development of institutional support was essential for social science research to emerge and flourish, thereby, allowing social scientists to devote systematic professional energy to research on human communities and the environment. From the 1950s through 1986, four major institutional developments facilitated the conduct and growth of social science research on natural resources and the environment: 1) formation of research centers and training programs in government and universities, 2) recognition of human communities and their relationship to the environment as legitimate sessions at annual meetings of professional societies, 3) the introduction of scholarly journals and natural resource management book series with social science content, and 4) federal legislation that contained within it the legitimization of social science research.

Social science research on people and natural resources prior to 1960 was associated with recreation and the formal study of leisure. The work was basically descriptive of visitors and their activities, and not particularly analytical. Little of the research conducted advanced our understanding of the relationship of people and public lands. The first concerted social science research effort was sponsored by the Outdoor Recreation Resources Review Commission (ORRRC), created in 1958 by the U.S. Government. As the Commission began to look at the burgeoning use of public land for recreation, it commissioned studies that examined recreation behavior and patterns of recreation use and the demographics of human populations participating in outdoor recreation.

Research Centers and Training Programs
ORRRC's work was followed by the establishment or expansion of research programs in federal land management agencies. Beginning in 1962, the USDA Forest Service (USFS) established recreation research units within the forest and range

experiment stations, many of which were located at universities. Next, the National Park Service established a small social science research program centered on a partnership concept called the *Cooperative Park Studies Units*. These units were often located on university campuses, as well. Other federal agencies (e.g., Bureau of Land Management, U.S. Army Corps of Engineers) hired social scientists, but lacking a formal research mandate, did not establish separate programs. These government programs provided the first steps toward practical knowledge about human behavior for public land management agencies.

Within the universities it was at the professional schools, and park and recreation departments, where instruction and research about human behavior associated with natural resources flourished. The addition of sociologists and social psychologists to these departments helped focus

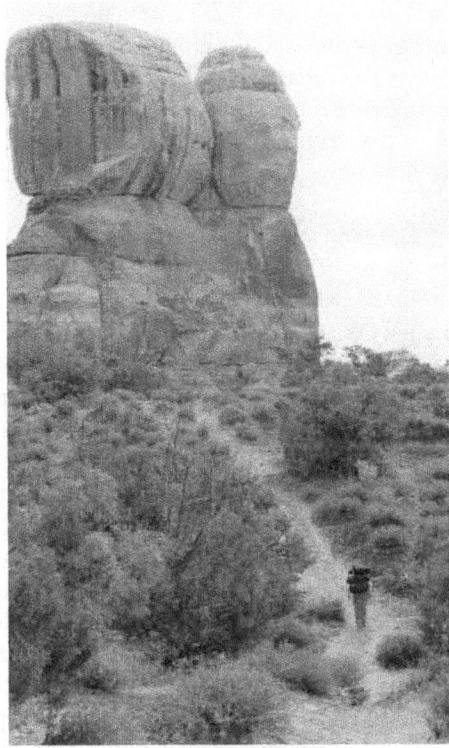

BRENT ERB

research on human behavior and social group analysis. Colleges of forestry began to expand their faculty to include social scientists who could address people-forestry issues that extended beyond just recreation behavior. Faculties from traditional academic departments were often involved as collaborators and used the research to support their graduate students.

Professional Societies and Annual Meetings
In the 1960s and 1970s, discipline-based professional societies began to organize sessions around people, natural resources and environmental concerns. The formation of the Natural Resource Research Group in 1967 within the Rural Sociological Society (RSS) was one of the first professional organizations to formally recognize the importance of environmental issues. The RSS included within its membership government social scientists and resource managers (neither of whom had advanced degrees in sociology or rural sociology). The Society of American Foresters provided a forum for research on recreation and forest-based communities. Research on fishing communities was presented at annual meetings of the Society for Applied Anthropology. But human behavior as it related to natural resource management was always at the fringe of these discipline-based societies, and the research was often too applied.

Elsewhere, small bands of social scientists were infiltrating meetings of biological scientists to focus attention on human-natural resource themes. One example is research on human-wildlife interaction (Hendee & Schoenfeld, 1973). Inspired by this early leadership, another group of scientists and practitioners gathered to organize the *Human Dimensions in Wildlife Study Group*. This group popularized the term "human dimensions" to refer to the *people* aspect of wildlife issues. That terminology has been adopted by several U.S. federal agencies to reflect both content of research on people/resource issues and in the case of the USFS, as an organizational entity within it.

Scholarly Journals and Book Series
The *Journal of Leisure Research* was first published in 1969 and many of the early contributions were from federal agency social scientists that used data from the original ORRRC studies. *Environment and Behavior* in 1971 published research on the environmental movement, public opinion on environmental issues and behavioral studies in park and outdoor recreation settings. *Leisure Sciences* and the *Journal of Park and Recreation Administration* both published research on human behavior in recreational settings in 1977 and 1979 respectively. Ann Arbor Science Press published five books under the series title *Man, Community and Natural Resources* between 1976 and 1980. Westview Press followed with a series entitled *Human Behavior and the Environment* between 1986 and 1990. There were occasional special issues of social science journals devoted to natural resource topics (e.g., the *Pacific Sociological Review* in 1971 on recreation, the *Natural Resources Journal* on public involvement in 1976), but one devoted exclusively to a comprehensive examination of human/natural resource relations did not exist. For a field of study to emerge, flourish and be sustained over time, publication outlets had to be established.

Federal Legislation
The environmental agenda of the U.S. Congress in the 1960s and early 1970s provided the impetus for social science research on natural resources to flourish. A key development was the reallocation of public land in Alaska. The Alaska Native Claims Settlement Act in 1980 allocated land rights to native groups, the State of Alaska, and the U.S. Departments of Agriculture and Interior. Additional federal legislation legitimated the public recreation on federal and state lands (e.g., Wilderness Act of 1964) and provided funding to states to expand their recreation opportunities. Other legislation called for public participation in land use planning and provided funds to do research on people and natural resources, or evaluate the impacts of public use of federal resources. Most notably, this included the National Environmental Policy Act in 1969, National Forest Management Act in 1976 and Federal Land Policy and Management Act in 1976.

The Next Step: Establishment of ISSRM
The 1970s was a period when natural resource researchers with a social science perspective were being produced by professional schools and programs of forestry, parks and recreation, and environmental studies. These new professional scholars were not from traditional social science departments and had little professional identity with professional social science or biological societies. Instead they sought an open interdisciplinary forum to present and discuss their research interests. Likewise, resource managers, foresters, park rangers, wardens, planners, policy

analysts and others were looking for a place where they could learn about the application of social science findings to resource management problems.

While improving the knowledge base on human behavior, natural resources and the environment, scientific information more often was segregated and isolated along disciplinary lines, thereby retarding the accumulation process. For example, research by rural sociologists on the adjustment of agricultural communities to farm consolidation was published in *Rural Sociology*. At the same time social scientists in colleges of forestry studying forest-dependent communities, or anthropologists studying fishing communities, or resource economists studying mining communities, would publish in their own journals. The chance to compare findings on similar resource issues seldom appeared in any annual meeting agenda. Nor would the space allotted to these issues at annual meetings be sufficient to accommodate their work and allow for an exchange of ideas.

The expansion of the research themes addressed by natural resource and environmental social scientists seldom fit with traditional academic interests. There was really no place for all to get together on a substantive issue. What was needed was a forum acknowledging and supporting interdisciplinary approaches to natural resources issues from the mix of theoretical perspectives and concepts outside of the traditional disciplinary focus. ISSRM filled a research and management niche and a new applied social science discipline was born.

Success of ISSRM Initiatives

ISSRM provided the incentive and support for both institutional and individual initiatives for interdisciplinary science and application of social science knowledge to resource management issues. The following are some of the ISSRM activities and achievements since the first symposium in 1986.

Scholarly Social Science Journals

Evaluations of the first symposium indicated a need for an interdisciplinary refereed publication for social science research on natural resources and the environment. To fill this gap, three new journals emerged. *Society and Natural Resources: An International Journal* began publication in 1988 with most of its initial articles based on papers from the first ISSRM. *Human Dimensions of Wildlife* was first organized as a session of ISSRM, and resulted in a journal by the same name in 1996. It is now offered as part of the membership package to IASNR. In the same year, a group of symposium participants started the *International Journal of Wilderness* which was later underwritten by more than a dozen institutional partners.

Expanding the Symposium Beyond North America

Hosting the ISSRM Symposium outside of North America began in 1997 when meetings were held on alternate years outside North America at the University of Belize (Belize) in 1997, University of Queensland (Australia) in 1999, and the University of Sassari in the Archipelago of LaMaddalena National Park (Sardinia, Italy) in 2002. The move to internationalize the Symposium recognizes that environmental problems and their solutions are not the same everywhere. Meeting outside North America has added new knowledge and cultural perspectives on how different countries approach natural resource issues.

As we approach the 20th year of ISSRM, attendance has grown from 300 to more than 700 researchers and managers representing the breadth of the social and biological sciences, and the resource management professions. ISSRM is indeed a forum where *managers and researchers come together* and discuss useable knowledge for addressing resource management issues. It is where science and application merge.

The International Association for Society and Natural Resources
In recent years, a group of scientists, resource extension specialists and land mangers have met and formed a new professional association. As one member pointed out, "We have a journal, we have a symposium, and we have a newsletter, now we have a professional society." (Burdge, 1999, p.261). IASNR was established in January, 2003.

IASNR is now the governing body managing ISSRM and overseeing the journal *Society and Natural Resources.* The membership and the Board of Directors have an opportunity to embrace a worldview involving scientists and resource managers and wardens from countries outside of North America. International membership is currently strongest in Australia and New Zealand, reflecting in part the 1999 meeting of the symposium in Brisbane, Australia.

New Directions for Symposium Themes
While many of the current themes will remain important for years to come, such as human dimensions of wildlife, resource dependent communities, eco-tourism and natural resource-based recreation, others need more attention. Global climate change, marine systems, water rights, the private-public interface on the boundaries of public lands, and the urban-wild land interface represent additional problem areas. However, of the important issues facing natural resource management over the next two decades, three stand out.

Diverse and Local Voices in Natural Resource Decision-Making
Social science input became more important during the 1980s as we began to recognize and enfranchise more voices in managing natural resources. These voices have added new definitions of resources, new perceptions of their value and use, personal and deep meaning of resources and places, new resource-based products and opportunities, and new means of learning and communicating about them. While some resource management institutions have been slow to recognize and hear these many voices, both social scientists and land mangers have been criticized for not considering local knowledge in decision-making. This apparent lack of attention has highlighted the importance for social science to at least focus some attention on understanding the public in agency planning, management and administration.

With the many voices of interested and affected people, the complexity of the decisions, and the long-term consequences associated with most decisions, how can we not know what is perceived, preferred, and required, and how natural resource managers impact people? As we discovered in developing forest management plans during the 1970s and 1980s, we need to develop techniques for people to effectively voice their observations and concerns, to affect collaboration in planning and decisions, and to provide continuing involvement long past the implementation of proposed actions. We must move past mere public input to active participation.

Realigning and Prioritizing the Multiple Uses of Public Lands
"Multiple-use" on public lands has traditionally emphasized extraction and consumption of resources over watershed management, wildlife habitat preservation and recreational use. In the decades ahead, the focus will be on sustainability of resources, endangered species, watershed management, wildlife, fire management, recreational opportunities, and a variety of non-traditional uses (e.g., mushroom gathering, plant collection, protection of cultural artifacts). Furthermore, cultural history is a key part of indigenous use of public lands. Meanings attached to natural resources by all people must be understood if we are to sustain the resources and provide new multiple use opportunities.

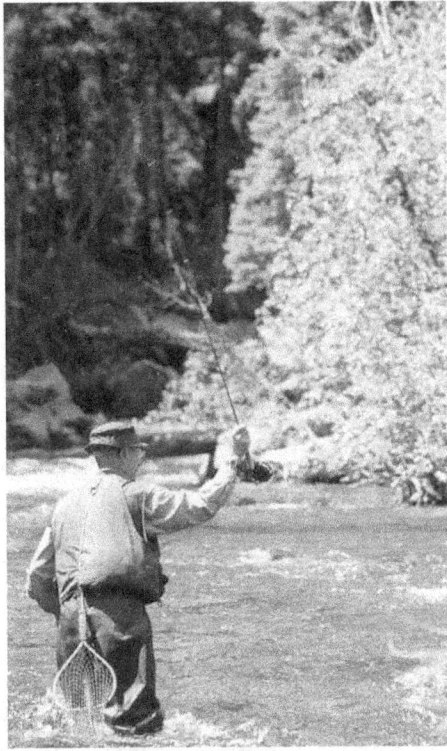

Communities and Collaboration
During the past two decades, it has become quite clear that persons living in communities either dependent upon or surrounded by natural resources desire more participation in decisions that affect their lives and livelihoods. As a result, collaborative models for discussion and decision-making are being developed and implemented. These models often go beyond local needs and concerns and attempt to enfranchise diverse local and national voices. As we consider the appropriate arrangements for governance of public lands particularly, a rich field of inquiry is before us as social scientists. We have an opportunity to learn how to help communities build capacity for their participation in natural resource decision-making, and to learn how to integrate across land ownerships, geographies, economic sectors and human concerns.

In Retrospect
Social scientists studying human behavior, natural resources and the environment are a diverse lot having arrived at their "calling" from programs in recreation and forestry, environmental studies, as well as a variety of traditional academic disciplines. They share an interdisciplinary spirit and a responsibility toward the application of their knowledge to assist public land managers. They share a conviction that human behavior and culture are integral, not separate, parts of natural resources.

Social and biophysical perspectives come together when considering natural resource and environmental questions. The issue is no longer one of whether or not humans are part of the ecosystem: The issue now is how we incorporate human community within ecosystem management and within management of resources. While interdisciplinary inquiry has matured in both theory and practice, it is the integration of social science knowledge with the practice of natural resource management that is only now unfolding in the public and private sector.

We can learn and slowly let our research seep into natural resource decisions, but the pace of change in natural resources does not allow such luxury. What the research shows should be used now; it is on our backs to help people see the relevance of the information and ideas we generate. Social scientists must work with administrators and managers to challenge and support their decisions, and to help them learn how to listen to people and apply research information.

We are in a place of unusual grandeur to celebrate the 10th ISSRM. The Rocky Mountains are a national treasure, a special place, and an asset of unparalleled importance. They, like the many other resources throughout the world, are to be sustained and protected for all present and future generations. In this place, as researchers and managers we must learn how to live in our mountains so that we prosper socially, economically, and spiritually while ensuring that the mountain heritage lives on. How we do this in the face of tremendous and rapid social change will challenge all of us, especially those of us most interested in human behavior, the human condition, and all that it supports. ISSRM is one vehicle we have to share what we are learning and to explore how we might best confront the future.

The chapters to follow will highlight the variety of topics covered during ISSRM's 20-year history and the lessons learned from interdisciplinary inquiry and exchange on the association of human behavior, natural resource and the environment. They provide a brief synthesis of our past, while pointing the way to tomorrow.

References

Burch, Jr., W. R. (1999). *Daydreams and nightmares: A sociological essay on the American environment*. Middleton: Social Ecology Press.

Burdge, R. J. (1999). We have journal, we have a meeting, why not a professional society? *Society and Natural Resources, 12*, 261-264.

Driver, B. L., & Tocher. S. R. (1970). Toward a behavioral interpretation of recreational engagements, with implications for planning. In B.L. Driver (Ed.), *Elements of outdoor recreation planning*, Ann Arbor, MI: University of Michigan Press.

Firey, W. (1999). *Man, mind and land*. Middleton: Social Ecology Press.

Hendee, J. C., & Schoenfeld, C. (Eds). (1973). *Human dimensions in wildlife programs*. Washington, DC: The Wildlife Management Institute.

Klausner, S. (1971). *On man and his environment*. San Francisco: Jossey-Bass.

2

Philosophical Perspectives on Natural Resources

Examining the Past to Understand the Future

Alan Ewert

Bill Stewart

"Philosophy is . . . the front trench in the siege of truth. Science is captured territory; and behind it are those secure regions in which knowledge and art build our imperfect and marvelous world."

—Will Durant, 1966

Philosophical perspectives on natural resources take several directions. Experts and scientists who study natural resources have a long history of such discussion (Catlin, 1832; Marsh, 1864; Williams & Stewart, 1998), and one that overlaps with issues related to philosophy of science (Carnap, 1966; Gergen, 1994). Dominant cultural values, as they reflect philosophies toward the environment, also provide direction for discussion (Botkin, 1990; Burke, 1985). In addition, natural resource management philosophies and approaches to decision-making have a meaningful history of thought (Manring, 1998; Minteer & Manning, 1999; Mohai & Jakes, 1996; Twight, 1983).

Philosophical perspective also are linked to the values and beliefs of park visitors, interest groups, and other publics – referred to as *stakeholders* – who use and enjoy natural resources and environments, and who become involved in planning processes (Cronon, 1992, 1995; Kruger & Shannon, 2000). The purpose of this chapter is to highlight each of these directions, and in doing so, develop linkages between philosophical perspectives and roles for social scientists who study society and resource management.

Philosophical Issues from Past ISSRM

Not surprisingly, numerous discussions from the previous ten International Symposia on Society and Resource Management (ISSRM) have focused on a variety of philosophical issues related to natural resource management. These issues include the following:

- The effect of personal experience in a place on

values, beliefs and philosophical orientations regarding personal meanings and knowledge toward natural resources.

- Relationships between socioeconomic factors, values, and philosophies assigned to natural resources by individuals and groups.

- The effect of culture and race on one's value orientation and understanding of natural resources. Different groups may expect different benefits from natural resources and these expectations may blend with events such as acculturation and assimilation.

- Values may influence, and may be influenced by, an individual's philosophical perspective of natural resources.

- Traditional dichotomies such as people-nature, individual-group, use-preservation and beliefs-knowledge may influence both individual and collective understandings of the natural world.

- Perspectives of natural resources representing market-related values may affect one's philosophy different than non-market values.

- There are philosophical concerns in moving from an authority-based paradigm of decision-making to a community-based process of decision-making.

Quite obviously, there is a broad spectrum of issues and topics related to philosophical perspectives of the natural environment. Moreover, it has become clear that there is a growing role for social scientists and academics involved in natural resource management, as society struggles to resolve the many issues germane to its natural resource base.

Definition, Importance and Process

For the purpose of this chapter, philosophical perspectives on natural resources are defined as a set of beliefs, precepts, or principles that underlie a particular evaluation or behavior regarding how natural resources should be used and how they should be managed. While defining the term *philosophical perspectives*, the simplicity of the definition belies the complexity and fluidity of the construct. And, in one sense, this complexity and fluidity speak to the very heart of the problem, that is, the wide and often divisive nature regarding how our natural resources should be valued and managed. In essence, underlying this chapter is the belief that a substantial portion of those disagreements can be traced to differences in the beliefs, precepts, and values that provide the under-girding for one's philosophical view about natural resources.

Aspects of Philosophy of Science

Scientific research is challenged to adequately capture the relationship between philosophy and practice. While science looks for uniformity and generalizability, philosophical perspectives speak to the affective side of human nature: feelings, intuition, attitudes. Thus, the scientific tendency of looking for a uniformity of nature principle tends to result in reductionism and an oversimplification of a complex issue (Goran, 1974).

Adding to this oversimplification are the paradoxes between permanence and change, stability and fluidity, certainty and uncertainty; paradoxes that have engaged philosophers, theologians, scientists, and poets for more than two thousand years (Gergen, 1994). If, indeed, our understanding of the world and the way it works is in a constant state of change, how does this fact mesh with Carnap's (1966) statement regarding the purpose of science: "The more systematic observations of science reveal certain repetitions or regularities in the world . . . The laws of science are nothing more than statements expressing these regularities as precisely as possible" (p. 3)? More precisely, if the underlying philosophy that serves to guide and inform us about natural resources changes over time, how does the management and use of these natural resources also change? As Gergen (1994) stated, "What is learned or 'known' at any given instant may be irrelevant to the next" (p. 1).

Understanding the often tacit philosophy an individual uses to make judgments concerning natural resources is a messy business and almost entirely within the purview of the social sciences. Gergen (1994) compared the natural and social sciences and saw very different results, and thus questioned their goals: "In contrast to the mighty oaks of the natural sciences, one might describe the social sciences as a sprawling thicket. The oaks . . . seem sturdy, powerful, and reliable. In contrast, the [social sciences] seem to have no clear and dependable product" (p. 3).

From a different approach, others have labeled natural resource issues as *wicked* problems (Brown & Harris, 1992; Shindler & Cramer, 1999), and suggest that goals for social science are related to developing the full complexity of issues. These goals of social science are often in direct contrast to the implied goals of the natural sciences, which generally are to reduce the natural world into simplified relationships (Patterson & Williams, 1998).

Finally, an individual's philosophical perspective is seldom isolated from the larger social concerns and movements that occur simultaneously. Toward this end, the next section examines the history of philosophical perspectives.

Dominant Cultural Values
As children we learned that our ancestors often had to wrestle the materials for food, shelter, and sustenance from the natural environment. Thus, the environment was usually viewed with hostile intent; an idea abetted by the Judeo-Christian tradition of believing the natural world belonged to humans for both their exploitation and development (Nash, 1968). Within the American context, it was not until after European settlement occurred and the problems of getting food, protection of hearth and home, and securing adequate shelter were addressed that developing philosophies concerning natural resources began to differ from a *multiply and conquer* mentality.

Prior to the Industrial Revolution in the U.S., nature was conceived as divinely created, perfectly ordered, and organic. Not surprisingly, this nicely coincided with the developing creation of science that searched for the regularities and order of the world. Thus, as epitomized in the early writings of George Catlin (1832) and George Perkins Marsh (1864), nature, if left undisturbed by humans, would assume an order and structure of both beauty and efficiency. Similar to this Romantic view of nature, the Trancendentalists viewed the natural world as epitomizing spiritual truth and morality (Thoreau, 1851).

BRENT ERB

In this world of dichotomies and paradoxes, it is not surprising that while proponents were extolling the Romantic and Transcendental views of nature, a broader social movement was developing that tended to look in another direction. In this case, Social Darwinism was proving to be an enticing philosophical perspective: It united the natural and social worlds (Burke, 1985). Instead of virtue and beauty, the natural world was based on survival of the fittest, and so was the social world. Natural resources were there to use and exploit. Likewise, individuals and groups in society were to be organized and controlled in order to produce wealth and material goods. And the role of government was simple: to facilitate individuals in the pursuit of their own self-interests.

Thus, our ancestors were faced with a mix of perspectives regarding not only what natural resources were for, but how they should be managed. Cahn (1995) argued that American political culture emerged, and operates from an awkward marriage of two disparate philosophies: 1) facilitation of individual self-interest (Lockean Liberalism), and 2) a primary concern for the public good (Civic Republicanism). The development of Lockean and Civic Republicanism perspectives may have manifested themselves into the current categorizations of *anthropocentrism* (i.e., human centered) and *biocentrism* (i.e., ecology centered), and further still into the "use vs. preservation" dichotomy.

Botkin (1990) suggested that by the 17th century, nature was also thought of as machine-like or as a creature. Nature, as machine, implied innumerable parts, all fitting together, like an engine full of gears. As a creature, the Earth was looked upon as being similar to an animal or plant. From a contemporary perspective, this view was extended by positing that the machine had a life of its own, as embodied in the Gaia hypothesis first proposed by Lovelock (1995) that the Earth behaves like a self-regulating, super organism that modifies its environmental components to meet threats and adjust to change.

Perhaps not surprisingly, the 1800s saw the emergence of a number of events that had profound influence on the public's view of natural resources. First was the emergence of the perception that natural resources were, indeed, limited and finite. With vast swaths of forests now falling to the axe, it wasn't necessarily true that the homesteader or lumberjack could always go over the next ridge for more. Second, the frontier came to an end with the announcement by Frederick Turner in 1893 that there was no longer a continuous line of undeveloped, and presumably uncivilized, lands. And finally, the philosophy of utilitarianism emerged. Utilitarianism embraced the concept that humans could be powerful change agents for good, particularly by using technical expertise and scientific management (Forbes & Lindquist, 2000) to produce the greatest good for the greatest number (Shideler & Hendricks, 1991). Once taming the natural environment was considered complete, Americans turned their attention to philosophical perspectives that were based less on survival, and more toward nature as divine creation, symbolic of truths, and aesthetic beauty (Thomas, 1983).

Management Philosophies

O'Riordan (1995) believed that four basic tensions affect the way environmental philosophies influence management of natural resources: 1) the desire for dominance versus the reality of dependence, 2) efficiency versus equity, 3) the demands and desires of the present versus those of future generations, and 4) the need for individual property rights versus belief in the public good.

In a fashion similar to the previously discussed terms of biocentrism and anthropocentrism, O'Riordan (1995) suggested that two fundamental environmental perspectives emerged since the 1970s: *technocentrism* and *ecocentrism*. The technocentric view is hierarchical, manipulative, and managerial. Its advocates believe that efficient, self-regulating markets, private property rights, technology, research, creativity, and ingenuity can ensure the proper use of natural resources for the betterment of humankind. Conversely, those individuals classified as ecocentrics have little or no faith in large-scale technology and development, and instead, embrace community-scale projects such as natural wetlands for local water purification, and believe in the morality of ecological principles. Not surprisingly, there is a growing body of literature that suggests any long-term solutions and approaches will lie in embracing tensions between technocentrism and ecocentrism, and charting some middle ground. For example, Norton (1991) posited that most environmental issues can be moved toward solution through a pragmatic, weakened version of anthropocentrism.

Based on the philosophical minds in the mid 1800s to early 1900s of Charles Peirce, William James, and John Dewey, pragmatism contends that truth is established by practicability, or things that actually work. From this standpoint, any philosophical perspective that leads to long-term solutions which will actually work is the one to support. Thus, if true, what the preceding statement suggests is that society is moving away from contentious debates over values and principles, and instead, toward a realm of discerning what management actions will actually work and be acceptable by stakeholders (Minteer & Manning, 1999). This approach often includes collaboration and partnerships in its process (Manring, 1999; Yaffee, Phillips, Frentz, Hardy, Maleki & Thorpe, 1996).

Stakeholder Philosophies

A starting point from which to understand stakeholders' philosophical perspectives is to appreciate their many different viewpoints and view them collectively as philosophical pluralism. For example, the commonly accepted "use vs. preservation" framework splits philosophical perspectives into two mutually exclusive camps. In doing so, it represents a false divide that oversimplifies the boundaries of environmental discussions (Gottlieb, 1993; O'Riordan, 1981). Resource managers must understand the various philosophical positions of their stakeholders and design planning processes that address the collection of these positions. There are several roles for social scientists that could facilitate managerial understanding and decision-making within a stakeholder context of philosophical pluralism.

The beliefs, precepts, and principles that underlie stakeholder perspectives on any given issue are intimately connected to meanings attributed to places. These meanings have been constructed through a variety of contexts, including: personal histories with a place, communities of friends and family, and organizational cultures of one's workplace. For the purposes of this chapter, the origins of these meanings are not as important as the recognition that these meanings are socially-constructed, yet typically viewed as "truths" by those who hold them.

By casting environmental meanings as stories we tell about ourselves and our landscapes, Cronon (1992) suggests that beliefs, values, and principles about natural environments become grounded in the places and events of our lives. At first glance, our stories about the places in our lives may not have the usual markings of philosophy, yet as Cronon (1992) and others (Bonnifield, 1979; Glover, 2003; Worster, 1979) have thoroughly developed, it is just such narratives that provide the underlying reasons for our evaluation and behavior toward natural resources. Several other scholars also have suggested that it is only through the use of narratives that humans are able to make meaning of the places and events in their lives (Linde, 1993; Polkinghorne, 1988; Rappaport, 2000).

By positioning environmental meanings as being best represented by individual and community narratives, philosophical perspectives of stakeholders become idiosyncratic to place. In short, decision-making forums each have their localized context in which to understand the pluralism of stakeholder perspectives (Brandenburg & Carroll, 1995). These localized contexts need recognition, and explicit understanding of the tensions that exists within the collection of stakeholder narratives. Philosophical pluralism of decision-making suggests that resource managers need to continue their efforts to know their stakeholders, and to enhance ways in which stakeholders represent themselves (Schroeder, 1996; Zube, Friedman & Simcox, 1989). The flip side of stakeholder representation is *social learning* where stakeholders not only represent themselves, but witness the representation of other stakeholders. In forums with a mutual exchange of narratives, stakeholders may learn about themselves and about other stakeholders, which carries potential for development of social capital and a stronger sense of community (Kruger & Shannon, 2000; Yankelovich, 1991).

Expectations for Future Philosophical Issues

The development of philosophical issues has been a fast-moving discourse since the first ISSRM. Expectations for the future are, at best, speculations from a particular vantage point in time. Our expectations include further development of philosophical perspectives that:

- Embrace urban land ethics directed at environmental responsibility in worked landscapes and stewardship for our daily lifestyle (see Halweil, 2002; White, 1995).

- Question concepts connected to "pristine" land, and cast preservation and other protected areas as ecological restoration projects, albeit ones in need of a vision or philosophical justification for restoration (see Abram, 1996; Cole, 2000; Jordan, 1999).

- Are sensitive to place and idiosyncratic to stakeholder and their localities in order to address movement away from authority-based paradigms to community-based processes of decision-making (Brandenburg & Carroll, 1995; Kruger & Shannon, 2000; Manring, 1998).

- Explicitly recognize meanings of nature as being socially constructed, and in doing so, expose problems with traditional philosophies by anchoring discourse in critical perspectives sensitive to gender, race, and class (Hayles, 1995; Merchant, 2003).

Continued Roles for Social Scientists

As a starting point for social scientists, the recognition that any collection of stakeholders embraces multiple philosophical perspectives affords at least two essential roles for social scientists: 1) representation of stakeholders, and 2) development of decision-making forums that allow for social learning.

Representation of stakeholders' philosophical perspective is a challenge. Dominant culture myths about society and nature (e.g., preservation, wise-use, pristine land) may not be a good fit for a given localized issue. Stakeholders may struggle with ways in which to represent their perspectives and inadvertently draw upon dominant cultural myths to help them articulate who they are and what they believe. Philosophical perspectives, even as reflected in narratives, are often difficult to articulate. Social scientists are trained for psychological and social assessment techniques, and should maintain and enhance this function they already serve. The important point for enhancement is to further appreciate community-based narratives as representations of philosophical perspectives. In other words, resist the urge to impose dominant cultural philosophies about society and natural resources.

American society is challenged to developed decision-making forums that are not adversarial, competitive, and dichotomizing. There are a growing number of forums for public land decision-making that provide opportunities to build community, improve one's sense of belonging, and create value within the decision-making process. Given an explicit pluralism of philosophies, rather than some opposing dualism, stakeholders need to recognize the complexity of decision-making. Forums that foster dialogue need further exploration regarding their potential for social learning and civic discovery (Manring, 1998; Walker & Daniels, 1996).

In their quest for a civic science, Kruger and Shannon (2000) championed approaches to inquiry that allow people to learn from one another. Helford (2000) also suggested that social learning should be an important part of natural resource management, but that forums for such learning are often not included in planning processes. Converging with trends in the planning literature, social scientists in natural resource management may become involved with collaborative learning processes in roles that mediate between stakeholders and facilitate decision-making, sometimes referred to as a *bricoleur* (Innes & Booher, 1999).

Conclusion

Philosophical issues that connect science, management, culture, and stakeholders to natural resources are important for researchers to understand. From a long-term perspective, the answers are often not as important as the development of questions that are posed. New questions ultimately foster creative responses to resource conflicts and improved ways of making decisions. Social scientists have many roles in the interplay between developing questions, responding to management problems, and improving human welfare. Several of the tensions, and suggestions for reconciliation, were highlighted in this chapter, including:

- In natural resource management, the natural and social sciences have fundamentally different perspectives on what should be studied and how it should be studied.

- Science is a human endeavor and not autonomous from the ambient social undercurrents in society.

- There is a wide diversity of philosophies regarding natural resources and the environment.

- There is not one *right* philosophy.

- It is complex and challenging for stakeholders to represent their philosophy on natural resources and the environment.

- Tensions exist between human-centered and ecologically-centered philosophies. The goal is not to reconcile the tension, but to reach acceptable decisions.

- Stakeholders learn about philosophies held by other stakeholders; they recognize tensions between various philosophies, and there is promise that such recognition leads to more acceptable natural resource decisions.

There is still much to learn regarding the relationship between philosophical perspectives and human behavior towards natural resource management. Perhaps the statement provided by Aldo Leopold (1949) who talked about the connection between philosophy and behavior, is the direction we should heed: *"I have read many definitions of what is a conservationist, and written not a few myself, but I suspect that the best one is not written with a pen, but with an axe. It is a matter of what a man thinks about while chopping, or while deciding what to chop. A conservationist is one who is humbly aware that with each stroke he is writing his signature on the face of the land. (p. 68)."*

References

Abram, D. (1996). *The Spell of the sensuous: Perception and language in a more-than-human world.* New York: Pantheon.

Bonnifield, P. (1979). *The Dust Bowl: Men, dirt, and depression.* Albuquerque, NM: University of New Mexico Press.

Botkin, D. B. (1990). *Discordant harmonies: A new ecology for the twenty-first century.* New York: Oxford University Press

Brandenburg, A., & Carroll, M. (1995). Your place or mine?: The effect of place creation on environmental values and landscape meanings. *Society and Natural Resources,* 8, 381-398.

Brown, J., & Harris, C. (1992). The U.S. Forest Service: Toward the new resource management paradigm?" *Society and Natural Resources,* 5, 231-245.

Burke, J. (1985). *The day the universe changed.* Boston: Little, Brown, and Company.

Cahn, M. A. (1995). *Environmental deceptions: The tension between Liberalism and environmental policymaking in the United States.* New York: State University of New York Press.

Carnap, R. (1966). *An introduction to the philosophy of science.* New York: Basic Books.

Catlin, G. (1832). *North American Indians: Being letters and notes on their manners, customs, and conditions, written during eight years' travel amongst the wildest tribes in North America,* 1832-1839. London.

Cole, D. (2000). Paradox of the primeval: Ecological restoration in wilderness. *Ecological Restoration,* 18 (2), 77-86.

Cronon, W. (1992). A place for stories: Nature, history, and narrative. *Journal of American History,* 78 (4), 1347-1376.

Cronon, W. (1995). The trouble with wilderness; Or, getting back to the wrong nature. In W. Cronon (Ed.), *Uncommon ground: Toward reinventing nature* (pp. 69-90). New York: Norton.

Forbes, W., & Lindquist, C. (2000). Philosophical, professional, and environmental ethics: An overview for foresters. *Journal of Forestry,* 98 (7), 4-10.

Gergen, K. J. (1994). *Toward transformation in social knowledge.* London: SAGE.

Glover, T. (2003). The story of the Queen Smith Memorial Garden: Resisting a dominant cultural narrative. *Journal of Leisure Research*, 35 (2), 190-212.

Goran, M. (1974). *Science and anti-science*. Ann Arbor, MI: Ann Arbor Science.

Gottlieb, R. (1993). *Forcing the Spring: The transformation of the American environmental movement*. Washington DC: Island Press.

Halweil, B. (2002). Farming in the public interest. In C. Flavin, H. French, & G. Gardner (Eds.), *State of the world 2002: A Worldwatch Institute report on progress toward a sustainable society* (pp. 51-74). New York: Norton.

Hayles, K. (1995). Simulated nature and natural simulations: Rethinking the relation between the beholder and the world. In W. Cronon (Ed.) *Uncommon ground: Toward reinventing nature* (pp. 409-425). New York: Norton.

Helford, R. (2000). Constructing nature as constructing science: Expertise, activist science, and public conflict in the Chicago wilderness. In P. Gobster & R. Hull (Eds.), *Restoring Nature: Perspectives from the social sciences and humanities* (pp. 119-142). Washington, DC: Island Press.

Innes, J., & Booher, D. (1999). Consensus building as role playing and bricolage: Toward a theory of collaborative planning. *Journal of the American Planning Association*, 65 (1), 9-26.

Jordan, W. (1999). Nature and culture. *Ecological Restoration*, 17 (4), 187-188.

Kruger, L., & Shannon, M. (2000). Getting to know ourselves and our places through participation in civic social assessment. *Society and Natural Resources*, 13, 461-478.

Leopold, A. (1949). *A Sand County almanac and sketches here and there*. New York: Oxford University Press.

Linde, C. (1993). *Life stories, the creation of coherence*. New York: Oxford University Press.

Lovelock, J. E. (1995). *Ages of Gaia: A biography of our living earth*. New York: W.W. Norton & Company.

Manring, N. (1998). Alternative dispute resolution and organizational incentives in the U.S. Forest Service. *Society and Natural Resources*, 11, 67-80.

Marsh, G.P. (1864). *Man and nature; Or, physical geography as modified by human action*. New York: Charles Scribner.

Merchant, C. (2003). *Reinventing Eden: The fate of nature in Western culture*. New York: Routledge.

Minteer, B. A., & Manning, R. E. (1999). Pragmatism in environmental ethics: Democracy, pluralism, and the management of nature. *Environmental Ethics*, 21(2), 191-207.

Mohai, P., & Jakes, P. (1996). The Forest Service in the 1990s: Is it headed in the right direction? *Journal of Forestry*, 94(1), 31-37.

Nash, R. (1968). *The American environment: Readings in the history of conservation.* Reading, MA: Addison-Wesley.

Norton, B. G. (1991). *Toward unity among environmentalists.* New York: Oxford University Press.

O'Riordan, T. (1981). *Environmentalism.* London: Prion.

O'Riordan, T. (1995). Frameworks for choice: Core beliefs and the environment. *Environment*, 37(8), 4-9; 25-29.

Patterson, M., & Williams, D. (1998). Paradigms and problems: The practice of social science in natural resource management. *Society and Natural Resources*, 11, 279-295.

Polkinghorne, D. E. (1988). *Narrative knowing and the human sciences.* Albany, NY: State University of New York Press.

Rappaport, J. (2000). Community narratives: Tales of terror and joy. *American Journal of Community Psychology*, 28(1), 1-24.

Schroeder, H. (1996). *Voices from Michigan's Black River: Obtaining information on "special places" for natural resource planning.* (General Technical Report NC-184). St. Paul, MN: USDA Forest Service North Central Experiment Station.

Shindler, B., & Cramer, L. (1999). Shifting public values for forest management: Making sense of wicked problems. *Western Journal of Applied Forestry*, 14(1), 28-34.

Shideler, J. C., & Hendricks, R.L. (1991). The legacy of early ideas of conservation: Tracing the evolution of a movement. *Journal of Forestry*, 89(10), 20-23.

Thomas, K. (1993). *Man and the natural world: Changing attitudes in England, 1500-1800.* London: Allen Lane.

Thoreau, H.D. (1851). *Excursion, the writings of Henry David Thoreau.* Boston: Ticknor and Fields.

Twight, B. (1983). *Organizational values and political power: The Forest Service versus the Olympic National Park.* University Park, PA: Pennsylvania State University Press.

Walker, G., & Daniels, S. (1996). The Clinton Administration, the Northwest Forest Conference, and managing conflict: When talk and structure collide. *Society and Natural Resources*, 9, 77-91.

White, R. (1995). "Are you an environmentalist or do you work for a living": Work and nature. In W. Cronon (Ed.) *Uncommon ground: Toward reinventing nature* (pp. 171-185). New York: Norton.

Williams, D., & Stewart, S. (1998). Sense of place: An elusive concept that is finding a place in ecosystem management. *Journal of Forestry*, 66 (5), 18-23.

Worster, D. (1979). *Dust Bowl: The Southern plains in the 1930s.* New York: Oxford University Press.

Yaffee, S., Phillips, A., Frentz, I., Hardy, P., Maleki, S., & Thorpe, B. (1996). *Ecosystem management in the United States: An assessment of current experience.* Washington, DC: Island Press.

Yankelovich, D. (1991). *Coming to public judgment: Making democracy work in a complex world.* Syracuse, NY: Syracuse University Press.

Zube, E., Friedman, S., & Simcox, D. (1989). Landscape change: Perceptions and physical measures. *Environmental Management*, 13 (5), 639-644.

3

Social Sciences and Natural Resources Management

An Assessment of Advances

George H. Stankey

Stephen F. McCool

Public debate over the sustainability and use of natural resources and ecosystems is increasingly contentious and divisive. The challenges for public and private sector decision-makers at local, regional and national levels are equally volatile, complex and contested. This chapter examines the impact, contributions and challenges facing the social sciences as they seek to contribute to efforts to address these challenges. It offers a foundation for understanding how the social sciences can contribute to community discourse and deliberation about the sustainability of natural resources and ecosystems. The observations are interpretive and indicative, and they derive from several sources: our collective 60+ years as social scientists working with natural resource managers, scientists and policy makers; an overview of trends in publication in *Society & Natural Resources* as well as the wider social science literature, and; discussions at previous International Symposia on Society and Resource Management (ISSRM).

Aspirations

In the inaugural issue of *Society & Natural Resources*, co-editors Burdge and Field established a goal to publish articles that featured the "interaction of the social with the biological and the social with the physical environment since we believe that the beginning steps in understanding a resource problem require an interdisciplinary perspective embracing the social and natural sciences" (Burdge & Field, 1988, p. 1).

The importance of this goal was reflected in the opening essay of that first issue: *Improving Interdisciplinary Research: Integrating the Social and Natural Sciences* (Heberlein, 1988). Like Burdge and Field, Heberlein expressed concern about the future of social science research in natural resources. He cited significant barriers facing efforts to integrate the social sciences into natural resource decision-making, including the perceived lack of rigor and relevancy, a lack of organizational support and rewards, and issues related to power and control. Although the world is an integrated place, government agencies, academics and scientific communities sometimes are not. Carved and molded by disciplines, bureaucracies, cultures, and egos, integrated research and application are faced with substantial challenges. Although the potential envisioned by Burdge, Field, Heberlein and others might be shared by some, for many, integration remains more of an obstacle and a burden than a desired condition.

But how well has that original motivating intent of *Society & Natural Resources* been met? More importantly, to what extent has social science research become an important and substantive component of the natural resource decision-making process and a source of understanding to facilitate the integration process (Clark, Stankey, Brown, Burchfield, Haynes & McCool, 1999)? To the extent that efforts to foster integrated management approaches have fallen short of this goal, has social science research improved understanding as to why this is so? To what extent have the social sciences moved beyond a passive and descriptive role to one in which they are actively engaged in framing questions and constructing answers? Have the social sciences helped fashion persuasive arguments in support of more integrative approaches, despite their admittedly more difficult and time-consuming character?

These are difficult issues. This chapter's effort to assess progress is grounded in both our experience as practicing social scientists, as well as a more systematic look at the research undertaken within the social sciences to address them. Culhane's (2001) analysis of the contents of the first 10 years of *Society & Natural Resources* provides a baseline from which to assess the topics and issues on which scientists have reported. Although obviously not all social science research on natural resources is limited to *Society & Natural Resources*, the assumption is that the journal's content resembles the type of research being conducted. Table 1 shows the breakdown of topics Culhane found in the first 10 years (i.e., Volumes 1-10). The data show that no one singular topic or question dominated social science research as reported in the journal during this period. But, have the questions changed? To address this issue, we conducted a similar analysis for volumes 11 though 16. While the number of articles per year has increased (from about 50 to nearly 80), content remained almost the same as reported for the first 10 years.

Several aspects of the data in Table 1 are noteworthy. First, there is little evidence of economic analyses. Advances in neo-classical and ecological economics have accelerated understanding in which resources are allocated and valued. Although economists have numerous journals in which to publish, given the aspirations for integration, the lack of economic articles might contribute to more provincialism on the part of other social sciences.

Second, identifying and evaluating the influences of institutions and cultural factors on individuals and their decisions continue to be a major line of inquiry. Since the inception of *Society & Natural Resources*, the role of institutions and cultural norms in influencing the acceptability or appropriateness of natural resource management actions has become increasingly apparent. Such work has the potential for contributing insights about how fundamental changes, such as in legal processes, can occur.

Third, there has been relatively little attention to methodology. The analysis did not include an assessment of methods used, but it appears likely that the foundation

Topic	Volumes 1-10	Percent	Volumes 11-16	Percent	Percent change
Public or protected Lands	75	10.3	23	5.2	- 5.1
Natural Resources, resource development	60	8.3	70	15.8	+7.5
Resource conservation, non-consumptive use	63	8.7	45	10.2	+1.5
Agriculture and fisheries	77	10.6	27	6.1	- 4.5
Rural sociology	94	12.9	28	6.3	- 6.6
Culture and individual behavior	85	11.7	74	16.7	+0.5
Decision Making and Institutional Behavior	100	13.8	60	13.6	- 0.2
Pollution Regulation and land use	49	6.7	17	3.8	- 2.9
Economics	45	6.2	21	4.8	- 1.4
Theory and philosophy	47	6.5	37	8.4	+1.9
Methodology	31	4.3	30	6.8	+2.5
Green Business	0	0	4	0.9	+0.9
Restoration	0	0	3	0.6	+0.9
Ecotourism	0	0	3	0.6	+0.6
Totals (non book review)	318	100	442	97.7	

Table 1. Topics addressed in *Society and Natural Resources* since 1988. (adapted from Culhane, 2001)

for social science remains a positivistic paradigm relying on quantitative models, despite critiques of post-modernism and growing interest in qualitative methodologies (Kruger & Sturtevant, 2003; Patterson & Williams, 1998).

In sum, the barriers to integration cited by Heberlein (1988) largely still exist, although progress has been made, such as on methodological weakness or perceived illegitimacy. However, there remain issues with respect to power differentials in large-scale, integrated ecosystem assessments. For example, to what extent are the basic assumptions of such exercises shared across disciplines. To what extent are problem definitions mutually constructed? To what extent does the assessment process foster mutual respect and equal access to information and participation in modeling exercises? Addressing these issues remains a major goal for many social scientists.

Social Science Contributions to Natural Resource and Ecosystem Policy

What factors have given rise to the growing recognition of the role of social science in natural resource policy development? First, there is a growing awareness among

BRENT ERB

natural resource managers and policy-makers that the dilemmas they face are fundamentally social in nature. This emerging recognition acknowledges that conflict over resource values and uses is a function of the meanings ascribed to landscapes, resources and ecosystems. Indeed, it is only with the perception of utility in any landscape element that society assigns the concept of resource, whether for commodity, spiritual or cultural values (Firey, 1960). Because U.S. society is increasingly pluralistic, the multiple meanings associated with natural resources will grow. These potentially conflicted meanings lead to a series of political and substantive issues such as for whose meanings we manage, what choice processes are employed, how meanings change over time and scale, and what underlying factors drive these changes.

Recognition that natural resource issues are largely social in nature has accelerated the need for increasing social science contributions to managing, mitigating and resolving conflicts. These contributions include ways in which agency decision-making structures and processes affect how decisions are made, the types of knowledge perceived as legitimate, and the processes relied upon to respond to a diversity of natural resource values and voices regarding natural resource and environmental issues. As understanding of the social foundations of problems improves, the ways in which ecosystems and resources intersect with human communities become more obvious. Although urbanization has distanced many from direct contact with nature and natural processes, interactions between society and natural resources remain. The character of interactions is dynamic, sometimes dramatic, and often subtle; social scientists play an important role in describing these changing relationships and the respective implications for resource management.

Second, the growing interest in deliberative or discursive forms of democracy, emphasizing dialogue, learning and evaluation of planned actions, presents important opportunities for social science research (Daniels & Walker, 1996; Dryzek, 2000). This interest is fed by growing concerns about the capacity of decision-making institutions to deal with contemporary natural resource issues. Alternative and largely collaborative modes of decision-making, ranging from community-based resource management (e.g., Kellert, Mehta, Ebbin & Lichtenfeld, 2000) to the landcare and catchment management programs in Australia (Ewing, Grayson & Argent, 2000) are gaining attention among both management organizations and the citizenry, although there are detractors (McCloskey, 2001). There is growing recognition of differing forms and values of knowledge for planning and of the need for innovative mechanisms for obtaining such knowledge (Daniels, Walker, Carroll & Blatner, 1996; Dissanayake, 1986). Collectively, such research on public engagement mechanisms (including collaborative processes) has informed managers on the details of facilitating, evaluating and using public participation.

Third, there is growing recognition of the limits of traditional expert-based and rational comprehensive planning processes that have dominated planning for the past 50 years. This recognition derives, in part, from high levels of uncertainty about cause-effect relationships and conflict over goals of ecosystem management (Allen & Gould, 1986). Such planning processes also have proven ill-equipped to deal with value conflicts; such situations require combinations of public engagement and technical planning. Although social science research has exposed the limits and liabilities of traditional planning models, it has been less successful in framing effective alternatives. Recent interest in collaborative approaches to planning (e.g., Wondolleck & Yaffee, 2000) can be interpreted as a critique of rational planning models and as an alternative, but implementation of such approaches remains constrained by a lack of institutional capacity.

A fourth observation is that a hierarchy of scales exists within society, each nested within the next. Each scale possesses emergent properties unrevealed at smaller scales. These can be defined as social organizational, rather than strictly spatial, scales: individual, household or family, neighborhood, community, county, state, nation and globe. Differing interests in the outcomes of particular decisions reveal themselves at different scales.

Social science disciplines focus differently on these scales: psychology with *individuals*, sociology and anthropology with *groups* and *communities*, geography with the *spatial dimensions of human activity*, political science with *institutions*, economics with *firms*. There is concern, however, that because the scales exist within a hierarchy, such disciplinary orientations, by themselves, ultimately will be unable to deal with the linkages among scales. Problems change with scale, but each serves as a context for smaller scales. Understanding that context is critical to resolving important issues.

Fifth, the social sciences can help frame natural resource issues and problems, both by offering processes that facilitate such problem-framing as well as in terms of the substance of the problems themselves. Bardwell (1991) has noted that the complexity of environmental problem-framing, if left to single or closely aligned disciplines, can lead to excessively narrow problem definitions. For example, defining the "snowmobile problem" in Yellowstone National Park as solely one of environmental pollution might lead to solutions, such as improved internal combustion engines, that effectively resolve the adverse biophysical consequences of such use. Such solutions, however, could fail altogether in dealing with the meanings and values that lie beneath the conflict. In many instances, the failure to gain consensus on the underlying problem stymies the solution-seeking efforts. The ongoing logging versus owl conflict in the Pacific Northwest (U. S.) is but one example. Within that debate, there is a failure to recognize the underlying social aspects of the problem, such as concerns about public access to the decision-making process, a strong desire to sustain a particular life style, and protecting the attributes of special places (FEMAT, 1993; Yaffee, 1994).

Sixth, serious challenges confront efforts to bring the social sciences into a more integrative role in natural resource policy and management processes. Integration involves relationships, and relationships necessarily involve power and how it is both distributed and wielded. Thus, for social science knowledge to "be at the table" in scientific and policy settings, there must be power-sharing. Differing world paradigms held by social scientists and biophysical scientists influence how, and if, power is shared.

There have been efforts to achieve integration in bioregional assessments, but the record of social science participation in, and influence upon these efforts, remains arguable (Cordell & Bergstrom, 1999; Johnson, Swanson, Herring & Greene, 1999). Again, both process and substantive issues are involved. Clark et al. (1999) argued that the lack of comparable data put social scientists at a disadvantage; McCool and Burchfield (1999) identified structural barriers to integration of social science, namely a lack of clarity regarding the criteria by which judgments are made regarding what constitutes integrative assessments. The problem is confounded by the fact that integration involves technical as well as social and political dimensions. Collectively, these elements contribute to problem-framing and solution-building components, but joining and executing these elements requires skills different from what most scientists—biophysical and social—possess.

Finally, there are signs that higher education is beginning to change its approach to natural resource management education. In many schools of forestry or natural resources, a number of social scientists were hired in the 1970s and 1980s to deal with recreation. Typically, recreation management courses were seen as independent of traditional forestry and wildlife management. In fact, many undergraduates in those majors often viewed recreation and aesthetics either as frivolous or as threats. Yet, as recreation management faculty gained experience through research and interaction with management, they frequently were called upon to deal with new problems and challenges, such as public involvement or social impact assessment, because of the skills, concepts and methods at their disposal related to dealing with people. This, in turn, helped create a cadre of social scientists with a broader set of experiences. It also set the stage for a generation of PhD students, who brought a broader (than recreation) range of interests to bear on natural resource issues.

Such changes constitute the needed foundation for improving integration between the social and biophysical sciences, particularly if natural resource schools are not forced into traditional domains such as forestry, wildlife, fisheries or recreation. These topic areas have much in common (e.g., measurement, planning, decision-making). However, external processes such as professional standards, accreditation requirements, job descriptions, and organizational pressures to maintain traditional identities, can be powerful forces that mitigate against integrative processes.

"Higher Order" Observations

In the future, the issue remains about what the key arenas will be within which the social sciences will have a particular opportunity, as well as an ability to contribute to the formulation and implementation of natural resource policies and programs. Many opportunities arise from the web of interactions occurring at the human/natural resource interface; natural resource policies are framed within high levels of technical and scientific complexity, they derive from a pluralistic and ambiguous socio-political context, and they remain in competition with a host of other goods, services and outcomes. From this contentious and volatile context, what core issues emerge for which social science research can provide important and needed input?

Changing Public Conceptions of Natural Resources

First, it is critical that the social sciences build upon the historical traditions in which natural resources and their associated goods, services and values are the product of human constructions. Both the scientific and popular literature characterize today's world as one of rapid and dramatic change; changes in population composition, structure and distribution hold major implications for both public perceptions and constructions of natural resources, as well as in the policies and strategies that govern their management.

For example, the continuing urbanization and suburbanization of the U.S. presents implications for a host of questions which the social sciences can help address. Do such changes signal shifts in the mix of goods and services sought from the nation's natural resources? Does the growing separation of production and consumption contribute to a disconnect between the body politic and the realities, limits and constraints of biophysical processes? Such questions have implications for a diversity of natural resource-based activities, ranging from commodity production (e.g., timber harvesting), consumptive recreation (e.g., hunting and fishing), or the management of natural processes (e.g., fire management).

Not only might changes in the structure, distribution and composition of society affect how resources are defined and valued, but they also can have dramatic impacts upon the particular strategies, policies and management actions undertaken. Since the work of Firey (1960), social scientists have acknowledged the importance of framing management prescriptions consistent with prevailing societal norms and beliefs. In the contemporary literature, the question of *social acceptability* and the factors that shape, sustain, and alter these judgments have drawn increasing attention (Brunson, Kruger, Tyler & Schroeder, 1996; Shindler, Brunson & Stankey, 2002). The professional literature, the experiences of natural resource managers, and anecdotal evidence in the form of letters to the editor and newspaper accounts abound with examples of policies and programs that have proven non-implementable, not because of limitations in the scientific principles upon which they are founded or in their ability to generate public benefits, but in the lack of public understanding and support.

How will natural resource management be affected by the nation's continually changing demographics, including age, ethnicity and urban-rural mix? For example, during the decade of the 1990s, the Pacific Northwest population grew 20 percent, driven largely by immigration. These new residents not only represent increased levels of impact on the region's resources, but they also brought new experiences, knowledge and expectations that can profoundly impact natural resource management. The nation's burgeoning Hispanic population means that cultural norms and beliefs that often stand in sharp contrast to those held by traditional white Anglo culture must be given attention by managers and policymakers. These may present important implications for natural resource programs and policies ranging from biodiversity conservation, to outdoor recreation, to commodity production.

In sum, social scientists are faced with both a great opportunity as well as an obligation to help the legal, policy and management sectors tailor programs that are responsive to the nation's democratic traditions while at the same time, remain consistent with biophysical and economic considerations.

Full Accounting of Costs, Implications and Consequences
A second major arena within which the social sciences can contribute to natural resource management lies in enhancing the identification and evaluation of the range of impacts associated with alternative policies and programs. This potential stems from long-standing social science involvement in *social impact assessment* (Interorganizational Committee on Principles and Guidelines for Social Impact Assessment, 2003). It includes not only an assessment of the impacts of a specific set of policies and activities on the land, but also the larger and contextual milieu within which policies and decisions are framed and implemented.

Such work is especially important given the rising dominance of assessment and evaluation protocols driven primarily, if not solely, by efficiency concerns. Resource policies and actions often have widespread, long-term equity consequences that affect people in diverse ways. They also have differential abilities to deliver on the effectiveness of their respective programs. These impacts also vary at differing scales. Effectiveness and equity are fundamentally different criteria by which programs are assessed, and it is unlikely that improved efficiency measures can either embrace them or be taken as surrogate indices of them. It is also unlikely that effectiveness and equity issues can be framed in commensurate terms (e.g., monetary expression). Although some extreme economic dogma would suggest that the lack of an explicit monetary measure is indicative that the issue is not of consequence, such a judgment is problematic.

Social scientists are challenged to help managers and policymakers understand the reality and significance of a host of non-efficiency issues and concerns. Indeed, if one reviews the record of public policy-making with regard to natural resource management in recent years, it is evident many of these issues (e.g., wilderness, biodiversity conservation, endangered species protection, protection of the rights of nature) have derived from a non-economic basis that includes the spiritual, moral and ethical. The inability or unwillingness to acknowledge these concerns and to embed them substantively and meaningfully into planning and decision-making processes has contributed to the acrimonious debate that typifies natural resource policy today. Developing measures and means through which these values are better recognized and accommodated remains a challenge.

Designing Integrative Decision-making Processes
As noted earlier, from the outset of *SNR* an important goal has been to promote a more integrative linkage among the biological, physical and social sciences. Despite ongoing rhetorical debate about the distinctions between interdisciplinary and integrative approaches, there has been a long tradition in the social sciences with how social systems interact with natural systems, and processes within which they are nested and to which they give meaning. In this field of inquiry, a critical topic concerns development of structures and processes that mediate the relationship between and among people and their environment. Fashioning innovative institutions remains an area where thoughtful deliberations by social scientists could be especially helpful. Indeed, within the recent literature concerning efforts to implement new approaches to natural resource management (e.g., ecosystem management, ecological stewardship, adaptive management, collaboration), there is a recurring similarity in the conclusions. Namely, it is institutional limitations that retard the potential contribution of these alternative management paradigms.

Despite calls for integration, a sober assessment of substantive progress suggests less than heroic gains. For example, if one reviews social science involvement in recent bioregional assessments (e.g., Cordell & Bergstrom, 1999), participation remains largely compartmentalized and separate. This is particularly so at the critical problem-framing stage, meaning that issues are defined largely in biophysical terms, with the role of the social sciences confined to describing impacts and consequences associated with implementation of some policy regime.

The social sciences have an important role in fashioning improved understanding of the social and political processes that give rise to natural resource problems, as well as in offering concepts and frameworks for crafting alternative policies, processes, and institutions to address crucial problems. Yet such contributions remain marginalized in efforts to frame effective responses to promote a more sustainable society; endeavors currently dominated by the biophysical and engineering fields. What steps must be taken to gain a greater awareness of, and appreciation for, the unique contributions the social sciences can bring to implementing integrative approaches to natural resource management?

The Challenges Facing Social Science

Although there are a number of specific suggestions that might be made in response to such questions, four fundamental points seem especially critical. First, based on our collective experience working in the natural resource management interface, it is clear that social scientists must learn the culture, norms, and language of the biological, physical and resource management communities with which they seek to collaborate. The challenge is not unlike that of living in a foreign country: one must learn the language, norms, beliefs and world views of the host country. This is difficult. It is time-consuming. It can be threatening. It takes considerably energy and personal investment, and there is no guarantee the effort will lead to a productive outcome. Coupled with demanding time frames and an emphasis on the bottom-line, it often is simply easier to not engage in such endeavors.

Second, we must work effectively to foster constituencies that support an expanded role for social scientists in resource management and policy-making. Social scientists must think creatively about how to better articulate the contributions of their expertise and to whom these contributions accrue. Such statements could help generate compelling arguments for the resource management community, policy-makers, legislators and their staff, and the public in general.

Such diverse support offers the potential for overcoming the constraints on further integration of social science with natural resource management. A key factor constraining such integration is the lack of organizational capacity within agencies to interpret, process, use, and evaluate social science. The social science presence in most federal management agencies today is dominated by economists while sociologists, rural sociologists, political scientists, geographers and anthropologists remain minorities. By building organizational capacity for the social sciences, the potential for effective integration likely will grow. But this will require support within the wider resource management community. Therefore, it remains incumbent upon the social science professions to better articulate the rationale for such support.

A major structural constraint on social science in general, and on its integration into decision-making in particular, lies in the various statutory strictures that limit public participation, involvement, and engagement. The Federal Advisory Committee Act (FACA) and the Paperwork Reduction Act are two examples. FACA constrains development of many collaborative-type operations, permitting their formation only under strict procedural guidelines which are an anathema to adaptive and collaborative processes. Although FACA arose from legitimate concerns about the domination of local decision-making by affected interests (e.g., livestock ranchers on grazing boards), it has created a burdensome framework that works against fashioning local-based groups who can bring knowledge and expertise to resource managers quickly (Nuszkiewicz, 1992).

The Paperwork Reduction Act is the legal basis for restrictions on the use of public surveys. Again, these restrictions derive from legitimate concerns (originating during the Depression) about excessive government intrusiveness into, and impacts upon, citizens. However, as presently implemented, it represents a major hurdle to systematically and rigorously investigating a host of public issues that could yield important information to the decision-making process.

Overcoming these and other structural barriers is difficult and will not occur quickly. However, support for their modification (rather than elimination) in ways that provide for legitimate social science inquiries and studies is crucial. Pressure for reform from the management and science community has had little impact; changes require intervention by legislators, legislative staffs and citizens. The challenge for social science is to develop compelling arguments for these interests to press for change.

Third, social scientists need to undertake a thoughtful synthesis and assessment of previous endeavors where their concepts, frameworks and methods have been applied in natural resource planning and policy-making. The purpose here would be to capitalize and build upon these experiences as a basis for informing subsequent behavior. In short, what characteristics, situational contexts and dynamics of these experiences might help frame equally contributory engagements in the future?

For example, in experiences developing and applying the Recreation Opportunity Spectrum (Clark & Stankey 1979; Driver & Brown, 1978) and Limits of Acceptable Change (Stankey, Cole, Lucas, Petersen & Frissell, 1985), the relationship with the management and policy-making communities was critical. In both cases, there was a high level of consensus among both managers and researchers regarding the presence of a problem that required an innovative approach for resolution. Thus, there was agreement on how the problem should be framed. In addition, there was a high level of organizational capacity and commitment among the key players: recreation managers, line officers, and agency and university researchers. There was time to undertake a thoughtful approach to problem resolution, providing opportunities for dialogue and mutual learning to improve problem definition and clarification of expectations as to what tools and approaches could be developed. This combination of factors made it possible to explore alternatives in actual situations, and test and evaluate ideas and approaches, develop protocols tailored to differences in areas and conditions, and build understanding and support among managers and citizens.

Finally, while these areas embrace short-term approaches, it is critical to also consider changes needed in the longer-term. These are particularly important because of the systemic nature of many of the challenges faced. Barriers to social science derive from deeply imbedded norms and beliefs that cannot be overcome easily or quickly. What is needed is fundamental reform in the educational process (Orr, 1992).

Reform is essential if integration is to be more than empty rhetoric. Although management agencies, supplemented by policy and legal processes, can work toward implementation of integrative approaches, the most effective strategy lies in developing professionals who bring an educational background, accompanied by appropriate concepts, theories, frameworks, and methods that enable integrative projects to take form from the outset (Clark et al., 1999). This condition, however, must await systemic changes in how professionals are educated. Disciplinary expertise remains important, but we need innovative ways to join substantive educational programs with education in ways that cultivates norms and beliefs that support open and integrative thinking. Until this occurs, the social sciences will remain peripheral to mainstream resource management and decision-making processes.

References

Allen, G. M., & Gould, E. M., Jr. (1986). Complexity, wickedness and public forests. *Journal of Forestry*, 84 (4), 20-24.

Bardwell, L. (1991). Problem-framing: A perspective on environmental problem-solving. *Environmental Management*, 15(5), 603-612.

Brunson, M, Kruger, L. E., Tyler, C. B., & Schroeder, S. A. (1996). *Defining social acceptability in ecosystem management: A workshop proceedings* (General Technical Report PNW-GTR-369). Portland, OR: USDA Forest Service, Pacific Northwest Research Station.

Burdge, R. J., & Field, D. R. (1988). A statement of editorial policy and content. *Society & Natural Resources*, 1(1), 1-3.

Clark, R. N., & Stankey, G.H. (1979). *The recreation opportunity spectrum: A framework for planning, management, and research* (General Technical Report PNW-GTR-98). Portland, OR: USDA Forest Service, Pacific Northwest Research Station.

Clark, R. N., Stankey, G. H., & Shannon, M. A. (1999). The social component of the Forest Ecosystem Management Assessment Team (FEMAT). In H. K. Cordell & J. C. Bergstrom (Eds.), *Integrating social sciences with ecosystem management: Human dimensions in assessment, policy and management* (pp. 237-264). Champaign, IL: Sagamore.

Clark, R. N., Stankey, G. H., Brown, P. J., Burchfield, J. A., Haynes, R. W., & McCool, S. F. (1999). Toward an ecological approach: Integrating social, economic, cultural, biological, and physical considerations. In N. C. Johnson, A. J. Malk, W. T. Sexton, & R. Szaro (Eds.), *Ecological stewardship: A common reference for ecosystem management* (pp. 297-318). Oxford, U.K.: Elsevier Science Ltd.

Cordell, H. K., & Bergstrom, J. C. (Eds). (1999). *Integrating social sciences with ecosystem management: Human dimensions in assessment, policy and management*. Champaign, IL: Sagamore.

Culhane, P. J. (2001). Research on Society & Natural Resources: A content analysis of the first decade. *Society & Natural Resources*, 14(5), 365-384.

Daniels, S. E., & Walker, G. B. (1996). Collaborative learning: Improving public deliberation in ecosystem-based management. *Environmental Impact Assessment*, 16, 71-102.

Daniels, S.E., Walker, G. B., Carroll, M., & Butler, K. (1996). Using collaborative learning in fire recovery planning. *Journal of Forestry*, 94(8), 4-9.

Dissanayake, W. (1986). Communication models and knowledge generation, dissemination, and utilization activities: A historical survey. In G. M. Beal, W. Dissanayake, & S. Konoshima (Eds.), *Knowledge generation, exchange, and utilization*, (pp. 61-75). Boulder, CO: Westview Press

Driver, B. L., & Brown, P. J. (1978). The opportunity spectrum concept and behavior information in outdoor recreation resource supply inventories: A rationale. In G. H. Lund, V. J. LaBau, P. F. Pfolliott, & D. W. Robinson (Eds.), *Integrated inventories of renewable natural resources: proceedings of the workshop* (General Technical Report RM-55) (pp. 24-31). Fort Collins, CO: USDA Forest Service, Rocky Mountain Forest and Range Experiment Station.

Dryzek, J. S. (2000). *Deliberative democracy and beyond: Liberals, critics, contestations.* New York: Oxford University Press.

Ewing, S. A., Grayson, R. B., & Argent, R. M.. (2000). Science, citizens, and catchments: Decision support for catchment planning in Australia. *Society & Natural Resources*, 13(5), 443-460.

Firey, W. (1960). *Man, mind, and land.* Glencoe, IL: The Free Press.

Forest Ecosystem Management Assessment Team (FEMAT). (1993). *Forest ecosystem management: An ecological, economic, and social assessment.* Portland, OR: U.S. Department of Agriculture.

Heberlein, T. A. (1988). Improving interdisciplinary research: Integrating the social and natural sciences. *Society & Natural Resources*, 1(1), 5-16.

Interorganizational Committee on Principles and Guidelines for Social Impact Assessment. (2003). Principles and guidelines for social impact assessment in the USA. *Impact Assessment and Project Appraisal*, 21(3), 231-250.

Johnson, K. N., Swanson, F. Herring, M., & Greene, S. (Eds.). (1999). *Bioregional assessments: Science at the crossroads of management and policy.* Washington DC: Island Press.

Kellert, S. R., Mehta, J. N., Ebbin, S. A., & Lichtenfeld, L. L. (2000). Community natural resource management: Promise, rhetoric, and reality. *Society & Natural Resources*, 13(8), 705-716.

Kruger, L. E., & Sturtevant, V. E. (2003). Divergent paradigms for community inquiry: An argument for including participatory action research. In L. E. Kruger (Ed.), *Understanding community-forest relations* (General Technical Report PNW-GTR-566). Portland, OR: USDA Forest Service, Pacific Northwest Research Station.

McCloskey, M. (2001). Is this the course you want to be on? Comments from the closing session of the 8th International Symposium on Society and Resource Management. *Society & Natural Resources*, 14(7), 627-634.

McCool, S. F., & Burchfield, J. (1999). Social sciences and ecosystems: An overview of the role of social sciences in the Interior Columbia Basin Ecosystem Management Project. In H. K. Cordell & J. C. Bergstrom (Eds.), *Integrating social sciences with ecosystem management: Human dimensions in assessment, policy and management* (pp. 297-318). Champaign, IL: Sagamore.

Nuszkiewicz, M. (1992). Twenty years of the Federal Advisory Committee Act: It's time for some changes. *Southern California Law Review*, 65, 920-970.

Orr, D. W. (1992). *Ecological literacy: Education and the transition to a postmodern world*. Albany, NY: State University of New York.

Patterson, M. E., & Williams, D. R. (1998). Paradigms and problems: The practice of social science in natural resources management. *Society & Natural Resources*, 11(3), 279-295.

Shindler, B., Brunson, M., & Stankey, G. H. (2002). *Social acceptability of forest conditions and management practices: A problem analysis* (General Technical Report PNW-GTR-537). Portland, OR: USDA Forest Service, Pacific Northwest Research Station.

Stankey, G. H., Cole, D. N., Lucas, R. C., Petersen, M. E., & Frissell, S. S. (1985). *The limits of acceptable change (LAC) system for wilderness planning* (General Technical Report INT-GTR-176). Ogden, UT: USDA Forest Service, Intermountain Forest and Range Experiment Station.

Wondolleck, J. M., & Yaffee, S.L., (2000). *Making collaboration work: Lessons from innovation in natural resource management*. Washington DC: Island Press.

Yaffee, S. L. (1994). *The wisdom of the spotted owl: Policy lessons for a new century*. Washington DC: Island Press.

4

Challenges of Change

Natural Resource Management Professionals Engage Their Future

R. Bruce Gill

More than seven years have passed since publication of *The Wildlife Professional Subculture: A Case of the Crazy Aunt* (Gill, 1996). That paper pointed out that many of the social and political problems confronting natural resource managers could be attributed to peculiarities of their professional culture. As resource professionals enter a new millennium, revisiting this old problem is warranted. The first part of this chapter reviews the challenges posed by the changing management environment that confronts natural resource managers now and into the future. The second part unabashedly challenges natural resource professions to adapt accordingly in order to effectively engage the challenges of change.

Challenges of Change

Rapid change is characteristic of today's world. Revolutionary developments in science and technology have spurred a global technological transformation. Although the transformation has brought a plethora of blessings to the short term, it threatens a profusion of curses in the longer term unless the downside of technological development can be managed successfully (Wilson, 2002). Unrestrained technological and economic developments are responsible for declining natural capital, decaying social capital, and eroding political capital (Brown, 2001).

Declining Natural Capital

Natural capital has been defined as "the resources we use, both nonrenewable (oil, coal, metal ore) and renewable (forests, fisheries, grasslands), and the services those resources provide (forest cover, parks, topsoil, clean air, rainfall, waste processing, medicines, erosion control)" (Hawkens, 1997, p. 41). It is intricately interwoven and interactive with social and political capital in complex and, as yet, unpredictable relationships, but which have serious consequences to the preservation of biodiversity, social harmony, and democratic institutions (Shutkin, 2000). Numerous examples attest to the continuing decay in the earth's natural capital.

Since the beginning of agriculture, the Earth has lost nearly half of its forests. In the decade between 1990 and 2000, forests shrunk by more than 90 million hectares globally. Although developed countries gained some 36 million hectares of forestlands, mainly due to conversion of abandoned agricultural lands to forestlands, developing countries lost 130 million hectares, or a rate of about 13 million hectares per year. Not surprisingly, loss of forest cover has significantly and adversely impacted available forest resources and services. As a result, climate regulation, flood control, soil conservation, nutrient cycling, and water conservation have been adversely impacted (Brown, 2001).

Faced with feeding, housing, and clothing some 1.3 billion citizens, Chinese rangelands have been overgrazed, farmlands overflowed, forestlands overcut, and aquifers overpumped. The result has been rapidly expanding desertification. From 1950 to 1960, the average rate of desert spread in China was 1,560 square kilometers per year. In the 1980s that rate increased by 35 percent to 2,100 kilometers per year; and through the 1990s the rate desert conversion increased still more to 2,460 kilometers per year (Brown, 2002).

In the United States, nearly 60 percent of the public grazing lands managed by the Bureau of Land Management and USDA Forest Service are in poor to fair condition. Nearly two-thirds of private grazing lands are in poor to fair condition. Although the trend over the past several decades has been toward gradually improving conditions, that trend will not continue into the future unless grazing policies change significantly (Box, 1990). In fact, it might not be possible to successfully reclaim the rangeland biodiversity on those lands unless domestic livestock grazing is eliminated entirely (Donahue, 1999).

Oceanic fishery populations are declining or, in some cases, collapsing completely. Over the past 50 years, catches of many of the most popular species of North Atlantic commercial fishes, such as cod, tuna, flounder, and hake, have declined by half while fishing effort has tripled (Larson, 2002). Woodward (2003) claims "one-third of the nation's assessed fish populations are being fished at unsustainable levels or have already crashed, and we don't even know the status of 655 (populations)" (p. 5). Both Woodward (2003) and Brown (2002) blame at least part of the collapse of commercial fisheries on a poor understanding of oceanic ecosystems, caused in part by insufficient human and economic resources, and also because the field of marine ecology is staffed with inappropriately qualified professionals.

Nearly one in four of the earth's 50,000 known species of vertebrate animals are declining precipitously, exist as only small populations, or are threatened with extinction primarily due to habitat conversion (Tuxill, 1998). As many as 1,200 of the 9,800 known species of birds face extinction in the 21st century (Youth, 2003). The number of U.S. species listed as threatened and endangered increased five-fold between 1980 and 2002. Fish species led the roster with an average of three new species listed annually, followed by one species of reptiles and amphibians added per year, three species of mammals every other year, and four species of birds every three years. Taken together, diminishing biodiversity and degradation of ecosystems combined with global climate change have resulted in a dramatic decline in natural resource capital essential to sustaining life, that includes human life. How to reverse declining biodiversity in the face of decreasing natural resource capital is the single greatest challenge to current and future natural resource management. This challenge is further complicated by a concurrent decay in social capital and erosion of political capital.

Decaying Social Capital
Social capital has been defined as the networks, norms, and social trust that facilitate coordination and cooperation among people for mutual benefit (Shutkin, 2000). In today's world, several trends occurring simultaneously create a kind of dry rot, consequently eroding the fabric of social capital.

The United States has become a metropolitan society, and as such, urban residents are detached from direct involvement with the land. A cultural breach has developed between those who till or graze the land and those who do not (Baden, 1998; Nelson, 2002). In addition, we are a rootless society in which immigration and transmigration of our citizenry is the norm, creating a rift between newcomers and long-term community residents (Krannich & Smith, 1998; Smith & Krannich, 2000).

In addition, the aging of the U.S. population is creating a gap between the values of the old and the values of the young (Manfredo & Zinn, 1996). Further, women comprise a significant segment of the workplace – including natural resource management agencies – compared to 50 years ago. Women in natural resource management are more likely to favor biodiversity protection and management for wildland amenities, while men incline more towards resource use and commodity production. Thus, a gender gap is created among environmental policy preferences both within natural resource management agencies and beyond (Sanborn & Schmidt, 1995; Vaske, Donnelly, Williams & Jonker, 2001).

Despite significant cultural change, the attitudes and philosophies of resource professionals towards the management of natural resources still more closely reflect those of resource users than those of the public at large (Harris & Brown, 1994). Commodity and production attitudes are reinforced by and contribute to iron triangles comprised of resource management agencies, commodity user clients, and political representatives (Nester, 1997), thereby limiting access to resource management decision processes to those outside the triangles, and creating still more social tension and conflict (Bengston, 1997; Gill, 1996; Harris & Brown, 1994; Waller, 1995).

Traditional economic systems undervalue or assign no value to environmental costs of natural resource production and utilization. Such undervaluing subsidizes resource consumption for short-term benefits, and the results include environmental degradation, resource scarcity, and pollution with its attendant health costs (Brown, 2001; Donahue, 1999; Wilson, 2002). Additionally, benefits and costs of natural resource consumption are conferred inequitably across socio-economic strata. Those highest on the economic ladder benefit most. Those lowest on the ladder pay the most in real costs such as poor health, blighted neighborhoods, environmental pollution, and crime; subsequently amplifying class, ethnic and racial tension (Shutkin, 2000).

Still another economic inequity results when environmental costs are deferred to the future. Environmental benefits enjoyed by current generations are denied later generations because current consumption rates are not sustainable. Cost-benefit ratios of resource consumption by future generations soar due to reduced benefits and deferred costs. This trans-generational inequity is neither fair nor moral, and decays social capital even further.

Competition for natural resources is increasing as resources become scarce. This is especially true regarding the competition between the commodity and amenity values of natural resources (Badden, 1998; Cawley, 1993; Echeverria & Eby, 1995; Krannich & Smith, 1998). Resource competition has spawned social conflict not only in North America, but throughout the world, especially among developing nations. Collectively, these factors have contributed to a gradual erosion of the social capital necessary to effective democratic functioning (Renner, 1996; Shutkin, 2000).

Eroding Political Capital

Social congruence around legislative policies and translated into political will constitutes political capital. There are abundant signs that political capital in the U.S has been eroding steadily over the past five decades.

A competitive tension is wedged between those who would protect the environment and those who would use it (Shutkin, 2002). However, in the 1960s that tension exploded into political warfare with the emergence of the modern environmental movement. Environmentalism arose largely in response to declining environmental health and the tremendous influence on natural resource policy-making by well-organized and well-financed commodity production interests (Shutkin, 2002). During the ensuing two decades, the environmental movement enjoyed tremendous success. The U.S. Congress passed a litany of environmentally protective legislation, including the Wilderness Act in 1964, National Environmental Policy Act in 1969, Endangered Species Act in 1973, National Forest Management Act in 1976, and the Federal Land Policy and Management Act in 1976. Each of these acts imposed new restrictions on the use of public lands, in addition to mandates for their management.

According to Gale (1986), successful social movements are intrinsically controversial, and inevitably inspire counter movements. So it was no surprise that the successes of the environmental movement began to spawn a backlash. Beginning in the late 1970s, a counter movement, the *Wise Use Movement*, began to organize to roll back the legislative gains of environmentalists (Echeverria & Eby, 1995; Beder, 2002). Subsequently, environmentalists and wise users have battled to a political stalemate in their efforts to implement competing land use agendas. As a result, legislative efforts to protect dwindling biodiversity have gridlocked (Rushmore, 1998).

Iron triangle relationships, such as USDA Forest Service, timber and mineral interests, and U.S. Congress; or Bureau of Land Management, grazing and energy development interests, and U.S. Congress; or state wildlife agencies, hunting and fishing interests, and state legislatures and/or wildlife commissions; have made access to policy-making difficult for those outside the triangle. In response, the disenfranchised have resorted to litigation and ballot initiatives to increase their political influence. Litigation may stop the implementation of undesired policies, but can significantly increase the costs of governing and consequently, necessitate funds that could be better applied to on-the-ground programs to preserve biodiversity. Ballot initiatives aimed at complex socio-political issues have to be simple in design to capture public attention. But simple policies that address complex issues often compound problems rather than resolve them. The combined effects of excessive litigation and making policy via ballot initiative serve to further erode political capital.

Iron triangle relationships foster another casualty of an element necessary to the creation of effective political capital: public credibility. When professional experts ally with one interest group against another, the credibility of the experts suffer (Gill, 2001). This "shadow side" of professionalism creates a dispossessed majority of citizens who increasingly know less and less about more and more of the world in which they live, leaving them at the mercy of experts who know more and more about less and less (Derber, Schwartz & Magrass, 1990).

When a majority of citizens are effectively stripped of their political influence by a minority of elites, political disinterest ensues, and the power of the special interests, politicians and professional is enhanced. In other words, political capital is lost. Surveys indexing public trust in government indicate a steep and relentless decline in public trust. In 1958, more than 70 percent of respondents reported they trusted government to do what is right most or all of the time. By 1996, the figure had dropped to around 30 percent (Orren, 1997).

Erosion of political capital has led to a diminished sense of community among citizens, and a disinclination to become politically engaged. And the consequences ripple through the natural and social fabrics that shape our communities and livelihoods (Shutkin, 2000).

Changing Professions

Natural resource professionals have not ignored these developments. To the contrary, they have begun to adapt scientifically by developing new and emerging scientific disciplines focused on biodiversity conservation, ecosystem restoration, and adaptive management. They have begun to adapt culturally by slowly changing their management emphasis from a lop-sided accentuation on commodity production to a more balanced consideration of resource commodities, amenities, and aesthetics. And, they increasingly engage their publics as partners both in biodiversity preservation and professional transformation.

Emerging Disciplines

Landscape ecology and *ecosystem management* emerged in the mid- to late-1980s largely in response to a need for a more comprehensive understanding of ecological processes at scales beyond species and community levels (Burel, 2003; Meefe, Nielson, Knight & Schenborn, 2002; Wu & Hobbs, 2002). Both disciplines focus on relationships between structure, function, and change, and both engage multi- and inter-disciplinary fields of science.

In the 1990s, *restoration ecology* emerged to develop a reliable body of knowledge concerning the restoration of altered or damaged ecosystems. It is focused primarily at an ecosystem level, and in fact integrates principles of ecosystem management. As its name implies, restoration ecology attempts to emulate current or former local ecosystems (Baldwin, De Luce & Pletsch, 1994; Jordan, Gilpen & Aber, 1990) through means that can include invasive species eradication, species reintroduction, re-vegetation, and similar efforts.

Conservation biology diverged from conventional wildlife biology in the mid-

1980s, because of an ill-attended need to develop reliable information and management practices to preserve biodiversity, especially animal diversity. Conservation biology, like ecosystem management, landscape ecology, and restoration ecology, is multi- and inter-disciplinary.

Human dimensions arose from the recognition that natural resource management is increasingly complex, involving not only the physical sciences of ecology and biology, but also the social sciences of economics, politics, and sociology. Social conflicts resulting from declining natural, social, and political capital threatened to paralyze natural resource management unless managers became more skilled at resolving conflicts. Human dimensions aimed to provide resource managers with those skills based upon a combination of social science and adaptive management (Manfredo, Decker & Duda, 1998; Riley et al., 2002).

Ecological economics arose in response to the neglect of conventional economics to account for environmental considerations in the calculations of costs and benefits of human commerce. Ecological economists argued that economics is not independent of ecology. Rather, all life, including human life and its attendant economic accounting practices, is dependent upon natural resources for sustaining subsistence.

Collectively, all of these emerging disciplines have begun to transform the focus of natural resource management from commodity production to sustainable development. In the process, they are becoming more responsive to public environmental values and, in the process, transforming the politics of environmental policy-making.

Greening Institutions

As new natural resource management disciplines emerged, professional cultures slowly began to change. Recruitment of a younger work force from a more diverse pool of applicants has contributed to a gradual "greening" of the natural resources professions where employees have become increasingly sensitive and dedicated to biodiversity conservation issues (Kennedy, 1991; Sanborn & Schmidt, 1995). This transition comes with a cost. Conflict and backlash within natural resource management agencies have delayed the rate of cultural change (Brown & Harris, 2000; Xu & Bengston, 1997). Greening of the professions has also stimulated a political backlash against the agencies themselves, prompting attempts by state and federal legislatures to reverse the greening by politicizing public natural resource management agencies (Freddy, 2003; Hedge & Johnson, 2002).

Increasing Participation

Faced with conflict both within and outside of natural resource agencies, management professionals have begun to experiment with processes to enhance and expand public participation in resource policy-making (Decker, Schluser, Brown & Mattfeld, 2000; Irwin & Freeman, 2000; Moore & Koontz, 2003; Moote & McClaran, 1997; Ryan, 2001; Waage, 2003). Enhancing and increasing citizen participation without, however, expanding their power and influence is only a hollow gesture that amplifies the erosion of political capital. For the time being, professionals seem less than eager to significantly share political power with ordinary citizens (Mortenson & Krannich, 2000).

Challenges to Change

Changes in the professions towards improved resource management science and practice, increased emphasis on biodiversity conservation, and expanding inclusion of citizens in resource decision-making are each a welcome trend. Unfortunately, time is not a friend in the race between professional evolution and environmental devolution (Woodwell, 2003). Biologist and philosopher E.O. Wilson (2002) warns that there are only a few decades remaining in which to act decisively to avoid the biodiversity crisis. Natural resource professionals can and must do more to act decisively. Following are several significant and worthy changes the professions can contribute toward reversing the biodiversity crisis.

Response to Agency Politicization

Professional societies must do a better job of insulating their members from expanding politicization of public resource management. Developments in state wildlife agencies serve as a noteworthy example. Appointed officials with the blessing of state legislatures are exerting increasing influence on the recruitment of new professionals. These recruits are being selected as much for their political orientations as for their expertise. Wildlife commissions look less and less like the publics they are supposed to represent, and more and more like the interests with whom they align. Consequently, more policy-making authority is being assumed by political appointees (Freddy, 2003). Resource professionals come under ever increasing pressure to support the political party line. Meanwhile, the professional societies have done little to resist these trends.

Interdisciplinary Collaboration

Natural resource decisions are made not just within ecological contexts, but social and political environments as well. Therefore, professional societies in natural resource management that include forest, range, and wildlife ecology; landscape ecology; restoration ecology, and; ecological economics must collaborate with other disciplines that include the political and social sciences. Social scientists and political scientists are necessary, but rare additions to professional staffs of federal and state resource management agencies (Mascia et al., 2003).

Adaptive Resource Management

Perhaps most important, professional societies need to begin the routine practice of adaptive resource management where knowledge is brought to policy as predictive hypotheses of biotic responses to various policy alternatives. Those hypotheses are then tested with management-level experiments designed to test the rigor of the predictions. The entire enterprise of adaptive resource management is fundamentally a process of learning-by-doing with the foresight of careful planning and the hindsight of rigorous evaluation (Holling, 1978; Oglethorpe, 2002; Walters & Holling, 1990).

Coupling Adaptive Resource Management to Adaptive Resource Policy-making

Better science alone will not suffice. Resource professionals also must routinely couple adaptive resource management with adaptive decision-making (Johnson, 1999). Lee (1993) referred to this coupling as the compass and gyroscope of policy-making. The compass is science, necessary so that public policy can maintain its sense of direction. The gyroscope is public collaboration, necessary to resolve intractable conflicts and keep our political balance amid stormy seas.

William Shutkin (2000) refers to the union of science and public participation as *civic environmentalism*. He argues that only by democratizing the environmental policy-making process can we begin rebuilding our diminishing supplies of natural, social and political capital. In the beginning, resource professionals should carefully design, implement, and evaluate relatively small experiments in adaptive resource management and democratic policy-making. For example, one might begin with species in trouble on local scales first. Then, as abilities to understand increasingly complex natural and social systems expand, the scale of management experiments can be expanded. Careful consideration must be given to the inclusiveness of the processes to assure legitimacy (Hibbard & Madsen, 2003; Mohan & Stokke, 2000; Paulson, 1998). Equally careful consideration also must be given to decision-making mechanisms to insure that the processes truly are democratic (Armour, 1995; Brechin, Wilshusen, Fortwangler & West, 2002; Crosby, 1995; Renn, Webler & Wiedemann, 1995; Yoder, 1999).

Conclusion

Established interests will regard the adaptive, democratic approach to natural resource management with skepticism and resistance because it requires the relinquishment of political power and because it is costly in time, dollars, and effort. But the "no change" alternative will be even costlier. In the bargain, natural resource professionals stand much to gain. If Lester Brown (2001) and Edward Wilson (2002) are correct in their forecasts of resource scarcity and social conflict, then natural resource professionals might not only profoundly affect the nature of life, but also the life of nature.

References

Armour, A. (1995). The citizen's jury model of public participation: A critical evaluation. In O. Renn, T. Weber, & P. Wiedemann (Eds.), *Fairness and competence in citizen participation*. (pp. 175-187). Dordrecht, Netherlands: Kluwer Academe Publishers.

Baden, J. A. (1998). A clash of cultures in the emerging west. In K. Hess, Jr. & J. A. Badden (Eds.), *Writers on the range* (pp. 3-13). Niwot, CO: University Press of Colorado.

Baldwin, Jr., A. D., De Luce, J., & Pletsch, C. (1994). *Beyond preservation: Restoring and inventing landscapes*. Minneapolis, MN: University of Minnesota Press.

Beder, S. (2002). *Global spin: The corporate assault on environmentalism*. White River Junction, VT: Chelsea Green Publishing Company.

Bengston, D. N. (1997). Trends in national forest values among forestry professionals, environmentalists, and the news media, 1982-1993. *Society and Natural Resources*, 10(1), 43-59.

Box, T. W. (1990). Rangelands. In R.N. Sampson & D. Hair (Eds.), *Natural resources for the 21st century* (pp. 101-120). Washington, DC: Island Press.

Brechin, S. R., Wilshusen, P. R., Fortwangler, C. L., & West, P. C. (2002). Beyond the square wheel: Toward a more comprehensive understanding of biodiversity conservation as social and political process. *Society and Natural Resources*, 15, 41-64.

Brown, G., & Harris, C.C. (2000). The US Forest Service: Whither the new resource management paradigm? *Journal of Environmental Management*, 58, 1-19.

Brown, L. R. (2001). *Eco-economy: Building an economy for the earth.* New York: W.W. Norton & Co.

Brown, L. R. (2002). Deserts invading China. In L. R. Brown, J. Larsen, & D. B. Fischlowitz-Roberts (Eds.), *The earth policy reader* (pp. 6-28). New York: W.W. Norton & Company.

Burel, F. (2003). *Landscape ecology: Concepts, methods, and applications.* Enfield, NH: Science Publishers.

Cawley, R. M. (1993). *Federal land and western anger: The sagebrush rebellion and environmental politics.* Lawrence, KS: University Press of Kansas.

Crosby, N. (1995). Citizens juries: One solution for difficult environmental questions. In O. Renn, T. Weber, & P. Wiedemann (Eds.), *Fairness and competence in citizen participation* (pp. 157-174). Dordrecht, Netherlands: Kluwer Academe Publishers.

Decker, D. J., Schusler, T. M., Brown, T. L., & Mattfeld, G. F. (2000). Co-management: An evolving process for the future of wildlife management. *Transactions of the North American Wildlife and Natural Resources Conference*, 65, 262-277.

Derber, C., Schwartz, W.A., & Magrass, Y.R. (1990). *Power in the highest degree – professionals and the rise of the new mandarin order.* New York: Oxford University Press.

Donahue, D. L. (1999). *The western range revisited : Removing livestock from public lands to conserve native biodiversity.* Norman, OK: University of Oklahoma Press.

Echeverria, J. D., & Eby, R. B. (1995). *Let the people judge: Wise use and property rights movement.* Washington, DC: Island Press.

Freddy, D. J. (2003). *The systematic extirpation of checks and balances in the governance of Colorado's wildlife resources.* Paper presented at the meeting of the Colorado Chapter of the Wildlife Society, Ft. Collins, CO.

Gale, R. P. (1986). Social movements and the state: The environmental movement, countermovement, and government agencies. *Sociological Perspectives*, 29(2), 202-240.

Gill, R. B. (1996). The wildlife professional subculture: The case of the crazy aunt. *Human Dimensions of Wildlife*, 1(1), 60-69.

Gill, R. B. (2001). Professionalism, advocacy, and credibility: A futile cycle? *Human Dimensions of Wildlife*, 6(1), 21-32.

Harris, C. C., & Brown, G. (1994). Constituency bias in a federal resource management agency: A confirmatory analysis. *Journal of Environmental Management*, 43, 317-331.

Hawkens, P.l (1997). Natural capitalism. *Mother Jones*, 22(2), 40-51.

Hedge, D., & Johnson, R. J. (2002). The plot that failed: The Republican revolution and Congressional control of the bureaucracy. *Journal of Public Administration Research and Theory*, 12(3), 333-351.

Hibbard, M., & Madsen, J. (2003). Environmental resistance to place-based collaboration in the U.S. West. *Society and Natural Resources*, 16, 703-718.

Holling, C. S. (1978). *Adaptive environmental assessment and management.* New York: John Wiley and Sons.

Irwin, E. R., & Freeman, M. C. (2002). Proposal for adaptive management to conserve biotic integrity in a regulated segment of the Tallapoosa River, Alabama, U.S.A. *Conservation Biology*, 16(5), 1212-1222.

Johnson, B. L. (1999). Introduction to the special feature: Adaptive management – scientifically sound, socially challenged? *Conservation Ecology*, 3(1), 10-14.

Jordan III, W. R., Gilpin, M. E., & Aber, J. D. (1990). *Restoration ecology: A synthetic approach to ecological restoration.* New York: Cambridge University Press.

Kennedy, J. J. (1991). Integrating gender and interdisciplinary professionals into traditional U.S. Department of Agriculture-Forest Service culture. *Society and Natural Resources*, 4, 165-166.

Krannich, R. S., & Smith, M. D. (1998). Local perceptions of public lands natural resource management in the rural West: Toward improved understanding of the "revolt in the West." *Society and Natural Resources*, 11, 677-695.

Larson, J. (2002). Fish catch leveling off. In L. R. Brown, J. Larsen, & B. Fischlowitz-Roberts (Eds.) *The earth policy reader* (pp. 99 – 102). New York: W.W. Norton & Company.

Lee, K. N. (1993). *Compass and gyroscope: Integrating science and politics for the environment.* Washington, DC: Island Press.

Manfredo, M. J., & Zinn, H. C. (1996). Population change and its implications for wildlife management in the New West: A case study of Colorado. *Human Dimensions of Wildlife*, 1(3), 62-74.

Manfredo, M. J., Decker, D. J., & Duda, M. D. (1998). What is the future for human dimensions? *Transactions of the North American Wildlife and Natural Resources Conference*, 63, 268-293.

Mascia, M. B., Brosius, J. P., Dobson, T. A., Forbes, B. C., Horowitz, L., McKean, M. A., & Turner, N. J. (2003). Conservation and the social sciences. *Conservation Biology*, 17(3), 649-650.

Meefe, G. K., Nielson, L. A., Knight, R. L., & Schenborn, D. A. (Eds.). (2002). *Ecosystem management: Adaptive, community-based conservation.* Washington, DC: Island Press.

Mohan, G., & Stokke, K. (2000). Participatory development and empowerment: The dangers of localism. *Third World Quarterly,* 21(2), 247-268.

Moore, E. A., & Koontz, T. M. (2003). A typology of collaborative watershed groups: Citizen-based, agency-based, and mixed partnership. *Society and Natural Resources,* 16, 451-460.

Moote, M. A., & McClaran, M. P. (1996). Viewpoint: Implications of participatory democracy for public planning. *Journal of Range Management,* 50(5), 473-481.

Mortenson, K. G., & Krannich, R. S. (2000). Wildlife managers and public involvement: Letting the crazy aunt out. *Human Dimensions of Wildlife,* 6(4), 277-290.

Nelson, P. B. (2002). Perceptions of restructuring in the rural West: Insights from the "cultural turn". *Society and Natural Resources,* 15(11), 903-921.

Nester, W. R. (1997). *The war for America's natural resources.* New York: St. Martin's Press.

Paulson, D. D. (1998). Collaborative management of public rangeland in Wyoming: Lessons in co-management. *Professional Geographer,* 50(3), 301-315.

Oglethorpe, J. (2002). *Adaptive management: From theory to practice.* Washington, DC: Island Press.

Orren, G. (1997). Fall from grace: The public's loss of faith in government. In J. S. Nye, Jr., P. D. Zelikow, & D. C. King (Eds.), *Why people don't trust government* (pp. 77-107). Cambridge, MA: Harvard University Press.

Renn, O., Webler, T., & Wiedemann, P. (1995). The pursuit of fair and competent citizen participation. In O. Renn, T. Weber, & P. Wiedemann (Eds.), *Fairness and competence in citizen participation* (pp. 339-369). Dordrecht, Netherlands: Kluwer Academe Publishers.

Renner, M. (1996). *Fighting for survival: Environmental decline, social conflict, and the new age of insecurity.* New York: W.W. Norton & Co.

Riley, S. J., Decker, D. J., Carpenter, L. H., Organ, J. F., Siemer, W. F., Mattfeld, G. F., & Parsons, G. (2002). The essence of wildlife management. *Wildlife Society Bulletin,* 30(2), 585-593.

Rushmore, B. (1998). Wise use and the limits of public lands. In K. Hess, Jr. & J. A. Baden (Eds.), *Writers on the range* (pp 15-26). Niwot, CO: University Press of Colorado.

Ryan, C. M. (2001). Leadership in collaborative policy-making: An analysis of agency roles in regulatory negotiations. *Policy Sciences,* 34(3-4), 221-245.

Sanborn, W. A., & Schmidt, R. H.(1995). Gender effects on views of wildlife professionals about wildlife management. *Wildlife Society Bulletin,* 23, 583-587.

Shutkin, W. A. (2000). *The land that could be: Environmentalism and democracy in the twenty-first century.* Cambridge, MA: IT Press.

Smith, M. D., & Krannich, R. S. (2000). "Culture clash" revisited: Newcomer and longer-term residents' attitudes toward land use, development, and environmental issues in rural communities in the Rocky Mountain West. *Rural Sociology,* 65(3), 396-421.

Tuxill, J. (1998). Losing strands in the web of life: Vertebrate declines and the conservation of biological diversity. *Worldwatch Paper* 141.

Vaske, J. J., Donnelly, M. P., Williams, D. R., & Jonker, S. (2001). Demographic influences on environmental value orientations and normative beliefs about national forest management. *Society and Natural Resources,* 14(9), 761-776.

Waage, S. (2003). Collaborative salmon recovery planning: Examining decision making and implementation in northeastern Oregon. *Society and Natural Resources,* 16(4), 295-307.

Waller, T. (1995). Knowledge, power, and environmental policy: Expertise, the lay public, and water management in the western United States. *The Environmental Professional,* 17, 154-166.

Walters, C. J., & Holling, C. S. (1990). Large-scale management experiments and learning by doing. *Ecology,* 71, 2060-2068.

Wilson, E. O. (2002). *The future of life.* New York: Alfred A. Knopf.

Woodward, C. (2003). Saving the seas. *Trust,* 6(2), 1-8.

Woodwell, G. M. (2003). World enough and time? *Conservation Biology,* 17(2), 356-357.

Wu, J., & Hobbs, R. (2002). Key issues and research priorities in landscape ecology: An idiosyncratic synthesis. *Landscape Ecology,* 17, 355-365.

Xu, Z., & Bengston, D. N. (1997). Trends in national forest values among forestry professionals, environmentalists, and the news media, 1982-1993. *Society and Natural Resources,* 10(1), 43-59.

Yoder, D. E. (1999). A contingency framework for environmental decision-making: Linking decisions, problems, and processes. *Policy Studies Journal,* 16(3/4), 11-35.

Youth, H. (2003). Winged messengers: The decline of birds. *Worldwatch Paper* 165.

5

Conservation Psychology

Joanne Vining
Carol D. Saunders

A growing body of psychological research is addressing the need to better understand the human aspects of conservation. In particular, the past decade has witnessed a greater appreciation for the reciprocal aspects of human interactions with the natural world. On the one hand, studies continue to document how human activity affects the environment both positively and negatively. On the other hand, social scientists are beginning to pay more attention to understanding what nature means to people. Indeed, the goal of environmental sustainability emphasizes the need to understand and reshape the relationships between people and their environment (Becker & Jahn, 1999).

In this chapter, the lens of caring relationships with the natural world will be used to view past and future environmental psychology research, and as a way to discuss the emerging field of conservation psychology. Much of the past research has explored factors that promote behavior change. There have been fewer studies that investigate the emotional or developmental dimensions of people's relationship to nature. In addition, this chapter discusses management implications and identifies future research needs.

Definition

Worldwide, natural resources are under unprecedented pressure. Consequently, it is vital to ask how human relationships with the natural world might be improved. As experts in human behavior, psychologists have provided a number of approaches for understanding the cognitions, attitudes, motives, beliefs, values, and types of behaviors related to conservation issues (Bechtel & Churchman, 2002; Cvetkovich & Werner, 1994; Gardner & Stern, 1996; Nickerson, 2003). Recently, there has been increasing attention given to psychology's role in promoting environmentalism and environmental sustainability (e.g., Kurz, 2002; Oskamp, Howard, Winter,

Stern & McKenzie-Mohr, 2000; Schmuck & Schultz, 2002; Werner 1999; Winter, 2003; Zelezny & Schultz, 2000). Despite the ways psychology has explored conservation-related problems, however, it is far from reaching its full potential (Kidner, 1994).

A number of researchers have been exploring a new way for psychologists and other social scientists interested in conservation issues to organize themselves; a discipline called *conservation psychology*. As recently described by Saunders (in press), conservation psychology is the scientific study of the reciprocal relationships between humans and the rest of nature, with a particular focus on how to encourage conservation of the natural world. In addition to being a field of study, conservation psychology is also the actual network of researchers and practitioners who work together to understand and promote a sustainable and harmonious relationship between people and the natural environment. It differs from environmental psychology in that it places a greater emphasis on relationships with nature, as well as its strong mission to conduct psychological research oriented toward environmental sustainability. Conservation psychology is more closely related to what Bonnes and Bonaiuto (2002) call *environmental psychology of sustainable development*.

Ideas about conservation psychology, as a distinct approach to the study of conservation behavior, were explored at the eighth International Symposium on Society and Resource Management (ISSRM) in June 2000. A series of sessions were presented under the general theme of *conservation psychology*, with more than 35 papers that addressed a variety of topics, including: a) sense of self/sense of place, b) perceptions of the environment, c) environmental experience and development, d) relational caring/ethic of care, e) cultural aspects of caring/cultural constructions of nature, f) meanings and values of nature, and g) caring for nature/conservation behaviors. Participants also discussed how to build a broader professional identity for psychological research about conservation issues. To promote an exchange of ideas, the discussion was deliberately organized around the controversial idea of whether a new field was needed. The history of conservation biology was used as a model. With its strong mission focus, it offered helpful comparisons (Saunders & Myers, 2001).

Since then, the conservation psychology field has continued to grow through a network of websites, list-serves, workshops and publications. Throughout its development, the language of caring has been a helpful organizing framework. The word *care* is deceptively simple because it actually includes many dimensions (Brown, 1997). First, it always has a subject and an object. Usually the subject is a person (e.g., I care). The word itself can refer to different psychological processes related to thinking, feeling and acting. For example, when we say we "care about" something, it usually has an affective meaning, whereas "to care for" or "take care of" often has a behavioral connotation.

Myers and Saunders (2002) point out that the object of care can vary in levels; from the individual to animal to ecosystem. They speculate about possible pathways from natural care to environmental care. However, as Noddings (1984) notes, care most naturally extends to individuals that visibly respond to the caring. Abstract entities such as ecosystems do not provide such tangible feedback.

This chapter focuses on a review of the research from two specific outcome areas: 1) how humans behave towards (i.e., take care of) nature (with the goal of creating durable behavior change at multiple levels and sustainable relationships), and 2) how humans care about and value nature (with the goal of creating harmonious relationships and an environmental ethic).

Research Findings in Conservation Psychology

Conservation Behavior

There has been a wealth of psychological studies on conservation behavior conducted during the past three decades. Conservation behavior has been defined by Monroe (in press) as any behavior or specific action that supports sustainability. She notes that most conservation behaviors are actually made up of several behaviors. For example, consider the conservation behavior of commuting to work by bicycle. There are many behaviors associated with commuting by such means.

Applied behavior analysis, or behaviorism, was one of the earliest frameworks from which conservation behavior was addressed. The seemingly simple idea of rewarding appropriate behavior and punishing inappropriate behavior was appealing in principle, but problematic in practice. At the most basic level, rewards are expensive, and when they are removed, the target behavior tends to return to baseline. Moreover, as Deci and Ryan (1985) demonstrated, when altruistically-motivated behavior is paired with a reinforcer, the original altruistic motivation is diminished. If it is possible to persuade people to conserve because they think it is the right thing to do (or by making it convenient, as noted below), then reinforcers are not only unnecessary, but also ill-advised. Reward and punishment tends to work better in a market sense, such as when energy prices increase and consumers react with conservation. Nonetheless, Geller (1995), one of the most dedicated of applied behavior analysts, departed from strict behaviorism and proposed a mediating factor: the actively caring individual. Such internal psychological variables dominate the conservation psychology literature.

One of the most obvious internal psychological variables is knowledge, which can include stored memories and learned items as well as the current understanding of conservation issues. Many psychologists, and even more practitioners and managers, have suggested that greater knowledge about the environment will lead to greater pro-environmental behavior. However, there is little evidence to show that this is true, and a number of studies indicate that people require very little understanding of environmental issues in order to conserve resources (Hungerford & Volk, 1990; Kollmuss & Agyeman, 2002; Vining & Ebreo, 1990). What does seem to matter is that different forms of knowledge must work together in a convergent manner to foster conservation behavior (Kaiser & Fuhrer, 2003). As it happens, at least with respect to recycling behavior, what people need is for the behavior to be made convenient (DeYoung, 1986; Vining & Ebreo, 1990).

Often the most important type of knowledge is knowing how to do the behavior (Marcinkowski, 2001). Among residents of North American and European countries, attitudes regarding conservation and the environment are largely very positive, and it appears that these individuals have sufficient information to form those attitudes. Thus, making conservation easier, whether by providing required information or by modifying infrastructure, is a major step toward encouraging such behavior. Moreover, it is possible that by facilitating behavior in accordance with pro-environmental attitudes, those attitudes may be strengthened and even generalized to other pro-environmental behaviors. Evidence for this direct experience effect is mixed, but it remains an intriguing possibility that deserves further study.

Other cognitive precursors to conservation behavior, such as attitudes, values, motives, and beliefs, have received the lion's share of attention. Motives were the subject of early attempts to distinguish between recyclers and non-recyclers. DeYoung (1989) and Vining and Ebreo (1990) found that these groups differed only to the extent that they perceived recycling to be an inconvenience or a nuisance; personal and social norms, as well as altruistic motives, did not distinguish between the two groups. There appear to be few, if any, studies that have extended this analysis to other conservation behaviors.

Much of the literature on precursors to conservation behavior has also focused on attitudes, and associated constructs such as values and beliefs. The models that have received the most attention are variants of either the Theory of Reasoned Action (TRA, Fishbein & Ajzen, 1975), the subsequent Theory of Planned Behavior (TPB, Ajzen, 1991) or Schwartz's (1977) Norm Activation model. Because general environmental attitudes are poorly related to conservation behavior (Vining & Ebreo, 1992), a great deal of effort has gone into finding cognitive structures that might have more predictive power.

With Fishbein and Ajzen's (1975) TRA, psychologists successfully used beliefs, intentions and social norms to modify the path between attitudes and behavior, significantly improving predictive validity. Ajzen's (1991) TPB has received somewhat less attention in the conservation psychology literature. With this model, the element of perceived behavioral control (i.e., the extent to which the target behavior is perceived to be inhibited or facilitated), is added as a modifier of intentions. Research based on these models has shown that attitudes that are strongly related to intentions are most likely to predict conservation behaviors.

The Schwartz (1977) Norm Activation Model has been used by a number of researchers to predict conservation behavior. In this model, an individual's awareness of consequences and perceived responsibility result in a personal norm that predicts the target behavior. Mixed results have been achieved with this model, as some of the constructs have been found to be effective alone or in different combinations than the model specified. More recently, Schwartz (1994) has suggested a model of values with two dimensions: 1) self transcendence versus self-enhancement, and 2) conservatism versus openness to change. Stern and his colleagues have then integrated the Schwartz constructs with value orientations described as egoistic, altruistic, and biospheric (Stern, 2000; Stern, Dietz, Abel, Guagnano & Kalof, 1999).

Caring About and Valuing Nature
The ways that people care about and/or value nature have sometimes been included

as important variables in behavior change models, but this needs to be highlighted as an area valuable on its own. Understanding the psychology of how humans experience nature provides important insights about how people develop connections with nature, communicate about such relationships, influence others and shape related social norms.

One body of research related to forming connections with nature has looked at the psychological benefits of experiences in nature. There have been a number of studies that document human preference for natural settings (e.g., Kaplan & Kaplan, 1989), how humans benefit from and are affected by the natural world (e.g., Ulrich, 1993), how interactions with nature positively affect multiple dimensions of human health (e.g., Irvine & Warber, 2002), and the effect of nature on spiritual well-being (e.g., Driver, Dustin, Baltic, Elsner & Peterson, 1996). Nevertheless, this literature could be better integrated. In addition, many unanswered questions remain.

An increasing number of researchers are studying how caring about the natural world develops (Kahn & Kellert, 2002); emotional affinity and empathy for nature (Kals, Schumacher & Montada, 1999; Schultz, 2000); the formation of an environmental identity (Clayton & Opotow, in press); relationships between a psychological connection with nature and environmental sustainability (Schultz, 2002); significant life experiences as precursors of environmental commitment (Chawla, 1999; Tanner, 1980); development of a sense of place and place attachment (Bott, Cantrill & Myers, in press; Giuliani, 2003); moral development (Kahn, 1999) and moral functioning (Opotow & Weiss, 2000) in relation to the natural environment, and; the links between environmental values, concern and action (Kempton, Boster & Hartley, 1995; Shultz & Zelezny, 1998).

Early work on emotions and decisions showed that negative emotions such as disgust and fear are associated with preservation decisions (Vining, 1987; Vining & Schroeder, 1989). This was interpreted as a framing effect, in that preservation decisions almost always bring to mind loss of a treasured resource while development decisions were framed as potential gains. Kals, Schumacher and Montada (1999) demonstrated that conservation behavior was negatively associated with feelings of indignation and resignation. Vining and Ebreo (2002) suggested that the self-aware emotions, such as shame, embarrassment or guilt may arise through cognitive dissonance when individuals who care about the environment fail to act in accordance with that feeling. Defense mechanisms such as denial and rationalization then help protect the individual from these negative emotions, possibly resulting in beliefs that, for example, one's own contribution to the problem is too small to matter.

Although the relationship between positive emotions and conservation behavior has not been studied extensively, it seems logical that there should be such a link. For example, pride associated with doing something for the environment should serve as a reinforcer for such behavior. Kaplan (1990) argues that the psychological state of "being needed" is a powerful motivator and source of satisfaction. This concept has three basic requirements: 1) perceiving there is something worthwhile to be done, 2) a feeling that one's own contribution is necessary, and 3) a sense of competence.

Future Directions

Previous research has set the stage for several directions of future studies in conservation behavior. In the past, there has been an emphasis on cognitive structures, or products, that influence conservation behavior. It is important to see more research on the processes by which these cognitive structures and conservation behaviors came to be. In other words, it is good to know that intentions, measured just prior to a behavior, are a good predictor of the behavior, and that intentions are predicted by beliefs and perceived norms, but it is worth wondering where those beliefs and perceived norms came from in the first place.

This leads us to a related second point, which is the need for more explanatory models of behavior in addition to predictive models. Although it may be argued that predictive models are vital to develop applications, an application based on a measure of a behavioral intention or a basic value is not very practical. A focus on explanations of conservation behavior and its precursors would be of greater practical and theoretical value.

These suggestions require more use of qualitative research. The significant life experiences research makes use of multiple qualitative methodologies to uncover the formative influences that lead to a commitment to the environment (Chawla, 1998). Childhood experiences in the outdoors such as camping, hiking or other outdoor exploration were common experiences among environmentalists interviewed (Chawla, 1999). Other factors she discovered were the presence of family members who valued the environment, pro-environmental organizations, negative experiences of environmental degradation, and school-based education, especially if there were opportunities to take action. Although the generalizability of this research is limited (see Gough,1999; Tanner, 1998), many common themes continue to be identified.

Another example of qualitative research is provided by Daitch, Kweon, Tyler, and Vining (1996). They conducted interviews with ten individuals of varying backgrounds to construct environmental biographies. These biographies indicated that environmental experiences during childhood are important in forming the ways individuals interact with the environment as adults. Similarly, Chenoweth and Gobster (1990) performed a qualitative exploration of peak aesthetic experiences, discovering that such events were typically experienced in outdoor settings.

Finally, emotions are vital components of conservation psychology research, but they have been all but ignored in the empirical literature. Over the past two decades, psychological research has demonstrated that emotions are stored and retrieved along with cognitive structures such as memories (Ben-Ze'ev, 2000). Thus, emotions are a vital component of cognitive processing that should be included when considering conservation behavior. Moreover, recent theories of emotion suggest that they are important, valid and adaptive cognitive forces that play vital roles in organizing cognitions, communication and motivation (Lewis & Haviland-Jones, 2004). Because values and attitudes are affective in nature, emotion needs more research attention, and both negative and positive emotions must be examined.

In sum, although research is needed in many areas, we have emphasized the gaps in our understanding about how relationships with nature are formed, the need for more explanatory models to assist practitioners, the value of qualitative research, and the need for more research about the emotional dimensions of conservation.

Conclusion

The study of the human aspects of conservation is currently fragmented and unfocused. Given the urgency of our environmental problems, we need more efficient interdisciplinary networks working together on real-world conservation problems. We also need more strategic methods for social scientists and conservation practitioners to work together. Conservation psychology offers some ideas for how to promote such outcome-oriented networks. Measuring success and documenting how the public talks about ideas related to nature and conservation provides a feedback loop that can lead to future social change.

Psychologists have brought valuable principles and methods to the study of the human aspects of conservation, but more research is needed. Most of the contributions to date have been in the area of understanding and promoting pro-environmental behaviors. Some of the findings are: the limitations of using reinforcers, knowledge as a weak component of behavior change and convenience as a key variable, recognition that the relationship between attitudes and behaviors strengthen when they are more specific, and identification of conditions under which social norms can influence personal norms.

Using a caring framework, conservation psychologists have emphasized the reciprocal nature of how people relate to nature. Much of the research related to how people take care of nature has focused on using psychological approaches to encouraging or discouraging certain behaviors. Less research has been done on how people develop caring relationships with nature. There is a need for more explanatory models, qualitative research, and studies of the emotional connections with the natural world. There is also a need for more studies linking the ways people value nature with how they express that caring in terms of pro-environmental action.

References

Ajzen, I. (1991). The theory of planned behavior. *Organizational Behavior and Human Decision Processes*, 50, 179-211.

Bechtel, R.B., & Churchman, A. (2002). *Handbook of environmental psychology.* New York: John Wiley & Sons.

Becker, E., & Jahn, T. (1999). *Sustainability and the social sciences: A cross-disciplinary approach to integrating environmental considerations into theoretical reorientations.* New York: Zed Books.

Ben-Ze'ev, A. (2000). *The subtlety of emotions.* Cambridge, MA: The MIT Press.

Bonnes, M., & Bonaiuto, M. (2002). Environmental psychology: From spatial-physical environment to sustainable development. In R. B. Bechtel & A. Churchman (Eds.), *Handbook of environmental psychology* (pp. 28-54). New York: John Wiley and Sons.

Bott, S., Cantrill, J., & Myers Jr., O.E. (in press). Place and the promise of conservation psychology. *Human Ecology Review.*

Brown, G. (1997). *Is 'care for nature' a wise focus for educational efforts?* Paper presented at the annual meeting of the North American Association for Environmental Education, Vancouver, B.C.

Chawla, L. (1998). Significant life experiences revisited: A review of research on sources of environmental sensitivity. *Environmental Education Research,* 4, 369-382.

Chawla, L (1999). Life paths into effective environmental action. *Journal of Environmental Education,* 3, 15-26.

Chenoweth, R.E., & Gobster, P.H. (1990). The nature and ecology of aesthetic experiences in the landscape. *Landscape Journal,* 9, 1-8.

Clayton, S., & Opotow, S. (Eds.) (in press). *Identity and the natural environment.* Cambridge, MA: MIT Press.

Cvetkovich, G.T., & Werner, R. (1994). *How can psychology help save the planet: A research agenda on environmental problems.* Washington, D.C.: American Psychological Association.

Daitch, V., Kweon, B., Tyler, L., & Vining, J. (1996). Personal environmental histories: Expressions of self and place. *Human Ecology Review,* 3, 19-31.

Deci, E.L., & Ryan, R.M. (1985). *Intrinsic motivation and self-determination in human behavior.* New York: Plenum Press.

DeYoung, R. (1986). Some psychological aspects of recycling: The structure of conservation satisfactions. *Environment & Behavior,* 18, 435-449.

DeYoung, R. (1989). Exploring the difference between recyclers and non-recyclers: The role of information. *Journal of Environmental Systems,* 18, 341-351.

Driver, B.L., Dustin, D., Baltic, T., Elsner, G., & Peterson, G. (1996). *Nature and the human spirit: Toward an expanded land management ethic.* State College, PA: Venture Publishing.

Fishbein, M., & Ajzen, I. (1975). *Belief, attitude, intention and behavior: An introduction to theory and research.* Reading, MA: Addison-Wesley.

Gardner, G.T., & Stern, P.C.. (1996). *Environmental problems and human behavior.* Boston, MA: Allyn and Bacon.

Geller, E.S. (1995). Actively caring for the environment: An integration of behaviorism and humanism. *Environment and Behavior,* 27, 184-195.

Gough, S. (1999). Significant life experiences (SLE) research: A view from somewhere. *Environmental Education Research,* 5, 353-363.

Hungerford, H., & Volk, T. (1990). Changing learner behavior through environmental education. *Journal of Environmental Education,* 21, 8-22.

Irvine, K.N., & Warber, S.L. (2002). Greening healthcare: Practicing as if the natural environment really mattered. *Alternative Therapies*, 8, 76-83.

Kahn, Jr., P.H. (1999). *The human relationship with nature: Development and culture.* Cambridge, MA: The MIT Press.

Kahn, Jr., P.H., & Kellert, S.R. (Eds.) (2002). *Children and nature: Psychological, sociocultural and evolutionary investigations.* Cambridge, MA: The MIT Press.

Kaiser, F.G.,& Fuhrer, U. (2003). Ecological behavior's dependency on different forms of knowledge. *Applied Psychology: An International Review*, 52, 598-613.

Kals, E., Schumacher, D., & Montada, L. (1999). Emotional affinity toward nature as a motivational basis to protect nature. *Environment and Behavior*, 31, 178-202.

Kaplan, S. (1990). Being needed, adaptive muddling and human-environment relationships. *Proceedings of the Environmental Design Research Association*, 21, 19-25.

Kaplan, R., & Kaplan, S. (1989). *The experience of nature: A psychological perspective.* Cambridge, MA: Cambridge University Press.

Kempton, W., Boster, J.S., & Hartley, J. (1995). *Environmental values in American culture.* Cambridge, MA: MIT Press.

Kidner, D.W. (1994). Why psychology is mute about the environmental crisis. *Environmental Ethics*, 16, 359-376.

Kollmus, A., & Agyeman, J. (2002). Mind the gap: Why do people act environmentally and what are the barriers to pro-environmental behavior? *Environmental Education Research*, 8, 239-260.

Kurz, T. (2002). The psychology of environmentally sustainable behavior: Fitting together pieces of the puzzle. *Analyses of Social Issues and Public Policy*, 2, 257-278.

Lewis, M., & Haviland-Jones, J. (Eds.). (2004). *Handbook of emotions, 2nd edition.* New York: Guilford Press.

Marcincowski, T. (2001). Predictors of responsible environmental behavior: A review of three dissertation studies. In H. Hungerford, W. Bluhm, T. Volk, & J. Ramsey (Eds.), *Essential readings in environmental education* (pp. 247-276). Champaign, IL: Stripes Publishing L.L.C.

Monroe, M. (in press). Two avenues for encouraging conservation behavior. *Human Ecology Review.*

Myers, G., & Saunders, C.D. (2002). Animals as links toward developing caring relationships with the natural world. In P.H. Kahn, Jr., & S.R. Kellert (Eds.), *Children and nature: Psychological, sociocultural, and evolutionary investigations* (pp. 153-178). Cambridge, MA: The MIT Press.

Nickerson, R.S. (2003). *Psychology and environmental change.* Mahwah, NJ: Lawrence Erlbaum Associates.

Noddings, N. (1984). *Caring: A feminine approach to ethics and moral education.* Berkeley, CA: University of California Press.

Opotow, S., & Weiss, L. (2000). Denial and the process of moral exclusion in environmental conflict. *Journal of Social Issues, 56,* 475-490.

Oskamp, S., Howard, G.S., Winter, D.N., Stern, P.S., & McKenzie-Mohr, D. (2000). Environmental sustainability. *American Psychologist, 55,* 496-537.

Saunders, C.D. (in press). The emerging field of conservation psychology. *Human Ecology Review.*

Saunders, C.D., & Myers, Jr., O.E. (2001). Using conservation biology as a model for thinking about conservation psychology. *Population and Environmental Psychology Bulletin, 27,* 7-8.

Schmuck, P., & Schultz, W.P. (Eds.). (2002). *Psychology of sustainable development.* Boston: Kluwer Academic Publishers.

Schultz, P.W. (2000). Empathizing with nature: The effects of perspective taking on concern for environmental issues. *Journal of Social Issues, 56,* 391-406.

Schultz, P.W. (2002). Inclusion with nature: The psychology of human-nature relations. In P. Schmuck, & W.P. Schultz (Eds.), *Psychology of sustainable development,* (pp. 61-78). Boston: Kluwer Academic Publishers.

Schultz, P.W., & Zelezny, L. (1998). Values and proenvironmental behavior: A five-country survey. *Journal of Cross-Cultural Psychology, 29,* 540-558.

Schwartz, S.H. (1977). Normative influences on altruism. In L. Berkowitz (Ed.), *Advances in experimental social psychology, Vol. 10,* (pp. 221-279). New York: Academic Press.

Schwartz, S.H. (1994). Are there universal aspects in the structure and content of human values? *Journal of Social Issues, 50,* 19-45.

Stern, P.C. (2000). Psychology and the science of human-environment interactions. *American Psychologist, 55,* 523-530.

Stern, P.C., Dietz, T., Abel, T., Guagnano, G.A., & Kalof, L. (1999). A value-belief-norm theory of support for social movements: The case of environmentalism. *Human Ecology Review, 6,* 81-97.

Tanner, T. (1980). Significant life experiences: A new research area in environmental education. *Journal of Environmental Education, 11,* 20-24.

Tanner, T. (Ed.) (1998). Special issue about significant life experiences research. *Environmental Education Research, 4,* 365-464.

Ulrich, R.S. (1993). Biophilia, biophobia, and natural landscapes. In S. R. Kellert, & E. O. Wilson (Eds.), *The biophilia hypothesis,* (pp. 73-137). Washington, D.C.: Island Press.

Vining, J. (1987). Environmental decisions: The interaction of emotions, information, and decision context. *Journal of Environmental Psychology*, 7, 13-30.

Vining, J., & Schroeder, H. W. (1989). The effects of perceived conflict, resource scarcity and information bias on emotions in environmental decision-making. *Environmental Management*, 13, 199-206.

Vining, J., & Ebreo, A. (1990). What makes a recycler? A comparison of recyclers and non-recyclers. *Environment & Behavior*, 22, 55-73.

Vining, J., & Ebreo, A. (1992). Predicting recycling behavior from global and specific environmental attitudes and changes in recycling opportunities. *Journal of Applied Social Psychology*, 22, 1580-1607.

Vining, J., & Ebreo, A. (2002). Emerging theoretical and methodological perspectives on conservation behavior. In R. Bechtel & A. Churchman (Eds.), *Handbook of environmental psychology*, (pp. 541-558). New York: John Wiley and Sons.

Werner, C.M. (1999). Psychological perspectives on sustainability. In E. Becker, & T. Jahn (Eds.), *Sustainability and the social sciences. A cross-disciplinary approach to integrating environmental considerations into theoretical reorientation.* (pp. 223-242). London: Zed Books.

Winter, D.D. (2003). *The psychology of environmental problems*. Mahwah, NJ: Lawrence Erlbaum Associates.

Zelezny, L.C., & Schultz, P.W. (Eds.) (2000). Promoting environmentalism. *Journal of Social Issues*, 56, 365-578.

6

Global Forces in Social Science Approaches to Natural Resource Management

Jill M. Belsky

During the last few decades, social scientists have contributed enormously to understanding how environmental and natural resource management issues have become increasingly global phenomena (Stern, Young & Druckman, 1992), and alternately, that the global environment itself has much to offer the social sciences (Redclift & Benton, 1994). The global dimensions of environment and society are central chapters in today's textbooks and courses (e.g., Bell 1998; Harper, 2001; Humphrey, Lewis & Buttel, 2002). This is occurring as biophysical scientists realize that their work may help society achieve some end or objective, but determining the objective is largely a social decision, and one made more difficult as the scope for whose views are to be included becomes wider and more diverse. This chapter is a preliminary synthesis of natural resource sociology studies, and one that draws heavily from political ecologically-inspired geographers, anthropologists, and sociologists. After a brief discussion of the complexities involved in defining global forces (including globalization), the chapter discusses four topics that illustrate our engagement with global forces, and how they have changed over the last decade or so. It ends with suggestions for future research.

Social Science and Global Forces

A recent editorial in *Conservation Biology* acknowledged the importance of understanding social forces in environmental transitions, especially as they increasingly recognize the broad disconnect between their biological knowledge and conservation success on the ground (Mascia et al., 2003). However, these authors also acknowledge that the idea that conservation is as much about people and human behavior as it is about species or ecosystems is still insufficiently recognized in some conservation circles.

The complexity of these issues is heightened when their global context is considered. Environmental social scientist Fred Buttel (2002) argues that, with some important exceptions, the two key sub-fields of *environmental sociology* and *natural resource sociology* have not had a particularly distinguished record of dealing with global perspectives. Buttel suggests this may be due to the vague and imprecise notions of globalization and global forces themselves, and especially the lack of clear exemplars for incorporating global forces into the conceptualization of research problems. He suggests that the units or scale of analyses have been insufficient to develop a global sociology of resources and environment. The *sociology of natural resources* tends to stress local and regional units of analysis and has not dealt systematically with late 20th world economic and political integration, while the principal unit of analysis in *sociology of environment* has tended to be a homogeneous nation-state. Even when globalization is mentioned in the latter case, there is limited theorization. It has tended to be viewed as outside or exogenous to societies or as extensions of societal-level dynamics such as capitalism, interacting with an undifferentiated and un-ecological environment, such as in Schnaiberg's (1980) otherwise important theory of the "treadmill of production."

Trans-disciplinary perspectives that take seriously the *politics* and *ecology* in political ecology can help us bridge internal disciplinary differences, and better understand global forces (Belsky, 2002). Political ecology with its explicit attention to seeking out chains of explanations across multiple spatial and temporal scales, and to historical processes such as colonialism and economic development, is particularly attendant to embracing global forces.

Understanding Global Forces and Globalization

What do *global forces* and *globalization* mean? There is not one global perspective that provides an over-riding and widely agreed upon definition of globalization: what it is, how important is it, what drives it, its effects, or how best to study it. Each of the social sciences holds a different perspective on globalization. Controversies within and across disciplines range from fundamental issues regarding globalization's definition, importance, scope, timing and politics. Globalization is commonly defined as the integration of economic forces on a world scale, emphasizing in particular deregulation or "freeing" of trade markets. It is also often described as being shaped by technological change (especially information and communications technologies) reconfiguration of states, regionalization, and as an uneven process across the world (Pieterse, 2004).

Sociologists have been highly involved in articulating a vision of globalization, and especially in setting out an agenda for asking and responding to such concerns as who or what directs this process and who benefits or loses from it (Sklair, 1994). McMichael (2000) defines the globalization project as "an emerging vision of the world and its resources as a globally organized and managed free trade/free enterprise economy pursued by a largely unaccountable political and economic elite" (p. 354). While McMichael and social scientists informed by a political economy perspective emphasize an historical and largely structural understanding of global economic forces and institutions, and especially the inequities they have fostered between the North and South, other sociologists emphasize the non-economic aspects of globalization. For example, Ritzer (2004) defines globalization as "the worldwide diffusion of practices, expansion of relations across continents,

BRETT BRUYERE

organization of social life on a global scale, and growth of a shared global consciousness" (p. 72). Pieterse (2004) provides a definition that takes into consideration the multiple and contested notions of globalization:

> Globalization is an objective, empirical process of increasing economic and political connectivity, a subjective process unfolding in consciousness as the collective awareness of growing global interconnectedness, and a host of specific globalizing projects that seek to shape global conditions (pp. 16-17).

Among the many issues raised by trying to define globalization and its implications are the relations between the local and the global, and their influence on nation-states and citizens. While some suggest globalization is an extremely influential force that overshadows the local and inevitably leads to homogenization, others focus on the historically specific and hybrid ways global and local forces interact. With regard to global forces and the nation-state, McMichael (2000) suggests states are being pulled not only from *below* in terms of demands from civil society, but also from *above* by transnational (or even supranational) connections. Detachment from nation-states and national identities is leading people, information, ideas and organizations to find meaning and meeting space in a more global, transnational space, no doubt facilitated by the Internet and other forms of electronic communication.

In this view, the state is viewed as losing its reason to exist; it is either too small to deal with macro-global processes, or too big to be relevant to regional or local concerns (McMichael, 2000). Others are not as quick to bury the nation-state as a key unit of action and analysis. Burawoy et al. (2000) emphasize that transnational connections are not autonomous or "arbitrary patterns crossing in the sky" but are importantly "shaped by the strong magnetic field of nation states… Taxation, welfare, labor markets, regional centers of economic agglomeration, natural resources, education, political regimes, and ideologies—all mark out national grids for the transnational" (pp. 34-35).

A more fundamental question regarding global forces is whether they are really happening and if so, are they any different than in earlier times? Burawoy et al. (2000) outlined three competing views on this question. First, there are the *skeptics* who, referring to the period between 1870 and 1914, maintain that world trade, capital mobility, labor migration and monetary regulation were as open then as any time since. While there has been further internationalization of money, capital markets, foreign direct investment, and trade within supranational economic blocs (e.g., European Union, North American Free Trade Agreement, or NAFTA), they argue these are not new forms of globalization. They also point out that contrary to a popular idea, most production in bigger national economies is for domestic consumption. Furthermore, nation-states are not powerless to regulate economic activities. Indeed some of the success of the newly industrializing Asian countries is due to state regulation of national economies (McMichael, 2000).

A second group, the *radicals*, supports the notion of globalization. They believe that globalization does mark something new, different and more widespread than anything that has come before. They draw support for their view in large part from the global spread of ideology, and especially capitalist ideology, as proof that globalization is indeed a reality. Within this group, globalization is the culmination of modernity and late capitalism. Interrogating globalization requires a confrontation with essentially the spread of neoliberal capitalism which, in this view, has literally become the global standard.

A third group, the *perspectivalists*, suggests that the above view reflects merely one perspective, and largely an American perspective. This group contends that the concept of globalization is a creation of U.S. policy makers, financial planners and their allies. To the charge that globalization reflects the global spread of neoliberal capitalism, they would argue it reflects instead a relatively thin, ungrounded account that is more of a projection of their socio-political location and privilege, and a strategy to defend the status quo. Perspectivalists suggest that it is highly questionable whether there is one monolithic position across the U.S. with regard to *globalization as neoliberal* capitalism, that neoliberalism itself is a homogenous or coherent policy (economically, politically or culturally), or that the U.S. remains an imperial power. The last point has been dramatically brought home in the wake of the Enron corporate accounting scandal; the contentious World Trade Organization (WTO) meeting in Cancun, Mexico in 2003 where negotiations collapsed amid divisions between 1) the United States, European Union, and Japan and 2) the group of 23 (G-23), lead by Brazil, South Africa, India and China; and most tragically in light of the September 11th terrorist events.

Major Themes

There are significant differences in how social scientists in the 1960s and early 1970s understood global forces in environmental change with how we examine them today. Many of the topics have changed as well. We can see some of these differences as well as possibilities for improving our understanding of global forces in environmental change in the future through tracing four broad topics.

Trans-border and Global Forms of Environmental Problems

Attention to and understanding global climate change, as well as environmental disasters such as in Chernobyl and Bhopal, are visible markers of an increasingly global environment, as well as the growing political divisions of how we go about understanding and dealing with it. Social scientists have served on panels to identify human causes of global environmental change (Stern, Young & Druckman, 1992). Similarly, environmental social scientists have helped to identify the multitude of factors contributing to episodes such as Chernobyl and Bhopal. This includes consideration beyond place-based technical malfunctions, and questions about the meaning of development, progress, identity, and the arrogance of western science (Rajan, 2002). We are offering particularly important insights on the political and ideological underpinnings of how climate change and other scientific data are generated and strategically interpreted and utilized by and for different interests (Buttel, Hawkins & Power, 1990; Buttel & Taylor, 1994).

The social causes and consequences of both northern temperate and southern tropical forest change is another arena of transborder environmental change that social scientists are addressing. As wide expanses of forests are converted to alternate uses (often industrial and/or agricultural), or as they burn up (as with fires in Southeast Asia), national, regional and global concern has risen to the extent that there is now a serious question regarding their long-term existence. Social scientists have given close attention to both the material and discursive dimensions of such efforts at varying levels, and how ideas about forest and forest change influence policy makers and managers (Leach & Fairhead, 2000). Literally hundreds of studies produced over the years highlight a wide array of ongoing forest struggles, conflicts, and movements involving forest dwellers, users, state and other elites, transnational timber companies, and forest conservationists from near and afar. They also indicate a long list of academic debates: issues concerning the "nature" of forests and forest change; notions of forest access, control and rights; environmental accounting, accountability and sustainability; gender, class and race aspects; discourse on local and indigenous knowledge; resource-extraction development, and; governance institutions and strategies (Doornbos, Saith & White, 2000). A particularly important sub-topic concerns understanding the variable ways common-pool resources have been understood (and misunderstood) and the methodological questions these differences suggest (Agrawal, 2001).

"Greening" of Multilateral Institutions and Development

In recent years there has been a new emphasis on nature-society relations, and attempts to legislate environmental dangers through inter-state agreements and multilateral organizations. A striking trend over the last decade has been the "greening" – and with limited success – of multilateral institutions such as the World Bank (e.g., the Global Environmental Facility), WTO, and regional associations and agreements such as the European Union and NAFTA (Watts, 2000).

Attention to development and environmental sustainability, and especially the role of states and multilateral institutions in rethinking and managing the relationship between the two, assumed center stage with publication of the Brundtland Report (1987). This report was influential in identifying connections between environmental crises and global inequality (and especially to dependency and poverty created through colonial and post-colonial terms of trade), and the value of linking today's conditions with those in future generations. The report's call to address sustainable development awoke many global institutions to the much-discussed subject of *sustainability*.

Sociologists have provided many contributions to this discussion. Of particular importance are studies that critiqued global institutions for appropriating the concept. While acknowledging that (finally) they were paying attention to the relationship between income and environmental degradation, global institutions have been criticized for using it as a means to justify continued conventional development (and capital accumulation) and avoid addressing political and economic structural change (Redclift, 1987). Not only has this debate provided additional evidence for critiquing (modernization-style) development, but it has raised questions regarding whether there is a certain level of material well-being that nations must achieve to support environmentalism (Brechin & Kempton, 1994). Environmental sociologists continue to examine the material and ideational dimensions of connections between different approaches to economic development and sustainability, and from many different angles: production, consumption, rationality, risk, modernity, feminist, etc. (Redclift & Benton 1994). From a managerial perspective, this has led to an explosion of works claiming the compatibility of capitalist capital accumulation with modernization (Mol, 1997), and support for green technologies, industries and practices such as eco-tourism and eco-labeling. These claims are currently some of the most hotly debated topics, and are likely to remain so in coming decades.

Restructuring of Global Capitalism and Expansion of Transnational Corporate Capitalism

Attention to global forces has become particularly important over the last decade given global economic restructuring, especially in the wake of the Soviet Union collapse and the experiences of newly industrializing countries in Asia and Latin America. Environmental and natural resource social scientists have played important roles in specifying the variable conditions of global economic restructuring and their implications for environmental and social change. Many address the implications of changes mandated by International Monetary Fund structural adjustment programs (e.g., deregulation, privatization, export-led development, natural resource extraction) on local economies and resources, often specifying particularly harsh consequences for marginal environments, ethnicities, classes and genders (Redclift & Woodgate, 1997).

Lastly, the development of a growing global political ecology has been important for documenting the actions of transnational corporations as they maximize profits by exploiting cheap sources of labor and natural resources, and take advantage of increasingly easy movement of capital, labor, technology, and commodities. Perhaps one of the most striking contributions of environmental and resource social scientists to revealing connections between transnational corporations and what happens on the ground and in our bodies is work on the global food economy. Many studies (e.g., McMichael, 1998) chart the rise of agri-businesses, abetted by use of institutional and multilateral mechanisms such as the General Agreement on Tariffs and Trade (i.e., GATT) and WTO policies, that monopolize control of world agriculture and food flows. Such works have specified the implications of the food and agricultural corporate giants on land degradation, petrochemical dependency, petro-violence, malnutrition and hunger, and corrosion of traditional agro-ecosystems and local food systems (Odman & Watts, 1997). The rise of bio-technologies and what many have seen as the hegemonic control of (northern) agribusiness over both the image and material products of genetically modified organisms through WTO-sponsored intellectual property rights, is perhaps one of the most widely contested and researched topics over the last decade. This debate indicates how far environmental and resource social scientists have come in critically engaging global forces (Humphrey, Lewis & Buttel, 2002).

Transnational Environmental and Environmental-Social Justice Advocacy Movements and Networks
The fourth topic refers to the rise of new social movements that strive to link environmental conservation with a range of fair trade, sustainable production, and human rights, or what is framed as *environmental justice.* Much of the attention of environmental and resource social scientists over the last decade has changed focus from large-scale environmental organizations and campaigns to local and community efforts. These efforts are strongly influenced by attention to local livelihood, property rights, and local participation. For example, environmental and resource social scientists have played key roles in articulating, debating and influencing resource management philosophies and programs that build on and assess models of participatory conservation and development. In theory, these offer alternatives to conventional scientific expert-driven development and conservation in such arenas as forestry, fisheries and grassland management. Many have gone on to influence community based movements in the U.S. such as community-based ecosystem management (Johnson, 2001) and community forestry (Baker & Kusel, 2003). In trying to understand these community-based movements, social scientists have drawn on understandings of rural life, social stratification, property systems, livelihood strategies, local knowledge, and governance. Of great importance are studies that identify obstacles at local to global levels that hinder local management, such as when participatory mechanisms serve to contain dissent (Few, 2001).

Debates over the meaning and practices of global biodiversity conservation provide a particularly acute lens for seeing the controversies and politics of what can happen when approaches and concepts developed in one part of the world are transferred to others. Brechin and West's (1991) co-edited volume, *Resident People and National Parks,* was an important milestone in articulating the limitations of the largely American exclusionary model of conservation (i.e., strict preservation in which historical human uses are prohibited) and defending the development of alternative models of locally-designed, participatory models of conservation.

Western and Wright's (1994) co-edited volume *Natural Communities* followed soon thereafter with descriptions of case studies and analyses learned from experiments in community-based conservation programs. Works by Peluso (1993), Neumann (1998), Agrawal and Gibson (1999) and ecological anthropologists such as Brosius, Tsing and Zerner (1998) have pushed forward our theoretical understandings of the concepts and on-the-ground efforts that make claims about *nature, society, community* and *conservation.* Rather than de-centering the value of community conservation (and global biodiversity conservation more generally) as some have charged, these efforts have significantly propelled our scholarship and its practical application in advance of international biodiversity with social justice for the next century.

Future Issues: Theoretical and Managerial Considerations

The above review merely hints at the range of topics and debates social scientists around the world are engaging in as they seek to make sense of and suggest ways to study increasingly globalized people and environments. There are many who remain sympathetic to the plight of marginalized peoples who have lost access and control over natural resources in the name of biodiversity conservation. Further, there remain huge theoretical, methodological and strategic differences regarding how each makes sense of these debates and objectives. A deeper question goes to the gulf among environmental and resource social scientists regarding the extent to which we think managerial strategies themselves are useful without deeper socio-political change. Another division revolves around the ability of actors from the North and South to be able to put aside historical experiences and inequities to forge partnerships and coalitions as equals. Developing such global collaboration is hampered by the views of citizens, institutions and governments in the North that treat tropical forests as "global heritages," a stance that is highly resisted among residents of the South who see it as hypocritical and imperialistic.

These differences will no doubt persist. The important challenges are how we can be more reflexive about our own (social) location and locality, and foster dialogue and meaningful partnerships among people in our own disciplines, as well as with biophysical scientists, movement activists, professional resource managers and historic resource users and managers. In thinking about how to understand and identify global forces in ways that can link theory to practice, we have much to learn from the notion of grounding globalization and to lessons from political ecology that take seriously politics, culture and ecology.

Burawoy et al. (2000) refer to *grounding globalization* "…as the process of capturing and extending observations out from micro processes to macro forces such as global forces" (p. 29). They utilize the extended case method to do so. It begins with an event or case for situational observations, but then branches out to social processes in the broader geographical and historical field (similar to the regional political ecology approach of "bottoms up"). The advantage of the extended method is explicit attention to using the case to discover extra-local influences which are not just approached as something specific to each case study, but as subjects of investigation and theorizing in their own right.

Taking seriously the *grounding globalization* approach would also assist us in another future challenge, and that is how to identify and work towards conservation practices that are more effective and socially just, and to do so through collaborative action. Multiparty collaborations can be an extremely valuable tool for environmental and resource sociologists given that conservation goals and procedures are socially contentious. Consequently, working closely with other scientists and stakeholders becomes critical to anticipate and actually implement multiple solutions. Doing so through a grounded globalization approach offers some hope to transcend "analysis paralysis," especially given the often

PONTUS OBERG

numbing experience of having to confront powerful global institutions and forces.

Engaging a wide array of scholars and practitioners from within, but also outside, the two subfields of environmental and resource sociology can help tremendously in thinking through these issues. Ecological anthropologists and legal scholars Brosius, Tsing and Zerner (1998) have provided some of the most trenchant and insightful statements on why and how conservation practitioners can understand not only our human impact on the physical and biotic environment, but why and how we must pay close attention to the politics of language and knowledge claims. Attention to ideas in their political-historical context is extremely important, even though the authors are aware that their analyses have been perceived by some as unhelpful criticism. On the contrary, their work demonstrates the incomparable value of critical analyses that reveal the cultural politics underlying research questions, concepts and strategic practices.

Conclusion

In addition to providing an overview of topics, this chapter has suggested some challenges ahead of us and some promising trends for meeting them. With regard to the latter, we need to pay close and critical attention to both the *material* political-economic (e.g., restructured capitalism, altered nation-states, inequitable access to and control over resources) and *symbolic* (e.g., discourse, values, culture) dimensions of human and nature relationships, and especially the interactions between them.

We should embrace the complexity of seeking chains of explanations as they wind around nested scales of analysis and most importantly, situating our analyses within particular peoples, places and practices. And lastly, we ought to ground our intellectual discoveries and theories further by constantly seeking collaboration with other social and biophysical scientists, private and government-agency resource managers, and citizens at-large to engage multiple perspectives on nature/society interactions, and work towards improving conservation and natural resource management practices that can be both ecologically effective and socially just.

References

Agrawal, A. (2001). Common property institutions and sustainable governance of resources. *World Development*, 29 (19), 1649-1672.

Agrawal, A., & Gibson, C. C. (1999). Enchantment and disenchantment: The role of community in natural resource conservation. *World Development*, (27), 629-649.

Baker, M. & Kusel, J. (2003). *Community forestry in the United States: Learning from the past, crafting the future.* London: Island Press.

Bell, M. (1998). *An invitation to environmental sociology.* Thousand Oaks, CA: Pine Forge Press.

Brechin, S., & Kempton, W. (1994). Global environmentalism: A challenge to the postmaterialism thesis? *Social Science Quarterly* (75), 245-269.

Brechin, S. & West, P. (Eds.). (1991). *Resident people and national parks.* Tucson, AZ: University of Arizona Press.

Brosius, J.P., Tsing, A. & Zerner, C. (1998). Representing communities: Histories and politics of community-based natural resource management. *Society & Natural Resources*, 11 (2), 157-168.

Brundtland, G. H. (1987). *Our common future.* London: Zed Books.

Burawoy, M., Blum, J. A., George, S., Gille, Z., Gowan, T., Haney, L., Klawiter, S., Lopez, S. H., Riain, S. O., & Thayer, M. (2000). *Global ethnography: Forces, connections and imaginations in a postmodern world.* Berkeley, CA: University of California Press.

Buttel, F.H. (2002). Environmental sociology and the sociology of natural resources: Strategies for synthesis and cross-fertilization. *Society & Natural Resources,* 15 (3), 205-211.

Buttel, F. H., & Taylor, P. J. (1994). Environmental sociology and global environmental change: A critical assessment. In M. Redclift & T. Benton (Eds.), *Social theory and the global environment* (pp. 228-256). London: Routledge.

Buttel, F.H., Hawkins, A., & Power, A.G. (1990). From limits to growth to global change: Contrasts and contradictions in the evolution of environmental science and ideology. *Global Environmental Change*, 1, 57-66.

Doornbos, M., Saith, A., & White, B. (Eds.) (2000). *Forests: Nature, people and power.* United Kingdom: Blackwell.

Few, R. (2001). Containment and counter-containment: Planner/community relations in conservation planning. *The geographical journal*, 167(2), 111-131.

Harper, C. (2001). *Environment and society: Human perspectives on environmental issues.* Upper Saddle River, NJ: Prentice Hall.

Humphrey, C.R., Lewis, T. L., & Buttel, F. H. (2002). *Environment, energy, and society: A new synthesis.* Australia: Wadsworth.

Johnson, N., Belsky, J., Benavides, V., Goebel, M., Hawkins, A., & Waage, S. (2001). Global linkages to community-based ecosystem management in the United States. *Journal of Sustainable Forestry*, 12 (3/4), 35-63.

Leach, M., & Fairhead, J. (2000). Fashioned forest pasts, occluded histories? International environmental analysis in western African locales. *Development and Change*, 31, 35-59.

Mascia, M.B., Brosius, J. P., Dobson, T. A., Forbes, B. C., Horowitz, L., McKean, M. A., & Turner, N. J. (2003). Editorial: Conservation and the social sciences. *Conservation Biology*, 17(3), 649-670.

McMichael, P. (1998). Global food politics. *Monthly Review*, 50, 97-111.

McMichael, P. (2000). *Development and social change.* Thousand Oaks, CA: Pine Forge Press.

Mol, A. P. (1997). Ecological modernization: Industrial transformations and environmental reform. In M. Redclift & G. Woodgate (Eds.), *The international handbook of environmental sociology* (pp. 138-149). Cheltenham, U.K.: Edward Elgar.

Neumann, R.P. (1998). *Imposing wilderness: Struggles over livelihood and nature preservation in Africa.* Berkeley, CA: University of California Press.

Odman, D., & Watts, M. (Eds.) (1997). *Globalising food.* London: Routledge.

Peluso, N.L. (1993). Coercing conservation: The politics of state resource control. *Global Environmental Change*, June, 199-217.

Pieterse, J. N. (2004). *Globalization & culture: Global melange.* Oxford, U.K.: Rowman & Littefield Publishers.

Rajan, S.R. (2002). Disaster, development and governance: Reflections on the "lessons" of Bhopal. *Environmental Values*, 11(3), 369-394.

Redclift, M. (1987). *Sustainable development.* London: Methuen Press

Redclift, M. & Benton, T. (Eds.) (1994). *Social theory and the global environment.* London: Routledge.

Redclift, M. & Woodgate, G. (Eds.) (1997). *The international handbook of environmental sociology.* Cheltenham, U.K.: Edward Elgar,

Schnaiberg, A. (1980). *The environment: From surplus to scarcity.* Oxford, U.K: Oxford University Press.

Sklair, L. (1994). Global sociology and global environmental change. In M. Redclift & T. Benton, (Eds.) *Social theory and the global environment* (pp. 205-227). London: Routledge.

Stern, P.C., Young, O. R., & Druckman, D. (Eds.) (1992). Global environmental change: Understanding the human dimensions. Washington, D.C. National Academy Press.

Watts, M. (2000). Political ecology. In T. Barnes & E. Sheppard (Eds.), *A companion to economic geography* (pp. 257-274). Oxford, U.K.: Blackwell.

Western, D., & Wright, R.M. (1994). *Natural connections: Perspectives in community-based conservation.* Washington, D.C.: Island Press.

7

Cultural Diversity and Natural Resource Management

Myron F. Floyd

A substantial body of research on the relationship between race, ethnicity, culture and natural resources has developed in recent decades. This development is due in large part to the growth, increasing visibility and political activism of racial and ethnic minority groups in the United States. It also reflects the increasing degree to which natural resource management takes places within multi-cultural contexts, and the limited social science understanding of natural resource use and values among ethnic minority and indigenous populations (Schelhaus, 2002).

The International Symposia on Society and Resource Management (ISSRM) has emerged as a major forum for disseminating findings from empirical and conceptual studies of cultural diversity. This chapter reviews research on cultural diversity presented at ISSRM since 1986. It presents findings from the symposia with the goal of identifying the major themes emerging from published abstracts, as well as findings which later appeared in peer-reviewed journals. The chapter concludes with a series of future issues and challenges.

The chapter is developed around four major themes: 1) extractive and subsistence use, 2) recreation use and settings, 3) environmental beliefs and worldviews, and 4) environmental justice. These themes overlap as the lines of separation are somewhat arbitrary. Nevertheless, they exemplify various ways ethnic minority and indigenous populations interact with natural resources and interface with natural resource management.

Extractive and Subsistence Resource Use

Several studies demonstrated that extractive and subsistence resource use is influenced by ethnicity and culture. Values and beliefs associated with ethnicity and cultural traditions have been linked to what types of resources are harvested (Anderson, Blahna & Chavez, 2000; Richards & Creasy, 1996), social organization of resource use (Endter-Wada & Levine, 1996), application of conservation technology (Mountjoy, 1996) and ecosystem impacts (Richards & Creasy, 1996; Schelhaus, 2002). These studies shed light on the critical knowledge needed to inform management and policy decisions regarding extractive and subsistence uses.

Several specific findings are worthy of note. First, sustainability of natural resources is linked to the values and norms of distinct ethnic groups. Mountjoy (1996) found that ethnic group membership influences adoption of effective soil conservation practices, farm management style, and use of technical assistance to mitigate erosion. Richards and Creasy (1996) documented differences in mushroom harvesting on national forests, and sources of conflict between Native Americans in the U.S. Pacific Northwest and immigrants from southeast Asia. They observed that harvesting among southeast Asian groups was primarily commercial activity and resource intensive in terms of amounts harvested and disturbance to duff and leaf litter. In contrast, Native Americans engaged in less intensive traditional harvesting, taking only what could be used in cultural rituals or exchanged with families. They also took steps to minimize disturbance of duff and leaf litter, and perceived increasing commercial harvesting as a threat to the resource. In another study, Anderson et al. (2000) found fern gathering among forest users of Korean and Japanese backgrounds was motivated by social and recreational reasons rather than commercial reasons or economic necessity. The authors used these findings to caution researchers and managers against treating Asian sub-populations as a single Asian category.

Second, previous studies highlight the importance of achieving an appropriate balance between commercial and traditional subsistence uses of natural resources. For example, Endter-Wada and Levine (1996) showed that ethnicity was associated with the social organization of subsistence activities. In their study of Native, non-Native, and part-Native households in Bristol Bay, Alaska, Natives and part-Native households exhibited higher levels of subsistence participation, greater diversity of resources harvested, and greater participation in sharing networks made up of kin and friends. The research concluded that subsistence activities, apart from economic benefits, provide an important context for sharing and sustaining cultural heritage. This aspect of subsistence use is often overlooked in conventional policy and economic impact analysis (Dick, 1996).

Third, differences in resource values and cultural practices are often the underlying basis for natural resource conflicts. As suggested above, Native Americans believed the commercial use-orientation of southeast Asian immigrants threatened their established cultural practices (Richards & Creasy, 1996). Similarly, Travis' (1998) analysis of Hawaii's tuna fishery described how conflict between Vietnamese-Americans and native Hawaiian long-line fishers had more to do with cultural differences in resource values, norms and history, than differences in actual gear and technology.

While the study of ethnicity and culture in relation to extractive and subsistence use has not developed as rapidly as other areas related to cultural diversity (e.g., recreation), it is likely to attract more research attention given increasing immigration from Latin America and Asia to the United States. Immigrant populations from these regions have been associated with non-traditional uses of public lands (Dick, 1996). In addition, accommodating the legal rights of indigenous populations to use natural resources for subsistence use will continue to be a management concern.

Outdoor Recreation

Studies related to outdoor recreation represent the largest topic area in research on ethnicity and natural resources. Systematic studies on racial and ethnic differences have been reported since the 1960s beginning with studies completed for the Outdoor Recreation Resources Review Commission. In recent years, investments in recreation research on race, ethnicity and demographic change by the Southern, Pacific Southwest and North Central research stations of the USDA Forest Service have contributed significantly to the development of this topical area.

The focus of concerns in outdoor recreation research can be grouped into two broad areas: 1) sorting out theoretical explanations for low levels of participation by ethnic minorities in natural resource recreation, and 2) investigation of ethnic patterns in on-site behaviors. Within the first area of inquiry, researchers have evaluated the role of economic marginality, subcultural variation between ethnic groups, and discrimination as explanations for disproportionately low participation among ethnic minorities. Subcultural variation has emerged as the predominant explanation. For example, Dragon and Ham (1986) concluded from their study of Native Americans that ethnicity was a better explanation of national park visitation than socioeconomic status. Dwyer and Hutchison (1988) found that socioeconomic variables could not account for differences in outdoor recreation activities between White and Black Illinois households. Based on a comparison of white and African-American adolescents, Floyd and Bixler (1994) concluded that race was a significant predictor of wildland recreation preferences, even when controlling for environmental preference, gender, and socioeconomic status. Controlling for socioeconomic status, Scott and Burr (1994) observed differences between Black and White Ohio residents in attitudes and opinions about recreation development alternatives.

Evidence on the role of discrimination effects has also begun to accumulate. Latino, Asian and African-American residents in the Chicago area cited instances of interpersonal and institutional discrimination as barriers to using area parks and forests (Blahna & Black, 1992). Violent threats made by Whites and institutional discrimination have been shown to affect African-Americans visitation to the Shawnee National Forest in southern Illinois (Outley & Floyd, 1996). In addition, findings from a national survey data suggest that institutional barriers such as poorly maintained facilities impact African-Americans more than Whites (Johnson, Bowker & Cordell, 2000). This finding provides empirical evidence that institutional barriers are not limited to isolated regions.

The second area of recreation research involves on-site use patterns and preferences (e.g., Bass, Ewert & Chavez, 1993; Carr & Williams, 1992, 1993; Gobster & Delgado, 1992). This work has contributed to understanding how ethnicity correlates with site use, and therefore provides guidance to managers and resource planners. The research has documented significant variations in on-site use between Anglo-Americans and Hispanic population, while identifying intra-ethnic variation among Hispanic Americans as well.

The distinctive on-site use patterns of Hispanics recreation groups are well-

documented. Compared to Whites, Hispanic recreationists have been found to visit forests in large groups composed of immediate and extended families (Carr & Williams, 1993), place more importance on tangible site features (e.g., picnic tables) and appear to be more tolerant of high user density (Pfister & Simcox, 1992). Studies have also shown that a significant proportion of Hispanic recreationists were born outside of the U.S. (Bass et al., 1993; Pfister, 1990) and that foreign-born Hispanics expressed greater concern about site degradation and general environmental issues (Pfister, 1994).

These studies demonstrate the extent of diversity that exists within ethnic groups, as well. For instance, Bass et al. (1993) found differences in on-site recreation activity participation between U.S. born and Mexican-born Hispanics. Similarly, Gobster and Delgado's (1992) research in an urban park setting showed that on-site participation in team sports varied by ancestral origin. Carr and Williams (1993) found that group composition varies by ancestral ties. In their study, Mexican origin groups included more immediate and extended family, while Central American groups participated as organized groups. Because of the extent of diversity within the Latino population, Chavez and Winter (1994) have questioned whether ethnic identity, ancestry, group size or national origin are the most meaningful independent variables for ethnic diversity research. Nevertheless, research findings on recreation use patterns are beginning to be translated into site design. Chavez (1998) described how research findings on Hispanic recreation behavior were applied to the re-design of the Applewhite

Picnic Area on the Angeles National Forest to reflect the ethnic transformation in southern California.

Environmental Attitudes and Worldviews

Research on ethnicity, culture and environmental attitudes has received extensive treatment in the literature. In ISSRM, studies have examined such topics as differences between European Americans and African-Americans on environmental concern (Parker & McDonough, 1999), effect of acculturation on environmental concern among Hispanic subpopulations (Caro & Ewert, 1995; Floyd, 1992), implications of environmentalism among Asian-Americans (Jeong, 2000), and environmental beliefs and worldviews among Native American tribal groups (Jostad, McAvoy & McDonald, 1996).

With regard to differences between African-Americans and European Americans, Parker and McDonough's (1999) research found little difference between environmental concern of these groups using a sample of Detroit residents. Similarly, Treadwell and Manning (1998) concluded that there were few differences between Blacks and Whites on environmental concern based on a Massachusetts sample. These findings are consistent with Jones's (2002) comprehensive analysis of environmental opinion data covering a 20-year period. He found no evidence of a "concern gap" between Blacks and Whites. In fact, in several instances environmental concern among Blacks exceeded concern expressed by Whites. In view of the broader literature (e.g., Jones, 2002), these findings help to dispel myths about lack of environmental concern among African-Americans.

With regard to Hispanic Americans, Caro and Ewert (1995) found that length of residence in the U.S. and arrival age accounted for most of the variance in environmental concern among Hispanic visitors to California national forests. Using the New Environmental Paradigm instrument (Dunlap & Van Liere, 1978), Floyd (1992) found that among Cuban Americans, age and acculturation were significantly related to utilitarian beliefs (e.g., agreement with statements like "plants and animals exist primarily to be used by humans"). Pfister's (1994) comparison of US-born and foreign-born Hispanic showed that foreign-born visitors expressed greater concern about general environmental issues such as oil spills and water quality. As suggested earlier, such studies demonstrate that ethnic labels can mask considerable variation within ethnic groups.

Environmental beliefs among Asian populations have been addressed to a lesser extent. Jeong (2000) described the relationship between pro-social behavior and resource impacts associated with Asian Americans. He noted that natural resources play an important role in traditional medicine among many Asian cultures, and that many Asian-Americans retain the social norms, attitudes and values of their native cultures.

Studies on environmental beliefs held by Native people illustrate the extent to which environmental worldviews can differ between ethnic groups. For example, based on interviews with members of several tribal groups, Jostad et al. (1996) described a four part system of environmental ethics among Native Americans based on 1) sacredness of all things, 2) respectful actions to preserve the balance of the system, 2) all is interrelated, and 4) a "contextually alive" (p. 572) relationship with

Mother Earth. These spiritual views of the environment contrast sharply with rational and scientific-utilitarian beliefs associated with natural resource agencies and European-American culture. Morris (1992) explored the utility of indigenous knowledge of Native Americans of the pre-colonial era to inform current resource management. Rikoon's (1996) analysis of the incorporation of Native American beliefs in a public education campaign by the USDA Soil Conservation Service revealed that such efforts are inherently problematic. He argued that irreconcilable value differences exist between Native American and Western environmental thought, and that these differences make such cultural transfers complex.

Environmental Justice

The rise of the environmental justice movement in the 1980s generated a flurry of research activity and initiated a new climate of environmental policy-making. At the center of this activity was growing awareness of the link between race, class and exposure to environmental hazards (Bullard, 1994). Social scientists from several disciplines have provided both conceptual and empirical analyses of environmental injustice claims.

In one of the first studies to address the topic at ISSRM, Gelobter (1988) examined correlations between air quality, race, and class from 1970 to 1986. He found that differences in exposure to poor air quality by income have decreased over time, while racial differences persisted. Moreover, he found that minority exposure to U.S. Environmental Protection Agency criteria pollutants were 40 to 60 percent higher than exposure among Whites.

There are few examples of environmental justice research set in a context of natural resource amenities or outdoor recreation (e.g., Tarrant & Cordell, 1999). As cited earlier, however, Johnson et al. (1994) found that pollution is more likely to be a barrier to outdoor recreation among ethnic minority groups than among Whites. Bowker and Leeworthy (1998) found that increased fees for access to public lands has a differential impact on non-Hispanic Whites than Hispanics: Fee increases exerted a greater negative effect on visitation among Hispanics.

Research examining ethnic minority group influence on natural resource decisions and policy-making also falls under the heading of environmental justice. Austin (1998) suggested that Native Americans are often neglected in environmental impact assessments, even when significant environmental risks are present. Using two case studies involving longstanding disputes over water and land rights, Bidol-Padva (1992) sought to identify the level of protection the regulatory process provided the natural and cultural heritages of the Seminole and Miccosukee tribes in Florida. Raish (2000) analyzed the conflict between Hispano communities of northern New Mexico, environmental groups and USDA Forest Service policy. Her study included an historical analysis of how USDA Forest Service policies have denied or limited Hispano access to natural resources. She describes how such communities have asserted their ethnic identity and cultural heritage to form economic and stewardship cooperatives to regain land and resource access. Like other communities with environmental injustice claims, they have used protests, litigation and formation of community action groups to exert influence on natural resources decisions affecting their communities.

Summary of Findings

ISSRM has become a major forum for research on race, ethnicity, culture and their relationships to natural resource management. Major findings from previous symposia and other research can be summarized as follows:

- Ethnic and cultural patterns are reflected in extractive, subsistence and natural resources uses, and these patterns have implications for resource conditions and sustainability.

- Visits to outdoor recreation areas by African-Americans appear to be influenced by ethnic factors, rather than income or class factors.

- Hispanic on-site use patterns tend to be characterized by larger groups with more varied social composition and greater emphasis on site features.

- A core set of environmental beliefs and values appears to exist among Native American tribal groups. Among Hispanic sub-populations, acculturation appears to be a significant predictor of environmental concern. There was no evidence of lack of environmental concern among African Americans.

- Although empirical findings are limited, ethnic minority groups experience differential access to environmental quality and natural resource decision-making.

Conclusions and Implications

The overriding theme to emerge from research presented at ISSRM is the need for culturally diverse perspectives in natural resources management. In light of this need, a better understanding of the relationship between ethnicity, culture and natural resources should be a high research priority for the 21st century. The research themes highlighted in this chapter provide several ideas about direction for future studies.

Shifting Paradigms in Outdoor Recreation Research

Outdoor recreation has received the greatest amount of research attention. While this research area has shown signs of maturation, new perspectives will be needed to capture new forms of ethnic diversity. The current paradigm of research is centered around bipolar analyses (e.g., Black-White, Anglo-Hispanic). Yet, as demographic trends suggest, the bases of cultural diversity are becoming more complex. Alternative perspectives are needed to address resource management implications associated with multi-ethnic situations, intra-ethnic diversity, and multiracial ancestry.

Promoting Social Justice in Natural Resource Management

It will become increasingly important to recognize the legitimacy of diverse meanings and values of natural resources among different ethnic and cultural groups. Historically, natural resource management agencies have used ethnic and cultural differences to legitimize resource values and meanings associated with Anglo/Western European values while devaluing the culture and values of minority groups and indigenous people. Currently, there is greater awareness of social justice concerns due to the emergence of the environmental justice movement and subsequent policy actions (Floyd & Johnson, 2002). More research is needed to identify various understandings of natural resource uses and values to promote greater participation of minority groups and indigenous populations in decision-making. Research attention should also focus on monitoring the distribution of costs and benefits associated with natural resource management.

Organizational Change and Cultural Diversity
Organizational change is a prerequisite for fostering cultural diversity in natural resources management. While few studies within ISSRM addressed diversity within natural resource agencies, monitoring the effectiveness of organizations to address cultural diversity internally and externally will continue to be important. Resource management agencies in the U.S. have experienced some success in increasing workforce diversity (e.g., Mohai, Stillman, Jakes & Liggett, 1994; Thomas & Mohai, 1995). While such success is recent, research should begin to examine whether and how cultural diversity in natural resource agencies impact overall agency culture and whether diversification makes a difference in the formulation and implementation of resource management policy (Brown & Harris, 2000).

Research Methods for Cultural Diversity
As natural resource agencies and researchers engage members of ethnic minority groups and indigenous populations in research, the appropriateness of particular methodological tools and approaches should be considered. McAvoy, Winter, Outley, McDonald and Chavez (2000) challenged researchers to carefully consider their choice of methods when conducting research with communities of color. Drawing on their experiences from past studies in Latino, African-American, and American Indian communities, they emphasized awareness of negative experiences people of color have experienced with scientific research, realization of personal biases, development of trust with communities under study, employment of multiple methods, culturally-diverse research teams, and recruitment of co-researchers from the community in the study setting.

Ethnicity and Park Management in Global Perspective
Examination of the research on ethnicity and culture in natural resources reveals a bias toward North American (primarily U.S.) studies. There is a need to better understand the various ways ethnicity and culture relate to parks and protected areas in other geographical contexts. Discussions on the relationship between ethnicity and natural resources, and between indigenous populations and resource management, rarely converge. This fails to occur despite over-lapping theoretical concerns and management challenges (Constantinides & Brechin, 1992). Clearly, differences in social, geographical and cultural contexts limit the degree to which these two issues can be integrated. Nevertheless, commonality between the literature which focuses on ethnicity and natural resources, and that which focuses on indigenous populations and resource management in developing nations, should be explored.

References

Anderson, J.A., Blahna, D.J., & Chavez, D.J. (2000). Fern gathering on the San Bernandino National Forest: Cultural versus commercial values among Korean and Japanese participants. *Society and Natural Resources*, 13, 747-762.

Austin, D. (1998, May). *Enhancing Native American cultural revitalization through EIS-motivated activities.* Paper presented at the 5th International Symposium on Society and Resource Management, Fort Collins, CO.

Bass, J., Ewert, A., & Chavez, D.J. (1993). Influence of ethnicity on recreation and natural resource use patterns: Managing recreation sites for ethnic and racial diversity. *Environmental Management*, 17, 523-529.

Bidol-Padva, P. (1992, May). *Impacts on collaborative mediation of the protection of the natural and cultural heritage of the Seminole and Miccosukee tribes of Florida.* Paper presented at the 4th International Symposium on Society and Resource Management, Madison, WI.

Blahna, D., & Black, K. (1992). Racism a concern for recreation managers. In P. Gobster (Ed.), *Managing urban and high-use recreation settings* (General Technical Report NC-163) (pp. 111-118). St. Paul, MN: USDA Forest Service.

Brown, G., & Harris, C.C. (2000). The US Forest Service: Whither the new resource management paradigm? *Journal of Environmental Management*, 58, 1-19.

Bullard, R.D. (1994). Introduction. In R.D. Bullard (Ed.), *Unequal protection: Environmental justice and communities of color* (pp. xv-xxiii). San Francisco: Sierra Club Books.

Caro, V., & Ewert, A. (1995). The influence of acculturation on environmental concerns: An exploratory study. *Journal of Environmental Education*, 26, 13-21.

Carr, D.S., & Williams, D.R. (1993). Understanding the role of ethnicity in outdoor recreation experiences. *Journal of Leisure Research*, 25, 22-38.

Chavez, D.J. (1998). *Redesigning social spaces to serve ethnic diversity: The case of the Applewhite Picnic Area.* Paper presented at the 7th International Symposium on Society and Resource Management, Columbia, MO.

Chavez, D.J., & Winter, P.L. (1994, June). *Research addressing culturally diverse visitor populations: Searching for the independent variable.* Paper presented at the 5th International Symposium on Society and Resource Management, Fort Collins, CO.

Constantinides, J., & Brechin, D.R. (1992, May). *Parks, protected areas, and racial and ethnic minorities: A review of the literature and future research needs.* Paper presented at the 4th International Symposium on Society and Resource Management, Madison, WI.

Dick, R.E. (1996). Subsistence economics: Freedom from the marketplace. *Society and Natural Resources*, 9, 19-29.

Dragon, C., & Ham, S.H. (1986, May). *Native American underrepresentation in national parks: Tests of the marginality and ethnicity hypotheses.* Paper presented at the First International Symposium on Society and Resource Management, Corvallis, OR.

Dunlap, R., & Van Liere, K. (1978). The new environmental paradigm. *Journal of Environmental Education*, 9, 10-19.

Dwyer, J.F., & Hutchison, R. (1988). Outdoor recreation participation and preferences by black and white households. In J. Vining (Ed.), *Social science in natural resource recreation management* (pp. 49-67). Boulder, CO: Westview.

Endter-Wada, J., & Levine, D.W. (1996). Comparison of subsistence activities among natives and non-natives in Bristol Bay, Alaska. *Society and Natural Resources*, 9, 595-609.

Floyd, M.F. (1992, May). *Understanding intra-ethnic environmental attitude variations: Cuban origin population views.* Paper presented at the 4th International Symposium on Society and Resource Management, Madison, WI.

Floyd, M. F., & Bixler, R. D. (1996). *The significance of race as a predictor of wildland recreation activity preferences.* Paper presented at the 6th International Symposium on Society and Resource Management, University Park, PA.

Floyd, M.F., & Johnson, C.Y. (2002). Coming to terms with environmental justice in outdoor recreation and tourism: A conceptual discussion with research implications. *Leisure Sciences*, 24, 59-77.

Gelobter, M. (1988, June). *The distribution of outdoor air pollution, by income and race.* Paper presented at the Second Symposium on Society and Resource Management, Urbana-Champaign, IL.

Gobster, P.H., & Delgado, A. (1992). Ethnicity and recreation use in Chicago's Lincoln Park: In-park user survey findings. In P. Gobster (Ed.), *Managing urban and high-use recreation settings* (General Technical Report NC-163) (pp. 75-81). St. Paul, MN: USDA Forest Service.

Jeong, W. (2000, June). *Asian Americans: Attitudes, values and behaviors toward natural resources.* Paper presented at the 8th International Symposium on Society and Resource Management, Bellingham, WA.

Johnson, C., Bowker, J.M., & Cordell, H.K. (2000, June). *Outdoor recreation barriers in the South: An examination of race, gender, and rural dwelling.* Paper presented at the 8th International Symposium on Society and Resource Management, Bellingham, WA.

Jones, R.E. (2002). Blacks just don't care: Unmasking popular stereotypes about concern for the environment among African-Americans. *International Journal of Public Administration*, 25, 221-251.

Jostad, P.M., McAvoy, L.H., & McDonald, D. (1996). Native American land ethics: Implications for natural resource management. *Society and Natural Resources*, 9, 565-581.

McAvoy, L., Winter, P.L., Outley, C., McDonald, D., & Chavez, D.J. (2000). Conducting research with communities of color. *Society and Natural Resources*, 13, 479-488

Mohai, P., Stillman, P., Jakes, P., & Liggett, C. (1994, June). *Changing perceptions and attitudes in the USDA Forest Service: What differences does workforce diversification make?* Paper presented at the 5th International Symposium on Society and Resource Management, Fort Collins, CO.

Morris, J.D. (1992, May). *Pre-contact Native American land use patterns: Historic basis for future answers.* Paper presented at the 4th International Symposium on Society and Resource Management, Madison, WI.

Morrissey, J., & Manning, R.E. (2000). Race, residence and environmental concern: New Englanders and the White Mountain National Forest. *Human Ecology Review*, 7, 12-23.

Mountjoy, D.C. (1996). Ethnic diversity and the patterned adoption of soil conservation in the Strawberry Hills of Monterey, California. *Society and Natural Resources*, 9, 339-357.

Outley, C., & Floyd, M.F. (1996, May). *Perceived discrimination and recreation choice among African Americans.* Paper presented at the 6th International Symposium on Society and Resource Management, University Park, PA.

Parker, J.D., & McDonough, M.H. (1999). Environmentalism of African Americans: An analysis of the subcultural and barrier theories. *Environment and Behavior*, 31, 155-177.

Pfister, R.E. (1990, May). *Ethnicity in outdoor recreation: Observations of Hispanic forest visitors.* Paper presented at the 3rd International Symposium on Society and Resource Management, College Station, TX.

Pfister, R.E. (1994, June). *Environmental issues: The significance of age, gender, and place of birth.* Paper presented at the 5th International Symposium on Society and Resource Management, Fort Collins, CO.

Pfister, R.E., & Simcox, D.E. (1992, May). *Effects of varying user density levels on Hispanic perceptions of outdoor recreation and environmental values and landscape perceptions of Hispanic forest visitors.* Paper presented at the 4th International Symposium on Society and Resource Management, Madison, WI.

Raish, C. (2000). Environmentalism, the Forest Service, and the Hispano communities of Northern New Mexico. *Society and Natural Resources*, 13, 489-508.

Richards, R.T., & Creasy, M. (1996). Ethnic diversity, resource values, and ecosystem management: Matsutake mushroom harvesting in the Klamath Bioregion. *Society and Natural Resources*, 9, 359-374.

Rikoon, J.S. (1996). Imagined culture and cultural imaging: Cultural implications of the USDA-SCS "Harmony" campaign. *Society and Natural Resources*, 9, 583-593.

Schelhaus, J. (2002). Race, ethnicity, and natural resources in the United States: A review. *Natural Resources Journal*, 42, 723-763.

Scott, D., & Burr, S. (1994). *African-Americans' and Whites' views about recreation development and preservation of park lands.* Paper presented at the 5th International Symposium on Society and Resource Management, Fort Collins, CO.

Tarrant, M.A., & Cordell, H.K. (1999). Environmental justice and the spatial distribution of outdoor recreation sites: An application of geographic information systems. *Journal of Leisure Research*, 31, 18-34.

Thomas, J., & Mohai, P. (1995). Racial, gender, and professional diversification in the Forest Service from 1983 to 1992. *The Policy Studies Journal*, 23, 296-309.

Travis, M.D. (1998, May). *Conflict in Hawaii's fisheries: The Influence of ethnicity and culture on institutional structure.* Paper presented at the 7th International Symposium on Society and Resource Management, Columbia, MO.

Wang, G.A., Anderson, D.H., & Jakes, P.J. (1996). Legislating the past: Cultural resource management in the U.S. Forest Service. *Society and Natural Resources*, 9, 3-18.

8

Recreation Planning Frameworks

Robert E. Manning

The frameworks that now guide much of contemporary planning and management of parks, wilderness and related outdoor recreation areas had their genesis in the mid 1980s, as the first International Symposium on Society and Resource Management meeting was convened in 1986. Development, refinement, and application of these frameworks have been well-represented in the abstracts of this important series of national and international symposia. This chapter briefly outlines the emergence of contemporary recreation planning frameworks; their application by park and wilderness management agencies; the research and management agendas they have spawned, and; theoretical, methodological and empirical issues surrounding their use.

From Carrying Capacity to Rational Planning

Perhaps the most fundamental issue in the planning and management of parks, wilderness, and related outdoor recreation areas is the inherent tension between *use* and *preservation*. The legislation creating the U.S. National Park Service illustrates this fundamental tradeoff by defining the twofold mission of national parks "to provide for the enjoyment of the public" while also "to conserve the scenery and the natural and historic objects therein." This mission is embodied, explicitly or implicitly, in the planning and management guidelines of virtually all parks, wilderness, and related outdoor recreation areas.

The issue of how much recreation use can be accommodated without threatening the preservation of parks and related protected areas has conventionally been addressed under the rubric of *carrying capacity*. Carrying capacity has a rich history in the natural resources professions of wildlife and range management where it refers to the number of animals that can be ecologically sustained in a given habitat (Dasmann, 1964). It has obvious parallels and intuitive appeal in the social aspect of park planning and management. In fact, it was first suggested as a park planning and management concept in the context of the U.S. national parks in the 1930s (Sumner, 1936). However, the first rigorous applications of carrying capacity to park and outdoor recreation planning and management did not occur until the 1960s (e.g., Wagar, 1964).

Burgeoning visitor use in parks, wilderness, and related outdoor recreation areas in the 1960s and 1970s gave rise to a number of legislative and policy initiatives designed to address social carrying capacity (Cole & Stankey, 1997; Hof & Lime, 1997). For example, the 1978 General Authorities Act (U.S. Public Law 95-625) requires national parks to develop *visitor carrying capacities*. Similarly, regulations emerging from the 1976 National Forest Management Act (U.S. Public Law 94-588) specified that national forest wilderness areas must "provide for limiting and distributing visitor use of specific portions in accord with periodic estimates of the maximum levels of use that allow natural processes to operate freely and that do not impair the values for which wildernesses were created."

However, application of carrying capacity proved challenging. Despite a blossoming base of scientific literature documenting the ecological and experiential impacts of increasing outdoor recreation use, the question remained of how much impact should be allowed, or what are the *limits of acceptable change* (Frissell, 1963; Frissell & Stankey, 1972). Subsequent research and management experience suggested that the limits of acceptable change can be determined only within the context of specific management objectives. For example, what degree of resource protection should be maintained, or what type of recreation opportunity should be provided? Research generally illustrates that adverse impacts to natural resources and the quality of the visitor experience are caused by even relatively low levels of use, and that increasing levels of use may cause greater levels of impact (Hammitt & Cole, 1998; Manning, 1999).

The concept of limits of acceptable change and the associated need for management objectives is illustrated in Figure 1. In this figure, two hypothetical relationships between 1) recreation use and 2) resource and social impacts (e.g., soil erosion and crowding, respectively) are shown. It is clear from both lines that recreation use and impact are related: even relatively low levels of use cause impacts, and increasing levels of use cause increasing amounts of impact. However, it is not clear at what point carrying capacity has been reached. The hypothetical relationships in Figure 1 suggest that some resource and/or social impact is inevitable, even with relatively low levels of visitor use. Thus, some level of environmental and social impact must be tolerated if parks and related outdoor recreation areas are to remain open. For the relationship defined by line A, X1 and X2 represent levels of visitor use; use that results in differing levels of resource and social impacts as defined by points Y1 and Y2. But which of these points -- Y1 ,Y2, or some other point along the axis -- represents the maximum amount of acceptable impact? Ultimately, this is a judgment that must be expressed within the context of management objectives. Empirical relationships such as those in Figure 1 can be helpful in making effective decisions about carrying capacity, but they must be supplemented with management objectives.

This perspective has given rise to a number of recreation planning and management frameworks based on the principle of management-by-objectives.

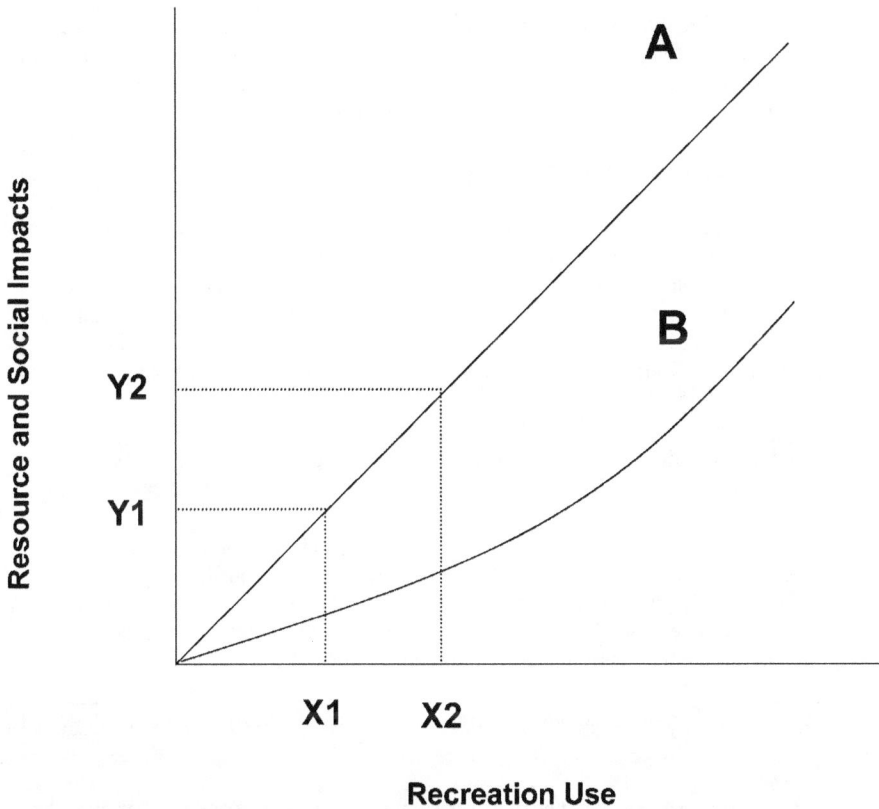

Figure 1. Hypothetical relationships between recreation use & resource and social impacts

While these frameworks were originally designed to address carrying capacity , or the fundamental tension between use and preservation, they can be (and have been) applied to multiple outdoor recreation issues across a spectrum of park and related protected areas. Now, these frameworks constitute an increasingly important and expanding guidance for rational, comprehensive outdoor recreation planning and management (Cole & McCool, 1997c).

Management-by-Objectives Frameworks
The initial management-by-objectives framework to emerge was limits of acceptable change (LAC), developed for application to USDA Forest Service wilderness (Stankey, Cole, Lucas, Peterson & Frissell, 1985). Similar frameworks have evolved, including Management Process for Visitor Activities (VAMP) developed by Parks Canada (1985); Carrying Capacity Assessment Process (C-CAP) developed by Shelby and Heberlein (1986); a generic outdoor recreation planning and management framework outlined by Manning (1986, 1999); Visitor Impact Management (VIM) developed with the National Parks and Conservation

Step 1. Agree that two or more goals (e.g., recreation and preservation) are in conflict. Contemporary, recreation planning frameworks can be seen as a means of resolving such conflict. Goals conflict whenever it is impossible to simultaneously optimize conditions for all management goals.
Step 2. Establish that all goals must be compromised to some extent.
Step 3. Decide which conflicting goal(s) will ultimately constrain the other goal(s). In other words, a hierarchy of goals must be established. If there are multiple constraining goals, either these constraining goals cannot conflict with each other or it must be possible to establish a hierarchy among the constraining goals. For parks and related areas, protection of natural resources and the quality of the visitor experience is generally considered the ultimately constraining goal.
Step 4. Formulate indicators and standards of quality and monitor the ultimately constraining goal(s). Indicators and standards of quality must be measurable.
Step 5. Allow the ultimately constraining goal(s) to be compromised until the standard of quality is reached. The process of balancing conflicting goals begins by allowing the most important goal(s) – the one(s) for which standards of quality have been written – to be compromised somewhat. Standards of quality define the maximum amount of compromise that will be accepted.
Step 6. Compromise the other goal(s) so standards of quality are not violated.

Table 1. Basic logic underlying contemporary recreation planning frameworks. (adapted from Cole and McCool, 1997b)

Association (Graefe, Kuss & Loomis, 1986); Visitor Experience and Resource Protection (VERP) developed by the U.S. National Park Service (Manning, 2001a; National Park Service, 1997;); and a generic goal-achievement framework outlined in the text, *Wilderness Management* (Hendee & Dawson, 2002).

Despite the apparent diverse and alphabet soup nature of these frameworks, most observers agree that they are more similar than different (Brunson, 1997; Cole & McCool, 1997c; Hof & Lime, 1997; McCool & Cole, 1997; Nilsen & Tayler, 1997). Each share common procedural and rational foundations, as well as fundamental procedural elements, including the following:

1. Formulation of management objectives that are expressed by quantitative indicators and standards of quality.

2. Monitoring of indicator variables to determine their condition relative to standards of quality.

3. Application of management actions to ensure that standards of quality are maintained.

A common rationale or logic underlying these frameworks is outlined in Table 1 (Cole & McCool, 1997b; Cole & Stankey, 1997).

Distinctions among contemporary recreation planning frameworks are mostly a matter of terminology and sequencing, although some differences might be considered more substantive. For example, LAC explicitly incorporates the Recreating Opportunity Spectrum concept (Clark & Stankey, 1979; Driver, Brown, Stankey & Gregoire, 1987), an approach that encourages zoning and development of a spectrum of recreation experiences. VIM emphasizes analysis of the potential causes of recreation-related impacts as a means of enhancing the selection and implementation of management actions. VERP requires that planning begin with an analysis of park purpose as a way to help formulate management objectives, and design a public involvement strategy.

The frameworks outlined above provide a strong professional basis for outdoor recreation planning (McCool & Cole, 1997; Shelby, Stankey & Shindler, 1992). They provide a conceptual basis for addressing the tradeoffs that are inherent in outdoor recreation, a structured process in which values are more explicitly considered and presented, and a context in which more transparent, traceable, and defensible recreation plans can be derived. In addition, these planning frameworks emphasize the consideration of desired future outcomes or conditions: the appropriate output measures of outdoor recreation planning. Their inclusion of long-term monitoring helps ensure that planners and managers are explicitly aware of changing resource and experiential conditions, and thus enhances the capability of park and wilderness management agencies to respond to changing conditions.

Applications

The planning frameworks noted above have been applied in both the United States and internationally, and the literature suggests these applications have generally been successful (Absher, 1989; Graefe, Kuss & Loomis, 1986; Graefe et al., 1990; Hendee & Dawson, 2002; Kaltenborn & Emmelin, 1993; Ritter, 1997; Warren, 1997). Two relatively prominent examples illustrate this. The initial application of LAC focused on the Bob Marshall Wilderness area in the northern Rocky Mountains of the U.S., and culminated in a plan adopted in 1987. This application employed a transactive planning approach – an extensive process of public involvement designed to enhance dialogue, mutual learning and societal action among stakeholders – to complement the rational nature of LAC and related frameworks (Friedmann, 1973; Yankelovich, 1991). The resulting plan divided the wilderness into four zones, or opportunity classes, each defined by a series of indicators and standards of quality for both resource and social conditions. For example, Opportunity Class 1, the most pristine zone, specifies that the barren core of campsites should not exceed 100 square feet, and that visitors should have an 80 percent probability of not encountering any other groups. An evaluation found that both managers and citizens believed this application would lead to better maintenance of natural conditions while providing high quality wilderness recreation opportunities (Ashor, 1985). In addition, a lack of appeals to management directives in this potentially contentious wilderness area further indicates that such an approach can be successful (McCoy, Krumpe & Allen, 1995). This result coincides with the results of a broader evaluation of LAC in national forests in six U.S. western states (McCoy et al., 1995).

A second prominent applied example of successful contemporary recreation planning frameworks involves the initial application of VERP to Arches National Park in the Colorado Plateau region of the U.S. (Manning, 2001a; Manning, Lime, Hof & Freimund, 1995; National Park Service, 1995). This application included a program of ecological and social research designed to provide a strong scientific basis for the formulation of indicators and standards of quality (Belnap, 1998; Hof et al., 1994; Manning, Lime, Freimund & Pitt, 1996; Manning, Lime & Hof, 1996). The park was ultimately divided into nine zones, each defined by management objectives, associated resource and experiential indicators, and standards of quality. For example, the pedestrian zone specified that 30 percent or more of soil samples adjacent to trails should be rated as less than four (4) on the soil crust index and that no more than 30 people at one time should be present at Delicate Arch more than 10 percent of the time. This application resulted in the first comprehensive carrying capacity plan implemented in the U.S. National Park system (National Park Service, 1995).

Other environmental issues and areas subject to the basic rationale or logic underlying these frameworks (as outlined in Table 1) may be amenable to this planning approach. In fact, a recent analysis concludes that "the LAC process [and related frameworks] has widespread applicability to issues other than recreation management and in places other than protected areas" (Cole & McCool, 1997b, p. 71). Consideration is now being given to more expansive applications of these recreation planning frameworks, including to a spectrum of protected areas that extends beyond national parks, wilderness and similar areas (Brunson, 1997; Brunson & Rodriquez, 1992); incorporation of non-recreational values into park and wilderness planning (Manning, 1992); and application to non-recreation issues such as fire management, air pollution, exotic plant and animal invasion, domestic livestock grazing, and fish stocking (Cole, 1995; Cole & McCool, 1997b; Cole & Stankey, 1997; Merigliano, Cole & Parsons, 1997).

Issues

Standards of Quality

Research and management experience with the recreation planning frameworks described above have revealed a number of conceptual, methodological, and managerial issues associated with their design and application. Standards of quality play an especially important role in contemporary recreation planning frameworks, but their formulation can be challenging and sometimes contentious. Consequently, standards have received substantial attention by researchers, planners and managers. First, what are standards of quality? Contrary to common first impressions, standards do not necessarily represent desired future conditions. Rather, they define the limits of acceptable change. Given that recreation planning frameworks can be viewed as processes for conflict resolution, standards might be most appropriately defined as a desirable compromise (Cole & Stankey, 1997).

A related issue considers whether management action should commence before a given condition deteriorates to the point that standards of quality may be violated. The answer to this issue is unclear. Management practices are often classified as

BRENT ERB

indirect or direct, the former preserving freedom of choice for visitors and the latter imposing use restrictions (Manning, 1999; Peterson & Lime, 1979). It may be appropriate to implement indirect management practices in an effort to maintain areas in a desired condition, but it is probably not appropriate to restrict visitor use before standards of quality are in danger of being violated (Cole & McCool, 1997a). A number of observers have noted that standards of quality should meet several criteria, including characterized as being quantitative, time or space-bounded, expressed as a probability, impact-oriented, and realistic (Brunson, Shelby & Goodwin, 1992; Manning, 1999; Whittaker & Shelby, 1992). Standards of quality can be derived from several sources, including legal and policy mandates, historic precedent, interest group politics, regional context, and information received via public involvement.

Indicators
Other elements of recreation planning frameworks have received less attention. Additional research is needed to help identify and define a broad range of indicators of the quality of recreation experiences. Much of the previous research has focused on crowding-related standards of quality, and this is in keeping with the emphasis

89

on solitude defined by the U.S. Wilderness Act in 1964 and other relevant legislation. However, research suggests that the quality of wilderness and other recreation experiences is multidimensional, and a broad array of potential indicators of quality should therefore be defined. Several observers have noted desirable criteria for indicators of quality, including being specific, objective, reliable and repeatable, related to visitor use, sensitive, manageable, efficient and effective to measure, and significant (Manning, 1999; Stankey et al., 1985; Whittaker & Shelby, 1992).

Monitoring

More research and management attention is also needed on monitoring indicators of quality (Manning & Lime, 2000). Monitoring of indicator variables is an inherent and important part of contemporary recreation planning frameworks. It determines when and where management action is needed to maintain standards of quality. However, monitoring can be time-consuming and costly, and it can challenge the personnel and financial resources of park and outdoor recreation management agencies. There is little guidance to be found in the professional and scientific literature on cost-efficient and effective monitoring approaches and techniques.

Management Action

Management actions also warrant more consideration, particularly their potential effectiveness (Manning & Lime, 2000). A wide range of management practices is available to maintain standards of quality (Manning, 1999). However, most research has focused on the effectiveness of only two basic management approaches: information/education programs and use rationing. While these are important management approaches, other management practices warrant additional attention, including rules and regulations, law enforcement, zoning, and site design and management. As indicator variables reveal a deteriorating condition that begins to threaten standards of quality, more research attention will be needed on the efficiency and equity of allocation techniques (Warren, 1997). In addition to issues of effectiveness, more attention to management actions in the planning process can be useful as a way to enhance understanding of the potential costs of alternative standards of quality (Cole & McCool, 1997a). High standards of quality will help protect important natural resources and the quality of the visitor experience, but their cost may entail restrictive management actions.

Finally, foresight and analysis are needed to anticipate and circumvent potential barriers to applying contemporary recreation planning frameworks (Hendee & Dawson, 2002; McCool & Cole, 1997; Stankey, 1997). Of course, availability and commitment of adequate agency personnel and financial resources are necessary. But several structural and procedural barriers must also be overcome. The "compartmentalism" of many park and related agencies (e.g., separate divisions for planning, management, and research) can weaken the integrated nature of contemporary recreation planning frameworks. Government agencies in the U.S. have traditionally struggled with public involvement, and this has sometimes been exacerbated by laws such as the Federal Advisory Committee Act that, while ostensibly designed to curtail influence by special interests, may in fact make it more difficult to seek democratic public involvement in planning. Similarly, the Paperwork Reduction Act may inhibit efforts to involve the public through survey research. Professional education and socialization of agency staff may place too much emphasis on the role of conventional, positivistic science in the planning process, while denigrating the potential role of local citizens and other non-experts. Finally, agencies must exercise the political will and leadership needed to make decisions that require value judgments and that may be controversial.

Conclusions

Emergence of the recreation planning frameworks described in this chapter has been instrumental in guiding contemporary management of parks, wilderness, and related outdoor recreation areas, and applications of these frameworks are likely to become more numerous and expansive in both outdoor recreation and environmental planning. Key elements of these recreation planning frameworks, along with the research and management activities needed to support them, can be summarized as follows.

- Management-by-objectives frameworks have shifted the emphasis and definition of conventional carrying capacity from *how many recreation visits can be accommodated in an area* to *desired future conditions* of such areas. This clarifies and elevates recreation planning by formulating positive and output-oriented measures of success (or failure), and opens and exposes the process of planning to public participation and scrutiny by explicitly emphasizing the tradeoffs and value judgments inherent in recreation planning.

- While the frameworks outlined in this chapter are conventionally defined by a series of steps or elements, they should be considered more iterative than linear (Cole & McCool, 1997a; Hof & Lime, 1997; Manning, 1999). There are strong connections among the elements, including feedback and "feed-forward" loops, and recycling through portions of the process may be both necessary and desirable during their application.

- Recreation planning is fundamentally adaptive in nature (Brunson, 1997; Manning & Lime, 2000; McCool & Cole, 1997). By definition, contemporary recreation planning frameworks require monitoring to measure the existing conditions of indicator variables and to implement or modify management actions to ensure that standards of quality are maintained. This is a fundamentally adaptive process. Further, as more information becomes available, planning should be revisited, though experience suggests this may be resisted (Ritter, 1997).

- Recreation planning is a *process*, not a *product*, as its adaptive nature would suggest. Consequently, planning and management cannot be fully disentangled (Cole & McCool, 1997a; McCool & Cole, 1997). Obviously, plans emerge from the planning process, but they require management for their implementation. The lessons learned from the experience of management should be used to refine plans when and where appropriate. It is common to hear criticism of planning as "taking too long," but in reality, planning is an on-going and long-term process that is coupled with management.

- Application of recreation planning must be a careful blend of science and public values (Manning & Lawson, 2002; McCool & Cole, 1997; Shelby et al., 1992). The rational nature of management-by-objectives planning frameworks suggests a deterministic process that is driven by technical experts and derived exclusively from scientific research. However, recognition of the inescapable role of value judgments in carrying capacity analysis and recreation planning has more broadly been an important advancement in the professional and scientific literature. Contemporary recreation planning frameworks make such value judgments more explicit by means of formulating indicators and standards of quality, and by opening this process to public participation and scrutiny. Nevertheless, recreation planning can (and should) be informed by the best science available, including research on public values (Manning & Lawson, 2002).

- Finally, recreation planning frameworks should be seen as helping to guide management of outdoor recreation by design rather than by default. In its most generic form, planning might be defined as a deliberate and thoughtful consideration of desired future conditions. Contemporary recreation planning frameworks are designed to enable this process and to shape its expression in the form of management objectives and associated, measurable indicators and standards of quality. Without such design, parks, wilderness and related outdoor areas may evolve by default in ways that unacceptably degrade natural resources and the quality of the visitor experience, diminish the diversity of recreation opportunities, and otherwise fail to meet the needs of society, both now and in the future.

References

Absher, J. (1989). Applying the limits of acceptable change model National Park Service Wilderness: An example from Cumberland Island National Seashore. In *Proceedings of the 1988 Southeastern Recreation Research Conference* (pp.143-152) Athens, GA: University of Georgia.

Ashor, J. (1985). *Recreation management in the Bob Marshall Wilderness Complex: An application of the limits of acceptable change concept and transactive planning theory.* Unpublished master's thesis, University of Montana, Missoula.

Belnap, J. (1998). Choosing indicators of natural resource condition: A case study in Arches National Park, Utah, USA. *Environmental Management, 22,* 635-642.

Brunson, M. (1997). *Beyond wilderness: Broadening the applicability of limits of acceptable change* (USDA Forest Service INT-GTR-371). Washington DC: US Government Printing Office.

Brunson, M., & Rodriquez, D. (1992). Standards for managing non-wilderness recreation areas. In USDA Forest Service, *Proceedings – Limits of acceptable change and related planning processes: Progress and future directions* (pp.44-49). Washington DC: US Government Printing Office.

Brunson, M., Shelby, B., & Goodwin, J.(1992). Matching impacts with standards in the design of wilderness permit systems. In USDA Forest Service, *Defining wilderness quality: The role of standards in wilderness management* (pp. 101-106). Washington DC: US Government Printing Office.

Clark, R., & Stankey, G. (1979). *The recreation opportunity spectrum: A framework for planning, management, and research.* (USDA Forest Service PNW-GTR-98). Washington DC: US Government Printing Office.

Cole, D. (1995). Defining fire and wilderness objectives: Applying limits of acceptable change. In USDA Forest Service, *Proceedings: Symposium on fire and wilderness and park management* (pp.42-47). Washington DC: US Government Printing Office.

Cole, D., & S. McCool. (1997a). The limits of acceptable change process: Modifications and clarifications. In USDA Forest Service, *Proceedings – Limits of acceptable change and related planning processes: Progress and future directions* (pp. 61-68). Washington DC: US Government Printing Office.

Cole, D., & McCool, S. (1997b). Limits of acceptable change and natural resources planning: When is LAC useful, when is it not? In USDA Forest Service, *Proceedings – Limits of acceptable change and related planning processes: Progress and future directions* (pp. 69-71). Washington DC: US Government Printing Office.

Cole, D., & McCool, S. (1997c). Limits of acceptable change and related planning processes: A workshop. In USDA Forest Service, *Proceedings – Limits of acceptable change and related planning processes: Progress and future directions* (pp. 1-2). Washington DC: US Government Printing Office.

Cole, D., & Stankey, G. (1997). Historical development of limits of acceptable change: Conceptual clarifications and possible extensions. In USDA Forest Service, *Proceedings – Limits of acceptable change and related planning processes: Progress and future directions* (pp. 5-9). Washington DC: US Government Printing Office.

Dasmann, R. (1964). *Wildlife biology.* New York: John Wiley and Sons.

Driver, B., Brown, P., Stankey, G., & Gregoire, T. (1987). The ROS planning system: Evolution, basic concepts, and research needed. *Leisure Sciences*, 9, 201-212.

Friedmann, J. (1973). *Retracking America: A theory of transactive planning.* Garden City, NJ: Anchor Press/Doubleday.

Frissell, S. (1963). *Recreational use of campsites in the Quetico-Superior Canoe Country.* Unpublished master's thesis, University of Minnesota, Minneapolis.

Frissell, S., & G. Stankey. (1972). Wilderness environmental quality: Search for social and ecological harmony. *Proceedings of the Society of American Foresters Annual Conference* (pp. 170-183). Hot Springs, AR: Society of American Foresters.

Graefe, A., Kuss, F., & Loomis, L. (1986). Visitor impact management in wildland settings. In USDA Forest Service, *Proceedings of the National Wilderness Research Conference: Current research* (pp. 432-439). Washington DC: US Government Printing Office.

Graefe, A., Kuss, F. & Vaske, J. (1990). *Visitor impact management: The planning framework.* Washington, DC: National Parks and Conservation Association.

Hammitt, W., & Cole, D. (1998). *Wildland recreation: Ecology and management.* New York: John Wiley and Sons.

Hendee, J., & Dawson, C. (2002). *Wilderness management*. Golden, CO: Fulcrum Publishing.

Hof, M., & Lime, D. (1997). Visitor experience and resource protection framework in the national park system: Rationale, current status, and future direction. In USDA Forest Service, *Proceedings – Limits of acceptable change and related planning processes: Progress and future directions* (pp. 29-36). Washington DC: US Government Printing Office.

Hof, M., Hammitt, J., Rees, M., Belnap, J., Poe, N., Lime, D., & Manning, R. (1994). Getting a handle on visitor carrying capacity: A pilot project at Arches National Park. *Park Science, 14*, 11-13.

Kaltenborn, B., & Emmelin, L. (1993). Tourism in the high north: Management challenges and recreation opportunity spectrum planning in Svalbard, Norway. *Environmental Management, 17*, 41-50.

Manning, R. (1986). *Studies in outdoor recreation*. Corvallis, OR: Oregon State University Press.

Manning, R. (1992). Beyond standard standards: Incorporating nonrecreational values into wilderness management. In USDA Forest Service, *Defining wilderness quality: The role of standards in wilderness management* (pp. 67-75). Washington DC: US Government Printing Office.

Manning, R. (1999). *Studies in outdoor recreation (2nd Ed)*. Corvallis, OR: Oregon State University Press.

Manning, R. (2001). Visitor experience and resource protection: A framework for managing the carrying capacity of national parks. *Journal of Park and Recreation Administration*, 19, 93-108.

Manning, R., & Lawson, S. (2002). Carrying capacity as "informed judgement": The values of science and the science of values. *Environmental Management, 30*, 157-168.

Manning, R., & Lime, D. (2000). Defining and managing the quality of wilderness recreation experiences. In USDA Forest Service, *Wilderness science in a time of change conference, Volume 4: Wilderness visitors, experiences, and visitor management* (pp. 13-52). Washington DC: US Government Printing Office.

Manning, R., Lime, D., Hof, M., & Freimund, W. (1995). The visitor experience and resource protection process: The application of carrying capacity to Arches National Park. *The George Wright Forum, 12*, 41-55.

Manning, R., Lime, D., Freimund, W., & Pitt, D. (1996). Crowding norms at frontcountry sites: A visual approach to setting standards of quality. *Leisure Sciences*, 18, 39-59.

Manning, R., Lime, D & Hof, M. (1996). Social carrying capacity of natural areas: Theory and application in the U.S. National Parks. *Natural Areas Journal*, 16, 118-127.

McCool, S., & Cole, D. (1997). Experiencing limits of acceptable change: Some thoughts after a decade of implementation. In USDA Forest Service, *Proceedings – Limits of acceptable change and related planning processes: Progress and future directions* (pp. 72-78). Washington DC: US Government Printing Office.

McCoy, K., Krumpe, E., & Allen, S. (1995). Limits of acceptable change planning – Evaluating implementation in the U.S. Forest Service. *International Journal of Wilderness*, 1, 18-22.

Merigliano, L., Cole. D., & Parsons, D. (1997). Application of LAC-type processes and concepts to nonrecreation management issues in protected areas. In USDA Forest Service, *Proceedings – Limits of acceptable change and related planning processes: Progress and future directions* (pp. 37-43). Washington DC: US Government Printing Office.

National Park Service. (1995). *Visitor experience and resource protection implementation plan: Arches National Park.* Denver, CO: National Park Service.

National Park Service. (1997). *VERP: The visitor experience and resource protection (VERP) framework – A handbook for planners and managers.* Denver, CO: National Park Service.

Nilsen, P., & Tayler, G. (1997). A comparative analysis of protected area planning and management frameworks. In USDA Forest Service, *Proceedings – Limits of acceptable change and related planning processes: Progress and future directions* (pp. 49-58). Washington DC: US Government Printing Office.

Parks Canada. (1985). *Management process for visitor activities.* Ottawa, Ontario, Canada: National Parks Directorate.

Peterson, G., & Lime, D. (1979). People and their behavior: A challenge for recreation management. *Journal of Forestry*, 77, 343-346.

Ritter, D. (1997). Limits of acceptable change planning in the Selway-Bitterroot Wilderness: 1985-1997. In USDA Forest Service, *Proceedings – Limits of acceptable change and related planning processes: Progress and future directions* (pp. 25-28). Washington DC: US Government Printing Office.

Shelby, B., & Heberlein, T. (1986). *Carrying capacity in recreation settings.* Corvallis, OR: Oregon State University Press.

Shelby, B., Stankey, G., & Shindler, B. (1992). The role of standards in wilderness management. In USDA Forest Service, *Defining wilderness quality: The role of standards in wilderness management* (pp. 1-5). Washington DC: US Government Printing Office.

Stankey, G. (1997). Institutional barriers and opportunities in application of the limits of acceptable change. In USDA Forest Service, *Proceedings – Limits of acceptable change and related planning processes: Progress and future directions* (pp. 10-15). Washington DC: US Government Printing Office.

Stankey, G., Cole, D., Lucas, R., Peterson, M. & Frissell, S., (1985). *The limits of acceptable change (LAC) system for wilderness planning* (USDA Forest Service General Technical Report INT-176). Washington DC: US Government Printing Office.

Sumner, E. (1936). *Special report on a wildlife study in the High Sierra in Sequoia and Yosemite National Parks and adjacent territory.* Washington, DC: National Park Service.

Wagar, J. (1964). The carrying capacity of wild lands for recreation. *Forest Science Monograph 7.*

Warren, G. (1997). Recreation management in the Bob Marshall, Great Bear, and Scapegoat wildernesses: 1987-1997. In USDA Forest Service, *Proceedings – Limits of acceptable change and related planning processes: Progress and future directions* (pp. 21-25). Washington DC: US Government Printing Office.

Whittaker, D., & Shelby, B. (1992). Developing good standards: Criteria, characteristics, and sources. In USDA Forest Service, *Defining wilderness quality: The role of standards in wilderness management* (pp. 6-12). Washington DC: US Government Printing Office.

Yankelovich, D. (1991). *Coming to public judgement: Making democracy work in a complex world.* Syracuse, NY: Syracuse University Press.

9

Social Impact Assessment

Seldom Used & Rarely Understood

Rabel J. Burdge

Vicky Sturtevant

This chapter discusses the field of social impact assessment (SIA) and its prevalence within the International Symposia on Society and Resource Management (ISSRM) during the past 20 years. Specifically, this chapter is based on a review of abstracts from previous ISSRM, and seeks to:

- Report the number of ISSRM abstracts submitted about SIA

- Summarize key words used to describe SIA

- List the types of natural resource projects for which SIAs were reported

- Illustrate the content and breadth of SIA variables

- Identify the institutional setting of the authors of the SIA abstracts

- Provide comment on future direction for SIA

Why Social Impact Assessment?

Definition
Social impact assessment began in the United States in response to the National Environmental Policy Act of 1969 (NEPA) and subsequent Council on Environmental Quality (CEQ) directives which mandated that effects on human communities be included in environmental impact assessments (EIA) of proposed U.S. federal government actions. It describes the systematic analysis, in advance, of the likely impacts a proposed action will have on the life of individuals and communities (Burdge, 2004b). In a research context, SIA is a sub-field of the integrated social sciences that provides a knowledge base about social impacts for different policies, plans, programs and projects (Burdge, 2004b). The Interorganizational Committee on Principles and Guidelines for SIA (2003) defines SIA *as all social and*

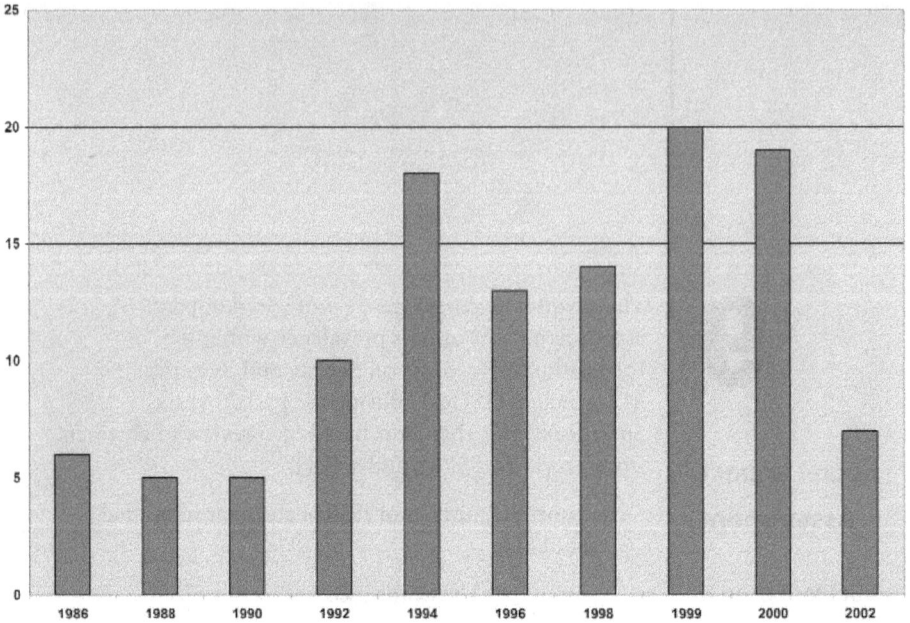

Figure 1. Number of SIA-related abstracts in previous ISSRM.

cultural consequences to human populations of any public or private actions that alter the ways in which people live, work, play, relate to one another, organize to meet their needs, and generally cope as members of society.

Rationale

The goal of SIA is to help individuals, communities, as well as government and private sector organizations, understand and better anticipate the possible social consequences for human populations and communities of planned and unplanned social change resulting from proposed policies, plans, programs and projects. Its benefits are numerous and extend to all aspects of the traditional impact assessment processes that are typically conducted within environmental and social contexts. Specifically, these benefits include:

- description of how a proposed action will affect the lives of individuals and communities in the primary and secondary zone of influences.

- alert planners, decision-makers and project proponents about changes in the community and region of impact.

- identify qualitative and quantitative indicators that are understood by both decision-makers and citizens.

- provide pre-emptive action before a decision is made; thereby serving as a valuable tool in planning.

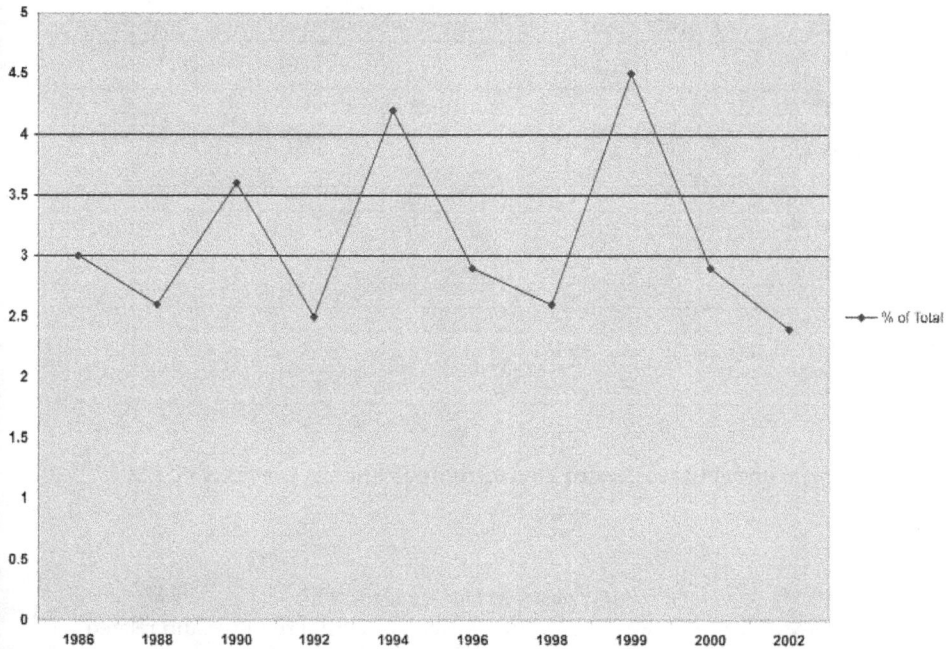

Figure 2. SIA-related abstracts as a percent of total abstracts at previous ISSRM.

- create suggestions for alternatives to the proposed action, as well as procedures for enhancement and mitigation.

Prevalence of SIA Content at ISSRM

The field of SIA represents a steady but relatively minor portion of previous ISSRM presentations. Based on a content analysis of the ISSRM Book of Abstracts distributed at the ten previous symposia, it appears that the number of abstracts about SIA has remained steady. The most, both in numbers and as a percent of the total, were submitted for the 1999 symposium. With the exception of 1990, 1996 and 2002, both the number of abstracts and overall attendance increased with each symposium (see Figures 1 & 2).

Identifying Social Impact Assessment Papers
The field of SIA research is more likely to expand if there is agreement on terminology. While *social impact assessment* is arguably the most often-used terminology, there are many terms and phrases used to describe processes, including: social analysis, social assessment, social impacts, and others. See Table 1 for a list of additional terms, as well as how often each of those terms, or keywords, appeared as an abstract topic in previous ISSRM.

Key Word	1986	1988	1990	1992	1994	1996	1998	1999	2000	2002	Total
Social Impact Assessment	14	17	3	2	8	8	1	31	12	2	100
Social Assessment	-	-	-	-	2	4	6	5	18	3	38
Social Analysis	3	-	-	-	-	-	1	-	-	2	6
Socio-economic Ass'ment	4	-	-	1	7	-	-	-	-	-	12
Social Impacts	-	5	10	4	15	13	9	27	16	8	107
Psycho-Social Impacts	-	-	-	-	-	-	-	-	1	-	1
Social Effects	-	2	-	-	-	-	-	-	2	-	4
Social Issues	-	-	-	-	-	-	-	3	-	1	4
Human Impact Assessment	-	-	-	-	-	-	-	-	1	-	1
Socio-economic Impacts	1	1	-	5	5	3	-	-	3	-	18

Table 1. Social impact assessment keyword prevalence at previous ISSRM.

Project Settings and the Focus of Social Impact Assessment
SIA's relevance and application extends to a variety of natural resource and related issues and circumstances. Many SIA processes have been applied to land use management, and parks and preserves (see Table 2). This includes situations involving watersheds, forest ecosystems, forest plans, use of fire as a management tool, and pesticide application. Within parks and protected areas, SIAs are often integrated within management plans, introduction of indigenous species to present eco-systems, and tourism development.

Projects dealing with mines and minerals, reservoir development and trade facilities are also commonplace. In addition, previous published work on SIA has also included theory and methods, including its relevance to the use of public involvement techniques as a component of environmental and social impact assessment.

Why Study Social Impacts?

As previously mentioned, *social impacts* refer to changes to individuals and communities due to a proposed action (Burdge, 2004b). SIA variables point to measurable change in human populations, communities, and social relationships resulting from planned (i.e., a proposed action) and unplanned interventions.

Gleaned from research on local community change, rural industrialization, reservoir and highway development, natural resource development, and social change in general, the *Interorganizational Committee on Principles and Guidelines for Social Impact Assessment* (2003) recommended a list of SIA variables under the general headings of 1) *population change* (i.e., present population and change due to the proposed action), 2) *community and institutional structures* (i.e., size, structure and level of organization of local government), 3) *political and social resources* (i.e., distribution of power authority, interested and affected parties, leadership capacity), 4) *individual and family changes* (i.e., factors that influence daily life, attitudes, values,

Setting	1986	1988	1990	1992	1994	1996	1998	1999	2000	2002	Total
Mineral Extraction	-	-	-	-	1	1	-	1	-	-	3
Hazard/Sanitary Waste	-	-	-	-	-	-	1	-	-	-	1
Reservoirs	-	1	1	-	2	-	-	-	-	-	4
Industrial Plants	-	-	-	-	-	-	-	-	1	-	1
Land Use Management	-	-	1	7	6	4	3	8	6	4	39
Linear Developments	-	-	-	-	-	-	-	1	-	-	1
Trade Facilities	-	-	-	-	-	2	1	-	2	-	5
Parks & Preserves	5	-	1	2	7	3	5	2	6	2	33
Housing Projects	-	-	-	-	1	-	-	-	-	-	1
Theory/Methods	1	4	2	1	1	3	4	7	4	1	28

Table 2. SIA settings as reported in previous ISSRM abstracts.

perceptions and social networks), and 5) *community resources* (i.e., patterns of land use, community services, indigenous people). Similar lists of SIA variables have been identified by others (see Burdge, 2004b; Vanclay, 2002).

On the following page, the sidebar indicates the number of times each of the SIA variables developed by the Interorganizational Committee was reported in ISSRM abstracts. Our findings show that the SIA variables used by symposium participants are similar to those recommended by the Interorganizational Committee (2003). In all, the summary suggests that similar SIA variables appear in ISSRM abstracts regardless of the type of natural resource settings. For example, assessments of land use management, parks and preserves often used population change, employment and income characteristics, presence of planning and zoning, interested and affected parties, perceptions of risk, health and safety, attitudes toward the proposed action and indigenous populations as key SIA variables of interest.

SIA Researchers and Authors

SIA is both a practice and a field of research (Burdge, 2003). University-based participants are likely to focus on the research contribution of SIA. Government and consulting firm participants generally report on the assessment process, rather than how the results might contribute to the SIA knowledge base. Table 3 illustrates the institutional location of the authors. Seventy two percent (137 abstracts) of the 191 names listed were from academic institutions with 18 percent (35 abstracts) from state and federal agencies. SIA practitioners in agencies and consulting firms seldom have the time (and in some cases, due to confidentiality, are not permitted) to publish in the refereed literature. As a result, these SIAs are seldom reported in a form easily located by a search of the serialized literature. The findings in Table 3 provide encouragement; they suggest that ISSRM is a reasonable and valid venue for SIA research papers.

Frequency of SIA variables in previous ISSRM abstracts

Population Change	
Population Size, Density & Change	4
Ethnic & Racial Comp & Change	2
Relocating People	2
Influx & Outflow of Temporaries	-
Presence of Seasonal Residents	-

Political & Social Resources	
Distribution of Power & Authority	4
Conflict: Newcomers & Old-timers	-
Identification of Stakeholders	3
Interested & Affected Parties	9
Leadership Capability & Characteristics	1
Interorganizational Cooperation	7

Community & Institutional Structures	
Voluntary Associations	-
Interest Group Activity	4
Size & Structure of Government	5
Historical Experience W/Change	1
Employment/Income Characteristics	8
Employment Equity of Disadvantaged Groups	1
Local/Regional/National Linkages	2
Industrial/Commercial Activity	7
Presence of Planning & Zoning	10

Individual & Family Changes	
Perceptions of Risk, Health & Safety	9
Displacement/Relocation Concerns	5
Trust in Political/Social Institutions	2
Residential Stability	1
Density of Acquaintanceships	5
Attitudes Toward Proposed Action	18
Family & Friendship Networks	1
Concerns about Social Well-being	7

Community Resources	
Change in Community Infrastructure	1
Indigenous Populations	7
Changing Land Use Patterns	3
Effects on Cultural, Historical, Sacred & Archaeological Resources	2

Myths Surrounding SIA

Compared with biophysical components, SIA in North America has not been as widely adopted in the assessment process for environmental and natural resource decision-making. Unfortunately, a series of myths and misunderstandings has historically limited the use of SIA in planning and decision-making processes (Burdge, 2004a). These misinterpretations include:

1. *Social impacts cannot be measured; therefore they should be ignored.* One can always find an indicator! It may be qualitative, such as the perception of health risks from polluted groundwater. It may be quantitative, as the population influx to a destination tourist facility.

2. *Social impacts are common sense and everyone knows what they are.* Knowledge is the forerunner to common sense. The disruption of the lives of individuals and communities due to water impoundments is only well known, for example, after decades of social science research (Cernea, 1995).

Institutional Setting	1986	1988	1990	1992	1994	1996	1998	1999	2000	2002	Total
University/College	4	3	4	6	22	16	13	10	41	18	137
Local/State/Federal Agency	3	1	4	2	5	2	2	3	6	7	35
Private Sector Organization	-	-	-	2	-	1	1	3	1	-	7
Consulting Firm	-	-	-	-	-	-	-	2	-	-	2
Non-government organizations	-	-	1	-	-	-	-	8	-	-	9
Not Specified	-	1	-	-	-	-	-	-	-	-	1

Table 3. Institutional setting of SIA authors at previous ISSRM

3. *Social impacts seldom occur and therefore need not be assessed.* Social impacts, like biophysical and financial impacts, *always occur*, but may not always be significant. Road building in rural communities disrupts daily living and movement patterns, but local populations see the benefits as access to outside employment, markets and reduced isolation.

4. *Social impacts deal with costs, not benefits, and SIA slows down or stops projects.* Change brings social costs to some and benefits to others. Building an access road to a garbage dump around the town was more expensive, but it improved company and community relations, and reduced in–town traffic congestion.

5. *SIAs increase the price of projects and do not enhance benefits.* Project failures and narrow cost-benefit analysis led to the NEPA legislation. The U.S. Congress passed the environmental policy act in large degree because environmental and social costs to local communities were not a part of the planning process. In developing countries, the donor agency or the host government generally bears the cost of failed projects.

6. *The SIA Process is not important.* In fact, it is the major benefit! Helping the affected population understand, participate in and cope with a proposed action may be the most important benefit of the SIA process.

Future Directions

While the numbers of SIA abstracts at ISSRM have increased with nearly each symposium, the growth has been small. Most federal and many state land management agencies have a mandate to do SIA, therefore one might reasonably expect more papers on the topic. Based on the initial content analysis reported here, a review of the literature, and our long history of SIA, we advocate for a number of directions.

First, we need to reach consensus as to the definition and the label for SIA. Information shown in Table 1 indicates that not all practitioners and agencies are using the same terminology. Second, although much improved, we need better models to understand the linkages between biophysical, land use, financial and subsequent social impacts. Social and environmental assessments should not be stand-alone processes. SIA follow-ups and comparative analysis must be used to better integrate all elements of the assessment process. We must study events in a location where planned environmental change has occurred, and to extrapolate from that analysis what is likely to happen in another location where a similar action is proposed.

Third, administrative and political steps need to be taken to insure that SIA is a required part of the planning process. The Interorganizational Committee on Principles and Guidelines for Social Impact Assessment has revised and updated an earlier 1994 version. The new principles and guidelines are being reviewed by the National Marine Fisheries Service and the Council on Environmental Quality for possible inclusion in an updating by CEQ of EIA-SIA procedures. Federal and state regulations must mandate the use of SIA; otherwise it will not be used in the assessment process.

Fourth, there needs to be a coherent body of research findings that can direct SIA. The previous 10 ISSRM have advanced the body of knowledge about the impacts of natural resource development on human communities. Although not specifically labeled as SIA, much of the research reported expands our knowledge about community change resulting from development.

Fifth, we need more consensus as to the variables to include when doing a social impact assessment. As shown in Table 1, we are beginning to isolate and develop a series of indicators for variables that repeatedly occur in most natural resource development and policy settings.

Finally, we need examples where a social impact assessment has actually made a difference or been followed in the planning-appraisal-decision process. Although a series of recent articles have depicted SIA as the poor cousin of EIA, there remains hope (Barrow, 2000; Burdge, 2002; Chadwick, 2002; Glasson, Thérivel & Chadwick, 1999; Lockie, 2001).

During the 20 year history of ISSRM, more than 100 papers and posters about SIA have been presented. Most call for more SIAs on resource management decisions, but little is said about how the SIAs might be used. Part of the confusion is from so many labels. But the more important problem is that decision-makers do not understand the benefits and the process of SIA. That is our challenge for the next decade.

References

Barrow, C. J. (2000). *Social impact assessment: An introduction*. London: Arnold.

Branch, K., Hooper, D. A., Thompson, J., & Creighton, J. C. (1984). *Guide to social impact assessment*. Boulder, CO: Westview Press.

Burdge, R. J. (2004a). *The concepts, process and methods of social impact assessment*. Middleton, WI: Social Ecology Press.

Burdge, R. J. (2004b). *A community guide to social impact assessment (3rd Ed.)*. Middleton, WI: Social Ecology Press.

Burdge, R. J. (2002). Why is social impact assessment the orphan of the assessment process? *Impact Assessment and Project Appraisal*, 20(1), 3-9.

Cernea, M. M.(Ed.) (1995). *Putting people first: Sociological variables in rural development (2nd Ed.)*. Oxford, UK: Oxford University Press.

Chadwick, A. (2002). Socio-economic impacts: Are they still the poor relations in UK environmental statements? *Journal of Environmental Planning and Management*, 45(1), 3-24.

Glasson J., Thérivel, R., & Chadwick, A. (1994). *Introduction to environmental impact assessment: Principles, procedures and processes*. London: UCL Press.

Interorganizational Committee on Principles and Guidelines for Social Impact Assessment (2003). U. S. principles and guidelines for social impact assessment. *Impact Assessment and Project Appraisal*, 21(3), 231-250.

Lockie, S.(2001). SIA in review: Setting the agenda for impact assessment in the 21st century. Impact Assessment and Project Appraisal, 19(4), 277-287.

Vanclay, F. (2002). Conceptualizing social impacts. *Environmental impact assessment review*, 22(3), 183-211.

10

Environmental Impacts of Outdoor Recreation in Wildlands

David N. Cole

Although often considered to be a non-consumptive use, outdoor recreation inevitably alters attributes of the environment, including: soil, vegetation, wildlife, and water. This chapter includes a brief review of how and when recreation ecology developed, and a synthesis of the primary research findings of this discipline. Recreational impacts on vegetation and soil are emphasized, particularly those caused by non-motorized use of wildlands; our understanding of those impacts is most advanced and sophisticated. The chapter concludes with a discussion of the managerial significance of this topic and some thoughts on future directions for recreation ecology.

Historical Development of Recreation Ecology

Although informal studies of recreational impacts on the environmental had been conducted occasionally since at least the 1920s (Meinecke, 1928), it was not until the 1960s that more rigorous recreation ecology studies were first conducted (Frissell & Duncan, 1965; Wagar, 1964). In the 1970s, the first long-term research programs were initiated. During this decade, Bayfield (1973) began his work on trail and trampling impacts in Scotland, Liddle (1975) began his work on trampling effects in Great Britain and Australia, and Cole (1978) embarked on his work on trail, camping, and hiking impacts in wildernesses in the United States. During the 1980s and 1990s, the number of recreation ecology studies increased greatly, although few researchers ever conducted more than one study. Nevertheless, considerable progress was made in applying recreation ecology research to the development of impact monitoring protocols, management strategies, and low-impact educational messages, especially in national parks and wilderness areas (e.g., Cole, 1981a, 1989; Hampton & Cole, 1988; Marion, 1995). This led to publication of the first recreation ecology textbook in 1987 (Hammitt & Cole,

1987). Descriptive field studies became more sophisticated, with the adoption of cross-sectional and longitudinal designs, and were augmented by experimentation. Although general principles and consistent findings emerged from this work, theory remains poorly developed today.

Rigorous and cumulative research programs concerning impacts on vegetation and soil developed before similar programs devoted to wildlife and water impacts. By the 1980s, research was accumulating on disturbance of animal species (e.g., bighorn sheep in MacArthur, Geist & Johnston, 1982) and the first textbook on recreation impacts on wildlife was published in the 1990s (Knight & Gutzwiller, 1995). Despite the conduct of hundreds of studies, however, little progress has been made in uncovering broad generalizations and principles regarding recreational disturbance of wildlife. Research on the impacts of recreation on water remains even more sparse and disparate.

Research Findings

Descriptive Knowledge

As is common during the first decades of a new field of inquiry, most recreation ecology studies have been largely descriptive. Substantial progress has been made in describing the nature and quantifying the magnitude of recreational impacts, particularly on vegetation and soil. Trampling, the most prevalent recreation impact, damages and kills plants, displaces soil organic horizons, and compacts mineral soils. These immediate and direct trampling effects, in turn, have additional longer lasting and cascading effects (Liddle, 1997). Models of trampling impacts often contain positive feedback loops. For example, trampling eliminates vegetation cover, which reduces inputs of organic matter and root exudates into the soil. Along with the physical effects of soil compaction, this alters the microorganisms that live in the soil. Since soil microorganisms are critically important both to the alleviation of soil compaction and the establishment and growth of vegetation, soil and vegetation are further altered by these changes to the soil biota. Consequently, sites can remain compacted and barren, even in the absence of further trampling.

The ultimate result of even modest levels of repetitive trampling is a severe but localized (and often long-lasting) alteration of virtually all aspects of the structure, composition and function of ecosystems. The most commonly studied ecosystem attributes are readily observable vegetation and soil characteristics (e.g., plant cover, species composition, soil compaction) and the most common scale of analysis is the site scale (e.g., 0.1 ha). Recent studies, however, have enlarged the array of ecosystem effects that have been documented. For example, Zabinski and Gannon (1997) documented reductions in the functional diversity of microbial populations growing on campsites, and Belnap (1996) showed that disturbance of surface cyanobacterial-lichen soil crusts reduces nitrogenase activity and, therefore, alters nitrogen cycles. In addition to trampling, substantial environmental impacts are caused by such activities as firewood collection and campfire building, trail construction and maintenance, grazing of pack animals, human intrusion into wildlife habitat, and the use of motor vehicles. Many of these impacts are described in detail in recent textbooks (Liddle, 1997; Newsome, Moore & Dowling, 2002).

Magnitude of impact is a function of both the intensity of impact (i.e., impact per unit area) and the extent (i.e., area) of impact. Many studies assess the size of impacted sites and several have aggregated data over large areas to informally enlarge the scale of analysis. For example, Cole (1981b) reported that vegetation loss from camping, at the scale of several wilderness watersheds, was less than 0.2 percent, despite exceeding 90 percent on individual campsites. This illustrates the importance of carefully choosing the appropriate scale of analysis and of explicitly defining a study's scale when reporting results that quantify the magnitude of impact. More useful, but virtually nonexistent, would be studies that describe the effects of recreation on attributes that are unique emergent properties of large-scale ecological systems. For example, even highly localized trampling can result in a loss of global biodiversity if it happens to be concentrated on the only population of a rare plant species.

Lack of information about impacts at critical scales of analysis may partially explain our poor understanding of wildlife impacts and their significance, despite the large number of impact studies that have been conducted. Numerous studies assess the short-term responses of individual animals to recreational disturbance. For example, Cassirer, Freddy & Ables (1992) document, for a portion of Yellowstone National Park, that elk typically flee from cross-country skiers when approached within 400 meters. But little is known about whether such disturbances have significant long-term impacts on the elk, or other wildlife. However, more experimental studies are being conducted in an attempt to understand the impacts of recreation on wildlife. Examples include studies of reproductive success after elk were approached and displaced by study personnel during peak calving season (Phillips & Alldredge, 2000), studies of trail effects on bird communities (Miller, Knight & Miller, 2001) and studies of human intrusion on avian richness and abundance (Riffell, Gutzwiller & Anderson, 1996).

Spatial and Temporal Patterns
Although Leung and Marion (1999a) discussed spatial strategies for managing recreation impacts, spatial patterns of impact have received little attention. At large spatial scales (i.e., >10 ha), a given aggregate area of impact may be distributed as either a few large impacts or a larger number of smaller impacts. These impacts can be distributed in a pattern that is either more clumped (i.e., underdispersed) or more regular (i.e., overdispersed) than a random pattern. The significance of recreation impacts is likely to vary as much with spatial pattern as it does with nature and intensity of impact.

The primary general findings of longitudinal studies of recreation impact are that (1) impacts often occur rapidly, (2) for many environmental variables, amount of impact can be stable over long periods of sustained use, and (3) recovery rates are highly variable but almost always slower than rates of deterioration. For example, most of the impact that occurred over six years following the initial creation of canoe campsites along the Delaware River occurred during the first year of use (Marion & Cole, 1996). Evidence of camping largely disappeared in six years along the river after campsites were closed (Marion & Cole, 1996), where soils are fertile and growing seasons are long. In the alpine meadows of Glacier National Park, in

BRENT ERB

contrast, residual effects of trampling remain 30 years after disturbance ceased (Hartley, 1999). At larger spatial scales, unless recreation use distribution is tightly controlled, impacts tend to increase over time, more from the creation of newly impacted sites than from the deterioration of established sites (Cole, 1993). Site proliferation occurs because, as use shifts across the landscape, deterioration of new sites occurs more rapidly than recovery of old sites.

Knowledge About Functional Relationships

Perhaps the best measure of progress in recreation ecology is the knowledge that has accumulated regarding factors that influence the magnitude of recreation impact. As first proposed in a state-of-knowledge review (Cole, 1987), characteristics of use, environment, and management all combine to influence the magnitude of recreation impact. The most important factors are *amount of use, type and behavior of use, timing of use, resistance and resilience of the environment, and the spatial distribution of use.*

Numerous studies show that the relationship between amount of use and amount of impact is not linear. In most situations, soil and vegetation has little ability to resist impact by recreation use, and the use-impact relationship is asymptotic. Initially, small increments of use cause substantial impact, with the rate of increase in impact decreasing as use increases. This relationship was first documented on campsites in the Boundary Waters Canoe Area (Frissell & Duncan, 1965). However, it was sometime later (Cole, 1981a) that the important management implications of this relationship were highlighted. Impacts can usually be minimized by encouraging the repetitive use of a small number of sites (i.e., *concentrating* use). This consistent finding is now at the core of management policies (e.g., requirements that visitors camp on designated sites) as well as the curriculum of Leave-No-Trace messages that encourage concentrating use and impact in popular locations (Hampton & Cole, 1988).

The asymptotic nature of the use-impact relationship is among the most important generalizations produced by recreation ecology. However, it should be noted that in some situations, use levels are so low and/or environmental parameters are so resistant (e.g., organic soil horizons, Marion & Cole, 1996), that the initial increments of recreation use have virtually no impact. For example, the relative lack of documentation regarding effects of recreation on water bodies (Hammitt & Cole, 1987) may reflect the resistance of water bodies to low levels of recreational disturbance. Hylgaard and Liddle (1981) were correct in hypothesizing that the general shape of the use-impact relationship approximates that of a logistic function. In most situations, however, vegetation in particular is not sufficiently durable for the initial exponential portion of the curve to be expressed. Where use levels are sufficiently low and/or environmental characteristics sufficiently durable, impact can be reduced by dispersing use.

Although more resistant to empirical quantification, the relationship between impact and type of use is also profound. There are *qualitative* differences in the nature of impacts caused by different users. Groups that gather firewood and build campfires cause impacts that groups that forego campfires do not. Groups that graze recreational pack stock cause impacts that groups that travel by foot do not.

There are also *quantitative* differences in the magnitude of impact caused by different user groups. Horses have been shown to cause substantially more trail erosion than hikers, llamas or mountain bikers (DeLuca, Patterson, Freimund & Cole, 1998; Wilson & Seney, 1994). Hikers with dogs disturb wildlife more than hikers without dogs (MacArthur et al., 1982; Miller et al., 2001).

In recent experimental work in France, Gallet and Rozé (2002) demonstrated that heathlands are more tolerant of trampling in winter than in summer. Tolerance is also dependent on weather conditions at the time of trampling, but the nature of the effect varies between species (Gallet & Rozé, 2002). Trail erosion is often greater when soils are wet than when they are dry (DeLuca et al., 1998). Wildlife are more vulnerable to disturbance at certain times of the year, such as during birthing, as well as at certain times of the day, such as when feeding (Knight & Gutzwiller, 1995).

Perhaps the largest and most diverse body of knowledge concerns the myriad of environmental factors that influence the magnitude of impact. Beginning with the early work of Wagar (1964), much of this knowledge has been developed from careful application of controlled levels and types of use and under experimental conditions. Such studies have shown that it is important to distinguish between a site's *resistance* (its ability to tolerate use without being damaged) and its *resilience* (its ability to recover from damage). Some vegetation types can tolerate more than 30 times as much use as others (Cole, 1995). Leung & Marion (1996) provide a useful review of how environmental conditions influence trail impacts, while several of the textbooks (Hammitt & Cole, 1987; Liddle, 1997) provide access to the voluminous literature on this topic.

Managerial Significance of Recreation Ecology
Descriptive studies of the nature of recreation impacts and studies relating magnitude of impact to influential factors have contributed directly to knowledge about how to efficiently monitor recreation impacts and effectively manage them. Monitoring methods are well developed for trail and campsite impacts, but poorly developed for the impacts of grazing and impacts on wildlife and water bodies. For campsite impacts, protocols have been developed ranging from quick assessments of condition classes (Frissell, 1978) to more precise and informative but time-consuming detailed measures (Cole, 1989). Marion and his associates (e.g., Leung & Marion, 1999b) have been particularly diligent in working to increase the efficiency of campsite and trail monitoring methods. When replicated over time, impact studies also document how conditions are changing over time, suggesting either the success of management or the need for alternative or more aggressive approaches.

Relatively few studies have directly assessed the effectiveness of actions taken to mitigate recreation impact, using a before-and-after experimental design. However, the knowledge that has developed about how various factors influence the magnitude of impact provides the foundation for development of management strategies. Management suggestions are often included in descriptive papers on recreation impact. In fact, recreation ecology research has provided the foundation of message content for the Leave-No-Trace educational program.

Issues for the Future
As the future unfolds and trends and fads in outdoor recreation develop, recreation ecology will consistently be faced with the need to understand the impacts of new activities in new environments. Recently, for example, substantial literature has developed on the impacts of scuba diving and snorkeling (e.g., Rouphael & Inglis, 2002). And, the ecotourism literature generally has borrowed heavily from recreation ecology (Newsome et al., 2002) and will continue to do so.

Currently, the impacts we understand best are those that occur at the human meso-scale. Future work needs to provide a better perspective on the large-scale implications of recreation impacts. We know that recreation causes severe impacts at small scales, but does recreation cause substantial impacts on watersheds and landscapes, or on entire units of parks and wilderness? Attempts to address this question should increase our ability to draw useful conclusions about the ecological significance of impacts. Equally important is the need to understand impacts occurring at the microscale, such as impacts on soil biota and soil-plant interactions. Managers often close recreation sites in attempts to restore them. They are often not very successful, and a major contributor to poor success is our rudimentary understanding of microscale and below-ground impacts.

Finally, we need to better integrate social and ecological research regarding recreation impacts. As managers consider how to limit impacts, they are faced with difficult decisions that often affect users. There is little clarity about the criteria to use or the stakeholders to include. Attempts to describe visitor perceptions of impact suggest that most visitors abhor the idea of impact, but fail to recognize it. There is little evidence that the experiences and behaviors of most visitors are significantly affected by recreation impacts (Farrell, Hall & White, 2001). Should limits be set on the basis of concerns about ecological integrity, about aesthetics, or about the symbolic nature of human impacts on the environment? Answers to these questions lie at the intersection of social and ecological science, and offer an excellent opportunity for interdisciplinary research.

Conclusion

Recreation ecology is only about 30 years old and only a handful of people have ever identified themselves as recreation ecologists. Nevertheless, approximately 1,000 recreation ecology studies have been conducted and substantial progress has been made in integrating this body of work in such a way that it has a high degree of managerial relevance. Progress is constrained by the small number of recreation ecologists, the relative lack of theory (and funding for more conceptual and theoretical work) and by insufficient attention to impacts at scales that are larger and smaller than the human scale.

First among the primary conclusions of recreation ecology is the simple notion that impact is inevitable with recreation. Avoiding impact is not an option, unless all recreation use is curtailed. Managers must make conscious decisions about tolerable levels of impact, and implement strategies that keep impacts within acceptable levels. Impacts occur rapidly and recover slowly. This effectively negates management strategies based on periodically resting sites. It emphasizes the importance of proactive management focused on avoiding impacts instead of repairing them. This can be counter to visitor management principles that stress avoiding regulation until indirect management has failed.

The primary factors that influence magnitude of impact (i.e., amount of use, type of use, timing of use, spatial distribution of use, and environmental attributes) can all be manipulated by managers to develop strategies for limiting impacts. In particular, our understanding of the curvilinear relationship between use and impact provides a foundation for visitor and site management, as well as education programs.

References

Bayfield, N.G. (1973). Use and deterioration of some Scottish hill paths. *Journal of Applied Ecology*, 10, 639-648.

Belnap, J. (1996). Soil surface disturbances in cold deserts: Effects on nitrogenase activity in cyanobacterial-lichen soil crusts. *Biology and Fertility of Soils*, 23, 362-367.

Cassierer, E.F., Freddy, D. J., & Ables, E. D. (1992). Elk responses to disturbance by cross-country skiers in Yellowstone National Park. *Wildlife Society Bulletin*, 20, 375-381.

Cole, D.N. (1978). Estimating the susceptibility of wildland vegetation to trailside alteration. *Journal of Applied Ecology*, 15, 281-286.

Cole, D.N. (1981a). Managing ecological impacts at wilderness campsites: An evaluation of techniques. *Journal of Forestry*, 79, 86-89.

Cole, D.N. (1981b). Vegetational changes associated with recreational use and fire suppression in the Eagle Cap Wilderness, Oregon: Some management implications. *Biological Conservation*, 20, 247-270.

Cole, D.N. (1987). Research on soil and vegetation in wilderness: A state-of-knowledge review. In R.C. Lucas (Comp.), *Proceedings - National wilderness research conference: Issues, state-of-knowledge, future directions* (pp. 135-177). (General Technical Report INT-220). Ogden, UT: U.S. Department of Agriculture, Forest Service, Intermountain Research Station.

Cole, D.N. (1989). *Wilderness campsite monitoring methods: A sourcebook.* (General Technical Report INT-259). Ogden, UT: U.S. Department of Agriculture, Forest Service, Intermountain Research Station.

Cole, D.N. (1993). *Campsites in three western wildernesses: Proliferation and changes in condition over 12 to 16 years.* (Research Paper INT-463). Ogden, UT: U.S. Department of Agriculture, Forest Service, Intermountain Research Station.

Cole, D.N. (1995). Experimental trampling of vegetation: Relationship between trampling intensity and vegetation response. *Journal of Applied Ecology*, 32, 203-214.

DeLuca, T.H., Patterson, W.A., Freimund, W.A., & Cole, D.N. (1998). Influence of llamas, horses, and hikers on soil erosion from established recreation trails in western Montana, USA. *Environmental Management*, 22, 255-262.

Farrell, T., Hall, T. E., & White, D. D. (2001). Wilderness campers' perception and evaluation of campsite impacts. *Journal of Leisure Research*, 33, 229-250.

Frissell, S.S. (1978). Judging recreation impacts on wilderness campsites. *Journal of Forestry*, 76, 481-483.

Frissell, S.S., & Duncan, D.P. (1965). Campsite preference and deterioration in the Quetico-Superior canoe country. *Journal of Forestry*, 65, 256-260.

Gallet, S., & Rozé, F. (2002). Long-term effects of trampling on Atlantic Heathland in Brittany (France): Resilience and tolerance in relation to season and meteorological conditions. *Biological Conservation*, 103, 267-275.

Hammitt, W.E., & Cole, D.N. (1987). *Wildland recreation: Ecology and management.* New York, NY: John Wiley.

Hampton, B., & Cole, D. (1988). *Soft Paths.* Harrisburg, PA: Stackpole Books.

Hartley, E. (1999). Visitor impacts at Logan Pass, Glacier National Park: A thirty-year vegetation study. In D. Harmon (Ed.), *On the frontiers of conservation* (pp. 297-305). Hancock, MI: The George Wright Society.

Hylgaard, T., & Liddle, M. J. (1981). The effect of human trampling on a sand dune ecosystem dominated by *Empetrum nigrum*. *Journal of Applied Ecology*, 18, 559-569.

Knight, R.L., & Gutzwiller, K.J. (Eds.) (1995). *Wildlife and recreationists: Coexistence through management and research*. Washington, DC: Island Press.

Leung, Y., & Marion, J.L. (1996). Trail degradation as influenced by environmental factors: A state-of-knowledge review. *Journal of Soil and Water Conservation*, 51, 130-136.

Leung, Y., & Marion, J.L. (1999a). Spatial strategies for managing visitor impacts in national parks. *Journal of Park and Recreation Administration*, 17, 20-38.

Leung, Y., & Marion, J.L. (1999b). The influence of sampling interval on the accuracy of trail impact assessment. *Landscape and Urban Planning*, 43, 167-179.

Liddle, M.J. (1975). A selective review of the ecological effects of human trampling on natural ecosystems. *Biological Conservation*, 7, 17-36.

Liddle, M.J. (1997) *Recreation ecology*. London: Chapman & Hall.

Macarthur, R.A., Geist, V., & Johnston, R.H. (1982). Cardiac and behavioral responses of mountain sheep to human disturbance. *Journal of Wildlife Management*, 46, 351-358.

Marion, J.L. (1995). Capabilities and management utility of recreation impact monitoring programs. *Environmental Management*, 19, 763-771.

Marion, J.L., & Cole, D.N. (1996). Spatial and temporal variation in soil and vegetation impacts on campsites. *Ecological Applications*, 6, 520-530.

Meinecke, E.P. (1928). *The effect of excessive tourist travel on the California redwood parks*. Sacramento, CA: California Department of Natural Resources, Division of Parks.

Miller, S.G., Knight, R.L., & Miller, C.K. (2001). Wildlife responses to pedestrians and dogs. *Wildlife Society Bulletin*, 29, 124-132.

Newsome, D., Moore, S.A., & Dowling, R.K. (2002). *Natural area tourism: Ecology, impacts and management*. Cleveland, UK: Channel View Publications.

Phillips, G.E., & Alldredge, A.W. (2000). Reproductive success of elk following disturbance by humans during calving season. *Journal of Wildlife Management*, 64, 521-230.

Riffell, S.K., Gutzwiller, K.J., & Anderson, S.H. (1996). Does repeated human intrusion cause cumulative declines in avian richness and abundance? *Ecological Applications*, 6, 492-505.

Rouphael, A.B., & Inglis, G.J. (2002). Increased spatial and temporal variability in coral damage caused by recreational scuba diving. *Ecological Applications*, 12, 427-440.

Wagar, J.A. (1964). *The carrying capacity of wild lands for recreation* (Forest Science Monograph 7). Washington, DC: Society of American Foresters.

Wilson, J.P., & Seney, J.P. (1994). Erosional impact of hikers, horses, motorcycles, and off-road bicycles on mountain trails in Montana. *Mountain Research and Development*, 14, 77-88.

Zabinski, C.A., & Gannon, J.E. (1997). Effects of recreational impacts on soil microbial communities. *Environmental Management*, 21, 233-238.

11

Communication Research in Outdoor Recreation and Natural Resources Management

James D. Absher

Alan D. Bright

It is often suggested in the recreation and natural resources management fields that simply communicating with or educating the public about a particular issue can solve management problems. If we could create a stronger environmental ethic among visitors, for example, we would eliminate or decrease problems with litter and vandalism. If we explain the biological consequences of prescribed fires and mechanical thinning, we could ultimately have greater public support for fire management policies (and consequently, a healthier ecosystem). These examples illustrate the often unrealistic expectations that managers and researchers have of their ability to develop information that will inform and/or influence the public. Unfortunately, attempts to influence or educate the public achieve only moderate success, and quite often are a complete failure (Manfredo, 1992).

There are a number of reasons that the success of persuasion and education is limited. First, people come into contact with a huge amount of information everyday in all types of places and situations. Much of this information competes with recreation and natural resource messages for the attention of the public, and is consequently screened out or misunderstood. Second, recreation and natural resource managers and researchers have relatively limited experience with, and understanding of, communication and persuasion processes.

This chapter explores the nature of recreation and natural resource communication research. In terms of communication, we focus primarily on studies that include either a persuasion (attitude/ behavior change) or informational/ educational focus. The analysis begins with a brief examination of the prevalence of communication research within several sub-disciplines. Second, examples of communication research are described. Third, some of the primary theoretical frameworks of communication in recreation and natural resource contexts are presented. Finally, suggestions for future research needs that should be explored in the recreation and natural resource fields are provided.

Communication Research in Recreation and Natural Resource Management

Visitors to parks, forests and protected areas routinely seek out information before and during their travels. The venues and media are varied. Written materials such as brochures, guidebooks, or signs are common. Personal communications from desk personnel, interpreters or field staff, while more costly to provide, are often preferred. The potential mix can be a dizzying array of communication techniques and approaches. Communicating effectively requires that managers be sensitive to both visitors' needs and preferences, and to the capabilities of the communication channels (i.e., media) used. Communicating well also requires a broad program of research on the effectiveness of such communication devices and programs.

This section provides a discussion of the prevalence and types of communication research applied to recreation and natural resource management. The review begins by examining the books of abstracts from the International Symposia on Society and Resource Management (ISSRM). Also reviewed were scientific journals such as *Society and Natural Resources, Human Dimensions of Wildlife, Journal of Environmental Education, Journal of Interpretation Research, Journal of Leisure Research,* and *Leisure Sciences.* The initial focus was to examine both the relative amount of communication research conducted within the recreation and natural resource fields, as well as an assessment of the nature of that research.

The Prevalence of Communication Research

In general, empirical research on communication processes and effectiveness comprises a small amount of the total research base. Even studies with a focus on attitudes and/or behavior rarely included a communication component beyond recognizing that an understanding of attitudes, behavior, and other constructs has implications for communication research and management.

The predominant location for reporting communication research was within the books of abstracts of the ISSRM. Over the past 15 years, there have been approximately 75 reports of empirical research about the effectiveness of communication programs (an average of about six abstracts per symposium). The prevalence of communication research in the ISSRM proceedings is considerable compared to the peer-reviewed journals. For example, there was an average of about one empirical study of communication and its effectiveness per year in *Society and Natural Resources.* Far fewer were found in *Human Dimensions of Wildlife,* where there was less than one empirical communication study per year since its inception in 1996. In the recreation field, only five and six empirical tests of communication were found in *Leisure Sciences* and *Journal of Leisure Research,* respectively, in the past 15 years.

The review of empirical communication research also included the *Journal of Environmental Education* and *Journal of Interpretation Research.* While the primary focus of these journals is primarily communication, only about 15 percent of the articles fit our definition of empirical communication research. Two-thirds of those (or 10 percent overall) represented the use or test of a communication theory; the remaining 90 percent represented descriptive studies of the effects of communication on attitudes, behaviors, and knowledge. Many of the articles and research focused on topics such as 1) the need for environmental education for different populations, 2) subjective assessments of the quality of environmental education or specific types of programs, 3) a descriptive report of a particular group's environmental attitudes or behavior without a persuasion or information component, 4) assessments of change in environmental attitudes with time as the only independent variable, and 5) philosophical discussions about the role of environmental education in classrooms.

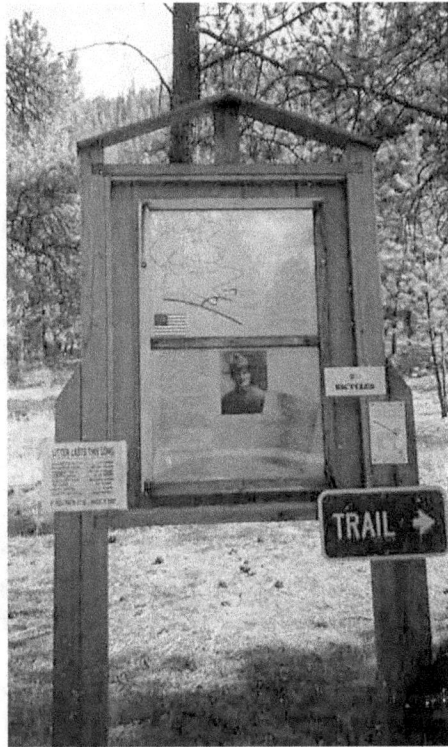

BRENT ERB

Types of Communication Research
Along with an examination of the prevalence of empirical communication research in the selected symposia and journals, the general nature of recent communication research was also examined. A number of research threads were identified that seem to organize these papers and presentations thematically. Some studies that are clearly focused on a program or policy context are largely descriptive in nature. These provide valuable information about how or why a communication strategy was a success (or not), including insight into the status of communication in natural resource management. A special case of this type of empirical research focuses attention on communication, per se, either as part of an environmental education or interpretive program. Finally, studies exist, albeit few, that investigate the theoretical underpinnings of visitor communication from a social psychological standpoint, including those that employ persuasion theory.

General communication and information studies. Most of the empirical studies are descriptive in nature, examining the effect of a variety of communication and information programs on a dependent variable such as attitudes, behavior or knowledge. Generally, these fail to be nested within a theoretical framework. Further, such non-theoretical studies made up nearly three-fourths of the communication research.

There are a number of basic foci of the descriptive research. Empirical studies focused on environmental education and interpretation services have generally focused on program effectiveness for specific populations. Environmental education and programs for school groups are an especially prominent topic of communication research (e.g., Culen & Volk, 2000; Gillett, Tomas, Skok & McLaughlin, 1991; Ramsey,

1993; Tomsen & Disinger, 1998). Many school-based environmental education articles offer specific programmatic curricula as exemplars for success (e.g., Keen, 1991; Leeming, Porter, Dwyer, Coburn & Oliver, 1997). Many employ some methodological sophistication through sampling and the use of descriptive or inferential statistics (Saslaw, 2000; Wallace & Gaudry, 2002; Weiler, 1999). Some compare different approaches of providing interpretive and environmental education messages such as adventure versus ecology programming (Hanna, 1995), traditional versus non-traditional classroom education (Dettmann-Easler & Pease, 1999; Zelezny, 1999), and traditional versus constructivist teaching (Lord, 1999). Some examine and compare the effects of specific medium such as brochures (Young & Witter, 1994); radio, television, and in-store information (Gillilan, Werner, Olson & Adams, 1996), and; interpretation programs directed toward youth versus adults (Morgan, Absher, Louden & Sutherland, 1997).

Communication theory studies. The remaining 25 percent of the communication studies identified either tested or used a theoretical framework to examine the effectiveness of communication programs and/or the process by which these programs work. While there has been relatively few theoretically-based studies on communication and attitude-change, those that have occurred represent solid methodological attempts to understand the process by which information influences attitudes and behaviors.

Communication theory has been used to inform studies about the key functions of visitor information. One thread looked generally at communication theory and argued that models from that discipline, such as agenda-setting, uses and gratifications (U&G) or text analysis (i.e., print media) could be readily adapted to natural resource management (Absher, 1998; Absher, Thapa & Graefe, 2002;

Bengston & Fan, 1999; Maher, 1997). Such approaches bring a deeper understanding of the role of information to agency efforts (Absher, Graefe & Kyle, 2000; Graefe, Absher, Confer & Thapa, 2000, 2003; James & Absher, 1999). For instance, newspaper coverage of forest management issues can be linked to community support for ongoing programs (Bengston & Fan, 1999). U&G scales can differentiate way finding from information needs for a user segment (Absher, 1999; James & Absher, 2000) or better understand the information needs of under-served populations (Thapa, Graefe & Absher, 2002). Overall, these perspectives move the task of providing information for visitors forward by placing these efforts into a broader context that treats communication more strategically and more differentially according to function, media, message, and audience (Absher, 1997; Ham, 1997).

Analysis of print media has been done on a limited number of related forest management topics, such as recreational fee demonstration, and general forest values (Bengston & Fan, 1999). In general, this approach provides a feedback mechanism through the newspaper and other print media. Although the methodology has been accepted by the mass media, it is subject to some criticism over coverage and validity issues. That notwithstanding, the results are similar to those obtained through more conventional social science surveys, and the process is arguably quicker and less expensive to conduct. Utility, or lack thereof, will be borne out over further applications and use of the technique.

As mentioned above, the U&G approach has been adapted from communication theory for use in visitor center and recreational information studies. Beginning with the work of Absher and Picard (1998), four basic U&G dimensions were proposed: labeled orientation, education, regulatory/policy information, and safety/reassurance. For each U&G dimension, a set of Likert scaled items were developed and tested. Subsequent research (Absher, 1999; James & Absher, 2000; Thapa, Graefe & Absher, 2002) showed that the approach could be used to differentiate user groups in ways that reflected in staffing and message delivery systems. Loker, Shanahan and Decker (1999) applied this theoretical approach to mass media and stakeholder beliefs about suburban wildlife and its management.

Other prominent theories have been borrowed from social psychology as a way of understanding the processes by which information influences attitudes and behavior. The theory most prominently applied in the field is the Elaboration Likelihood Model (ELM, Petty & Cacioppo, 1986). Research utilizing ELM examines the extent to which a number of factors influence whether individuals carefully consider a message (i.e., elaboration) and the extent to which that elaboration influences attitudes and behavior. High elaboration of information may lead to attitude change (referred to as the *central route to persuasion*) that is considered to be highly enduring. Low elaboration may lead to attitude change (referred to as the *peripheral route to persuasion*), which is likely to be less enduring. In addition, ELM suggests that factors such as involvement, argument quality, source credibility, and working knowledge (among others) influence an individual's motivation and ability to elaborate on information. This model has been used to examine the elaboration and effects of information on attitudes toward wilderness behavior in the Boundary Waters Canoe Area Wilderness (Manfredo & Bright, 1991), drilling for oil in the Alaska National Wildlife Refuge

(ANWR, Bright, Teel, Manfredo & Brooks, 2003), and ecosystem management (Tarrant, Bright & Cordell, 1996).

Another prominent social psychology model applied to communication is the Theory of Reasoned Action (TRA, Fishbein & Ajzen, 1975). While originally developed as a model of attitudes and behavior, its tenets can be applied to the attitude change and persuasion process as well. This model suggests that one's attitude toward a behavior as well as one's perceptions of how other's feel about a behavior (i.e., subjective norms) are prominent predictors of *behavior intention* and *behavior*. In turn, one's attitudes and subjective norms are driven by the salient beliefs an individual has about the behavior. This may be applied to attitude-change by noting that providing information to people that changes their beliefs may result in a change of attitudes, subjective norms, and ultimately behavior. TRA has been applied as a model of attitude and behavior change, including examination of the effects of information about controlled burn policies (Bright, Manfredo, Fishbein & Bath, 1993; Manfredo & Fishbein, 1992) bear encounters (Lackey, 2002), and wilderness behavior (Hanna, 1995).

Finally, Teel, Brooks, Bright and Manfredo (2001) questioned many assumptions that natural resource managers and researchers have about the direct effect of information on attitudes and behavior. They examined the potential for *biased processing* of information about drilling for oil in ANWR and found that people who received information about drilling for oil in ANWR did not change their attitudes toward the issue, but rather, processed the information consistent with their original attitudes, and actually became more extreme as a result of the information. This occurred regardless of the direction of the original position toward the issue. Our assumption that merely providing the public with information through education will change their attitudes and behaviors in a desired direction may not be true, at least in some cases.

Conclusions and Future Research Needs

We came to two general conclusions through our review of communication and attitude change research. First, while the development of information programs targeted for the public is often identified by researchers as a key implication of recreation and natural resources research, testing the effects of information programs on attitudes and behaviors has not been a particularly prominent area of research in the recreation and natural resource fields.

Second, most of the communication research that does occur is descriptive in nature, limiting itself to examining the effects of a particular information or education programs on attitudes, behavior, or knowledge. There is relatively little application of communication theory, though interest appears to be growing. As noted in the introduction, this limited use of theory could be both a cause and result of the lack of understanding of the process by which information influences attitudes and behavior.

Our recommendations for future research in communication are threefold. First, given the importance that natural resource and recreation agencies place on communication with the public, research into the effects of communication on attitudes, behaviors, and other factors should be increased. It is an area ripe for creative social science that can have immediate and far-reaching implications for how well resource and recreation managers do their jobs. Second, there is growing recognition that recreationists and natural resource management constituencies are very diverse. This implies that recreation and natural resource managers serve multiple value systems. These systems include European and non-European viewpoints represented by native/indigenous peoples, Hispanics, African-Americans and other increasingly prominent ethnicities with a stake in recreation opportunities and natural resource management. Research on communication across diverse cultures, values, and generations will enhance the ability of managers to be responsive to an increasingly complex society. Third, where possible, communication research should be based on sound communication theory. This will further researchers' and managers' understanding of the process by which information works (and does not work). Basing communication studies on theory also will allow for a broader interpretation of a given study beyond the particular situation in which it was conducted.

References

Absher J.D. (1997). Introduction: Interpretation as communication. *Trends, 34* (4), 2–3.

Absher, J.D. (1998). *Parables and paradigms: An introduction to using communication theories in outdoor recreation research* (General Technical Report NE–241). Radnor, PA: USDA Forest Service, Northeastern Research Station.

Absher, J.D. (1999). *The utility of a uses and gratifications approach to assess the information needs of forest visitors: An activity–based market segmentation test* (General Technical Report NE–255). Radnor, PA: USDA Forest Service, Northeastern Research Station.

Absher, J.D., & Picard, R. (1998). *Applying a well-known communication theory (Uses and Gratifications) to National Forest recreation use.* Paper presented at the Seventh International Symposium on Society and Resource Management, Columbia, MO.

Absher, J.D., Graefe, A.R., & Kyle, G. (2000). *Information use and preferences at Mono Basin Scenic Area* (General Technical Report PNW-GTR-497). Portland, OR: USDA Forest Service, Pacific Northwest Research Station.

Absher, J.D., Thapa, B., & Graefe, A.R. (2002). *Assessing information needs and communication behaviors of national forest summer visitors* (General Technical Report NE-289). Newtown Square, PA: USDA Forest Service, Northeastern Research Station.

Bengston, D.N., & Fan, D. P. (1999). The public debate about roads on the national forests: An analysis of the news media, 1994-1998. *Journal of Forestry,* 97(8), 4-10.

Bright, A.D., Manfredo, M.J., Fishbein, M., & Bath, A. (1993). Application of the theory of reasoned action to the National Park Service's controlled burn policy. *Journal of Leisure Research,* 25(3), 263-280.

Bright, A. D., Teel, T., Manfredo, M. J., & Brooks, J. (2003, November). *Attitudes toward drilling in the Alaska National Wildlife Refuge: An application of the elaboration likelihood model of persuasion*. Paper presented at the Conference on Human Dimensions in Natural Resources, Sun Valley, ID.

Culen, G., & Volk, T. (2000). The effects of an extended case study on environmental behavior and associative variables in 7th and 8th grade students. *Journal of Environmental Education, 31*(2), 9-15.

Dettmann-Easler, D., & Pease, J. L. (1999). Evaluating the effectiveness of residential environmental education programs in fostering positive attitudes toward wildlife. *Journal of Environmental Education, 31*(1), 33-39.

Fishbein, M., & Ajzen, I. (1975). *Belief, attitude, intention, and behavior: An introduction to theory and research*. Reading, MA: Addison-Wesley.

Gillett, D. P., Tomas, G. P., Skok, R. L., & McLaughlin, T. F. (1991). The effects of wilderness camping and hiking on the self-concept and environmental attitudes and knowledge of twelfth graders. *Journal of Environmental Education, 22*(3), 33-44.

Gillilan, G., Werner, L. L., Olson, L., & Adams, D. (1996). Teaching the concept of precycling: A campaign and evaluation. *Journal of Environmental Education, 28*(1), 11-18.

Graefe, A.R., Absher, J.D., Confer, J.J., & Thapa, B. (2000). *The role of user surveys in the development of an information and education plan for the Allegheny National Forest.* (General Technical Report PNW-GTR-497). Portland, OR: USDA Forest Service, Pacific Northwest Research Station.

Graefe, A.R., Absher, J.D., Confer, J.J., & Thapa, B. (2003). *Communication needs and approaches for visitor management: A case study of the Allegheny National Forest.* Unpublished report.

Ham, S. (1997). *Environmental education as strategic communication: A paradigm for protected area managers and teachers in the 21st century*. Paper presented at the 1997 International Symposium on Society and Resource Management, Fort Collins, CO.

Hanna, G. (1995). Wilderness related environmental outcomes of adventure and ecology education programming. *Journal of Environmental Education, 27*(1), 21-32.

James, K., & Absher, J.D. (1999). Forest information van: Message form, content and uncertainty reduction. Unpublished report. Riverside, CA: USDA Forest Service, Pacific Southwest Research Station.

James, K., & Absher, J.D. (2000). *Use of information services at Big Bear Discovery Center.* Unpublished report.

Keen, M. (1991). The effect of the Sunshine Earth Program on knowledge and attitude development. *Journal of Environmental Education, 22*(3), 28-32.

Lackey, B. K. (2002). *Conflicts*. Paper presented at Proceedings of the Eighth International Symposium on Society and Resource Management. Bloomington, IN.

Leeming, F. C., Porter, B. E., Dwyer, W. O., Coburn, M. K., & Oliver, D. P. (1997). Effects of participation in class activities on children's environmental attitudes and knowledge. *Journal of Environmental Education*, 28(2), 33-42.

Loker C. A., Shanahan, J., & Decker, D. J. (1999). The mass media and stakeholders' beliefs about suburban wildlife. *Human Dimensions of Wildlife*, 4(2), 7-26.

Lord, T. R. (1999). A comparison between traditional and constructivist teaching in environmental science. *Journal of Environmental Education*, 30(3), 22-28.

Maher, M. (1997). *Application of mass communications research to natural resource management*. Paper presented at the 1997 International Symposium on Society and Resource Management, Fort Collins, CO.

Manfredo, M. J., & Bright, A. D. (1991). A model for assessing the effects of communication on recreationists. *Journal of Leisure Research*, 23(1), 1-20.

Manfredo, M. J. (Ed.) (1992). *Influencing human behavior: Theory and applications in recreation, tourism, and natural resource management*. Champaign, IL: Sagamore.

Manfredo, M. J., & Fishbein, M. (1992). A theory of behavior change. In M. J. Manfredo (Ed.), *Influencing human behavior: Theory and applications in recreation, tourism, and natural resource management* (pp. 29-50). Champaign, IL: Sagamore.

Morgan, J. M., Absher, J., Louden, B., & Sutherland, D. (1997). The relative effectives of interpretive programs directed by youth and adult naturalists in a national forest. *Journal of Interpretation Research*, 2(1), 13-26.

Petty, R. E., & Cacioppo, J. T. (1986). The elaboration likelihood model of persuasion. In L. Berkowitz (Ed.), *Advances in experimental social psychology*: Vol. 19 (pp. 123-205). San Diego, CA: Academic Press.

Ramsey, J. M. (1993). The effects of issue investigation and action training on eighth grade students' environmental behavior. *Journal of Environmental Education*, 24(3), 31-36.

Saslaw, D. (2000). *How wonderful is it? Providing environmental education opportunities for underserved youth*. Paper presented at the Eighth International Symposium on Society and Resource Management, Portland, OR.

Tarrant, M. A., Bright, A. D., & Cordell, H. K. (1996). *The effect of persuasive communication strategies on rural resident attitudes toward ecosystem management*. Paper presented at the Sixth International Symposium on Society and Resource Management, University Park, PA.

Teel, T. L., Brooks, J. T., Bright, A. D., & Manfredo, M. J. (2002). *Evidence of biased processing in a study of attitudes toward drilling for oil in the Alaska National Wildlife Refuge*. Paper presented at the Ninth International Symposium on Society and Resource Management, Bloomington, IN.

Thapa, B., Graefe, A.R., & Absher, J.D. (2002). Information needs and search behaviors: A comparative study of ethnic groups in the Angeles and San Bernardino National Forests, California. *Leisure Sciences*, 24(1), 89-107

Tomsen, J. L., & Disinger, J. F. (1998). A method for assessing effects of an introductory environmental history course on student worldviews. *Journal of Environmental Education*, 29(2), 11-20.

Wallace, G. N., & Gaudrey, C. J. (2002). An evaluation of the "authority of the resource" interpretive technique by rangers in eight wilderness/backcountry areas. *Journal of Interpretation Research*, 7(1), 43-68.

Weiler, B. (1999). Improving interpretive services in guided tours: Lessons from field-based research on Australian ecotour guides. *Proceedings of Application of Social Science to Resource Management in the Asia-Pacific Region*. Brisbane, Australia: University of Queensland.

Young, C. A., & Witter, J. A. (1994). Developing effective brochures for increasing knowledge of environmental problems: The case of the Gypsy Moth. *Journal of Environmental Education*, 25(3), 27-34.

Zelezny, L. C. (1999). Educational intervention that improves environmental behaviors: A meta-analysis. *Journal of Environmental Education*, 31(1), 5-14.

12

Collaborative Resource Management

Discourse-based Approaches and the Evolution of TechnoReg

Steven E. Daniels

Antony S. Cheng

Collaboration. Consensus. Council. Compromise. These words have flooded into the jargon of natural resource management in recent years. This chapter discusses the dramatic rise in the interest in what might collectively be called *discourse-based approaches to natural resource management.* The goal is to provide a broader understanding of the social and political forces that are giving rise to collaboration in resource management approaches, as well as a glimpse into the lessons learned through these experiments in participatory governance.

Defining the Topic Area

The phenomenon under examination is one where the academic community struggles to keep up with the practitioners and community activists. Across the globe there are groups of people, often adhering to very different and competing viewpoints, trying to work through natural resource issues that have not been adequately addressed through other means. It is a truly emergent process, with the different groups developing their own rules of engagement and shared language along the way to fit their unique situations. The process also cuts across a number of academic disciplines, both drawing upon and generating substantial literatures in communication, law, natural resource management, geography, human ecology, anthropology, political science, public administration, and sociology. As a result, there is no standard terminology. What is the difference between *collaboration* and *consensus?* Is a *dispute* also a *conflict?* Is there an important distinction between *conflict management* and *conflict resolution?* Rather than expend time attempting to draw arbitrary or arcane distinctions, we prefer to lump them into an inclusive set: discourse-based approaches.

Defining Discourse-based Approaches
The unifying characteristic of all discourse-based approaches is an emphasis on multi-party communication

among stakeholders. These processes are undertaken to promote creativity, to resolve misunderstandings of fact, to surface value differences, and to seek mutually acceptable outcomes. While they are often local (e.g., watershed councils, community-federal land partnerships), these dialogues can also be regional or national in scope (e.g., Seventh American Forest Congress, Colorado Ranching Roundtables). They are sometimes facilitated or mediated, and sometimes not. They often strive for specific implementable agreements, and sometimes not. But in all cases, the emphasis is on the discourse; the thoughtful process of deliberating on complex and often controversial issues. Listening and speaking are done as much to learn as to convince. It draws upon rich traditions of participatory governance that characterize civic life in America: town hall meetings, Chautauquas, salons, the Grange movement, etc. Contemporary examples include study circles, design charettes, and citizen/value juries.

It is important to distinguish these discourse-based approaches from the public participation processes that agencies have been enacting since the 1970s. Agency-driven public participation is a much more controlled communication interaction. The agenda has been largely established by the convening agency in the sense that the purpose and need for proposed action—and perhaps the proposed action itself—have already been identified. The limitations of the public participation model have been extensively catalogued by others, (e.g., Blahna & Yonts-Shepard, 1989; Thomas, 1995; Wondolleck, 1988) and the interest in discourse-based approaches may be understood at least in part as arising out of dissatisfaction with the agency-driven public participation model.

Interest in discourse-based approaches is also growing among the natural resource social science community. This interest is evident in the steadily increasing number of presentations at sessions of the International Symposium on Society and Resource Management (ISSRM) and articles published in *Society and Natural Resources* (SNR) (see sidebar).

Defining the Historical Context

The authors have crafted a concept of *TechnoReg* to represent the dominant paradigm that drove natural resource management in the public estate in the 20th century, and thus created the context within which discourse-based approaches arose.

Techno refers to the assumption that there are technically correct or preferable approaches to natural resource issues. Natural resource management is seen at its core as a scientific or engineering problem with technical solutions. Oftentimes the implicit presumption when people do not agree with a proposal is "they just don't understand the science." The *techno* mindset also tends to underestimate the likelihood that differences in preferences can arise from deeply-seated value differences that exist largely independent of technical issues that therefore defy technical solutions.

Reg refers to the major ways through which various techno solutions were institutionalized into widespread practice. A long series of court cases, legislative solutions, and regulations have dominated the evolution of natural resource management. An embedded presumption in *reg* is that it is possible to craft regulations consistent with the *techno* science that can then be implemented in a routinized manner across the entire jurisdiction to which the regulations apply.

Discourse-based approaches (DBA) in ISSRM and SNR

A frequency count of papers in the Book of Abstracts for the International Symposium on Society and Resource Management from 1992, 1996, and 2000, and in *Society and Natural Resources* from Volume 1-16 (1988-2003) clearly shows an increase in the percentage of papers related to discourse-based approaches (Figure 1). Concepts and terms in the tally include, but are not limited to, U.S. and international cases in alternative dispute resolution, conflict management/resolution, collaboration, co-management, consensus, deliberation, democracy, negotiation, partnerships, public involvement/ participation, stakeholder involvement/participation, and watershed councils. Frequency counts of values/attitudes studies were not included unless that was input into a larger DBA project or evaluation of DBA.

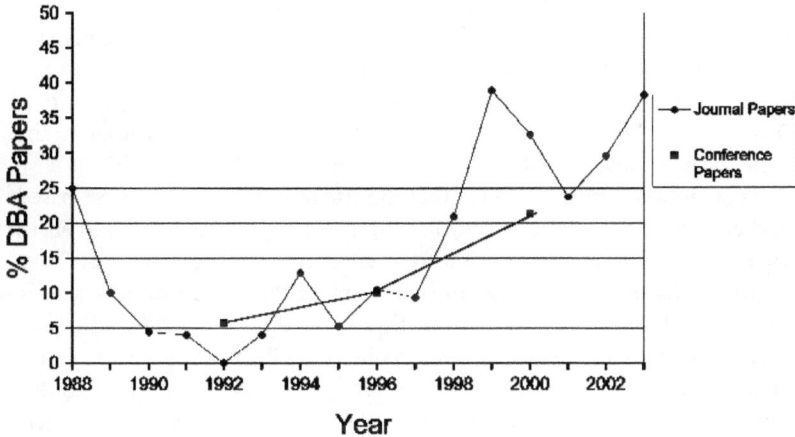

Figure 1. Percentage of papers on discourse-based approaches in Society and Natural Resources, 1988-2003 and Proceedings of ISSRM, 1992-2000.

The biggest jump occurs between 1996 and 2000, when there was a two-fold increase in DBA presentations at ISSRM and a four-fold increase in articles in SNR. This increase reflects the "coming out" period of collaborative partnerships, such as the Applegate Partnership and Quincy Library Group, in 1993 and 1994. The publicity of these and other partnerships signaled an exciting, emerging social dimension in natural resource management.

TechnoReg is the hybridization of two different rationalities—science and law—and was the unifying cultural mindset that drove natural resource management throughout the 20th century.

The emergence of *TechnoReg* was embedded in the social and political culture that gave rise to natural resource management in the United States. Germanic forestry, the progressive political era, the formation of forestry schools to train professionals for the new agencies, and the American predilection to solve conflicts through litigation all played a part. The high watermark for *TechnoReg* in the U.S. was the 1970s, with the passage of the National Environmental Policy Act (which required interdisciplinary analysis and public disclosure) and the National Forest Management Act (which required comprehensive plans for all National Forests in the U.S., and ultimately involved huge linear programming optimization models). *TechnoReg* also spread far beyond the U.S., as young professionals came to the U.S. for training or as other countries' legal and administrative structures for natural resource management were cloned from American rootstock.

But even as *TechnoReg* hit its zenith in the 1970s, the limitations of the approach became apparent. Federal land management agencies began to devote larger portions of their budgets and personnel to a cycle of planning-disclosure-appeals-litigation-legislation. Not surprisingly, the decision space around natural resource management became populated with analysts, attorneys, advocates, and administrators. A phrase that Dick Behan (1991) crafted embodied much of this cycle: "Potomocentric statutory fixes" (p. 1). These were attempts to have Congress craft legislation that somehow solved problems that could not be resolved in other venues.

The contention in this chapter is that the rise of interest in discourse-based approaches is an attempt to move beyond the *TechnoReg* paradigm and to enrich the participation of concerned citizens and non-governmental organizations. That is not to say that *TechnoReg* is wrong. Indeed, many of the conservation successes we have experienced in this country are directly attributable to *TechnoReg*. But any approach has its limits and *TechnoReg* is no different. People's connections to natural lands are often deeply nuanced and very personal. *TechnoReg*, in contrast, tends to result in sweeping policy decrees that are justified on the basis of often abstract concepts such as forest health, risk, range of historic variability, habitat connectivity, etc. The challenge in discourse-based approaches is to weave these very different ways of understanding and caring about land into a fabric that is stronger than either could be alone.

Synthesis and Integration of Research Findings

Discourse-based approaches are not unique to natural resource management; they have sprung forth in other areas of public affairs: regional transportation planning, land use, public schools, public health, and so forth (Fullinwider, 1999). This interest in civic engagement has co-evolved with a body of social and political theory that is known as *deliberative democracy*. Discourse-based approaches in natural resource management are also not confined to the United States. Indeed, community-based resource management absent *TechnoReg* has been commonplace internationally and brought to light by collective action scholars such as Elinor Ostrom (1990, 1998). This section provides an overview of the theoretical underpinnings of discourse-based approaches in natural resource management, describes research findings concerning the key attributes and lessons learned for effective discourse, and highlights critiques of discourse-based approaches.

Theoretical Underpinnings

The rise of discourse-based approaches in natural resource management and other areas of public affairs manifests what political scientist John Dryzek (2000) calls the deliberative turn in democratic theory. The theoretical development and critiques of deliberative democracy has grown in recent years (Dryzek, 1990; Fishkin, 1991; Fishkin & Laslett, 2003; Miller, 1992). Benjamin Barber (1984) refers to this transformation in how citizens engage in public affairs as "strong democracy." Barber highlights four points that underlie strong democracy: (1) strong democratic talk among citizens based on active listening, thoughtful argument, and reflection, (2) public action towards shared goals and values, (3) redefining citizens as active participants in civic discourse, and (4) redefining community as the fundamental unit of deliberation. The discourse-based approaches emerging in the natural resources field embody all four attributes.

Daniel Yankelovich (1991) echoes these themes in calling for a form of public deliberation that involves citizens in a process of working through conflicting goals and values, carefully weighing information, and arriving at public judgment as a community of citizens. Deliberative democratic theory has been applied to examinations of various natural resource management contexts (Gunderson, 1995; Moote, McClaran & Chickering, 1997; Press, 1994). The potential for public deliberation to flourish at a large scale is still a matter of debate. Robert Putnam (2000) suggests that an essential ingredient of public deliberation is social capital: the reservoir of norms and social networks that enable cooperative collective action toward a common goal. Discourse-based approaches also require a transformation in the roles of public administrators—including natural resource managers—from *objective technical analysts* to *facilitators of social learning* (Dukes, 1996; Reich, 1985).

Social and political theories of deliberative democracy are one foundation for understanding and exploring discourse-based approaches in natural resource management. A second, equally important body of theory comes from work in collective action to resolve common property resource dilemmas (Berkes, 1989; Bromley, 1992; Burger, Ostrom, Norgaard, Policansky & Goldstein, 2001; Ostrom, 1990; Western, Wright & Strum, 1994). Elinor Ostrom has been one of the leaders in developing a theory of collective action to conserve natural resources held in common that does not rely on *TechnoReg* (see Ostrom, 1998). Central to Ostrom's theory of collective action is communication among parties that results in transferring information, exchanging mutual commitment, increasing trust by affecting expectations of others' behaviors, clarifying values, reinforcing social norms of reciprocity, and developing and sustaining group identity. In short, communication discourse among parties is the glue that binds parties to norms of cooperative behaviors. These norms result in more durable social, economic, and ecological outcomes than externally-imposed *TechnoReg*.

It is critical to note the importance of discourse-based approaches in international natural resource management contexts where *TechnoReg* is not as

131

prevalent as in the U.S. Indeed, many of the models and concepts that are surfacing in the analysis of discourse-based approaches in resource management in the U.S. have their origins in international community-based conservation. Taken together, the theories of deliberative democracy and collective action in resource management comprise a foundational point of departure for explorations into discourse-based approaches to natural resource management.

What Makes for Effective Discourse? Attributes and Lessons Learned
Research in discourse-based approaches in natural resource management began with public involvement in agency planning and decision-making processes (Blahna & Yonts-Shepard, 1989; Gericke, Sullivan & Wellman, 1992; Wondolleck, 1988) and has moved into the various forms of partnerships, collaborations, councils, and the like (Brick, Snow & Wetering, 2001; Cestero, 1999; Daniels & Walker, 2001; Selin & Chavez, 1995; Williams & Ellefson, 1997; Wondolleck & Yaffee, 2000). The research generally falls into two methodological camps: survey questionnaires and case studies. Survey questionnaires are used to identify common attributes, processes, organizational structures, and outcomes across a large number of approaches. Case studies provide more in-depth analysis of the dimensions and nuances associated with multi-party communication by using qualitative, ethnographic methods.

The key attributes and lessons learned for moving discourse-based approaches in natural resource management into the future include the following:

- *Define common purpose.* Discourse requires a clear organizing principle (e.g., sense of place, sense of community, shared problems or fears, shared goals or interest). Defining the common purpose for discourse brings people to the table and keeps them there.

- *Actively search for new ways to frame and re-frame the situation.* Situational frames define what issues are important, why they are important, what the critical cause-and-effect relationships are, what the boundaries of the issues are, and what parties should be involved in the discourse. Natural resource issues likely have many different frames. Exploring these different frames can help people break out of linear ways of thinking and view the situation as a system of inter-related and inter-connected components.

- *Strive for an open and inclusive process.* All interested and affected parties should be invited and have access. One of the persistent challenges of discourse-based approaches is the constant arrival of new people, ideas, concerns, values, and ways of knowing and expressing. Although great care is needed to manage the discourse, newcomers can enrich the dialogue and offer new perspectives in deliberations.

- *Encourage broad participation rather than formal representation.* It is more important to have a wide spectrum of viewpoints, knowledge, and experiences than formalized representation. Representation may actually hamper discourse due to the cognitive burden of being accountable to one's organizational mission.

- *Develop multiple approaches for interactive communication among all parties.*

Discourse is more than simply talking. There are many ways in which people can share ideas, discover common values, and constructively work through differences. Small group discussions, participatory mapping, charrettes, study groups, shared history timelines, field trips, and web forums are but a few examples of numerous techniques that can enrich discourse.

- *Work at a scale appropriate to the community or place.* Discourse about natural resource management works best when focused on a landscape scale with which people can identify. Issues and concerns are tangible, potential improvements are more feasible, and parties can actually see results happen on the ground.

- *Start with a level playing field.* Productive discourse can only happen when every voice has equal influence on defining the issues, analyzing improvements, final decision-making, and appropriate actions. Voices that are privileged over others, or are marginalized or suppressed, will lead to a short and potentially contentious discourse.

- *Use third-party neutral facilitators.* Facilitators do more than manage meetings: They are guardians of a fair and open process by reminding parties about ground rules, ensuring all voices have opportunities to be expressed and heard, and keeping the discourse on track.

- *Emphasis on mutual learning before arriving at judgments.* Each party brings values, knowledge, and experiences to the table. Each party is not likely to know all dimensions of an issue. Learning about the diverse values and richness of others' experiences in an open, safe environment is more likely to result in durable public judgments about a natural resource issue.

Critiques of Discourse-Based Approaches

A common critique of discourse-based approaches is that communication among parties involved in a natural resource issue is necessary but insufficient for producing durable outcomes (Gunderson, 1995; Moote et al., 1997). There are parties who will still exhibit strategic behaviors and act on their own self-interest, regardless of the impact on others. Public natural resource agencies are still invested with the unilateral authority to enforce legal mandates and standards created by *TechnoReg* to protect the environment and the public from these strategic parties (Coggins, 1999; Dukes & Firehock, 2001). Indeed, many of the mandates that govern public natural resource agencies constrain their ability to actively engage in civic discourse. There is also the matter of conflicting mandates, goals, and missions of the various public natural resource agencies. No amount of discourse can resolve these conflicts outside of the courtroom.

Discourse-based approaches are also inefficient; they take a lot of time and require up-front financial and personnel resources, with payoffs that are uncertain at best (Daniels & Walker, 2001; Wondolleck & Yaffee, 2000). As a result, discourse-based approaches occur sporadically and tend to rely on strong personalities more than the availability of institutional structures to support civic discourse. In short, the supply of discourse-based approaches in natural resources lags behind the demand. The supply shortage has a systemic effect: Most citizens do not have the experience, practice, and skills to effectively participate (Dukes & Firehock, 2001). This lack of skills prevents many citizens from participating in the first place, creating a negative feedback loop.

Lastly, many of the discourse-based approaches that have emerged around the management of U.S. federal public lands have been criticized for being illegitimate, for they undermine existing venues for democratic deliberation, such as the legislature, courts, and administrative rule-making process (Coggins, 1999; McCloskey, 1996, 1999). Of particular concern are community-based collaborations which seemingly grant local citizens and communities a disproportionate role in federal public land and resource management decision-making. There is already a discourse-based system for deciding on goals and actions. Local discourse-based approaches shift power away from this system to the hands of the few parties who are physically able to participate. This is one of the primary reasons why many national environmental organizations are wary of supporting community-based collaboration in natural resources.

So Where Do Things Go From Here?

To echo a sentiment from the beginning of this chapter, the proliferation of discourse-based approaches is not an endeavor where academics or researchers are defining the agenda or leading the charge. Instead, this is an emergent social phenomenon that researchers are challenged to document and understand. Moreover, these episodes defy the traditional research model to a considerable extent. They are each unique, and lack the traditional experimental attributes of replication or random assignment. As a result, hypo-deductive remote sensing in search of generalizable findings is a research paradigm that doesn't fit well. Even categorizing discourse-based projects into successes and failures is a value-laden dichotomy that attempts to lump nuanced phenomena into coarse categories. Research on discourse-based approaches seemingly demands a participatory or qualitative, almost ethnographic research paradigm. This is a research style that may demand a new style of researcher.

But is this a fad or fundamental sea-change? If it is the former, it is likely to soon wane. If it is the latter, a new era of governance is dawning. In all likelihood, it is neither. This flurry of activity around discourse-based approaches is but the latest episode in an on-going political drama that both defines, and is defined by, the political culture in the U.S. It is merely the latest chapter in a debate that defines governance in this country because it poses a fundamental question for all democracies: Can citizens be entrusted with public affairs, or are the issues so complex and inherently politicized that they must be delegated to the technocratic regulators? This question has energized political tides that date back to the competition between Jeffersonian idealism and Madisonian pessimism. And it is likely to be with us, in one form or another, as long as the tides ebb and flow.

References

Barber, B. R. (1984). *Strong democracy: Participatory politics for a new age.* Berkeley, CA: University of California Press.

Behan, R. W. (1991). Forests and plantations and Potomo-centric statutory fixes. *Forest Perspectives*, 1(1), 5-8.

Berkes, F. (Ed.) (1989). *Common property resources: Ecology and community-based sustainable management.* London: Belhaven Press.

Blahna, D. J., & Yonts-Shepard, S. (1989). Public involvement in resource planning: Toward bridging the gap between policy and implementation. *Society and Natural Resources*, 2, 209-227.

Brick, P., Snow, D., & Wetering, S. V. (Eds.) (2001). *Across the Great Divide: Explorations in collaborative conservation and the American West.* Washington, DC: Island Press.

Bromley, D. W. (Ed.). (1992). *Making the commons work: Theory, practice, and policy.* San Fransisco: Institute for Contemporary Studies.

Burger, J., Ostrom, E., Norgaard, R. B., Policansky, D., & Goldstein, B. D. (Eds.) (2001). *Protecting the commons: A framework for resource management in the Americas.* Washington, D.C.: Island Press.

Cestero, B. (1999). *Beyond the hundredth meeting: A field guide to collaborative conservation on the West's public lands.* Tuscon, AZ: Sonoran Institute.

Coggins, G. C. (1999). Regulating federal natural resources: A summary case against devolved collaboration. *Ecology Law Quarterly*, 25, 602-610.

Daniels, S. E., & Walker, G. B. (2001). *Working through environmental conflict: The collaborative learning approach.* Westport, CT: Praeger.

Dryzek, J. S. (1990). *Discursive democracy: Politics, policy, and political science.* Cambridge, England: Cambridge University Press.

Dryzek, J. S. (2000). *Deliberative democracy and beyond: Liberals, critics, contestations.* Oxford, U.K.: Oxford University Press.

Dukes, E. F. (1996). *Resolving public conflict: Transforming community and governance.* Manchester, England: Manchester University Press.

Dukes, E. F., & Firehock, K. (2001). *Collaboration: A guide for environmental advocates.* Charlottesville, VA: University of Virginia.

Fishkin, J. S. (1991). *Democracy and deliberation: New directions for democratic reform.* New Haven, CT: Yale University Press.

Fishkin, J. S., & Laslett, P. (Eds.) (2003). *Debating deliberative democracy.* Malden, MA: Blackwell.

Fullinwider, R. K. (Ed.) (1999). *Civil society, democracy, and civic renewal.* Lanham, MD: Rowman & Littlefield.

Gericke, K. L., Sullivan, J., & Wellman, J. D. (1992). Public participation in national forest planning: Perspectives, procedures, and costs. *Journal of Forestry*, 90(2), 35-38.

Gunderson, A. G. (1995). *The environmental promise of democratic deliberation.* Madison, WI: University of Wisconsin Press.

McCloskey, M. (1996). The skeptic: Collaboration has its limits. *High Country News,* 28(9), 7.

McCloskey, M. (1999). Local communities and the management of public forests. *Ecology Law Quarterly,* 25, 624-629.

Miller, D. (1992). Deliberative democracy and social choice. *Political Studies,* 40, 54-67.

Moote, M. A., McClaran, M. P., & Chickering, D. K. (1997). Theory in practice: Applying participatory democracy theory to public planning. *Environmental Management,* 21(6), 877-889.

Ostrom, E. (1990). *Governing the commons: The evolution of institutions for collective action.* Cambridge, England: Cambridge University Press.

Ostrom, E. (1998). A behavioral approach to the rational choice theory of collective action. *American Political Science Review,* 92(1), 1-22.

Press, D. (1994). *Democratic dilemmas in the Age of Ecology: Trees and toxics in the American West.* Durham, NC: Duke University Press.

Putnam, R. D. (2000). *Bowling along: The collapse and revival of American community.* New York: Simon & Schuster.

Reich, R. B. (1985). Public administration and public deliberation: An interpretive essay. *Yale Law Journal,* 94(7), 1617-1642.

Selin, S., & Chavez, D. (1995). Developing a collaborative model for environmental planning and management. *Environmental Management,* 19(2), 189-195.

Thomas, J. C. (1995). *Public participation in public decisions: New skills and strategies for public managers.* San Francisco: Jossey-Bass Publishers.

Western, D., Wright, R.M., & Strum, S.C. (Ed.). (1994). *Natural connections: Perspectives in community-based conservation.* Covelo, CA: Island Press.

Williams, E. M., & Ellefson, P. V. (1997). Going into partnership to manage a landscape. *Journal of Forestry,* 95(5), 29-33.

Wondolleck, J. M. (1988). *Public lands conflict and resolution: Managing national forest disputes.* New York, NY: Plenum Press.

Wondolleck, J. M., & Yaffee, S. L. (2000). *Making collaboration work: Lessons from innovation in natural resource management.* Washington, DC: Island Press.

Yankelovich, D. (1991). *Coming to public judgment: Making democracy work in a complex world.* Syracuse, NY: Syracuse University Press.

13

Natural Resource Partnerships

Bridging Practice and Science

Steve Selin

During the past 15 years, partnerships have emerged as a mantra among policy-makers, managers, entrepreneurs, non-governmental organizations and citizens to achieve important conservation and sustainable development objectives. While a host of related terms such as *collaboration, co-management, community-based*, and *co-ordination* have also been used to describe these cooperative arrangements, partnerships generally refer to: 1) the voluntary pooling of resources (e.g., labor, money, information), 2) by two or more stakeholders to, 3) solve a set of problems that neither can solve individually (Gray, 1985).

Within the natural resource management literature, partnerships have been examined in the context of multi-party coalitions (Lichtman & Clark, 1994), gateway communities (Howe, McMahon & Propst, 1997), ecosystem management (Cortner & Moote, 1999), recreation resource management (Vaske, Donnelly & LaPage, 1995), and sustainable tourism (Bramwell & Lane, 2000) among others. While each partnership is unique and tailored to its own situation, they are generally based on the principles of voluntary participation, involving multiple partners, and seeking specific goals (Wondolleck & Yaffee, 2000).

The purpose of this chapter is to systematically examine the recent emphasis on partnerships within the conservation and sustainable development fields. Questions addressed include: How and in what form do partnerships address important resource management objectives? What economic, political, and social forces drive the increasing reliance on partnerships? What challenges or constraints tend to marginalize the full potential of partnerships within the natural resource domain?

In this chapter, the author synthesizes the emerging body of scientific literature on partnerships and identifies the lessons drawn to inform future research as well as public policy and management action to support effective partnerships within conservation and sustainable development.

Overview

Rise of Partnership Movement

Both internationally and in the United States, partnerships have grown from being a novel and alternative strategy to a way of life for many resource managers. Some suggest that partnerships are increasingly the only way to get the job done (Tuxill & Mitchell, 2001). A concrete example elaborates the point: The National Park Service (NPS) is perhaps best known for their direct management and ownership of the National Park System in the United States. However, it has expanded their mission considerably through technical and financial support for many community-based and regional conservation and heritage partnerships outside the National Park System. The National Heritage Areas and the Rivers, Trails, and Conservation Assistance Programs are both examples of NPS' provision of technical and financial assistance to local and regional conservation partnerships, though not getting involved in acquisition of new land or direct management. Regional partnerships like the Blackstone Valley National Heritage Area in Massachusetts are managed by a designated local management entity with representation from a diverse lot of local, regional and national partners that work cooperatively with NPS. These trends are representative of the recent partnership experience of other federal resource management agencies such as the USDA Forest Service, Environmental Protection Agency, Bureau of Land Management, and the Army Corps of Engineers.

Societal Forces at Work

The rising interest in partnerships within the natural resource domain reflects a number of broader political, economic, and social trends. Worldwide, many nations are navigating the transition from centralized, authoritarian government systems to more democratic and decentralized approaches that depend on an informed and active citizenry. This transition has provided a fertile ground for the design of more participatory approaches to natural resource policy-making and management.

Natural resource partnerships in the U.S. have also been forged by people frustrated with the protracted conflict and gridlock that has characterized federal land management in recent decades. For example, regional watershed coalitions like the Applegate Partnership in Oregon were formed to build a broader and shared vision for the future of the valley (Wondolleck & Yaffee, 2000). Planning models have also evolved in response to such societal trends, expanding from the expert systems and comprehensive, top-down approaches of the 1970s to more integrative approaches such as adaptive planning and ecosystem management where partnerships are considered a vital component (Cortner & Moote, 1999).

Many current partnership approaches to managing natural resources also reflect new economic realities facing public agencies. Downsizing, reinvention, and re-engineering have forced resource managers to look for alternative approaches to managing the natural resources under their care. Federally sponsored programs such as the Demonstration Fee Program and Challenge Cost-Share Grant Programs were implemented to stimulate management partnerships with the private sector, voluntary agencies, and other government agencies (Selin & Chavez, 1993). Other natural resource partnerships are championed by people and organizations with strong attachments to specific communities and special places: partnerships that often transcend the formal boundaries of public land management areas. The watershed movement is perhaps the best example of this. According to Moore and Koontz (2003), watershed partnerships bring together diverse stakeholders to transcend jurisdictional boundaries and fragmented policies while developing management strategies tied to local conditions and issues.

Challenges

While there is considerable hype surrounding the growth of partnerships in the conservation and sustainable development fields, many barriers limit their widespread adoption and support. Congressional oversight committees and agency directors have many questions regarding the accountability and control of multi-stakeholder partnerships that federal agencies support either directly through financial incentives, or indirectly through technical assistance and human resource support. For example, NPS' community outreach program, the Rivers, Trails, and Conservation Assistance Program, is currently under a Congressional inquiry investigating their use of public funds to support community-based conservation initiatives.

Partnerships are also hindered by traditional public agency culture and norms that discourage innovation and impose unrealistic bureaucratic hurdles to the nurturing of fragile partnerships with stakeholder groups. In study after study, partnership members complain about red tape and inflexible financial accounting and hiring practices (Selin & Chavez, 1995). Often, these problems are accentuated by agency staff who are unaware or resistant to adoption of partnership arrangements. Many blue ribbon panels and commissions have been authorized by federal agencies attempting to provide resource managers with more flexible policy and program tools to foster innovative partnerships. The USDA Forest Services' Partnership Authorities Workgroup, for example, was commissioned by the Chief of the Forest Service to recommend legislative and administrative improvements.

Against this backdrop of promise and contention, a growing body of social science research is examining the growth of partnerships in the conservation field. The following sections synthesize this accumulating work and draw both policy and management lessons as well as future research opportunities from this line of investigation.

Synthesis of Findings

Scholarly Interest in Partnerships
Social science research examining partnerships dates back to the mid-1980s with a growing recognition of the complexity and turbulence associated with modern societal problems, whether that be the safe storage of nuclear waste or preventing the spread of communicable diseases. Organizational scholars such as Barbara Gray recognized the need for creative solutions to these pervasive issues that included new ways for organizations to work together for the common good. Her book *Collaborating* (1989)

and subsequent special issues on collaborative alliances and partnerships in the *Journal of Applied Behavioral Science* catalyzed a generation of social scientists from the organizational behavior and management sciences, as well as other applied disciplines, interested in understanding these emerging partnership approaches.

Within the conservation field, partnerships have been subsequently examined within the context of sustainable tourism (Bramwell & Lane, 2000), ecosystem management (Cortner & Moote, 1999), protected area management (Kothari, Singh & Suri, 1996), watershed management (Moore & Koontz, 2003), heritage areas (Tuxill & Mitchell, 2001), and wilderness management (Selin, 1994), among others. Many natural resource scientists now routinely mention partnerships as at least one creative solution to thorny resource management problems. This growing body of knowledge is beginning to yield important insights into dynamics and processes of natural resource partnerships, as well as tools to support the care and feeding of effective partnerships.

Methodological Approaches

A number of methodological approaches have been used to analyze natural resource partnerships. As in any emerging area of social science inquiry, descriptive case studies and case study research dominates both the professional and research literature. Research varies from a detailed assessment and lessons learned from a single partnership case (Curtis & Lockwood, 2000) to research based on a large-scale database of partnerships (Wondolleck & Yaffee, 2000). Survey research has also been used extensively to gather behavioral data on partnership stakeholders as well as background information on the partnership itself. Researchers typically administer surveys to either partnership coordinators or to multiple participants of the partnership (Leach, 2002). In at least one case, partnership studies have also surveyed staff members of a public agency supporting partnerships to assess policy and program support for partnerships (Selin, Schuett & Carr, 1997). Leach (2002) critically compares these three survey approaches and emphasizes the need for a representative sample and advocating for the inclusion of informed non-participants in partnership studies to reduce the potential positive bias resulting from surveying only partnership stakeholders.

Much of the partnership research is based on the underlying assumption that conservation partners should adopt a domain level focus that includes "the set of actors (individuals, groups, and organizations) that become joined by a common problem or interest" (Gray, 1985, p. 912). Many resource managers and indeed social science research still embrace an organizational perspective (Evans, 1966) where their organization is thought to be the focal agency and others are considered to be external publics. Though this approach may be appropriate for a more predictable environment, a domain level focus is required for successfully navigating the modern era of turbulence and uncertainty.

Missing from the partnership research literature have been longitudinal study designs that are needed to examine the life cycle or development progression of partnerships (Selin, 1999). Life cycle models are routinely generated from case study research, but longitudinal study designs would prove more robust. However, they are perhaps limited due to the financial and time cost often associated with this type of research design.

Partnership Antecedents

Organizations that are potential partners in the conservation field operate in a dynamic social environment that exert many forces. Some of these forces are competitive or technological, while others are political, social or economic. Many work against cooperative relations while others tend to draw organizations together. In a multiple case study design, Selin and Chavez (1995) identified seven societal factors that served to catalyze partnership formation: 1) crisis, 2) broker intervention, 3) mandate, 4) common vision, 5) existing networks, 6) leadership, and 7) incentives. Long and Arnold (1995), examining environmental partnerships, describe four catalysts for partnership formation: 1) scientific uncertainty, 2) broad public interest, 3) existing or threatened regulation, and 4) a clearly identifiable opportunity. These factors serve as preconditions that tend to foster the formation of conservation partnerships.

These and other researchers have also identified social factors that tend to inhibit or constrain partnership formation in the conservation field. Wondolleck and Yaffee (2000), in their extensive study of innovation and excellence within the USDA Forest Service, reported many structural and institutional barriers to partnership formation including lack of incentives, conflicting goals and inflexible policies. The authors also cite barriers related to attitudes and perceptions that involve mistrust, group attitudes towards each other, and prevailing organizational culture and norms. Clearly, partnerships are born in a complex crucible of societal forces that social science research is beginning to map out, though additional work is needed.

Partnership Dynamics

Effective conservation partnerships, while complex and dynamic, conform to social, developmental and managerial norms that can be identified through social science research. Partnerships that do not conform to these norms are often doomed to failure. Research examining the internal dynamics of conservation partnerships can be grouped into two categories based on perspective: 1) those taking a structural view, and 2) those taking a process or developmental view.

The structural view of conservation partnerships is perhaps best exemplified by the work on developing typologies or classification systems. For example, Selin (1999) developed a typology for sustainable tourism partnerships based upon five classification dimensions: 1) geographic scale, 2) legal basis, 3) locus of control, 4) organizational diversity/size, and 5) time frame. Long and Arnold (1995) developed an analytic framework to understand environmental partnerships based on four types: 1) preemptive partnerships, 2) coalescing partnerships, 3) exploration partnerships, and 4) leverage partnerships. Other participant survey work has also adopted a structural view, assessing attitudes and perceptions of participants towards the partnership at one point in time. Several studies have used a structural approach to assess partnership members' level of satisfaction with the partnership, as well as to identify those individual and organizational factors that predict partnership effectiveness (Selin & Myers, 1995; Waddock & Bannister, 1991; Williams & Ellefson, 1997).

Other studies examining the dynamics of conservation partnerships have adopted a *process* or *developmental* approach. Past research on partnerships in the organizational behavior and conservation fields have been criticized for focusing primarily on formal transactions, being insensitive to multiple outcomes, and orienting toward individual actors at the expense of larger system dynamics (Gray, 1985).

One line of research in the sustainable tourism field is focused on design of a life cycle or developmental model for partnerships and community-based tourism planning (Caffyn, 2000; Jamal & Getz, 1995; Selin & Chavez, 1995). Building on the earlier work in the organizational behavior field by Gray (1985) and Waddock (1989), these researchers posit that partnerships evolve through predictable stages of development in their evolution. For example, Jamal and Getz (1995) developed a three-phase model for understanding the development of community-based tourism planning that included problem-setting, direction-setting and implementation phases. Selin and Chavez (1995), examining recreation and tourism partnerships, produced an evolutionary model with five stages and a feedback loop: 1) antecedents, 2) problem-setting, 3) direction-setting, 4) structuring, and 5) outcomes. Finally, Caffyn (2000), in a study of tourism partnerships, developed a life cycle model consisting of six stages: 1) pre-partnership, 2) take-off, 3) growth, 4) prime, 5) deceleration, and 6) continuation/after-life options. Much of this research has used case study research to confirm and extend hypothesized and a priori developmental models. Longitudinal research designs are needed to either confirm or refute these posited models.

Models for Success

Policy-makers, land management agencies and foundations providing resource support are concerned with measuring the performance of partnerships to ensure accountability and fiscal responsibility. Partnership members are also interested in monitoring outcomes to build public support and to learn how to be more effective. Researchers have responded to these concerns by conducting studies that begin to develop performance-based indicators for partnerships as well as to identify those factors that contribute to partnership success. Much of this research is driven by the question of how partnership success can be operationalized (Selin et al., 2000). Ecosystem health and community sustainability are often the long-term objectives of many partnerships, and performance indicators should reflect ecological and community changes affected by the partnership. Much of the current research, however, is based on surrogate measures of performance, such as partner or external observer perceptions of effectiveness and overall satisfaction.

A number of studies have identified common factors thought to contribute to partnership success. Yaffee, Philips, Frenz, Hardy, Malenki and Thorpe (1996), in a large-scale study of eco-system partnerships, found that broad-based support from stakeholders, public agencies and citizens often allowed these initiatives to proceed. Available resources and dedicated individuals to support project goals were identified as critical to partnership success. Williams and Ellefson (1997), in a survey of 40 natural resource partnerships, identified factors contributing to success including: recognition of common goals, an informal and open structure, and information sharing among partners. Finally, Selin, Schuett and Carr (2000), in a survey of participants in 30 natural resource partnerships, quantitatively linked a number of hypothesized predictors of partnership effectiveness to a multi-item dependent measure of partnership outcome achievement. Identified factors included: leadership, willingness to compromise, and having a broad representation of stakeholders.

There is great potential to expand on this early line of partnership monitoring research. Research is needed that develops long-term ecological and community indicators that assess the performance of individual partnerships. More work is also needed to build comprehensive models of those individual and organizational factors that predict partnership success.

Capacity-building Research

There has also been a good deal of effort, primarily sponsored by federal agencies and foundations, to build tool kits and resource centers to support the capacity building of conservation partnerships. For example, NPS recently sponsored several workshops and published technical bulletins on lessons learned in areas managed through partnerships (Tuxill & Mitchell, 2001). The USDA Forest Service has also been active, establishing a Partnership Task Force and establishing a *Leadership Guide for Partnerships* as well as a *Partnership Guide* for external partners. In November 2003, seven federal agencies co-sponsored a national conference titled *Partners in Stewardship* where more than 2,000 agency personnel and non-federal partners learned about the dynamics and skills of successful partnerships.

Conclusions

Clearly, the burgeoning interest in partnerships worldwide has stimulated scholarly inquiry from a number of social science disciplines to better understand the dynamics of natural resource partnerships. Below, several summary points are raised as a signpost to future partnership research as well as to support policy and management action to build the capacity of partnerships in the conservation and sustainable development fields.

Partnership research is in its early stages. The partnership literature to date has been dominated by case study research where researchers draw conclusions from a limited set of descriptive case studies. While this reflects the early stages of most fields of social science inquiry, partnership research needs to move on to more robust methodological designs.

Research must take a process and domain focus. Current research clearly demonstrates that partnership dynamics are complex; trying to understand them through cross-sectional research designs has limitations. Future research should adopt a process or developmental approach to reach a deeper understanding of the life cycle of partnerships. Researchers should also consider employing a domain focus which includes the complete set of actors jointly associated with the common problem or issue that defines the partnership (Gray, 1985).

Research must employ longitudinal designs. From the previous summary points, it is clear that partnership research must evolve to include longitudinal research designs that track partnership dynamics over time, as well as monitor partnership outcomes. While expensive and time consuming, longitudinal research is needed to fully explicate the complex life cycle of conservation partnerships.

Monitoring impacts is important. To convince skeptical oversight committees, donors and management authorities, monitoring research is needed to assess and quantify the social, ecological and economic outcomes resulting from the efforts of conservation partnerships. Funding is available for this type of research and should be vigorously pursued.

There is a need for multiple perspectives. Past partnership research has been criticized for only including partnership member elites, such as the coordinator or steering committee, in research designs. To avoid bias, future research should include all actors. In order to reduce bias, research might also include other third parties that may be knowledgeable of partnership activities, but are not vested in the process or outcomes.

Partnerships are not a panacea. From the buzz surrounding the talk of partnerships, one might conclude that they are the solution to many conservation problems and challenges. However, this is far from the truth. Partnerships, as a legitimate and acceptable management practice, face many challenges in the years to come.

Partnerships need a tailored approach. Rather than taking a cookie-cutter approach to using partnerships as an intervention strategy, partnerships must be tailored to their specific situation. In some cases, a partnership may be the appropriate management strategy to achieve desired future conditions. In other cases, another management strategy, such as a single management authority, regulation or incentives, may be a better way to achieve desired goals.

Partnerships are still marginalized. Despite the buzz, partnerships are often marginalized within policy-making and resource management circles. Agency culture is often resistant to change, particularly when those changes might require sharing decision authority with third parties. Congressional inquiries into partnership programs such as the NPS' Rivers, Trails and Conservation Assistance Program provide stark evidence of these fears.

Partnerships within the conservation and sustainable development fields have evolved from novel experiments to a way of life for many practitioners and managers. While partnerships hold much promise in achieving important conservation and economic objectives, much work is needed to bring partnerships into the mainstream of conservation and sustainable development practices. Social science research is beginning to shed light on the complex dynamics of partnerships and should be supported to inform thoughtful policy and management actions that build the capacity of conservation partnerships.

References

Bramwell, B., & Lane, B. (2000). Collaboration and partnerships in tourism planning. In B. Bramwell & B. Lane (Eds.), *Tourism Collaboration and Partnerships* (pp. 1-19). Clevedon, UK: Channel View Publications.

Caffyn, C. (2000). Is there a tourism partnership life cycle? In B. Bramwell & B. Lane (Eds.), *Tourism Collaboration and Partnerships* (pp. 200-229). Clevedon, UK: Channel View Publications.

Cortner, H., & Moote, M. (1999). *The politics of ecosystem management.* Washington, DC: Island Press.

Curtis, A., & Lockwood, M. (2000). Landcare and catchment management in Australia: Lessons for state-sponsored community participation. *Society and Natural Resources*, 13(1), 61-74.

Evans, W. (1966). *The organization-set: Towards a theory of interorganizational design.* Pittsburgh, PA: University of Pittsburgh Press.

Gray, B. (1985). Conditions facilitating interorganizational collaboration. *Human Relations*, 38(10), 911-936.

Gray, B. (1989). *Collaborating: Finding common ground for multiparty problems.* San Francisco: Jossey-Bass Publishers.

Howe, J., McMahon, E., & Propst, L. (1997). *Balancing nature and commerce in gateway communities.* Washington, DC: Island Press.

Jamal, T., & Getz, D. (1995). Collaboration theory and community tourism planning. *Annals of Tourism Research*, 22(1), 186-204.

Kothari, A., Singh, N., & Suri, S. (1996). *People and protected areas.* New Delhi: Sage Publications.

Leach, W. (2002). Surveying diverse stakeholder groups. *Society and Natural Resources*, 15(7), 641-650.

Lichtman, P., & Clark, T. W. (1994). Rethinking the "vision" exercise in the greater Yellowstone ecosystem. *Society and Natural Resources*, 7, 459-478.

Long, F., & Arnold, M. (1995). *The power of environmental partnerships.* Fort Worth, TX: The Dryden Press.

Moore, E., & Koontz, T. (2003). A typology of collaborative watershed groups: Citizen-based, agency-based, and mixed partnerships. *Society and Natural Resources*, 16(5), 451-460.

Selin, S. (1994). Current research in parks and recreation. *Parks and Recreation*, 29(11), 12-16.

Selin, S. (1999). Developing a typology of sustainable tourism partnerships. *Journal of Sustainable Tourism*, 7(3&4), 260-273.

Selin, S., & Chavez, D. (1993). Recreation partnerships and the USDA Forest Service. *Journal of Park and Recreation Administration*, 11, 1-8.

Selin, S., & Chavez, D. (1995). Developing an evolutionary tourism partnership model. *Annals of Tourism Research*, 24(4), 844-856.

Selin, S.W., & Myers, N. (1995). Correlates of partnership effectiveness: The Coalition for United Recreation in the Eastern Sierra. *Journal of Park and Recreation Administration*, 13(4), 38-47.

Selin, S., Schuett, M., & Carr, D. (1997). Has collaborative planning taken root in the national forests? *Journal of Forestry*, 95(4), 25-28.

Selin, S.W., Schuett, M., and Carr, D. (2000). Modeling stakeholder perceptions of collaborative initiative effectiveness. *Society and Natural Resources*, 13(8), 735-745.

Tuxill, J., & Mitchell, N. (Eds.) (2001). *Collaboration and conservation: Lessons learned in areas managed through National Park Service partnerships.* Woodstock, VT: Conservation Study Institute.

Vaske, J. J., Donnelly, M., & LaPage, W. (1995). Partnerships for the 21st century: A return to democracy. *Journal of Park and Recreation Administration*, 13(4), x-xi.

Waddock, S. (1989). Understanding social partnerships: An evolutionary model of partnership organizations. *Administration and Society*, 21(1), 78-100.

Waddock, S., & Bannister, B. (1991). Correlates of effectiveness and partner satisfaction in social partnerships. *Journal of Organizational Change Management*, 4, 74-89.

Williams, E. M., & Ellefson, P.V. (1997). Going into partnership to manage a landscape. *Journal of Forestry*, 95(5), 29-33.

Wondolleck, J., & Yaffee, S. (2000). *Making collaboration work.* Washington, DC: Island Press.

Yaffe, S., Phillips, A., Frenz, I., Hardy, P., Maleki,S., & Thorpe, B. (1996). *Ecosystem management in the United States.* Washington, DC: Island Press

14

Social Acceptability in Forest and Range Management

Bruce Shindler

Mark W. Brunson

Kristin Aldred Cheek

Social scientists as well as natural resource managers have long been interested in how people understand, evaluate, and respond to the management of nature. Public acceptance has become increasingly critical to the success of forest and rangeland management as debate intensifies worldwide over ecosystem protection and sustainable development. Indeed, management strategies that lack such acceptance are unlikely to be implemented. Yet the diverse factors that determine social acceptability of forest and range management are only now beginning to be understood and given credence by natural resource professionals. In this chapter we synthesize research on social acceptability to describe the disciplinary origins, conceptual framework, and management relevance of the acceptability concept. Our intent is to help organize the critical thinking and research from the past 15 years and provide a basis for continued research in this important area.

What is Social Acceptability?

The social acceptability concept in natural resource management can be traced to the work of rural sociologist Walter Firey (1960). Firey wanted to know why certain resource policies persisted in different societies, while others did not. He concluded that the adoption and retention of any particular program or policy depends on the extent to which it satisfies three requisites: it must be 1) physically possible, consistent with ecological processes; 2) economically feasible, generating revenue in excess of costs; and 3) culturally adoptable, consistent with prevailing social customs and norms. Similarly, Clawson (1975) argued that successful forest policies must meet five conditions: 1) biological and physical feasibility, 2) economic efficiency, 3) economic welfare or equity, 4) social or cultural acceptability, and 5) operational or administrative practicality. Both frameworks acknowledge a

BRENT ERB

fundamental notion: Policies and practices lacking societal acceptance and approval will ultimately fail, even if they are profitable and supported by sound science. Indeed, Stankey (1996) noted that Firey's three criteria are mutually constraining; each is necessary, but not sufficient, for sustainable ecosystem-based forest and rangeland management.

One need only look at daily headlines to appreciate the extent to which adverse public judgments can prevent or modify implementation of any management strategy. Rather than accept unpopular decisions, citizens have access to a wide variety of options to influence policy decisions and circumvent traditional agency authority. They can, for example, invoke the courts, lobby federal legislators, attract media attention for their cause, or organize statewide ballot initiatives to change existing laws (Shindler, List & Steel, 1993). There is sufficient evidence from the last two decades to indicate that citizens are both willing and able to employ such measures.

Thus while the view persists among many natural resource decision-makers that public opinion is a frustrating obstacle to the use of sound science or good economics, the need to produce socially acceptable decisions is acknowledged in definitions of ecosystem management (Cortner, Shannon, Wallace, Burke & Moote, 1996), adaptive management (Shindler & Aldred Cheek, 1999), and sustainable development (World Commission on Environment and Development, 1987). Accordingly, in recent years natural resource managers across the globe have sought to understand how citizens respond to proposed actions, and why. Social scientists increasingly are called upon to study factors that influence the acceptability of specific management actions or policies. Most of this work has been empirical and applied to specific management contexts, but gradually researchers are examining and reaching conclusions about the theoretical bases for public judgments about natural resource management.

The term *social acceptability* appears frequently in the natural resource literature, but has been used in subtly different ways. At various times it has been a synonym for actions that were described as *appropriate, preferred, desirable, supported, tolerated, adequate* and so on. Moreover, it is not a concept with a long history of use in basic social science, where a rigorous definition might have emerged. Brunson (1996) defined *acceptability* as "a condition that results from a judgmental process by which individuals 1) compare the perceived reality with its known alternatives, and 2) decide whether the real condition is superior, or sufficiently similar, to the most favorable alternative condition" (p. 9). Thus judgments about acceptability are made at the individual level, but they evolve in response to a host of typically social and external influences. Accordingly, Brunson (1996) reserved the term *social acceptability* to refer to aggregate forms of public consent whereby judgments are shared and articulated by an identifiable and politically relevant segment of the citizenry.

The distinction between *acceptability* and *social acceptability* is important because Western democracies tend to use sociopolitical processes rather than individual evaluations as a basis for decisions about what should occur for a larger community of interest (Cialdini, Reno & Kallgren, 1990; Ehrenhaldt, 1994). Sagoff (1988) reasoned that in the long-term, society is better off focusing on shared norms and values rather than on individual preferences. He argued that values are organized beliefs held by a community about what is right, and preferences are simply the desires of individual members and, as such, may not serve the larger society very well. Thus natural resource managers seek consensus (i.e., shared, organized beliefs) to guide many decisions.

One of the first uses of the term *acceptability* in natural resource management was in the Limits of Acceptable Change (LAC) planning system (Stankey, Cole, Lucas, Petersen & Frissell, 1985), a participant-oriented model developed originally to help establish acceptable and appropriate conditions for USDA Forest Service (USFS) wilderness areas. The authors did not explicitly define *acceptable* but used the word to describe both what is legally permissible under the U.S. Wilderness Act of 1964, and what wilderness users agree is desirable. Thus an unacceptable occurrence could imply circumstances of differing severity: a violation of federal law or a change in forest conditions beyond that preferred by users. In practice, it has been easier to achieve consensus about whether *unacceptable* conditions exist than about what constitutes *acceptable* conditions. Similarly, Brunson (1996) noted that acceptability is most often observed by its absence, because unacceptable conditions are what spark political action to restore prior or preferred conditions.

In forest management and research, efforts to address acceptability have historically focused on scenic quality. The rise of citizen protests against such practices as clear-cut logging can be traced to the impact of highly visible and rectangular harvests that affronted the aesthetic sensibilities of many who saw them. Bitter controversy over clear-cutting led to passage of the National Forest Management Act of 1976, which required the USFS to complete comprehensive forest management plans that take into account public concerns. This early history fostered an assumption that scenic impacts were the primary public concern about forestry, and aesthetics have often been used as a surrogate for social acceptability. Research on forest scenic quality began in earnest in the late 1960s. An in-depth review by Ribe (1989) of the burgeoning literature on the topic included nearly 90 papers exploring the complex origins and implications of public preferences for landscapes. This research continues today with many studies focusing on citizen surveys of alternative silvicultural treatments (e.g., Shelby, Thompson, Brunson & Johnson, 2003).

However, researchers have acknowledged problems with using scenic beauty as an indicator for social acceptability. Gobster (1996) observed that managing for scenic quality cannot adequately account for ecological disturbance processes such as wildfire, landslides, or floods. If the path of ecosystem management is to be followed, at times there will be unattractive forests and rangelands. Moreover, he points out that if citizens were to judge forests solely by scenic beauty, acceptance could be influenced by neither conscious thought about ecological processes nor by other senses such as the sound or smell of a healthy forest.

In further investigation, Shindler and Collson (1998) found that acceptability judgments about forest harvest treatments were linked to five criteria: 1) how sites will look once practices are implemented, 2) how natural characteristics of the forest will be affected, 3) level of trust in the information provided, 4) how the practice might benefit the local community, and 5) whether citizens had a meaningful role in the planning process. Nevertheless, visual images are what people remember most about the environment. Ecosystem management can produce disturbances that contribute to aesthetically less-desirable forests, and changing the public's mind about what they observe can be difficult.

Emergent Themes in Acceptability Research

This evolution of scientific understanding about scenic quality judgments exemplifies a growing body of work that examines social acceptability in forest and range management. This section briefly summarizes five crosscutting themes that have emerged from recent research (see Shindler, Brunson & Stankey, 2002).

Social Acceptability is a Dynamic Process

Social acceptability does not end with a particular outcome or result. Rather, it is an ongoing process. Many of the problems in natural resource management are wicked (Allen & Gould, 1986), not just because they are ecologically complex, but because they include moral and social issues that are debated in the political arena. Biological conditions and technical solutions evolve and continue to be influenced by the social and economic interests of the day. As factors change over time, acceptability judgments can change as well. After action is taken, costs and consequences become apparent. What seemed eminently reasonable in the past may now be less so, as is the case in contemporary wildfire management (Shindler & Toman, 2003) where the large-scale fire events of 2002 and 2003 piqued the public's attention. And because nature itself is a dynamic system, comparative judgments of alternative conditions may change over time. For example, scenic quality after timber harvest recovers at different rates depending on forest conditions and harvest treatments (Shelby et al., 2003).

As conditions and information keep changing, management action is needed to maintain acceptability. In a sense, the pot is constantly boiling and the resulting stew must be monitored and fed frequently. In the past, public acceptance often has been viewed in a stimulus-response sense: Managers act and people judge (Williams & Patterson, 1996). Now, part of the task of developing more durable and socially acceptable polices is to cultivate understanding. This involves creating, disseminating, and evaluating knowledge as well as methods for generating and implementing alternatives. The process is iterative: Discussion of problems and options results in more stakeholders surfacing, who then enrich the problem definition (Westley, 1995).

Multiple Factors Play a Role
While there are countless examples of people responding negatively to a particular resource management action, acceptability judgments generally are not the result of any single event. Instead they derive from complex circumstances within individuals and social contexts. This array of factors includes issue salience, prior experiences, personal values, social norms, knowledge about the problem, quality of information received, beliefs about the fairness of decision processes, trust in decision-makers, and risk perceptions (see Bright, Barro & Burtz, 2002; Lauber & Knuth, 1997; Winter, Vogt & Fried, 2002). Citizens can and do consider relatively subtle differences in management situations when judging acceptability. For example, Messmer, Brunson, Reiter and Hewitt (1999) found that the acceptability of predator control as a tool for bird conservation varied with the immediacy of the threat and the predator species being controlled. Because there is a multiplicity of factors, managers can easily be blind-sided by events. It is unlikely that any single solution will address every factor of interest to stakeholders. However, history has shown that if agencies fail to pay attention to the potential for multiple influences on citizen acceptance, they are condemned to continuously respond to the public's negative reactions.

Although resource managers may recognize this situation, many often believe that if they simply explain ecological processes to educate the public, they will gain support for management practices (Stankey & Shindler, 1997). But it is unlikely that people's judgments will change based solely on technical information. As managers focus on strategies and outcomes, the differences in stakeholders' various understandings of issues are frequently overlooked (Kearney, Bradley, Kaplan & Kaplan, 1998). Even when facts are agreed upon, different conceptions of causation or ethics often lead to widely differing interpretations (Brunson, 1992). Further, the likelihood and intensity of citizens' responses to unacceptable conditions depends in part on the strength and salience of attitudes toward the condition (Bright & Manfredo, 1995). Recognizing the variability and complexity of influences on acceptability judgments is an important part of an effective early warning system about potentially unacceptable conditions.

Context Influences Public Acceptance
Natural resource managers are trained to identify the best tools to apply to broad categories of problems. While this approach is efficient, it can also promote allegiance to one-size-fits-all solutions. This can be problematic; public acceptance tends to be situation-specific. Practices and conditions acceptable in one situation are not necessarily acceptable in another, even when the problem is the same as one encountered elsewhere. Thus, it is important for managers to identify and consider contextual influences on acceptability (Shindler, 2000).

Acceptability judgments are affected by the unique combination of spatial, temporal, political, and social contexts within which a proposed action occurs. For example, Winter et al. (2002) reported that the location of a fuels-reduction project relative to human habitation affected citizens' support for the methods that were used. Acceptability also varies with the scale of analysis, as residents of adjacent areas can interpret an action differently than those who live further away (Brandenburg & Carroll, 1995; Brunson & Steel, 1996). Brunson and Gilbert (2003) found that designation of a national monument in an area previously managed for multiple-use created a new constituency of recreation visitors who tended not to support livestock grazing on public lands, thereby reducing the overall acceptability of grazing management within the monument. Judgments are even affected by the setting in which they are expressed. For example, strident opinions voiced at loggers' meetings partly reflect the fact that a unifying theme of such groups is a negative evaluation of the USDA Forest Service (Carroll, 1989).

Importance of the Decision-making Process
Too often decision-makers focus on public acceptance of a decision (i.e., the outcome) without fully considering the process by which those decisions are made (Kakoyannis, Shindler & Stankey, 2001). A growing body of evaluative research throughout the last decade has shown that the public's idea of fairness and legitimacy involves the quality of the decision-making procedures. Of particular importance are opportunities for citizen participation (Lauber & Knuth, 1997; Tuler & Webler, 1999). When decision outcomes are emphasized at the expense of deliberative and inclusive processes, citizens often will seek alternative, and often less desirable, means to influence local policies.

Yet public participation processes do not generate acceptance merely because they exist. From a mechanistic standpoint, agency staff members have mastered the legal procedures by which the public can provide input on a plan or project. But these sessions frequently are sterile, rule-bound, and one-way exchanges that do not resonate with citizens (Cortner et al., 1996). The manner in which people are incorporated into decisions, especially those that affect their livelihood and quality of life, is critical to their judgments. Shindler and Aldred Cheek (1999) conducted an extensive examination of citizen-agency interactions and concluded that effective participation could be organized around six factors: 1) inclusiveness, 2) sincere leadership, 3) innovative and interactive methods, 4) early commitment and continuity, 5) sound planning skills with well-defined objectives, and 6) efforts that result in action.

Trust

Every land management unit has a history linked to its own particular pattern of actions to surrounding communities and to a legacy of previous decisions (Shindler & Aldred Cheek, 1999). A particularly important aspect of that history is the ongoing relationship between land managers and affected publics. No matter how meritorious a plan might be, nothing is validated unless the people involved trust one another. Trust and credibility in resource agencies are associated with perceptions of knowledge and expertise, openness and honesty, and concern and care (Peters, Covello & McCallum, 1997). If social acceptability is to be enhanced through interaction with citizens, resource professionals must be able to engage citizens through means perceived as genuine and trustworthy.

Because land management agencies are hierarchical, actions at one level affect trust at another. Recent research suggests that the public's negative feelings about forest and range management arise mainly from their general frustration with the federal bureaucracy, rather than with management personnel on the local level who themselves may be hindered from getting work done (e.g., Shindler & Toman, 2003). Yet local managers often bear the brunt of this distrust. As effective treatments are implemented and public awareness of success grows, so too will belief that the agencies can be trusted to manage responsibly.

Agency relations with constituents, and thus the acceptability of resulting plans and actions, are shaped by the cumulative nature of multiple interactions over time (Shindler & Aldred Cheek, 1999). Building trust takes great patience, requires many opportunities for citizen-manager interaction, and is a product of numerous factors that contribute to the endurance of relations. Achieving a balance point for acceptance among parties is a continual process of adjustment (Westley, 1995). In the long-term, building trust with stakeholders will come through the interaction process, particularly as people are able to see their concerns given consideration.

Why Social Acceptability Matters to Managers and Social Scientists

As we noted previously, the need for public acceptance of proposed actions may be seen as a nuisance by natural resource managers convinced of the ecological or economic validity of their plans. But there are good reasons for managers to pay heed to social acceptability. First, as a practical matter, few decisions in a democracy are simply a matter of objective science about a specific practice or condition. Technical information is critical in describing the alternatives, consequences, and implications of decisions, but such decisions ultimately express a prescriptive judgment reflecting the values of the decision-maker. The extent to which these views reflect wider public sentiment can be problematic (Brunson, 1992). Decisions that fail to adequately account for public values are unlikely to succeed, if they are implemented at all.

Second, accounting for social acceptability reflects a normative perspective. Simply put, the public has a right of access to decisions about resources of which they are the ultimate owners. Having made this argument, the fact remains that the public can make poor choices. The complexity of issues demands that scientific rigor and objectivity be included to help define alternatives, consequences, and rationale. However, managers often fail to present the technical information in a way that resonates with the value systems of the wider public (Brunson, 1992). To be most relevant, managers should provide situation-specific information about what changes in conditions will look like, how soon they could occur, how they will alter the character of the treated area, and how they might affect the surrounding community (Shindler, 2000).

The preceding points pose social acceptability as a constraint, focusing on how it can limit decisions and actions. However, it also can serve a positive function. Acceptability judgments are subject to change. In other words, learning is a key element of the acceptability process. Thus, as we consider social acceptability and its relation to management and decision-making, it can be seen as an opportunity for discussion, debate, and learning about the complex dimensions of the issues at hand. A legitimate effort to engage the issue of social acceptability can provide an important opportunity for an informed discussion, one based on mutual learning and recognition of participant interests.

From a scientific point of view, ongoing research on social acceptability is useful because it begins to tie in an important natural resource management concern (i.e., how to ensure public support for ecologically sustainable and economically viable policies) with time-tested social science concepts. Because acceptability is judged by comparing both cognitive and affective components of alternative conditions, social acceptability research provides a conceptual link between belief-attitude-behavior studies that focus on cognition (e.g., Bright & Manfredo, 1995; Bright et al., 2002) and scenic quality studies that emphasize affective aspects of judgment (Ribe, 1989; Zube, Sell & Taylor, 1982). Such thinking acknowledges these are complex and integrated problems that require resource professionals to account for a broad set of values.

Conclusion

Public acceptance of management policies is needed to secure the future of healthy public forests and rangelands. Without greater understanding of and attention to social acceptability, decisions will continue to be challenged, and our human and natural systems will continue to bear the brunt of our inability to reach agreement. Although each situation produces a unique set of circumstances that ultimately affect public judgments, it is possible to address social acceptability in a rigorous, formal, and systematic basis (see Shindler, Brunson & Stankey, 2002).

A central conclusion from our analysis is that social acceptability judgments are provisional. Public judgments about the acceptability or unacceptability of management practices, policies, and conditions are never absolute or final; they depend on many influences including factors both internal and external to management agency control. As a result, it is unlikely that any simple "index of acceptability" can or should be created. However, it does not mean that managers are powerless in the search for more broadly accepted management policies. Regardless of the provisional and idiosyncratic nature of social acceptability judgments, they still are subject to structure and critical thinking. Our analysis has revealed some of the consistent and predictable aspects of the concept. Most important may be that acceptability judgments reflect a political perspective; they are the product of interactions between citizens and management organizations over time, reflecting trust levels and beliefs that citizens hold about those responsible for the stewardship of resources. Continued research and management experimentation with public process will reveal additional features about the social acceptability concept.

References

Allen, G.M., & Gould, E.M. (1986). Complexity, wickedness, and public forests. *Journal of Forestry*, 84(4),20-23.

Brandenburg, A.M., & Carroll, M.S. (1995). Your place or mine? The effect of place creation on environmental values and landscape meanings. *Society and Natural Resources*, 8, 381- 398.

Bright, A.S., Barro, S.C., & Burtz, R. (2002). Public attitudes toward ecological restoration in the Chicago metropolitan area. *Society and Natural Resources*, 15(9), 763-785.

Bright, A.D., & Manfredo, M.J. (1995). The quality of attitudinal information regarding natural resource issues: Role of attitude-strength, importance and information. *Society and Natural Resources*, 8, 399-414.

Brunson, M.W. (1992). Professional bias, public perspectives, and communications pitfalls for natural resource managers. *Rangelands*, 14(5), 292-295.

Brunson, M.W., & L. Gilbert (2003). Recreationist responses to livestock grazing in a new national monument. *Journal of Range Management*, 56(6), 570-576.

Brunson, M.W. (1996). A definition of "social acceptability" in ecosystem management. In M. Brunson, L. Kruger, C. Tyler, and S. Schroeder (Eds.), *Defining social acceptability in ecosystem management: A workshop proceedings* (General Technical Report PNW-369, pp. 7-16). Portland, OR: USDA Forest Service.

Brunson, M.W., & Steel, B.S. (1996). Sources of variation in attitudes and beliefs about federal rangeland management. *Journal of Range Management*, 49, 69-75.

Carroll, M.S. (1989). Taming the lumberjack revisited. *Society and Natural Resources*, 2, 91-106.

Cialdini, R.B., Reno, R.R., & Kallgren, C.A. (1990). A focus theory of normative conduct: Recycling the concept of norms to reduce littering in public places. *Journal of Personality and Social Psychology*, 58, 1015-1026.

Clawson, M. (1975). *Forest for whom and for what?* Baltimore, MD: Johns Hopkins University Press.

Cortner, H.J., Shannon, M., Wallace, M., Burke, S., & Moote, M.A. (1996). *Institutional barriers and incentives for ecosystem management: A problem analysis* (General Technical Report PNW-354). Portland, OR: USDA Forest Service.

Ehrenhaldt, A. (1994). Let the people decide between spinach and broccoli. *Governing*, 7(10), 6-7.

Firey, W. (1960). *Man, mind, and land.* Glencoe, IL: The Free Press.

Gobster, P.H. (1996). Forest aesthetics, biodiversity, and the perceived appropriateness of ecosystem management practices. In M. Brunson, L. Kruger, C. Tyler, and S. Schroeder (Eds.), *Defining social acceptability in ecosystem management: A workshop proceedings* (General Technical Report PNW-369, pp. 77-97). Portland, OR: USDA Forest Service.

Kakoyannis, C., Shindler, B., & Stankey, G.H. (2001). *Understanding the social acceptability of natural resource decision-making process by using a knowledge base modeling approach.* (General Technical Report PNW-518). Portland, OR: USDA Forest Service.

Kearney, A., Bradley, G., Kaplan, R., & Kaplan, S. (1998). Stakeholder perspectives of appropriate forest management in the Pacific Northwest. *Forest Science*, 45(1), 62-72.

Lauber, T.B., & Knuth, B.A. (1997). Fairness in moose management decision-making: The citizens' perspective. *Wildlife Society Bulletin*, 25(4), 776-787.

Messmer, T.A., Brunson, M.W., Reiter, D., & Hewitt, D.G. 1999. United States public attitudes regarding predators and their management to enhance avian recruitment. *Wildlife Society Bulletin*, 27(1), 75-85.

Peters, R.G., Covello, V.T., & McCallum, D.B. (1997). The determinants of trust and credibility in environmental risk communication: An empirical study. *Risk Analysis*, 17, 43-54.

Ribe, R.G. (1989). The aesthetics of forestry: What has empirical preference research taught us? *Environmental Management*, 13, 55-74.

Sagoff, M. (1988). *The economy of the earth: Philosophy, law, and the environment.* Cambridge, UK: Cambridge University Press.

Shelby, B., Thompson, J., Brunson, M. & Johnson, R. (2003). Scenic quality after harvest: A decade of ratings for six silviculture treatments. *Journal of Forestry*, 101(2), 30-36.

Shindler, B. (2000). Landscape-level management: It's all about context. *Journal of Forestry*, 98(12), 10-14.

Shindler, B., & Aldred Cheek, K. (1999). Integrating citizens in adaptive management: A propositional analysis. *Journal of Conservation Ecology*, 3(1), 13-29.

Shindler, B., M. Brunson, & G. Stankey. (2002). *Social acceptability of forest conditions and management practices: A problem analysis* (General Technical Report PNW-537). Portland, OR: USDA Forest Service.

Shindler, B., & Collson, P. (1998). Assessing public preferences for ecosystem management practices. In D. Soden, B. Lamb & J. Tennert (Eds.), *Ecosystems management: A social science perspective.* Dubuque, IA: Kendall-Hunt.

Shindler, B., List, P., & Steel, B.S. (1993). Managing federal forests: Public attitudes in Oregon and nationwide. *Journal of Forestry*, 91(7), 36-42.

Shindler, B., & Toman, E. (2003). Fuel reduction strategies in forest communities: A longitudinal analysis of public support. *Journal of Forestry*, 101(7), 8-15.

Stankey, G.H. (1996). Defining the social acceptability of forest management practices and conditions: Integrating science and social choice. In M. Brunson, L. Kruger, C. Tyler, and S. Schroeder (Eds.), *Defining social acceptability in ecosystem management: A workshop proceedings* (General Technical Report PNW-369, pp. 99-112). Portland, OR: USDA Forest Service.

Stankey, G.H., Cole, D.N., Lucas, R.C., Petersen, M.E., & Frissell, S.S. (1985). *The Limits of Acceptable Change (LAC) system for wilderness planning*. (General Technical Report INT-176). Ogden, UT: USDA Forest Service.

Stankey, G.H., & Shindler, B. (1997). *Adaptive management areas: Achieving the promise, avoiding the peril* (General Technical Report PNW-394). Portland, OR: USDA Forest Service.

Tuler S., & Webler, T. (1999). Voices from the forest: What participants expect of a public participation process. *Society and Natural Resources*, 12, 437-453.

Westley, F. (1995). Governing design: The management of social systems in ecosystem management. In L.H. Gunderson, C.S. Holling & S.S. Light (Eds.), *Barriers and bridges to the renewal of ecosystems and institutions* (pp. 391-427). New York: Columbia University Press.

Williams, D.R., & Patterson, M.E. (1996). Environmental meaning and ecosystem management: Perspectives from environmental psychology and human geography. *Society and Natural Resources*, 9(5), 507-521.

Winter, G., Vogt, C., & Fried, J. (2002). Fuel treatments at the wildland-urban interface: Common concerns in diverse regions. *Journal of Forestry*, 100(1),15-20.

World Commission on Environment and Development. (1987). *Our common future*. Oxford, UK: Oxford University Press.

Zube, E.H., Sell, J.L., & Taylor, J.G. (1982). Landscape perception: Research, application, and theory. *Landscape Planning*, 9, 1-33.

15

The Social Aspects of Agriculture

Douglas Jackson-Smith

Despite dramatic changes over the last century, agriculture remains one of the most important natural resource industries in advanced industrialized economies. While the number of people employed in the primary agricultural production sector has declined by more than 70 percent since 1920 (Freudenburg, 1992), agricultural land uses continue to dominate the rural landscape. In the United States, cropland, pasture and rangelands comprised roughly two-thirds of the private land base in 1997 (USDA, 2001), and over half of the total land in the 15 European Union member countries is used for arable crops or permanent pastures (CIA World Factbook, 2003). At the turn of the century, U.S. gross farm receipts regularly approached $200 billion per year, and the production of raw agricultural commodities employed over three million people, or almost five times as many people as the logging, mining, and fishing industries combined (U.S. Census Bureau, 2002).

Meanwhile, the social organization of farming and ranching has changed dramatically during the last century (Cochrane, 1993; Friedland, Busch, Buttel & Rudy, 1991; Labao & Meyer, 2001). The most notable changes reflect a steady increase in the size of most agricultural operations, growing concentration of production in the hands of a relatively small number of very large firms, and an increased reliance on purchased inputs, commercial credit, and hired nonfamily workers and managers (Hoope & McDonald, 2001; Strange, 1988). In the most dramatic cases, extremely large farms have been created where the social organization of production activities more closely resembles industrial factories than traditional family-labor farms (Friedland, Barton & Thomas, 1981; Welsh, 1996).

These changes in the organization of agricultural production have led to dramatic increases in the output of farm commodities, averaging almost two percent per year since World War II (Ahearn, Yee, Ball & Nehring,

1998). However, they have also been linked to a range of modern environmental problems. The argument is frequently made that certain features of modern agricultural production systems (e.g., concentration of livestock on fewer and larger operations, separation of crop from livestock production, heavy use of purchased inputs) are responsible for a range of agricultural-environmental problems, including soil erosion, non-point pollution of ground and surface waters, mining of groundwater, and contributions to global warming from livestock emissions (USDA-ERS, 2003).

Although agriculture is a quintessentially human activity, many in the natural resource policy and research communities see little role for sociologists in the study and analysis of farming and ranching. The dominant view is that the agricultural sector is driven by an internal logic that is primarily technical and economic in nature (Nowak, 1993). Because the adoption of natural resource-conserving agricultural technologies has been relatively slow and incomplete (Fuglie & Kascak, 2001), sociologists have been brought in mainly to help understand why farmers fail to use best management practices and to devise ways to convince farmers to change their behaviors in the directions recommended by technical experts (National Research Council [NRC], 1993).

The relative low profile of sociological studies of agriculture within the natural resource scholarly community is evident in the record of papers presented at the first nine International Symposia on Society and Resource Management (ISSRM) and papers published in the associated journal, *Society and Natural Resources* (SNR). In both cases, farming and ranching activities were much less common than research addressing other natural resource-based industries (e.g., forestry, fishing, mining, outdoor recreation). A review of each of the ISSRM books of abstracts found an average of 14 abstracts with a primarily agricultural topic. This ranged from less than five at each of the first three meetings to a peak of 36 in the fourth meeting in Madison, Wisconsin. In recent years, there have been between nine and 21 agricultural papers presented at each meeting. Meanwhile, Culhane's (2001) review of SNR journal content between 1988 and 1997 suggests that less than five percent of published research articles examined conventional or sustainable farming topics. In both ISSRM books of abstracts and SNR articles, the most common agricultural topics were related to soil conservation behavior, agricultural watershed management programs, land use changes at the urban fringe, and sustainable farming systems.

Outside the natural resource management community, there is a long tradition in the sociology of agriculture that documents a much broader range of social influences that shape the fundamental dynamics of agricultural change at the individual, community, national, and global level (Albrecht & Murdock 1990; Buttel, Larsen & Gillespie, 1990). Implicit in much of this work is the argument that virtually all elements of agricultural systems have intrinsically "social" components. This chapter synthesizes the findings of these topics, and concludes with a discussion of the implications of these findings for the understanding and management of natural resource conflicts in agriculture.

What is "Social" about Agriculture?

Sociological Studies of Technological Change in Agriculture

The adoption-diffusion tradition. The most significant body of sociological research relative to natural resource management in agriculture has focused on the determinants of adoption of various types of conservation practices (Fuglie & Kascak, 2001; Guerin, 1999; Korsching & Hoban, 1990; Lovejoy & Napier, 1986; Nowak, 1993). Indeed, the first agricultural papers presented at the inaugural ISSRM meeting were on this topic (Bultena & Hoiberg, 1986; Napier, Thraen & McClaskie, 1986). Much of this research is grounded in a long tradition of adoption-diffusion (A/D) studies of general agricultural technologies in the United States (Rogers, 1995). The core assumptions of the A/D research tradition are: a) there is significant underlying variability in the social-psychological profile of farmers that differentiates them into "earlier" and "later" adopter categories, and b) that this is linked to the social position or role each type of farmer plays in local social networks. The A/D research tradition in agriculture has become an influential model for the study of the diffusion of innovations in other sectors of the economy (Wejnert, 2002).

In his recently updated book, *Diffusion of Innovations*, Everett Rogers (1995) summarizes the main conceptual and empirical accomplishments of the A/D tradition. Initially, A/D researchers identified a series of stages of adoption – awareness, evaluation, experimentation, implementation and confirmation – that described the cognitive steps leading up to actual adoption of a new technological practice. Because of the variability in the cognitive orientations of farmers, particularly with respect to risk aversion, many A/D researchers also discovered that adoption frequently follows an "s-curve" pattern, where adoption begins slowly as a small number of early adopters initially try out the innovation, followed by a period of rapid adoption by a majority of producers, and then a slowing of adoption rates as the last few producers (referred to as *laggards*) implement the new practice. Local social networks among farmers can affect the spatial diffusion of innovations across the landscape, where key early adopters serve as opinion leaders and examples for their neighbors who follow in their footsteps.

While farmer characteristics can be important determinants of agricultural technology use, not all innovations are likely to be adopted with equal rapidity. Instead, the most rapidly adopted technologies are those that: a) are less complex, b) are able to be adopted on a limited scale as an experiment, c) are easily seen by neighbors, d) have relative advantages over existing practices, and e) are compatible with other farming practices used by the operator.

While the A/D tradition in sociology is still quite active, a significant number of sociologists have been critical of many of the assumptions and conclusions of the traditional A/D approach. The most strident criticism has been that the A/D perspective tends to treat all new technologies in a positive light and ignores complexities. Similarly, many scholars reject the assumption that there are certain farmers who are innately innovative simply by virtue of the fact that they adopt production practices recommended by experts.

It is becoming apparent that many farmers have good reasons to not adopt a specific technology because it is not well-suited to their situation (Nowak, 1992).

For example, many new agricultural technologies have a strong scale-bias that makes them more suitable for considerably large operations (NRC, 2002). Meanwhile, there are other technologies that have lower capital or labor requirements, and are thus appropriate for smaller family labor farms. For each group of farmers, the definition of innovativeness might be conditioned on the proper fit between a specific practice and the farm's unique situation. To account for these factors, a growing number of scholars have added farm structural, socioeconomic and ecological variables to their adoption models (Napier, Tucker & McCarter, 2000; Nowak & Korsching, 1993).

The implications of a shift in focus from the personality of the farmer to the characteristics of the technology are quite striking. In the classic A/D approach, public programs are focused on the education of recalcitrant farmers and developing mechanisms to facilitate the social diffusion processes. By contrast, if the problem lies with the technologies, the emphasis should be placed on developing a range of technologies that are appropriate for different subgroups of agricultural producers (Hassenein, 1999; Kloppenburg, 1988). They then assume that most farmers can be expected to innovate when the technologies are well-suited to existing capital, labor and management resources.

A/D approaches to natural resource management. Much natural resource management policy in agriculture focuses on encouraging farmers to change their behavior by adopting new management practices and technologies that better protect natural resources (e.g., reducing soil and wind erosion, minimizing nutrient runoff, utilizing water resources more efficiently). However, the application of the A/D tradition in this area of natural resources has been met with mixed success. Early on, Pampel and van Es (1977) demonstrated that the sociodemographic and attitudinal predictors of the adoption of conservation technologies are quite different from those that predict commercial technology adoption. Repeated studies have failed to explain more than a small percentage of the variance in adoption of environmental practices using conventional A/D variables (Fuglie & Kascak, 2001; Napier, 2000). By the same token, the lack of widespread adoption of many environmental best management practices (BMPs) has been linked to the fact that they are inappropriate for many agricultural operations (Jackson-Smith & Barham, 2000; Shepard, 2000). This has led to suggestions that renewed emphasis be placed on developing a more diverse portfolio of technological and management solutions to environmental problems that will be suitable for diverse types of agricultural producers (NRC, 2002).

In addition to the mismatch between many technical solutions and diverse farming situations, a number of scholars have identified additional institutional and policy factors that can shape conservation-related behaviors (van Es & Notier, 1988). Specifically, Coughenour and Chamala (1989) compare conservation programs in the U.S. and Australia to illustrate how mandatory programs produce different behavioral outcomes than voluntary educational approaches. Even where conservation policies have been successful at changing farmers' behaviors, there is evidence that mandatory programs fail to instill a shift in the underlying beliefs, values, and motivations that might affect future agri-environmental behaviors (Makowski, Sofranko & van Es, 1990).

BRENT ERB

Sociological Perspectives on the Forces Underlying Agricultural Change

The agricultural economic model. While the microdynamics associated with adoption and diffusion of conservation practices have received the lion's share of attention in the social scientific literature, there is a much broader sociological tradition that examines the larger forces and dynamics underlying change in the farm sector.

Generally speaking, agricultural economists view changes in farm structure as the natural products of changes in the underlying technologies associated with production and the relative scarcity of agricultural inputs (Babb, 1979). In this view, changes in technology or the cost of inputs alter the efficient scale of production, and farm operations are forced to grow or adapt in order to remain competitive over the long run (Batte & Johnson, 1993; Cochrane, 1993). The tenacity with which inefficient small-scale producers have remained in business (often subsidized through federal commodity programs and with income from off-farm employment) usually has been viewed as an impediment to a socially-desirable allocation of agricultural resources (Tweeten, 1984). This economic model has dominated the way most natural resource scientists understand the forces of change in the agricultural sector of advanced industrial societies.

Social dimensions of agricultural change. From the point of view of theorists within the sociology of agriculture, however, it can seem that the operative question has usually been asked in the wrong way. Rather than ask "Why have we lost so many family farms?" many have sought to explain "Why does the family farm exist at all?" (Buttel, 1983). Certainly in virtually all other sectors of our economy we see the concentration of ownership and control of production by relatively small numbers of huge firms. Even in the larger food and fiber sectors, most of the input, processing, and marketing firms that sell to and buy from farmers are increasingly becoming consolidated into large enterprises (Bonnano & Constance, 2000; Friedland et al., 1991). By comparison, farm production is one of the only major sectors of modern capitalist society that is still dominated by family owned, sole-proprietor operations (Hoppe & McDonald, 2001). Despite the changes wrought by the last 100 years of technological change and rural restructuring, most of the nearly two million farm enterprises in the U.S. still depend principally on family members for their labor force, have (by industrial standards) relatively modest levels of investment and debt, and retain a remarkable amount of autonomy over their business decisions and work lives.

To help explain the persistence of non-capitalist forms of production, analysts have identified certain structural features of agriculture that make it a potentially unattractive site for capitalist investment. For example, the fact that agricultural production is fundamentally a biological process leads to a disjunction between labor-time and production-time that makes it difficult to accelerate the cycle of capital, and hence restricts the profit potential and rate of accumulation in farming (Mann & Dickinson, 1978). Additionally, the seasonality of demand for farm labor makes it difficult to support and maintain an efficient wage-labor force; family farms with a flexible supply of labor from the household are more able to adapt to natural labor rhythms (Reinhardt & Barlett, 1989). The dependence of agricultural production on vagaries of the weather makes it a particularly risky venture, and leads to unpredictable changes in labor needs on a day-to-day basis (Mann & Dickinson, 1978; Pfeffer, 1983).

Other structural features of agricultural production provide additional disincentives to large-scale capitalist investment. Because land is a key input for most kinds of agriculture, is fixed in quantity, and cannot be manufactured or relocated easily, tendencies toward centralization of production are constrained. The highly inelastic demand for food products leads farm-gate prices to be extremely volatile with fluctuations in output. The globalization of markets for agricultural products has tended to make this price volatility even more dramatic. The atomistic character of the farm sector in most industrial societies makes it one of the most competitive (and therefore, least profitable) sectors of the economy, and leads to persistent problems with overproduction and surplus capacity. Finally, unlike the manufacturing or heavy industrial sectors, economists have shown that there are few economies of scale to be realized beyond fairly modest-sized operations in the production of most agricultural commodities (Hallam, 1993).

Beyond disincentives to large-scale capitalist investment, there are also a number of distinctive structural, demographic, and cultural characteristics of family-farm units that can enable them to compete effectively with their more capitalist counterparts, particularly during difficult economic periods (Barlett, 1993; Friedmann, 1978a). First, and perhaps most critical, the costs of labor on a family farm operation are not fixed, but rather fluctuate with residual returns to the farm enterprise from year to year (Friedmann, 1978b). This suggests that in good years, relative returns to labor may be high, but in bad years, returns to labor may be quite low, or even negative. By contrast, a capitalist firm with a fixed hired labor force must pay prevailing wage rates and incur the same labor costs regardless of farm commodity prices.

Second, family-labor farms are able to minimize the costs of labor supervision. In an uncertain production environment, where a large number of small decisions and efforts can have significant impacts on farm performance, monitoring and supervision problems abound (Barham, Carter & Sigelko, 1995). Not only do family members, as the residual claimants of farm profits, have stronger incentives to work harder than do hired laborers, but they typically have a better understanding of the peculiarities of the local environment and landscape (Binswanger & Rosenzweig, 1986; Feder, 1985).

Unlike capitalist firms, which must earn an average rate of profit to survive, family farmers tend to have more complex subjective motivations for selecting farming as an occupation. Because family farm enterprises typically integrate household and business decisions, there are a number of non-economic benefits from farming that weigh in the decision to enter (and remain in) farming (Barlett, 1993; Bennett, 1982). Drawing on the classical Weberian categories, Mooney (1988) suggests that farmers in contemporary American agriculture utilize a substantive rationality, under which farmers pursue goals by some ultimate criteria other than strictly monetary economic calculations. *Substantive* rationality is contrasted to formal rationality, a businesslike approach that is oriented around maximizing profits and efficient use of available resources. Moreover, family farmers tend to adopt long-run planning horizons and organize their firms around the goal of passing the enterprise on to the next generation, rather than merely maximizing short-run profits (Hutson, 1987; Rogers, 1987; Salamon, 1985).

Barlett (1993) demonstrated the importance of cultural factors that mediate families and their farm enterprise decisions in her study of Georgia farm families during the 1980s. She contrasted farm families that had different management styles, consumption standards, and marital models, and found that attitudes towards debt, determinations of family consumption needs, and a commitment of the wife to the farm enterprise affected survival of family farms during the farm crisis years.

A number of scholars have suggested that family farm managers are not often single decision-makers, but rather are part of complex social and economic enterprises that pursue multiple objectives and have multiple decision-makers who must negotiate with other household members over a diverse set of firm and household priorities (Gasson, Crow, Errington, Hutson, Marsden & Winter, 1988). Substantial evidence supports the view that most agricultural operators select farming as a career not because they feel it is the best use of their skills, labor, and capital, but rather because it provides them with a certain quality of life and personal satisfaction. Changes in the farm enterprise that might reduce those more intangible non-economic benefits to the operator or household members are often avoided even if they might enhance their competitive position (Gasson & Errington, 1993).

Broader social forces of change in agriculture. Much of the impetus for change in agriculture originates in the diminishing ability of traditional farming operations to survive in an increasingly difficult economic climate. There is considerable evidence that net profit margins have been steadily declining and farms have been forced to increase the size of production units merely to maintain their historic levels of net income (Hallam, 1993). From a sociological point of view, however, the economic conditions prevailing in the farm sector are more a reflection of deeper social and political forces than a dynamic natural economic process. Two examples can be used to illustrate this macro-social aspect.

Initially, there is a wide range of government policies that shape the context within which microeconomic forces operate. Most obviously, the multi-billion dollar payments made annually by the U.S. government to producers of certain subsidized commodities provide distorted incentives that generate overproduction of certain commodities, create competitive advantages for some of the largest operations, and encourage the wasteful use of many natural resources (Gardner, 1981; Pasour, 1990). Federal and state tax policies also provide powerful incentives for capital-intensive production systems and disincentives for adoption of resource conserving practices (Hanson & Hewitt, 1997; Ward, Benfield & Kinsinger, 1989). In the environmental policy arena, the historic tendency of most state and federal governments to adopt a largely incentive-based educational and voluntary approach to managing agri-environmental problems lies in sharp contrast to the regulatory model used in other major industries (Poe et al., 2001). Within the United States, areas with relatively lax environmental oversight have seen much more rapid growth of potentially environmentally-risky agricultural production systems.

Second, dynamics of change at the farm level have been increasingly linked to changes in the broader agro-food industry (Buttel, 2001; Goodman, 2002). A number of scholars have looked at the exploitation of U.S. family farmers through adverse terms of trade with the input and output sectors. Upstream, many have noted the increasingly concentrated economic power in the agricultural input and service sector where farmers must buy their inputs (Heffernan, 1999). Meanwhile, downstream concentration in the food processing, marketing, and retailing sectors, and a long-run dependence on wholesale commercial markets for the disposition of their products, has led to erosion in the proportion of the typical food dollar which reaches the farm gate (Bonnano, Busch, Friedland, Gouveia & Mingione, 1994; Hendrickson, Heffernan, Howard & Heffernan, 2001). From a global perspective, increasing competition from overseas production and food processing has led to heightened competitive pressure on domestic agricultural producers and new pressures for change (Buttel, 2001; Goodman & Watts, 1997).

Finally, there is a growing appreciation for the crucial role that consumers and other non-farm rural interests can play in determining the trajectories of change within agriculture (Barham, 1997; Murdock & Miele, 1999). The growing importance of the organic and natural foods markets, combined with recurrent food scares (e.g., mad cow disease, E. coli outbreaks, pesticide contamination) have led to new pressures for change within agriculture in favor of more environmentally benign production systems (Green, 2000; Lockie & Kitto, 2000). Similarly, rapidly growing non-farm populations in agricultural regions have placed new demands on surrounding farmers to continue to supply the consumption benefits associated with the look of traditional rural agricultural landscapes, while refraining from imposing costs associated with production that generates noise, smells, dust and other nuisances (Daniels, 2000; Marsden, 1999).

The changing face of agricultural operations. Despite the obstacles to direct capitalist investment in agriculture and the competitive advantages of family labor farms mentioned previously, it is clear that these external societal forces have changed the nature of family labor farming in important ways during the previous few decades. Indeed, rather than being displaced by capitalist farms directly engaged in agricultural production, it can be argued that family farms have gradually been transformed in a number of more indirect yet significant ways.

There are number of mechanisms through which farmers have gradually lost some of their independent control over aspects of farm business decisions. Mooney (1986, 1988) has documented how increased use of rented land and commercial credit can draw farmers into exploitative relationships with absentee landlords and finance capitalists, respectively. In some specific commodity subsectors (e.g., poultry, processing vegetables, pork), contract production relationships between independent producers and large vertically-integrated processing firms have become the dominant form of production (Heffernan, 1984; Thu & Durrenburger, 1998). Contract production can relieve the producer of some degree of price risk (though they usually assume the risk of production failures), but typically requires contracting farmers to forfeit some of their decision-making autonomy (Davis, 1980; Roy, 1972). Finally, family farms have become increasingly reliant on income and benefits from off-farm employment by household members. While the availability of off-farm income can help farm households survive periods of depressed business income, they also reduce the availability of family members to contribute to the farm labor force and might induce farm operators to invest in labor-saving technological innovations or employ greater numbers of hired workers.

Implications of the Sociology of Agriculture for Natural Resource Management
This extended discussion of the sociological aspect of agriculture in advanced industrial societies has several implications for natural scientists seeking to solve pressing environmental and natural resource management problems in agriculture. It is apparent that the simple A/D approach to understanding agricultural producers' behavior with respect to natural resource management has proven to be inadequate.

Second, the nature of farmer decision-making is much more complex than often assumed. This complexity reflects the importance of several sociological aspects: a) the farm household as the key decision-making unit, b) the non-economic goals that many farmers seek, and c) the unique biophysical and social conditions in agriculture that provide disincentives for industrial-style production and competitive rewards for traditional family-labor types of operations. Conducting a narrow economic analysis of the impact of natural resource management practices on farm businesses without an appreciation for the broader sociological dimensions of farmer and farm household decision-making can lead to inaccurate assessments of the viability of new agricultural technologies.

Finally, the failure to appreciate the social aspects of agricultural production can lead researchers and practitioners to overestimate how quickly the farm sector is changing and to place too much emphasis on the importance of large, industrial-like facilities when they design natural resource management programs. While farming systems in the U.S. and Europe have changed dramatically in the last 30 years, when one compares the structure of agricultural production today with what people predicted our current situation would look like back in 1975, it can be argued that the similarities are more striking than the differences. In this regard, natural resource management practices and programs that are designed in anticipation of impending dramatic structural changes in the agricultural sector may well prove to be irrelevant or inappropriate for producers who may still be hanging on by using more conventional approaches.

Future Directions

Looking down the road, there are indications that the socio-political climate regarding agricultural policy may change in important ways. First, consumers have become more critical of the social and environmental conditions under which their food is produced. This may lead to the development and expansion of new markets for agricultural commodities that are as responsive to quality as they have been to cost and quantity. It may also lead to greater demands for more rigid regulation of the environmental practices of all types of farming operations. Second, in many places the rural countryside is changing from a place mainly used for the production of raw commodities into a landscape where aesthetics, recreation, and other forms of consumption can shape local markets, land use policies, and social relationships among farmers and their neighbors. As this takes place, a growing number of communities have placed limits on the ability of local agricultural operators to pursue a more industrial-style of production.

Despite the continued importance of farming and ranching activities on the rural landscape and environmental quality in most countries, the number of papers with an agricultural focus presented at ISSRM meetings and articles published in *Society and Natural Resources* has been slowly diminishing since the late 1990s. A future research agenda for a reinvigorated social analysis of natural resource management within agriculture should build on the insights outlined previously. In particular, the diversity of producers and complex social and economic context of land management decisions must be appreciated before designing new technologies, institutions, or policy interventions to solve agri-environmental problems. Finally, the growing presence of recreational and residential landowners in many agriculturally important areas presents new challenges and opportunities for natural resource management programs.

References

Ahearn, M., Yee, J., Ball, E., & Nehring, R. (1998). *Agricultural productivity in the United States*. (USDA-ERS Agricultural Information Bulletin No. 740). Washington, DC: U.S. Government Printing Office.

Albrecht, D. E., & Murdock, S. H. (1990). *The sociology of agriculture: An ecological perspective*. Ames: Iowa State University Press.

Babb, E. M. (1979). Some causes of structural change in U.S. agriculture, *In Structure issues of American agriculture* (Agricultural Economic Report No. 438) (pp. 51-64). Washington, DC: United States Department of Agriculture

Barham, E. (1997). Social movements for sustainable agriculture in France: A Polanyian perspective. *Society and Natural Resources*, 10, 239-50.

Barham, B., Carter, M. R., & Sigelko, W. (1995). Agro-export production and peasant land access: Examining the dynamic between adoption and accumulation. *Journal of Development Economics*, 46, 85-110.

Barlett, P. (1993). *American dreams, rural realities: Family farms in crisis.* Chapel Hill, NC: University of North Carolina Press.

Batte, M. T., & Johnson, R. (1993). Technology and its impact on American agriculture. In A. Hallam (Ed.), *Size, structure, and the changing face of American agriculture* (pp. 308-35). Boulder, CO: Westview Press.

Bennett, J. W. (1982). *Of time and the enterprise: North American family farm management in a context of resource marginality.* Minneapolis, MN: University of Minnesota Press.

Binswanger, H. P., & Rosenzweig, M. R. (1986). Behavioral and material determinants of production relations in agriculture. *Journal of Development Studies*, 22, 503-39.

Bonanno, A., Busch, L., Friedland, W., Gouveia, L., & Mingione, E. (1994). *From Columbus to ConAgra: The globalization of agriculture and food.* Lawrence, KS: University of Kansas Press.

Bonanno, A., & Constance, D. (2000). The powers and limits of TNCs: The case of ADM. *Rural Sociology*, 65, 440-60.

Bultena, G. L., & Hoiberg, E. O. (1986). Voluntarism in conservation behavior: Social factors affecting farmers' adoptions of recommended soil conservation practices. In *Program Abstracts of the First National Symposium on Social Science in Resource Management.* (CPSU/OSU Report 86-4) (p. 184). Corvallis, OR: Oregon State University.

Buttel, F.H. (1983). Beyond the family farm. In G. Summers (Ed.), *Technology and social change in rural areas* (pp. 87-107). Boulder, CO: Westview Press.

Buttel, F. H. (2001). Some reflections on the late twentieth-century agrarian political economy. *Sociologia Ruralis*, 41, 165-80.

Buttel, F. H., Larson, O. F., & Gillespie, G. W. Jr. (1990). *The sociology of agriculture.* New York: Greenwood Press.

CIA World Factbook. (2003). Retrieved September 3, 2003 from: http://www.cia.gov/cia/publications/factbook/

Cochrane, W. (1993). *The development of American agriculture: A historical analysis (2nd ed.).* Minneapolis, MN: University of Minnesota Press.

Coughenour, C. M., & Chamala, S. (1989). Voluntary and mandated institutional controls on soil conservation behavior of U.S. and Australian farmers. *Society and Natural Resources*, 2, 37-51.

Culhane, P. J. (2001). Research on Society & Natural Resources: A content analysis of the first decade. *Society and Natural Resources*, 14, 365-84.

Daniels, T. (2000). Integrated working landscape protection: The case of Lancaster County, Pennsylvania. *Society and Natural Resources*, 13, 261.

Davis, J. E. (1980). Capitalist agricultural development and the exploitation of the propertied laborer. In F. Buttel & H. Newby (Eds.), *The rural sociology of the advanced societies* (pp. 133-54). Montclair, NJ: Allanheld, Osmun & Co.

Feder, G. (1985). The relation between farm size and farm productivity: The role of family labor, supervision and credit constraints. *Journal of Development Economics*, 18, 297-313.

Freudenburg, W. (1992). Addictive economies: Extractive industries and vulnerable localities in a changing world economy. *Rural Sociology*, 57, 305-32.

Friedland, W. H., Barton, A. E., & Thomas, R. J. (1981). *Manufacturing green gold: Capital, labor and technology in the lettuce industry.* New York: Cambridge University Press.

Friedland, W. H., Busch, L., Buttel, F. H., & Rudy, A. P. (1991). *Toward a new political economy of agriculture.* Boulder, CO: Westview Press.

Friedmann, H. (1978a). World market, state, and family farm: social bases of household production in an era of wage labor. *Comparative Studies in Society and History*, 20, 545-86.

Friedmann, H. (1978b). Simple commodity production and wage labor in the American plains. *Journal of Peasant Studies*, 6, 71-99.

Fuglie, K. O., & Kascak, C. A. (2001). Adoption and diffusion of natural-resource-conserving agricultural technologies. *Review of Agricultural Economics*, 23, 386-403.

Gardner, B.L. (1981). *The governing of agriculture.* Lawrence, KS: University Press of Kansas.

Gasson, R., Crow, G., Errington, A., Hutson, J., Marsden, T., & Winter, D. M. (1988). The farm as a family business: A review. *Journal of Agricultural Economics*, 39, 1-41.

Gasson, R., & Errington, A. (1993). *The farm family business.* Wallingford, UK: CAB International.

Goodman, D. (2002). Rethinking food production-consumption: Integrative perspectives. *Sociologia Ruralis*, 42, 271-77.

Goodman, D., & Watts, M. (1997). *Globalizing food.* London: Routledge.

Green, G. P. (1984). Credit and agriculture: Some consequences of the centralization of the banking system. *Rural Sociology*, 49, 568-79.

Greene, K. (2000). U.S. organic agriculture gaining ground. *Agricultural Outlook*, April, 9-14.

Grieshop, J. I., MacMullan, E., Brush, S., Pickel, C., & Zalom, F. G. (1990). Extending integrated pest management by public mandate: A case study from California. *Society and Natural Resources*, 3, 33-51.

Guerin, T. F. (1999). An Australian perspective on the constraints to the transfer and adoption of innovations in land management. *Environmental Conservation*, 26, 289-304.

Hallam, A. (Ed.). (1993). *Size, structure, and the changing face of American agriculture*. Boulder, CO: Westview Press.

Hanson, J. C., & Hewitt, T. I. (1997). The use of United States' farm commodity programs in sustainable cash grain production systems. *Society and Natural Resources*, 10, 297-308.

Hassanein, N. (1999). *Changing the way America farms: Knowledge and community in the sustainable agriculture movement*. Lincoln, NE: University of Nebraska Press.

Heffernan, W. (1984). Constraints in the U.S. poultry industry. *Research in Rural Sociology and Development*, 1, 237-60.

Heffernan, W. (1999). *Consolidation in the food and agricultural system*. (Report to the National Farmers Union). Retrieved September 3, 2003 from: http://nfu.org/images/heffernan_1999.pdf

Hendrickson, M., Heffernan, W. D., Howard, P. H., & Heffernan, J. (2001). *Consolidation in food retailing and dairy*. (Report to the National Farmers Union). Retrieved September 3, 2003 from: http://nfu.org/images/heffernan.pdf

Hoope, R. A., & MacDonald, J. (2001). *Americas diverse family farms: Assorted sizes, types and situations*. (USDA-ERS Agricultural Information Bulletin No. 769). Washington DC: U.S. Government Printing Office.

Hutson, J. (1987). Fathers and sons: Family farms, family businesses and the farming industry. *Sociology*, 21, 215-29.

Jackson-Smith, D. B., & Barham, B. (2000). Dynamics of dairy industry restructuring in Wisconsin. In H. K. Schwartzweller & A. P. Davidson (Eds.), *Research in rural sociology and development* (pp 103-127). London: Elsevier Press.

Kloppenburg, J. R. (1988). *First the seed: The political economy of plant biotechnology, 1492-2000*. New York: Cambridge University Press.

Korsching, P. F., & Hoban, T. J. (1990). Relationships between information sources and farmers' conservation perceptions and behavior. *Society and Natural Resources*, 3, 1-10.

Labao, L. & Meyer, K. (2001). The great agricultural transition: Crisis, change, and social consequences of twentieth century U.S. farming. *Annual Review of Sociology*, 27, 10-34.

Lockie, S., & Kitto, S. (2000). Beyond the farm gate: Production-consumption networks and agri-food research. *Sociologia Ruralis*, 40, 3-19.

Lovejoy, S. B., & Napier, T. L. (Eds.) (1986). *Conserving soil: Insights from socioeconomic research*. Ankeny, IA: Soil Conservation Society of America.

Makowski, T. J., Sofranko, A. J., & van Es, J. C. (1990). Agroecological and policy influences on no-till adoption. *Society and Natural Resources*, 3, 361-371.

Mann, S. A., & Dickinson, J. M. (1978). Obstacles to the development of a capitalist agriculture. *Journal of Peasant Studies*, 5, 466-81.

Marsden, T. (1999). Rural futures: The consumption countryside and its regulation. *Sociologia Ruralis*, 39, 501-20.

Mooney, P. (1986) . The political economy of credit in American agriculture. *Rural Sociology*, 51, 449-70.

Mooney, P. (1988). *My own boss*. Boulder, CO: Westview Press.

Murdock, J., & Miele, M. (1999). "Back to nature": Changing "worlds of production" in the food system. *Sociologia Ruralis*, 39, 465-83.

Napier, T. L. (2000). Use of soil and water protection practices among farmers in the North Central region of the United States. *Journal of the American Water Resources Association*, 36, 723-35.

Napier, T. L., Thraen, C. S., & McClaskie, S. (1986). Adoption of soil conservation practices by farmers in erosion prone areas of Ohio. In *Program Abstracts of the First National Symposium on Social Science in Resource Management*. (CPSU/OSU Report 86-4, p. 185). Corvallis, OR: Oregon State University Press.

Napier, T. L., Tucker, M., & McCarter, S. (2000). Adoption of conservation production systems in three midwest watersheds. *Journal of Soil and Water Conservation, 2nd Qtr.*, 123-34.

National Research Council. (1993). *Soil and water quality: An agenda for agriculture*. Washington, DC: National Academy Press.

National Research Council. (2002). *Publicly funded agricultural research and the changing structure of U.S. agriculture*. Washington DC: National Academy Press.

Nowak, P. (1992). Why farmers adopt production technology. *Journal of Soil and Water Conservation, January-February*, 14-16.

Nowak, P. (1993). *The adoption of agricultural natural resource management practices: A critical overview*. Paper presented at SWCS Task Force on Socioeconomic Research, Minneapolis, MN.

Nowak, P., & Korsching, P. F. (1983). Social and institutional factors affecting the adoption and maintenance of agricultural BMPs. In F. W. Schaller & G. W. Bailey (Eds.), *Agricultural management and water quality* (pp. 349-73). Ames, IA: Iowa State University Press.

Pampel, F., Jr., & van Es, J. C. (1977). Environmental quality and issues of adoption research. *Rural Sociology*, 42, 57-71.

Pasour, E. C., Jr. (1990). *Agriculture and the state: Market processes and bureaucracy.* New York: Holmes and Meier.

Pfeffer, M. J. (1983). *The social relations of subcontracting: The case of contract vegetable production in Wisconsin.* (Working Paper #2). Madison, WI: Center for Comparative Studies in the Sociology of Agriculture, Department of Rural Sociology, University of Wisconsin.

Poe, G., Bills, N., Bellows, B., Crosscombe, P., Koelsch, R., Kreher, M., et al. (2001). Will voluntary and educational programs meet environmental objectives? Evidence from a survey of New York dairy farms. *Review of Agricultural Economics*, 23, 473-91.

Reinhardt, N., & Barlett, P. (1989). The persistence of family farms in United States agriculture. *Sociologia Ruralis*, 24, 203-225.

Rogers, E. M. (1995). *Diffusion of Innovations* (4th ed.). New York: Free Press.

Rogers, S. C. (1987). Mixed paradigms on mixed farming: Anthropological and economic views of specialization in Illinois agriculture. In Chibnik (Ed.), *Farm work and field work: American agriculture in anthropological perspective* (pp. 58-59). Ithaca, NY: Cornell University Press.

Roy, E. P. (1972). *Contract farming and economic integration.* Danville, IL: Interstate Printers and Publishers.

Salamon, S. (1985). Ethnic communities and the structure of agriculture. *Rural Sociology*, 50, 323-40.

Shepard, R. (2000). Nitrogen and phosphorus management on Wisconsin farms: Lessons learned for agricultural water quality programs. *Journal of Soil and Water Conservation*, 1st Qtr., 63-68.

Strange, M. (1988). *Family farming: A new economic vision.* Lincoln, NE: University of Nebraska Press.

Thu, K. M., & Durrenberger, E. P. (Eds.) (1998). *Pigs, profits and rural communities.* Albany, NY: SUNY Press.

Tweeten, L. (1984). *Causes and consequences of structural change in the farming industry.* (NPA Report No. 207, Food and Agriculture Committee). Washington, DC: National Planning Association.

U.S. Census Bureau. (2002). *Statistical abstract of the United States.* Washington, DC: U.S. Government Printing Office.

U.S. Department of Agriculture. (2001). *Summary report: 1997 national resources inventory.* Washington, DC: Natural Resources Conservation Service, U.S. Department of Agriculture. Retrieved July 22, 2002 from http://www.nrcs.usda.gov/technical/NRI/1997/summary_report/.

U.S. Department of Agriculture Economic Research Service. (2003). *Agricultural resources and environmental indicators*, 2000. Retrieved September 3, 2003 from: http://www.ers.usda.gov/publications/arei/arei2001/

van Es, J. C., & Notier, P. (1988). No-till farming in the United States: Research and policy environment in the development and utilization of an innovation. *Society and Natural Resources*, 1, 93-107.

Ward, J. R., Benfield, F. K., & Kinsinger, A. E. (1989). *Reaping the revenue code*. New York: Natural Resources Defense Council.

Wejnert, B. (2002). Integrating models of diffusion of innovations: A conceptual framework. *Annual Review of Sociology*, 28, 297-326.

Welsh, R. (1996). *The industrial reorganization of U.S. agriculture*. Greenbelt, MD: Henry A. Wallace Institute for Alternative Agriculture.

16

Social Aspects of Coastal Tourism

Rebecca L. Johnson

Jessica E. Leahy

Coastal areas provide a popular destination for tourists. Outdoor recreation activities in these areas, including swimming, visiting beaches and photography, have had high participation rates in recent years (Bringas-Robago, 2002; Gormsen, 1997). Coastal states account for 85 percent of all tourism revenues in the United States, with an estimated 180 million visits each year (Houston, 1996; Leeworthy, 2001; National Oceanic and Atmospheric Administration [NOAA], 1998). In the future, the importance of coastal tourism is expected to remain strong. "Of all activities that take place in coastal zones and the near shore coastal ocean, none is increasing more in both volume and diversity than coastal tourism and recreation" (NOAA, 1998, p. 1).

Coastal areas are also attractive locations for residents, including a growing retired population that is no longer tied to major metropolitan areas. Fifty-three percent of the U.S. population lives within 50 miles of a coastline, and this percent has been increasing (Bookman, Culliton & Warren, 1999; Cohen, Small, Mellinger, Gallup & Sachs, 1998).

Coastal ecosystems, an increasing concern to scientists and managers, are both fragile and resilient to significantly alterations by human activities. In addition to environmental impacts, coastal tourism has economic and social impacts. The competing demands of ecosystem preservation and tourism development have resulted in new and innovative approaches to sustainable tourism. Nature-based tourism, or ecotourism, can be one form of sustainable tourism; one whose demand has been increasing recently (Reynolds & Braithwaite, 2001).

Given the dual pressures of population and tourism growth in coastal areas, it is not surprising that the literature on social aspects of coastal tourism is rich with theory, case studies, and management implications. More than a decade ago, the Office of Technology Assessment (U.S. Congress, 1993) reviewed 68 articles related to coastal ecotourism. Previous International Symposia on Society and Resource Management (ISSRM) abstracts include at least 50 studies related to coastal tourism that have been presented at conferences since 1986. The purpose of this chapter is to summarize and synthesize the literature, elicit key concepts and findings, and discuss future research needs.

Definitions

There is no singular agreed-upon definition for *tourism* or *ecotourism*, although common elements appear in many definitions. Tourism can be broadly defined as *the act of traveling for leisure or pleasure and the industry that serves that type of travel*. The Ecotourism Society defines *ecotourism* as *responsible travel to natural areas which conserves the environment and improves the welfare of local people* (Lindberg & Hawkins, 1993). Coastal tourism draws from both categories, and has also been referred to as, or can resemble, *marine tourism, nature-based tourism, adventure tourism, mass tourism, commercial tourism, responsible tourism, green tourism* and *sustainable tourism*. Lesser-used terms are *soft tourism* and *tourism with understanding* (Gormsen, 1997).

Common elements among all types of coastal tourism are: 1) coastal natural resources serve as major attractions, and 2) benefits (e.g., economic, social, environmental) are derived from visitation. Beyond that, the differences are profound. One way to categorize coastal tourism is by types of development and impacts: 1) high development and low environmental impacts (e.g., artificial tide pools, visitor centers, developments built away from the coastline with scenic views as the main attraction), 2) high development and high environmental impacts (e.g., beach hotels, marinas, golf courses), 3) low development and low environmental impacts (e.g., camping, bird watching, beach walking), 4) low development and high environmental impacts (e.g., unregulated or little-regulated fishing and shellfish harvesting, off-road vehicle riding), and 5) everything in-between (see Figure 1).

Coastal tourism impacts can be environmental, economic and social. There is no necessary correlation between the magnitude or direction of these three types of impacts, although *ecotourism* by definition strives to have positive (or at least neutral) impacts in all three categories. Much of the coastal tourism research, however, examines the planning and management tools needed to minimize negative environmental and social impacts while maintaining economic benefits.

Synthesis and Integration of Research

Trends and Changes in Coastal Tourism

While coastal tourism has been growing rapidly, there have been differences in growth rates among its related activities. This has led to a change in the relative importance of different activities, which has implications for resource managers. Perhaps the most striking change has been the proliferation of non-consumptive marine activities, such as marine mammal-watching, scenic cruises and off-highway vehicle dune-riding. Of all wildlife-based tourism, whale-watching is the fastest growing (Lien, 2001). It was recently estimated that nine million people participate annually in whale-watching worldwide, and annual growth rates were around 12

More Development

More
Environmental
Impact

Less
Environmental
Impact

- Beach hotels
- Golf courses
- Marinas

- Visitor centers
- Artificial tidepools
- Development away
from shoreline

- Off-high vehicle riding
- Unregulated fishing
and shellfish harvesting

- Camping
- Beach walking
- Bird watching

Less Development

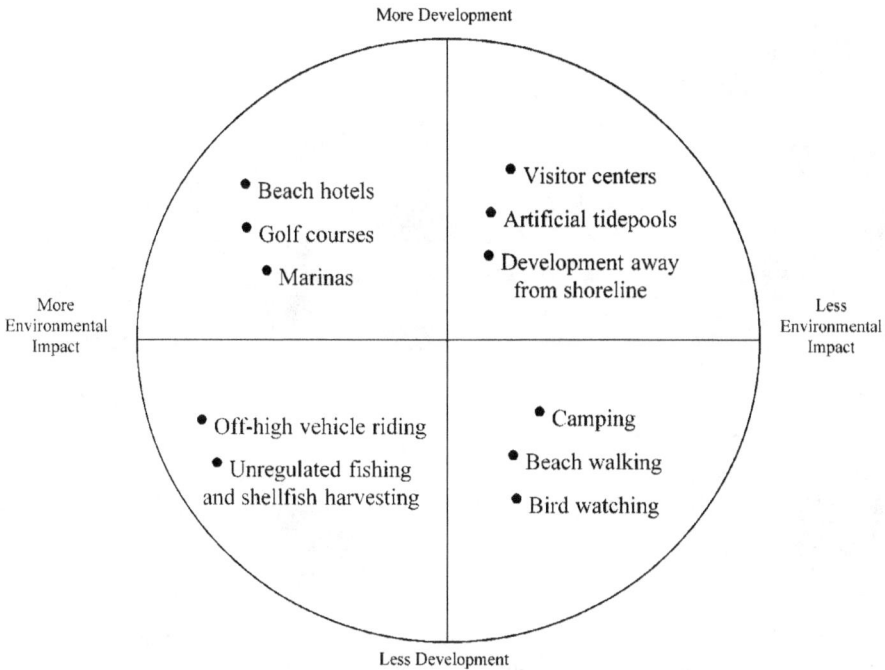

Figure 1: Development vs. environmental impacts

percent (Hoyt, 2001). Scenic cruises are growing at an average annual rate of approximately seven percent (Cruise Lines International Association, 2003). In Alaska, for instance, the amount of cruise ships nearly tripled between 1987 and 2002 (Jansen, Bengston, Boreng & Dahle, 2003). At the same time, consumptive activities, such as fishing, have had relatively slow or stable rates of participation (U.S. Fish and Wildlife Service, 2002).

As coastal tourism has been growing, there has also been a proliferation of tourism activities not directly related to coastal resources. These activities, such as amusement parks, golf courses, outlet malls, and casinos, simply take advantage of a ready market, and provide diverse opportunities for family members. In this sense, many coastal tourism businesses are complementary, and growth in one area spurs growth in others. How this growth and development is managed and impacts communities provides the basis for many coastal tourism studies.

Impacts of Coastal Tourism
Economic impacts. The economic impacts of coastal tourism have been documented in numerous case studies around the world. Some studies focus on direct impacts, assessing the magnitude of the tourism industry in terms of businesses, tourist expenditures, jobs, or income (Braun & Soskin, 2002; Gossling, 2001; Hoyt, 2001;

Leeworthy, 2001; Smith, 1994). For example, a recent study estimated that whale-watching produced $1 billion in revenue per year worldwide, and that humpback whales in Tonga alone create $700,000 in economic impact per year (Orams, 2002). Other studies use economic tools, such as input-output models, to further assess the indirect impacts of tourism on supplier industries, households and taxes (Jones & Tanyeri-Abur, 2001; Leeworthy & Vanasse, 1999; State of Hawaii Department of Business, Economic Development, and Tourism, 2003; Zhou, Yanagida, Chakravorty & Leung, 1997). In these studies, researchers measure the economic impacts generated by non-local tourists who bring new dollars into the local economy, or by local tourists who decide to stay home and spend money on local recreation activities, rather than visit a non-local destination. These tourist expenditures ripple through the local economy and create jobs and income. At the same time, increases in property values, sales, and room or head taxes contribute to city, county and state tax revenues. A hedonic study of property values on an island in South Carolina showed that for every quarter mile closer to the beach, there was a $4,000 average increase in value on developed property (Pompe & Rinehart, 1999). Coastal estuaries, wetlands and water use also positively contributed to property values in a hedonic study completed in Grays Harbor, Washington (Leahy, Huppert, Bell & Johnson, 2002). In both of these cases, the increased property values from coastal amenities return higher property tax revenue to local government.

While it would be useful for tourism planners and researchers to be able to estimate an average expenditure per day per coastal tourist, such a measurement is unrealistic, given the wide variations in coastal tourism. However, expenditures associated with a specific activity can reasonably be extrapolated beyond a study site to other sites with similar recreational and economic characteristics. Similarly, tourism multipliers estimated in one study can be used in another location with similar economic structure. NOAA has a marine recreation fisheries division that specializes in an ambitious recreation angler survey program. This division completes both valuation and expenditure surveys in three coastal regions: Northeast (Maine to Virginia), Southeast (North Carolina to Louisiana) and Pacific (Washington to California). The National Park Service uses the Money Generation Model to estimate total visitor spending (i.e., average spending per party day) and economic impact at each unit in the National Park System, including coastal sites.

Not all economic impacts, however, are perceived to be positive for local community members (Brenner & Aguilar, 2002; Diagne, 2001; Gormsen, 1997). Negative economic impacts include leakages of tourist expenditures out of the local economy, user fees for access to coastal resources that locals must also pay, seasonal or part-time employment instead of year-round or full-time employment, unstable and low-skilled employment, and the loss of traditional sources of income (e.g., commercial fishing).

Social impacts. The social impacts of coastal tourism have been the subject of many studies in both developed and less-developed countries. Social impacts documented in these studies are most often negative. However, positive impacts have more recently been assessed, such as improved economic conditions brought about by tourism growth, better infrastructure (e.g., schools, roads, water,) and lower poverty-associated measures (e.g., poor health, abuse rates, divorce rates) (Furlough & Wakeman, 1997; Sinha & Bushell, 2002; Smith, 1992; Yunnis, 2001). Other positive social impacts related to tourism include community pride, cultural appreciation between tourists and local residents, new ideas brought to the community and maintenance of traditional knowledge and culture. In Fiji, coastal ecotourism reinforced the local history and knowledge possessed by community residents (Sinha & Bushell, 2002). In Europe, coastal tourism led to an increase in commercial fishing, although the timing and techniques were modified. Tourists in this area desired a traditional and authentic cultural experience, and this actually led to the reinstatement of former fishing traditions (Furlough & Wakeman, 1997).

Unfortunately, many coastal tourism studies focus on negative social impacts. These include traffic congestion, crowding at recreation sites and in local communities, crime, loss of traditional knowledge and culture, and displacement of local businesses and residents (Brenner & Aguilar, 2002; Diagne, 2001; Gormsen, 1997; Gossling, 2001; Jansen et al., 2003). Lindberg and Johnson (1997) measured the willingness-to-pay of coastal Oregon community residents to reduce social impacts such as traffic congestion, noise reduction and high housing costs; residents were estimated to have a $110 to $186 mean annual household willingness to pay for a reduction in tourism-related traffic congestion. Diagne (2001) found many negative social impacts from coastal tourism in Senegal such as the prohibition of beach use for fish preparation (to prevent inconveniencing tourists on the beach), increased rates of prostitution and theft, resettlement of local residents away from coastal shorelines to allow for tourism development, and a change in the power roles between traditional elders and a new network of younger businessmen. Resettlement of local communities, in extreme cases, has involved combining several small individual communities into one larger community after relocation from the coastal zone (Smith, 1992).

Environmental impacts. Similar to social impacts, most studies of environmental impacts of coastal tourism focus on negative impacts. With coastal tourism encompassing so many different types of development, and coastal areas being unique around the world, it is clear that environmental impacts will vary widely. Therefore, general characterizations of impacts are difficult to determine.

Negative environmental impacts of coastal tourism are wide-ranging, from direct contact with marine resources to indirect impacts from increased development in the nearby communities (Gormsen, 1997; Poh-Poh, 1990; Smith, 1994; Uluocha, 1999). The former includes obvious impacts from consumptive activities like fishing and shellfish harvesting, to less obvious impacts from non-consumptive activities that trample tide-pools, introduce exotic species or inadvertently harass wildlife (Jansen et al., 2003; Liast, Knowlton, Mead, Collet & Podesta, 2001; Lien, 2001).

There are many case studies that highlight environmental impacts to a particular place from coastal tourism. Klug and Klug (1998), in a review of coastal environmental impacts from tourism in Germany, included loss of shoreline, wetlands and estuary habitats as negative environmental impacts. They specifically mentioned the impact of marinas on protected waters, where safe boating moorage can have ecologically significant effects. They also discussed the loss of vegetation from tourists driving vehicles on beaches, and the stress experienced by animals when being viewed or photographed. In the West Indies, negative environmental impacts included dredging, lack of sewage treatment, infrastructure development and sand mining (Baldwin, 2000). In the Caribbean, cruise ships have been faulted for harmful discharges of sewage, solid waste and oil in the ocean. Also, port development and dredging, have created harmful sediment conditions for coral reefs (Yunnis, 2001).

Harassment of marine mammals is regulated by the Marine Mammal Protection Act of 1972, which also outlines regional regulations and guidelines for wildlife-viewing, but negative impacts still persist. Jansen et al. (2003) observed changed behavior in Alaskan harbor seals, although the researchers were unable to determine if the decline in harbor seal population was due to cruise ships or hunting success by Alaskan Natives. Like harbor seals, whale behavior can change as the result of coastal tourism. Whales can become habituated to humans, which put them at risk when they encounter non-whale-watching ships (Lien, 2001). Ship strikes (i.e., collisions between whales and vessels) are increasing (Liast et al., 2001). Lien (2001) also noted that whale-watching tourists can disrupt regular whale behavior to the point that food gathering and rearing of young is negatively impacted.

Less direct impacts considered harmful to environmental resources include water demand and pollution from on-shore tourism businesses and run-off from paved surfaces (Diange, 2001; Klug & Klug, 1998). Water pollution can come from boats or the handling of wastewater at resorts and campgrounds (Klug & Klug, 1998). Loss of habitat due to tourism infrastructure has wide-ranging implications. Tussac grass communities on the Falkland Islands are used for various wildlife as sustenance; Hoppe and McAdam (1992) therefore advocated for the conservation of these grasses despite pressure for tourism development.

Based on the wealth of case studies from a wide range of tourism communities and associated economies, it is very difficult to make general statements about the overall impacts of tourism. It is clear that tourism can have both positive and negative economic, social and environmental impacts, and all stakeholders (including local community, tourists, managers and tourism developers) want to minimize the negative and maximize the positive impacts. For example, Gibson (1999) states that "most developers realize that the commercial success of their projects requires that the public perceive them as either environmentally benign or, better yet, as a positive contribution to the local ecology" (p. 577). However, it is difficult to classify impacts into *positive* and *negative* because, in some cases, the status quo is preferred by some, while others prefer the changes anticipated by tourism development.

Policy, Planning and Management Issues

Much of the coastal tourism literature focuses on planning and management to address or avoid adverse impacts. A number of case studies demonstrate the difference between carefully planned and managed coastal tourism destinations, and those that develop in an ad hoc fashion (Smith, 1992; Uluocha, 1999). Researchers have also studied several areas with potentially successful tourism development.

Smith (1994) found integrated tourism development in Indonesia as a promising management strategy. In these integrated tourist locations, planners clustered hotels together so that infrastructure and common facilities could be shared. These hotel clusters were then located near natural attractions, such as beaches and preserved natural areas. Smith (1994) suggested that these integrated developments were tourism-specific and future planning efforts should integrate all industries that rely upon the coastal ecosystem.

Sinha and Bushell (2002) recommend the use of local knowledge and culture to manage coastal tourism and environmental resources. Specifically, they suggested using the local spiritual belief system, which is focused on the connection between people and land, to plan for sustainable tourism that considers biodiversity conservation. In the Canary Islands, a national park and World Heritage Site was designated near a coastal resort area with very little objection or impact from local community members. The success of this conservation strategy was attributed primarily to two critical aspects of the area. First, people were not living in the area designated, so relocation was not necessary. Secondly, and perhaps more importantly, the designation was compatible with the conservation ethic of local residents (Bianchi, 2002).

The approach of the Mexican government to developing coastal tourism has received both praise and criticism (Brenner & Aguilar, 2002; Bringas-Robago, 2002). Unlike other countries, the government took a very active role in promoting coastal tourism. This included policies that provided tax credits and other mechanisms to support infrastructure development. It even included changes in the land ownership policies to allow for tourism uses. The criticism has come from isolating tourism development in enclave-like resorts too far away from local communities. This results in a lack of economic impact and basic services for existing communities that could have been achieved by placing large-scale resorts in closer proximity.

On the other hand, regional and national tourism policies are sometimes needed, and few countries appear to have them. Korea is establishing a national coastal tourism plan that includes marine park development (Tyrrell, Chang & Kim, 1999). These authors also report that Korean local governments are more involved in decision-making for coastal tourism than local governments in the U.S., United Kingdom or Canada.

In summary, much of the research on policy, planning and management of coastal tourism suggests the following lessons: 1) Tourism development must be compatible with the local environment, economy and culture; 2) tourism development must have local economic benefits, and must mitigate negative social and environmental impacts; 3) common property resources must be managed and their access should be controlled; 4) participatory decision-making and open communication between planners, managers, politicians, businesses and citizens must be facilitated; and 5) in fragile coastal environments, and where there is uncertainty about consequences of change, a precautionary approach that preserves future options is suggested.

Future Research

Continuing the trend of the recent past, future coastal tourism issues are likely to be centered on the concept of sustainable tourism development and management. This will include defining, measuring, and balancing positive and negative tourism impacts, as well as developing the best policy, planning and management tools to move toward sustainability. Researchers will have to tackle how to measure and monitor sustainable tourism to assess whether coastal tourism planning and development efforts were successful. For example, Adler, Zeller, Pitcher and Sumaila (2002) have already proposed a marine protected area evaluation model. The broad categories to monitor could include best coastal management practices, resource conditions, safety for tourists and locals, restoration of coastal areas (where needed) and policies for protection (Cicin-Sain & Knecht, 1999).

While many case studies point out the advantages of local involvement in coastal tourism planning and decision-making, more systematic research is needed on characteristics and processes that work best in different coastal tourism situations. Preliminary research from Australia suggests that in at least one country, "understanding better the decision-making process provides possibly the most important tool in the sustainable management of tourism development" (Richins & Pearce, 2000, p. 207).

Another trend that will continue is the use of more sophisticated technology in understanding coastal tourism issues and assisting with coastal tourism planning. Geographic information systems (GIS) are an obvious example of how economic, social and environmental data can be considered spatially. Integrated and comprehensive development teams can work together to evaluate potential economic, social and environmental impacts. They can use data such as political boundaries, existing infrastructure, beaches, other natural attractions, risk of natural disasters, and existing land uses to make informed decisions about future coastal tourism development (Joerger, DeGloria & Noden, 1999). There may also be possibilities of using GIS to understand historical trends and measure impacts from existing coastal tourism development.

While case studies of coastal tourism development have been extremely informative, in the future researchers need to move beyond case studies that simply list and describe impacts. Regional approaches, multi- and inter-disciplinary approaches, longitudinal studies, and syntheses across time and spatial scales are

PONTUS OBERG

needed. An example of this would be research that investigates how social and ecological tourism concerns are, and could be, incorporated into resource management decisions (Kline, 2001; Sharp & Lach, 2003).

Future public policy research in the U.S. might also address coordination of the many governmental organizations that have some interest in coastal resource issues. These include NOAA, Federal Emergency Management Agency, U.S. Fish and Wildlife Service, National Park Service, Environmental Protection Agency, Army Corps of Engineers, Coast Guard, and coastal zone management programs, among others. All have a role to play, but none are absolutely or exclusively responsible for coastal resource management.

Specific coastal tourism policy and management changes will occur over time that will also demand rigorous research. Recent examples include protected marine reserves or parks, and user fees for public coastal areas. As these new policies are proposed and implemented, coastal tourism researchers will have a significant role to play in assessing their impacts, especially in a sustainable tourism framework that takes into account economic, social and environmental aspects.

The future growth projected for coastal tourism will only increase the need for additional research. We must draw on results from previous studies and build more rigorous, comprehensive and integrated frameworks for addressing complex coastal tourism issues.

References

Adler, R., Zeller, D., Pitcher, T., & Sumaila, R. (2002). A method for evaluating marine protected area management. *Coastal Management*, 30, 121-131.

Baldwin, J. (2000). Tourism development, wetland degradation and beach erosion in Antigua, West Indies. *Tourism Geographies*, 2(2), 193-218.

Bianchi, R. (2002). The contested landscapes of World Heritage on a tourist island: The case of Garajonay National Park, La Gomera. *International Journal of Heritage Studies,* 8(2), 81-97.

Bookman, C., Culliton, T., & Warren, M. (1999). *Trends in U.S. coastal regions, 1970-1998: Addendum to the proceedings, trends and future challenges for U.S. national ocean and coastal policy.* Silver Spring, MD: National Oceanic and Atmospheric Administration.

Braun, B., & Soskin, M. (2002). The impact of day trips to Daytona Beach. *Tourism Economics,* 8(3), 289-301.

Brenner, L., & Aguilar, A. G. (2002). Luxury tourism and regional economic development in Mexico. *The Professional Geographer,* 54(4), 500-520.

Bringas-Rabago, N. (2002). Baja California and California's merging tourist corridors: The influence of Mexican government policies. *Journal of Environment and Development,* 11(3), 267-296.

Cicin-Sain, B., & Knecht, R. (1999). *Coastal tourism and recreation: The driver of coastal development.* Paper presented at the Trends and Future Challenges for U.S. National Ocean and Coastal Policy, Washington, D.C.

Cohen, J., Small, C., Mellinger, A., Gallup, J., & Sachs, J. (1998). Estimates of coastal populations. *Science,* 278(5341), 1211-1212.

Cruise Lines International Association (2003). *Cruise Lines International Association 2003 spring overview.* New York: Cruise Lines International Association.

Diagne, A. (2001). Impact of coastal tourism development and sustainability: A geographic case study of Sali in Senegalese Petite Cote. *Geographical Review of Japan,* 74(1), 62-77.

Furlough, E., & Wakeman, R. (1997). Composing a landscape: Coastal mass tourism and regional development in the Languedoc: 1960s-1980s. *International Journal of Maritime History,* 9(1), 187-211.

Gibson, J. W. (1999). Marine conservation as an advertising theme in coastal redevelopment for tourism. *Coastal Zone, Part COM,* 577-579.

Gormsen, E. (1997). The impact of tourism on coastal areas. *GeoJournal,* 42(1), 39-54.

Gossling, S. (2001). Tourism, economic transition and ecosystem degradation: Interacting processes in a Tanzanian coastal community. *Tourism Geographies,* 3(4), 430-453.

Hoppe, G., & McAdam, J. (1992). Management of a tussac grass community for wildlife, tourism, and agriculture. *Aspects of Applied Biology,* 29, 377-381.

Houston, J. (1996). International tourism and U.S. beaches. *Shore and Beach,* 64(2).

Hoyt, E. (2001). Whale-watching 2001: *Worldwide tourism numbers, expenditures, and expanding socioeconomic benefits.* Yarmouth Port, MA: International Fund for Animal Welfare.

Jansen, J., Bengston, J., Boreng, P., & Dahle, S. (2003). *Investigation of the potential disturbance of harbor seals by cruise ships in Disenchantment Bay, Alaska, May to August 2002.* (Draft Report No. 1: Field Activities and Preliminary Results). Seattle, WA: National Marine Mammal Laboratory, Alaska Fisheries Science Center, NOAA Fisheries.

Joerger, A., DeGloria, S., & Noden, M. (1999). Applying geographic information systems: Siting of coastal hotels in Costa Rica. *Cornell Hotel and Restaurant Administration Quarterly, 40*(4), 48-59.

Jones, L., & Tanyeri-Abur, A. (2001). *Impacts of recreation and commercial fishing and coastal resource-based tourism on regional and state economies* (TR-184). College Station, TX: Texas Water Resources Institute, Texas A&M University.

Kline, J. (2001). *Tourism and natural resource management: A general overview of research and issues* (PNW-GTR-506). Portland, OR: USDA Forest Service, Pacific Northwest Research Station.

Klug, H., & Klug, A. (1998). The impact of tourism on the natural ecosystems of the German coasts. In Kelletat (Ed.), *German geographical coastal research: The last decade.* (pp. 201-220). Institute for Scientific Cooperation.

Leahy, J., Huppert, D., Bell, K., & Johnson, R. (2002). Interactions between human communities and biophysical attributes of Pacific Northwest Coastal Ecosystems. In *2001 Annual Report for Pacific Northwest Coastal Ecosystem Regional Study* (pp. 1-14). Seattle, WA: University of Washington.

Leeworthy, V. (2001). *Preliminary estimates from versions 1-6: Coastal recreation participation.* Silver Spring, MD: National Oceanic and Atmospheric Administration.

Leeworthy, V., & Vanasse, P. (1999). *Economic contribution of recreating visitors to the Florida Keys/Key West: Updates for years 1996-97 and 1997-98.* Silver Spring, MD: Special Projects NOS.

Liast, D., Knowlton, A., Mead, J., Collet, A., & Podesta, M. (2001). Collisions between ships and whales. *Marine Mammal Science, 17*(1), 35-75.

Lien, J. (2001). *The conservation basis for the regulation of whale-watching in Canada by the Department of Fisheries and Oceans: A precautionary approach* (Canadian Technical Report of Fisheries and Aquatic Sciences 2363). Winnipeg, Manitoba.: Department of Fisheries and Oceans.

Lindberg, K., & Hawkings, D. (1993). *Ecotourism: A guide for planners and managers.* North Bennington, MA: The Ecotourism Society.

Lindberg, K., & Johnson, R. (1997). The economic values of tourism's social impacts. *Annals of Tourism Research, 24*(1), 90-116.

National Oceanic and Atmospheric Administration (1998). Coastal tourism and recreation. In *Year of the Ocean Discussion Papers.* Washington D.C.: U.S. Department of Commerce, National Ocean Atmospheric Administration.

Orams, M. (2002). Humpback whales in Tonga: An economic resource for tourism. *Coastal Management*, 30, 361-380.

Poh-Poh, W. (1990). Coastal resource management: Tourism in peninsular Malaysia. *ASEAN Economic Bulletin*, 7(2), 213-221.

Pompe, J., & Rinehart, J. (1999). Establishing fees for beach protection: Paying for a public good. *Coastal Management*, 27, 57-67.

Reynolds, P. C., & Braithwaite, D. (2001). Towards a conceptual framework for wildlife tourism. *Tourism Management*, 22(1), 31-42.

Richins, H., & Pearce, P. (2000). Influences on tourism development decision-making: Coastal local government areas in eastern Australia. *Journal of Sustainable Tourism*, 8(3), 207-231.

Sharp, S., & Lach, D. (2003). Integrating social values into fisheries management: A Pacific Northwest study. *Fisheries*, 28(4), 10-15.

Sinha, C., & Bushell, R. (2002). Understanding the linkage between biodiversity and tourism: A study of ecotourism in a coastal village in Fiji. *Pacific Tourism Review*, 6(1), 35-50.

Smith, R. (1992). Coastal urbanization: Tourism development in the Asia Pacific. *Built Environment*, 18(1), 27-40.

Smith, R. (1994). Planning and management for coastal eco-tourism in Indonesia: A regional perspective. *Indonesian Quarterly*, 22(2), 148-157.

State of Hawaii Department of Business, Economic Development and Tourism (2003). *Planning for sustainable tourism in Hawaii: A study on the carrying capacity for tourism* (Progress Report to the 2003 Legislature). Honolulu, HI: State of Hawaii Department of Business, Economic Development and Tourism.

Tyrrell, T., Chang, Y.-T., & Kim, S.-G. (1999). Coastal tourism development and EXPO 2010 in Korea. *Korea Observer*, 30(1), 187-210.

Uluocha, N. (1999). Mapping for the management of tourism values of Lagos coastal zone, Nigeria. *Coastal Zone, Part COM*, 446-448.

U. S. Congress (1993). Science and technology issues in coastal ecotourism. *Tourism Management*, 14(4), 307-316.

U.S. Fish and Wildlife Service (2002). *2001 National survey of fishing, hunting, and wildlife-associated recreation*. Washington, D.C.: Department of Interior, U.S. Fish and Wildlife Service.

Yunnis, E. (2001). *Sustainable development and management of tourism in coastal areas*. Retrieved 09/15/2003, 2003, from http://web.invemor.org.co/redcosteral/docs/518ManagementofTourism.pdf

Zhou, D., Yanagida, J., Chakravorty, U., & Leung, P.-S. (1997). Estimating economic impacts from tourism. *Annals of Tourism Research*, 24(1), 76-89.

17

Human Dimensions of Wildlife Management

Daniel J. Decker

Tommy L. Brown

Jerry J. Vaske

Michael J. Manfredo

Wildlife management during the last 35 years has increasingly relied on social science to improve understanding of: (a) how people value wildlife, (b) what benefits people desire from wildlife management, (c) acceptability of management practices, and (d) how various stakeholders affect or are affected by wildlife and wildlife management decisions. This suite of inquiry and application is referred to as the "human dimensions of wildlife management" (HDWM) (Decker, Brown & Siemer, 2001, p. 3; Manfredo, Vaske & Decker 1995, p. 17). Put simply, HDWM scholars describe what people think and do with respect to wildlife, develop knowledge to understand why, and determine how to incorporate that insight in wildlife management. This chapter synthesizes the knowledge development in HDWM in three interrelated domains of management interest and research innovation: wildlife-related activity description (describing what people do), social psychological (understanding what people think and why), and management application (incorporating HDWM insight into management). Presentations from each of these domains have been made at several International Symposia on Society and Resource Management (ISSRM).

Domain One: Wildlife-related Activity Description

Wildlife-related activity-participation studies: (a) inventory and characterize users, and (b) monitor and describe trends in participation. Understanding national trends in wildlife recreation has been facilitated by surveys of United States households conducted approximately every five years by the U.S. Fish and Wildlife Service (USFWS). Questions on hunter numbers, types of hunting, days afield, and hunters' expenditures have been included in the national survey since 1955. Information on nonconsumptive activities (e.g., wildlife observation, photography) has been collected since 1980. Unfortunately, the methodology for these surveys changed over time (e.g., the recall time frame for reporting frequency of participation questions), hampering use of these data to chart long-term trends in wildlife recreation participation (Chu, Eisenhower, Hay, Morganstein, Neter & Waksberg, 1992). Hunter surveys have also gathered harvest data for various game species to estimate population abundance and trends.

As it became evident in the 1980s that numbers of hunters, whose license fees are primary income for state wildlife agencies, were static or declining, the dynamics of hunting participation were examined in terms of recruitment, retention, continuous versus sporadic participation, and cessation. Results of this line of inquiry indicated that hunting is strongly culturally-driven from initiation through cessation (Decker, Provencher & Brown, 1984). Broad social trends affecting hunting (e.g., urbanization) suggest a continuing decline in participation (e.g., Brown, Decker, Siemer & Enck, 2000; Decker, Enck & Brown, 1993). By describing the complexity of hunting, this research highlighted the difficulties agencies face when attempting to stimulate sufficient recruitment or retention to curb the decline of hunters.

Nonconsumptive wildlife users became a focal point for management and research beginning in the 1980s (Manfredo, 2002). Wildlife observation around and near people's homes accounted for much of the time spent watching wildlife, though trips for the specific purpose of viewing wildlife were also common. The USFWS survey identified a demand for wildlife viewing that far exceeded the traditional clients of wildlife agencies. Concurrently, specific inquiries occurred about potential new clients for wildlife programs, such as wildlife viewers (e.g., Brown, Dawson & Miller, 1979; Witter & Shaw, 1979) and donors to state and private wildlife program funds (e.g., Manfredo, 1988; Witter, Tylka & Werner, 1981).

Domain Two: Social Psychological: Values, Attitudes, Norms and Motivations
This domain addresses three issues, including: 1) how different segments of the public value and evaluate wildlife and associated interactions, 2) what management actions are deemed acceptable in different situations, and 3) why people participate in wildlife-related activities. These practical directions of inquiry can be organized theoretically using the cognitive hierarchy: values, value orientations (i.e., basic belief patterns), attitudes and norms. In addition, motivation theory has been employed to understand the "why" questions about wildlife–related behavior.

Values and Value Orientations
Wildlife values were one of the first areas of investigation for HDWM researchers. Although there has been a lack of consistency in conceptual definition, values are typically used to denote stable, basic modes of thought about wildlife. Early HDWM studies attempted to develop values typologies that described how segments of society relate to wildlife. Kellert (1980), for example, postulated 10 basic views of Americans toward animals: naturalistic, ecologistic, humanistic, moralistic, scientific, aesthetic, utilitarian, dominionistic, negativistic and neutralistic. The *Wildlife Attitudes and Values Scale* (Purdy & Decker, 1989) was designed to understand people's orientations toward wildlife in human-wildlife conflict situations, emphasizing traditional conservation, social benefits, and problem acceptance perspectives. Simply revealing that such a diversity of perspective exists was insightful for the wildlife profession at the time.

BRENT ERB

In the mid-1990s Fulton, Manfredo and Lipscomb (1996) introduced the notion of *wildlife value orientations*, identifying a *protection-use* dimension and a *wildlife appreciation* dimension. Orientations were defined as the direction and pattern of basic beliefs about wildlife. Basic beliefs were seen as part of a cognitive hierarchy suggesting: values → basic beliefs → attitudes / norms → behaviors. Two people with the same value (e.g., respect for life) could be oriented differently in the expression of that value. Those with a more utilitarian view, for example, were more likely to engage in consumptive recreation and support more invasive forms of wildlife management than those with a protectionist orientation.

Contemporary efforts examining wildlife values are incorporating individual-level traits into models that reflect broader societal and cultural contexts, including cross-cultural research to enhance understanding different cultures within North America, as well as internationally.

Attitudes

Values and value orientations are believed to play an important role in shaping attitudes. An attitude is a person's favorable or unfavorable evaluation of an object (e.g., a situation, specific wildlife species, management action). Attitudes have both cognitive and evaluative elements or a combination of beliefs and negative/positive views about an object. Attitudes about specific objects (e.g., wolf restoration, trapping) are believed to influence behavior.

Given the central role of attitudes in the cognitive hierarchy, it is not surprising that the concept has had a major influence on HDWM research. Much of the HDWM research dealing with opinions, preferences and perceptions are actually attitudinal studies. The attitudes of rural landowners toward hunting access policies, for example, have received considerable attention (Brown, Decker & Kelley, 1984; Wright, Brown, Cordell & Rowell, 1988). Contrary to the assumptions of some state programs, these studies found most landowners were not opposed to hunting *per se*. Instead, the access restrictions reflected the landowners' poor image of hunters and concerns over liability risks. Influenced by this research, state wildlife agencies and hunting organizations embarked on efforts to address landowner concerns (e.g., hunter ethics, controlling access, incentives for allowing access for hunting, laws to reduce landowner liability).

Public attitudes toward potentially dangerous wildlife, especially among residents living in the wildland-urban interface, have spurred both empirical and theoretical work. Empirical examples include studies of mountain lions in Colorado (Manfredo, Zinn, Sikorowski & Jones, 1998) and Montana (Riley & Decker, 2000), and black bears in Colorado (Loker & Decker, 1995) and the northeast states (Organ & Ellingwood, 2000). Despite human deaths, the public is split with respect to how to control these mammals: findings that can be partially explained by differences in *perceived* versus *objective* risk (Riley & Decker, 2000). In a similar vein, HDWM attitude research has examined the social feasibility of restorations of large herbivores (e.g., elk, moose) that have potential for significant human impact. This typically involves predicting respondents' voting intentions on restoration initiatives using attitudinal measures.

While social psychologists use evaluative measures based on attitudes, economists employ contingent valuation and travel cost methods to estimate net and total economic benefits of wildlife. Bishop and Heberlein (1979), for example, showed that the amount Wisconsin goose hunters were willing to pay to hunt was of a similar order of magnitude as what hunters who already had received permits were willing to accept to give them up. Willingness to pay studies have been conducted over the years for a variety of types of wildlife recreation and for wildlife habitat preservation (Bowker, Newman, Warren & Henderson, 2003; Brown & Connelly, 1994; Teisl, Boyle & Record, 1999).

Norms

Norms are standards of behavior that specify what people should do or what most people are doing. They can be thought of as evaluative standards (i.e., acceptability measures) regarding individual behavior or conditions in a given context, and can be analyzed for various structural characteristics (e.g., range of tolerances for management actions, intensity or strength of the norm, level of agreement about the norm). Norm theory offers a paradigm for identifying and evaluating the public's tolerance for management actions.

Human tolerance for interactions with wildlife varies among different stakeholder groups for different situations, and for different species of wildlife. Traditional management methods (e.g., hunting, lethal trapping) can be effective in reducing problem wildlife populations, but may not be feasible in areas of dense human population and may not be acceptable to urban residents (Zinn, Manfredo, Vaske & Wittmann, 1998). An understanding of how stakeholders perceive particular management actions can help wildlife agencies minimize controversy when choosing among management alternatives (Loker, Decker & Schwager, 1999).

Differences in situational contexts in human-wildlife interactions have been shown to influence norms of acceptable management actions. The Wildlife Acceptance Capacity (WAC) idea (Decker & Purdy, 1988), for example, proposes that there is some "maximum wildlife population level in an area that is acceptable to people" (p. 53). Similar to the range of tolerable conditions in the norm literature (Vaske & Whittaker, 2004), the WAC concept suggests that a person's acceptance threshold is situation-specific and dependent on the severity of the human-wildlife interaction problem. These problems can be arranged along a continuum ranging from *nuisance* (e.g., raccoons dumping trash cans), to *economic or aesthetic* impacts (e.g., moose eating ornamental plants), to *health and safety threats* (e.g., Lyme disease transmitted by deer) (Decker, 1991). The more severe the problem, the more likely urban residents will accept lethal methods for managing wildlife. Suburbanites in New York, for example, were more willing to accept aesthetic or economic wildlife impacts (e.g., damage on ornamental plantings) than health risks (e.g., disease) (Connelly, Decker & Wear, 1987).

The WAC concept was refined (Carpenter, Decker & Lipscomb, 2000) with a more complex view of tolerance suggesting that WAC reflects the conditions necessary for optimum stakeholder acceptance of human-wildlife interactions. This view recognizes that people perceive both negative and positive impacts associated with wildlife, and that different stakeholders weigh the positives and negatives differently. While prior approaches suggest searching for a level of human-wildlife interactions that minimize negative impacts, this concept suggests looking for a level that maximizes net benefits.

Understanding public support for destroying problem wildlife is a complex phenomenon in even the most severe situations (Whittaker & Manfredo, 1997; Zinn et al., 1998). Although the same management tactics can be applied in a variety of situations, the acceptability of the tactic may vary depending on the species of animal. Variations in the animal's image, perceived abundance, and impact potential can also influence norms with respect to acceptability of destroying the animal. Coyotes, for example, are often portrayed as scavengers or pests (McIvor & Conover, 1994). As a result, destroying a coyote is more acceptable than destroying other animals (Wittmann, Vaske, Manfredo & Zinn, 1998).

An animal's potential to cause severe impacts also influences norms about their management. Beavers, coyotes, and mountain lions can all influence human activities, but in very different ways. Beavers can alter suburban landscapes with dams and resultant flooding, coyotes can kill pets, and mountain lions can kill humans. Each animal's behavior in conjunction with its reputation and potential for human impact influences the acceptability of destroying the animal (Zinn et al., 1998).

Overall, the structural norm approach and the WAC concept has provided the information necessary to: (a) define evaluative standards (i.e., acceptability) for specific management actions, (b) identify situations about which people feel strongly, and (c) describe the amount of agreement about a policy among the general public and/or various interest groups.

Motivation and Satisfaction
Substantial research in the 1970s was directed toward understanding recreationists' motivations or satisfactions. Motivation theory suggests that people are driven (i.e.,

BRENT ERB

motivated) to take actions to achieve particular goals (i.e., they seek certain outcomes from their experiences). Two enduring approaches to investigating motivations emerged in the literature. One, introduced by Hendee (1974), emphasized a multiple satisfaction approach to big game management. This approach suggested that we can identify and manage for groups of hunters who differ based on the types of satisfactions they receive.

Second, Driver and associates (Driver, Brown & Peterson, 1991) emphasized the importance of understanding the bundle of psychological outcomes recreationists desire and derive from participation. They also emphasized the insight gained by examining the setting and activity that is associated with those outcomes (e.g., benefits). Planning and managing for types of hunters were predicted to differ based on the mix of outcomes, activities and settings sought by participants (Hautolouma & Brown, 1978; Manfredo & Larson, 1993).

Several key understandings of hunters resulted from motivation and satisfaction research. First, hunters seek multiple satisfactions from hunting (e.g., companionship, nature appreciation) and are not homogeneous with respect to the satisfactions and benefits sought (Driver, 1976; Potter, Hendee & Clark, 1973). Second, hunters have a range of primary motivational orientations (e.g., affiliative, achievement, appreciative) (Decker, Brown, Driver & Brown, 1987). Third, the diversity of hunter motivations is manifested in a myriad of activity and experience preferences (Hautaluoma & Brown, 1978). Fourth, the primary motivations of hunters support several practical applications in hunting regulation (e.g., liberalized deer permits to increase utilization by permit holders) (Decker & Connelly, 1989).

Recognizing the diversity of experiences desired by participants in wildlife-related activities, researchers uncovered the importance of differentiating users into homogeneous and meaningful subgroups. Bryan (1977), for example, defines recreation specialization as a "continuum of behavior from the general to the particular, reflected by equipment and skills used in the sport" (p. 29). Within the continuum, individuals may range from the novice to the specialist. Variations between user classes reflect differences in motivations, the extent of prior experience with and commitment to an activity. As people become more specialized, they become more particular in their setting preferences and equipment. More specialized users are also more likely to have specific managerial requirements and more likely to communicate with managers. Research has applied the concept of specialization to angling (Bryan, 1977), hunting (Miller & Graefe, 2000), and wildlife viewing (McFarlane, 1996).

Domain Three: Management Application of HDWM Knowledge

The value of HDWM lies in the extent to which it leads to improved consideration of the *people aspects* of wildlife management. From our perspective, HDWM research has influenced wildlife policy and practice in three broad ways. First, the research has influenced wildlife policies. Illuminating Americans' interest in wildlife, for example, served as a building block for federal-level program initiatives that support non-game wildlife conservation. With respect to private land access, states have strengthened statutory protection against liability for landowners who allow uncompensated wildlife recreation on their property. In addition, landowner incentives have been created to allow access (e.g., state-run hunting cooperatives on private lands, posters indicating *access by permission only*, increased law enforcement consideration for cooperating landowners). Finally, states have established policies to improve recruitment (e.g., lowered hunting age, enhanced access) and retention of hunters (e.g., mentoring programs, land access programs, reduced license fees for older hunters).

Second, HDWM research has influenced wildlife management practices. For example, evaluative research has served to increase stakeholder involvement and improve decision making. Models have been developed that guide wildlife managers in designing stakeholder engagement (i.e., citizen participation, public involvement) processes. These efforts have identified key factors for community-based collaborative approaches, as well as elements leading to participant satisfaction with the process (Raik, Decker & Siemer, 2003; Schusler, Decker & Pfeffer, 2003).

Third, HDWM research has influenced education efforts and informed communication strategies. State hunter education programs, for example, have been expanded to include hunting ethics and landowner-sportsperson relations. State agencies have increased awareness among hunters of the importance of improving behavior and public image. Wildlife agencies have adopted proactive strategies for improving public understanding of hunting and trapping in North America and programmatic outreach for youth and women.

Conclusions

The evolution of HDWM has had a marked influence on wildlife management policy and practice. This chapter provided an overview of three broad, interrelated areas of research and application. Domain one concentrated on describing participants and monitoring trends in wildlife-related activities. Domain two emphasized understanding what people think and do with respect to wildlife, while domain three focused on incorporating the insights gained from HDWM research into management applications. The three domains represent a convenient way for summarizing the literature, but should not be construed as mutually exclusive. Work in all three domains continues today.

Many HDWM concepts and insights that now might be considered conventional wisdom are the result of what was regarded as pioneering effort a few years ago. While much has been learned from the integration of social sciences into wildlife management, much more remains to be explored. Those involved in HDWM need to (a) develop generalizations that can be used as tenets of management, (b) make existing knowledge more accessible to wildlife managers who do not have social science backgrounds, and (c) develop management models that integrate biological and human dimensions. The combination of more HDWM research and more effort to enhance wildlife managers' capacity to understand and integrate HDWM insights will lead to greater contributions to sound policy and management.

The need for establishing national baselines of public attitudes and values with respect to wildlife, human-wildlife interactions, and wildlife management approaches and practices is urgent. Public attitudes should be assessed at five to 10-year intervals to facilitate tracking of such attitudes, and determining possible shifts. Relating specific attitudinal orientations to demographic traits and socioeconomic trends regularly may lead to modeling, and even yield predictive ability that could prove valuable to wildlife management and wildlife recreation planners.

Looking forward, the role of community involvement and collaboration with wildlife management agencies will increase in importance, both internationally in situations involving communities located near protected areas, and in developed countries where overabundant wildlife are becoming a major concern in urban and suburban areas. In these and other situations research is needed to better understand how local communities and agencies can work together, including the processes of joint (social) learning and capacity-building for improved collaborative wildlife management.

As human-wildlife conflicts continue to grow globally, wildlife managers, elected officials and community leaders will continue to seek acceptable management actions. Human dimensions research can play a major role in helping managers and others identify the kinds of management actions that are appropriate for the kinds of impacts people experience from wildlife. This will continue to be a significant challenge for wildlife management, one that is likely to become even more daunting as new technologies (e.g., fertility control in wildlife) become available.

Experience has shown that human dimensions research is a valuable investment for effective management. The knowledge base needed for management of many wildlife issues often requires the output of sophisticated human dimensions inquiry. When the human and biological dimensions of wildlife management are well informed by research and effectively integrated, wildlife management can move forward. Although research into the human dimensions of wildlife management has made considerable progress over the last 35 years, many needs remain. These will be addressed as the changing nature and growing extent of interactions of people and wildlife indicate the need for continued human dimensions inquiry to serve wildlife management.

References

Barro, S. C., & Manfredo, M. J. (1996). Constraints, psychological investment, and hunting participation: Development and testing of a model. *Human Dimensions of Wildlife*, 1(3), 42-61.

Bishop, R. C., & Heberlein, T. A. (1979). Measuring values of extramarket goods: Are indirect measures biased? *American Journal of Agricultural Economics*, 61, 926-930.

Bowker, J. M, Newman, D. H., Warren, R. J., & Henderson, D. W. (2003). Estimating the economic value of lethal versus nonlethal deer control in suburban communities. *Society and Natural Resources*, 16, 143-158.

Brown, T. L., & Connelly, N. A. (1994). Predicting demand for big game and small game hunting licenses: The New York experience. *Wildlife Society Bulletin*, 22, 172-178.

Brown, T. L., Dawson, C. P., & Miller, R. L. (1979). Interests and attitudes of metropolitan New York residents about wildlife. *Transactions of the 44th North American Wildlife and Natural Resources Conference*, 44, 289-297.

Brown, T. L., Decker, D. J., & Kelley, J. W. (1984). Access to private lands for hunting in New York:1963-1980. *Wildlife Society Bulletin*, 12, 344-349.

Brown, T. L., Decker, D. J., Siemer, W. F., & Enck, J. W. (2000). Trends in hunting participation and implications for management of game species. In W. C. Gartner & D. W. Lime (Eds.), *Trends in outdoor recreation, leisure, and tourism* (pp. 145-154). New York: CABI Publishing.

Bryan, H. (1977). Leisure value systems and recreational specialization: The case of trout fishermen. *Journal of Leisure Research*, 9, 174-187.

Carpenter, L. H., Decker, D. J., & Lipscomb, J. F. (2000). Stakeholder acceptance capacity in wildlife management. *Human Dimensions of Wildlife*, 5, 5-19.

Chu, A., Eisenhower, D., Hay, M., Morganstein, D., Neter, J., & Waksberg, J. (1992). Measuring the recall error in self-reported fishing and hunting activities. *Journal of Official Statistics*, 8, 19-39.

Connelly, N. A., Decker, D. J., & Wear, S. (1987). Public tolerance of deer in a suburban environment: Implications for management and control. In N. R. Holler (Ed.), *Proceedings of the Third Eastern Wildlife Damage Control Conference* (pp. 207-218). Gulf Shores, AL: Auburn University.

Decker, D. J. (1991). Implications of the wildlife acceptance capacity concept for urban wildlife management. In E. A.Webb & S. Q. Foster (Eds.), *Perspectives in urban ecology* (pp. 45-53). Denver, CO: Denver Museum of Natural History.

Decker, D. J., Brown, T. L., Driver, B. L., & Brown, P. J. (1987). Theoretical developments in assessing social values of wildlife: Toward a comprehensive understanding of wildlife recreation involvement. In D. J. Decker & G. R. Goff (Eds.), *Valuing wildlife: Economic and social perspectives.* Boulder, CO: Westview Press.

Decker, D. J., Enck, J. W., & Brown, T. L. (1993). The future of hunting: Will we pass on the heritage? *Proceedings of the Annual Governor's Symposium on North American Hunting Heritage*, 2, 22-46.

Decker, D. J., Brown, T. L., & Siemer, W. F. (2001). *Human dimensions of wildlife management in North America.* Bethesda, MD: The Wildlife Society.

Decker, D. J., & Connelly, N. A. (1989). Motivations for deer hunting: Implications for antlerless deer harvest as a management tool. *Wildlife Society Bulletin*, 17, 455-463.

Decker, D. J., Provencher, R. W., & Brown, T. L. (1984). *Antecedents to hunting participation: An exploratory study of the social-psychological determinants of initiation, continuation, and desertion in hunting* (Outdoor Recreation Research Unit, Series No. 84-6). Ithaca, NY: Human Dimensions Research Unit, Cornell University.

Decker, D. J., & Purdy, K. G. (1988). Toward a concept of wildlife acceptance capacity in wildlife management. *Wildlife Society Bulletin*, 16, 53-57.

Driver, B. L. (1976). *Toward a better understanding of the social benefits of outdoor recreation participation.* Ashville, NC: Southeastern Forest Experiment Station, USDA Forest Service.

Driver, B. L., Brown, P. J., & Peterson, G. L. (Eds.). (1991). *Benefits of leisure.* State College, PA: Venture Publishing.

Fulton, D. C, Manfredo, M. J., & Lipscomb, J. (1996). Wildlife value orientations: A conceptual and measurement approach. *Human Dimensions of Wildlife*, 1(2), 24-47.

Hautaluoma, J. & Brown, P. J. (1978). Attributes of the deer hunting experience: A cluster-analytic study. *Journal of Leisure Research*, 10, 271-287.

Hendee, J. C. (1974). A multiple satisfaction approach to game management. *Wildlife Society Bulletin*, 1(2), 24-47.

Kellert, S. R. (1980). Americans' attitudes and knowledge of animals. *Transactions of the 45th North American Wildlife and Natural Resources Conference*, 45, 111-124.

Loker, C. A., & Decker, D. J. (1995). Colorado black bear hunting referendum: What was behind the vote? *Wildlife Society Bulletin*, 23(3), 370-376.

Loker, C. A., Decker, D. J. & Schwager, S. J. (1999). Social acceptability of wildlife management actions in suburban areas: 3 cases from New York. *Wildlife Society Bulletin*, 27, 152-159.

Manfredo, M. J. (2002). Planning and managing for wildlife viewing recreation: An introduction. In M. Manfredo (Ed.), *Wildlife viewing in North America: A management planning handbook* (pp. 1-8). Corvallis OR: Oregon State University Press.

Manfredo, M. J., & Larson, R. A. (1993). Managing for wildlife viewing recreation experiences: An application in Colorado. *Wildlife Society Bulletin*, 21, 226-236.

Manfredo, M. J., Zinn, H. C., Sikorowski, L., & Jones, J. (1998). Public acceptance of cougar management: A case study of Denver, Colorado, and nearby foothills areas. *Wildlife Society Bulletin*, 26, 964-970.

McFarlane, B. L. (1996). Socialization influences of specialization among birdwatchers. *Human Dimensions of Wildlife*, 1, 35-50.

McIvor, D. E., & Conover, M. R. (1994). Perceptions of farmers and nonfarmers toward management of problem wildlife. *Wildlife Society Bulletin*, 22, 212-219.

Miller, C. A., & Graefe, A. R. (2000). Degree and range of specialization across related hunting activities. *Leisure Sciences*, 22, 195-204.

Organ, J. F., & Ellingwood, M. R. (2000). Wildlife stakeholder acceptance capacity for black bears, beavers, and other beasts in the East. *Human Dimensions of Wildlife*, 5, 63-75.

Potter, D. R., Hendee, J. C., & Clark, R. N. (1973). Hunting satisfaction: Game, guns, or nature? *Transactions of the 38th North American Wildlife and Natural Resources Conference*, 38, 220-229.

Purdy, K. G., & Decker, D. J. (1989) Applying wildlife values information in management: The wildlife attitudes and values scale. *Wildlife Society Bulletin*, 17, 494-500.

Raik, D. B., Decker, D. J., & Siemer, W. F. (2003). Dimensions of capacity in community-based suburban deer management: The managers' perspective. *Wildlife Society Bulletin*, 31, 854-864.

Riley, S. J., & Decker, D. J. (2000). Risk perception as a factor in wildlife acceptance capacity for cougars in Montana. *Human Dimensions of Wildlife*, 5, 50-62.

Schusler, T. M., Decker, D. J., & Pfeffer, M. J. (2003). Social learning for collaborative natural resource management. *Society and Natural Resources*, 15, 309-326.

Teisl, M. F, Boyle, K. J., & Record, R. E. Jr. (1999). License-sales revenues: Understanding angler and hunter reactions to changes in license prices. *Human Dimensions of Wildlife*, 4(4), 1-17.

Whittaker, D., & Manfredo, M. J. (1997). *Living with wildlife in Anchorage: A survey of public attitudes* (Human Dimensions in Natural Resources Unit Summary Report No. 35). Fort Collins, CO: Colorado State University, Human Dimensions Unit.

Witter, D. J., & Shaw, W. W. (1979). Beliefs of birders, hunters, and wildlife professionals about wildlife management. *Transactions of the 44th North American Wildlife and Natural Resources Conference*, 44, 298-305.

Witter, D. J, Tylka, D. L., & Werner, J. E. (1981). Values of urban wildlife in Missouri. *Transactions of the 46th North American Wildlife and Natural Resources Conference*, 46, 424-431.

Wittmann, K., Vaske, J. J., Manfredo, M. J., & Zinn, H. C. (1998). Standards for lethal control of problem wildlife. *Human Dimensions of Wildlife*, 3(4), 29-48.

Wright, B. A., Brown, T. L., Cordell, H. K., & Rowell, A. L. (1988). *National private landowner study*. Athens, GA: USDA Southeast Forest Experiment Station.

Zinn, H., Manfredo, M. J., Vaske, J. J., & Wittmann, K. (1998). Using normative beliefs to determine the acceptability of wildlife management actions. *Society and Natural Resources*, 11, 649-662.

18

Human Dimensions of Fisheries

Robert B. Ditton

In their paper *Where's the Humanity? A Challenge and Opportunity for the Fisheries Community,* Voiland and Duttweiler (1984) challenged fisheries researchers to conduct human dimensions research, and fisheries managers to use it in decision-making. It is a relatively recent concern compared to biology, ecology, and other related fields of study. Fishery management is more than protecting common pool fish populations. It involves rules, regulations, conditions, methods and other measures which are required to maintain a fishery resource and which assure public benefits on a continuing basis (e.g., recreational opportunities, food production). Typically, this involves producing a maximum sustainable yield of fishery resources as modified by relevant economic, social, or ecological factors. It is important to note that fishery management involves more than just fish; it refers to a social system that includes fish, harvesters, as well as all involved with support infrastructure and related industries (Ditton, 1996). This chapter focuses on the human dimensions of recreational fisheries, provides background to human dimensions research, synthesizes important concepts, makes connections to management wherever possible, and points to future issues.

Definition of Recreational Fisheries
Three basic types of fishing exist in the United States: commercial, recreational, and subsistence. The social world of recreational fishing is substantial in size and of economic significance. In 2001, 34.1 million U.S. residents 16 years of age and older (about 16 percent) participated in recreational fishing. Overall, they spent $35.6 billion on fishing-related expenses during the previous year (U.S. Fish and Wildlife Service, 2002). Clearly, the reality exists to support human dimensions research related to fisheries.

Starting in 1955, the first of ten National Surveys of

Fishing, Hunting and Wildlife-Associated Recreation provided a national perspective on anglers and their fishing activity. Driver and Knopf (1976) first noted the need for fishery managers to better define the experiences they afford, and relate them to the needs of the angling public. To the extent managers understand the basic components of fishing motivation, Driver (1985) suggested they could be more effective in developing and extending programs and services.

While his research revealed a variety of reasons why people fish, Bryan (1974) concluded that catching and harvesting fish was relatively unimportant to anglers. Based on mean ranks and an assumption of group homogeneity, his findings were not well-received by fishery biologists and managers who interpreted this to mean fish were unimportant to the provision of fishing opportunities. To help managers get beyond their *average angler* focus, Bryan (1977) used an inductive research design to develop a conceptual framework for understanding and helping resource managers meet the wants and needs of the diversity of recreational anglers. He envisioned a continuum of participants that varied in terms of their behavior, attitudes, and preferences, and further, that some anglers progressed from one level of specialization to another over time.

Consideration of human dimensions in fisheries management ranges from being *optional* in most states to *required* in federal marine fisheries management. Since most fishery managers have natural science backgrounds with little if any background in the social sciences, there has been little overall integration of human dimensions information and understandings in fishery management decision-making.

Synthesis and Integration of Main Research Findings
The literature dealing with the human dimensions of recreational fishing is well developed for good reason. First, most fisheries management agencies have established research programs that are or can be easily expanded to include social science. Second, fishing is a potentially consumptive outdoor activity and thus of concern to management. Third, angler-generated license and tax revenues provide most of the funding needed for fisheries management, and consequently a means for funding related human dimensions research. Fourth, a licensing requirement provides a usable sampling framework for human dimensions studies not found with many other outdoor recreation activities.

Most of the basic deductive research in recreational fisheries has dealt with one or more of the following concepts and areas: 1) processes by which individuals are socialized into recreational fishing, 2) benefits sought from fishing, 3) demographics of the angler population in light of projected changes in the U.S. census and the implications for future participation, 4) diversity of the angler population in terms of specialization, and 5) how anglers make trade-offs in indicating preferences for management measures.

One important crosscutting area of concern in the understanding of fishing is the relatively recent epiphany that most previous outdoor recreation research studies focused mainly on Anglo males. Apparently, most researchers assumed that the male experience was representative of all participants (Henderson, 1994). While this group accounted for a majority of fishing participants when the studies were conducted (and still do today), understanding the remainder of the angler population (e.g.,

BRENT ERB

women, minority group members, urban dwellers, seniors) is now a high priority. Managers need better understandings of these groups to develop outreach programs that recognize basic differences in socialization processes, motivations, and recreation specialization levels. Management agencies will need to make use of stratified sampling designs (rather than simple random sample designs driven by least-cost factors) to understand these particular non-traditional angler groups.

Since 1992 there has been a significant decrease in the rate of fishing participation (the percent of the population that participates one or more days per year) at the national level (U.S. Fish and Wildlife Service, 2002). It appears that more people are being displaced from fishing than are being socialized into the activity despite numerous efforts to recruit new participants. That agency officials speak of *recruitment programs* rather than socialization processes perhaps suggests there is insufficient appreciation of the social processes involved.

Socialization to Fishing

Fishing is a social activity that typically involves family and friends. Within personal communities at home and at work, individuals share interests and activities and become socialized as a result (Burch, 1969). The nature of and process of social group composition is important for understanding the particular meanings that individuals attribute to their fishing participation. For example, going fishing with family is different in terms of experience outcomes sought than going fishing with friends from the neighborhood or workplace. Thus, the meanings attributed to fishing and the experiences sought are socially created by the groups involved.

Socialization into fishing involves the acquisition of the "skills, experience, relational norms, equipment, attitudes, and frequently the taste required for participation" (Kelly, 1974, p.182). While leisure socialization occurs from the cradle to the grave, much attention has been devoted to the childhood determination model of fishing participation (McGuire, Dottavio & O'Leary, 1987). Accordingly, participation in outdoor recreation activities is learned through childhood experiences. Particular skills and insights are learned from parents, peers, and educational programs during the early years (Kelly, 1974). Previous work has shown that most anglers started fishing during their pre-teen and adolescent years, and families and friends played a major role in providing opportunity, support and positive outcomes (Dann & Peyton, 1996; Siemer, Brown & Decker, 1989)

With a growing percentage of the U.S. population over 65 years of age, there is no guarantee that those who have been socialized into fishing will continue to participate when they become more constrained or lose their social circle of partners upon retirement or other life changes. Further, the size of the baby boom population cohort is too large to ignore those that were not socialized into fishing when they were young. Instead of concentrating programs only toward young people, efforts need to be focused on other age groups as well. Overall, little is known about the socialization processes of those with traditionally low rates of fishing participation previously; there is no reason to believe that results for young Anglo males will hold for young Anglo females or minority group members. And finally, it can be argued if current agency and non-governmental organization efforts to socialize young people into fishing were well-grounded, the rate of participation in recreational fishing would be increasing, rather than declining.

Demographic Change
Projected decreased rates of population growth, increased immigration, an aging population, and increased numbers and proportions of minority residents will all impact participation in recreational fishing in the U.S. (Murdock, Loomis, Ditton & Hoque, 1996). These conclusions are the result of linking age- and race/ethnicity-specific population projections with data on participation in recreational fishing to examine the future trends of angler numbers and characteristics. Results suggested that 1) the projected rate of increase in the angler population will not keep pace with population growth, and 2) that there will be older and larger minority sectors as a result of changes in population structure. The net growth in angler numbers will occur largely as a result of increases in the size of minority populations and immigration from other nations.

The increasing diversity of the angler population will require that managers have a better understanding of population subgroups with traditionally low rates of participation in fishing. We know the least about such groups in terms of their socialization processes and benefits sought from fishing. In addition, perhaps with greater attention to identifying and overcoming their constraints to participation, these groups will have higher rates of fishing participation in the future.

The demographic implications anticipated for recreational fishing (Murdock et al., 1996) have a high probability of occurring, but are not inevitable. If managers take no action in the face of demographic change, circumstances will be dictated solely by demographic forces, not by any managerial action. If managers make an effort to understand why some groups are more constrained from participating in recreational fishing than others, and take remedial action, the current trend in fishing participation rates may be reversed.

Fishing Motivations
Why people fish is a major topic of research interest; there are both catch and non-catch-related motivations involved. Most of the non-catch reasons for participating in recreational fishing are similar to other outdoor recreation activities: *relaxation, to be outdoors, to get away from the regular routine, be with friends.* Catch-related reasons, on the other hand, involve fishery resources, and the catching and retaining (or releasing) of fish caught. Fishery managers are concerned mainly with participants' catch-related motivations because: 1) fish are involved, and 2) managers often consider the remaining angler motivations to be exogenous to their responsibilities.

Various studies of angler populations have shown that motivations are diverse, just as they are for populations engaged in most other outdoor recreation activities. As Knopf, Driver, and Bassett (1973) first reported, anglers are motivated by four main factors: temporary escape, achievement, exploration, and experiencing natural settings. Besides the diversity of benefits sought from fishing, most previous research results indicate a low reported importance of catching and keeping fish (Fedler & Ditton, 1994). This has been frequently misinterpreted to mean that fishery resources are unimportant to recreational fishing, and this has led to disharmony between fishery managers and social scientists.

While the range of benefits sought is recognized on an intuitive basis, there has been a tendency to generalize motivation results from population studies to understanding angler motivations in specific contexts, (e.g., specific locations, fishing modes, species sought). From an ecological fallacy perspective (Babbie, 1998), motivational results from population studies would be expected to be artificial; they are an artifact of aggregating diverse angler groups. Overall, there are few motivational differences found between various populations of saltwater and freshwater anglers (Fedler & Ditton, 1994).

However, when anglers are grouped according to fishing mode or species sought, the importance of catch-related motivations varies significantly from population results. For example, the *challenge of fishing* and the *experience of the catch* were very important to angler sub-groups targeting large fish species, whereas they were less important to other angler groups (Fedler & Ditton, 1994). Likewise, some angler subgroups were much more interested to catch fish to eat, while others were fishing to obtain a trophy fish. Few differences were found at the sub-group level for non-catch motivations; thus, the non-catch reasons for participating in fishing appear to be almost universal to recreational fishing. While generalizations can be made from previous population-level studies as to why people fish, they are not very useful from a management perspective, which tends to be situation-specific.

Specialization

The concept of recreation specialization was first proposed by Bryan (1977) as a typology for understanding the diversity of participants in an activity. He defined specialization as "a continuum of behavior from the general to the particular as reflected by equipment and skills used in the sport and activity-setting preferences" (p. 175). Through interviews with trout anglers, he inferred a four-point continuum of specialization levels ranging *from occasional anglers* to *technique and setting specialists*. Significant differences have been observed in angler orientation, experience, relationships, and commitment along this theoretical dimension (e.g., Ditton, Loomis & Choi, 1992; Salz, Loomis & Finn, 2001). Accordingly, managers can use specialization as a conceptually-based means of segmenting anglers into groups. Since managers are not in a position to routinely administer in-depth questionnaires to anglers, however, they will require some basic indicators of specialization level that they can use to classify anglers for management purposes. Researchers need to develop some simple specialization indicators if this concept is to be implemented.

Much has happened in specialization research over the past 25 years. There is agreement that specialization involves a continuum of behavior, skills, and commitment, and therefore, single-item approaches to measuring specialization level have been replaced with multidimensional indices (e.g., Salz et al., 2001) to segment anglers into groups, despite concerns that an additive index "slights the complexity" of the specialization process (Kuentzel & McDonald, 1992, p. 269). However, disagreement remains as to the particular variables to be included, how they should be measured, and how the data should be analyzed.

There are several other issues regarding specialization worth noting: 1) specialization may be more appropriately applied at the *population*, rather than a *sub-population* or *site-specific* level, where anglers of a particular specialization level are already disproportionately represented, 2) many variables used to measure behavior and commitment are income-dependent; researchers may be measuring income rather than specialization, 3) Bryan's (1977) typology of four groups is negotiable; there may be any number of discrete specialization groups, 4) it is not clear how the specialization concept can be applied to other populations of recreational participants where there is no licensing provision or similar means for identifying the population, and 5) little is known about how gender, race and ethnicity groups fit with current identified specialization levels. A disproportionate number of anglers from these groups might be toward the low end of the specialization continuum because of their presumably recent socialization into fishing. Or, perhaps the variables historically used to measure specialization are not appropriate for today's more diverse population.

Also, as Scott and Shafer (2001) point out, specialization can be viewed as a developmental process with a progression in behaviors, skills, and commitment for some over time. The issue of movement along the specialization continuum has always garnered much attention, but requires a longitudinal study design to ascertain whether the process is linear or inevitable. Cross-sectional research designs will not be useful for answering these questions.

Specialization remains an exciting research area because of the complexity and enormity of the concept, and a lack of agreement on just about everything about it. A facilitated workshop involving the major players would help clarify where there is agreement and disagreement, and developing a meaningful research agenda for the future. This could lead to a comprehensive programmatic effort.

Preferences for Management Regulations

The area of angler preferences for particular harvest regulations has received much less research attention than most of the aforementioned research areas, yet it is one of the most important to fishery managers. Many managers want feedback from anglers on particular management strategies prior to final decision-making. They want to know which regulatory alternatives are more palatable. Traditional research designs require respondents to indicate if they support or oppose each of several harvest restrictions presented (e.g., a proposed minimum size of 14 inches, a bag limit of four fish). This is a *revealed preference* approach (Louviere & Timmermans, 1990). Unfortunately, the approach does not yield insight to the relative importance of each of the harvest restrictions to anglers and the tradeoffs they are willing to make when considering restrictions jointly. For example, when anglers indicate support for a decreased bag limit, they also may support the harvest of additional fish over the maximum size.

Discrete choice conjoint models (or *stated preference* or *choice* models) make use of hypothetical scenarios to derive individuals' preferences (Louviere & Timmermans, 1990). This approach assumes that complex decisions are based not on one factor or criterion, but on several considered jointly. Various forms of stated preference models have been used to understand angler preferences for management alternatives (Aas, Haider & Hunt, 2000; Gillis & Ditton, 2002; Roehl, Ditton, Holland & Perdue, 1993). Results allow investigators to understand how anglers combined their preferences for various management measures under consideration and the relative influence of each management measure. Also, as demonstrated by Hunt, Haider, and Armstrong (2002), this approach holds much potential for confirming that important human dimensions concepts such as social group, substitution, and motivations are statistically related to anglers' harvest decisions. This approach has potential for extending important lines of inquiry in research areas that appear stalled due to a reliance on revealed preference methods. However, due to the complexity of designs and results, managers may be reluctant to use these approaches to gain insight into the utility of various combinations of preference attributes and levels, and may choose instead to continue to believe that preference items should be rated independently.

Issues for the Future

While human dimensions is an emerging area in fisheries management, some managers still consider it exogenous to their responsibilities. Or perhaps, they are afraid that if they ask anglers too many questions, they may have to be responsive to their input. Further, many fisheries agencies depend mainly on available social and economic data from the National Survey of Fishing, Hunting, and Wildlife-Associated Recreation for their human dimensions understandings.

Other issues are whether human dimensions research by social scientists will be funded and used by fishery managers, and whether fisheries biologists should be conducting the human dimensions research. Managers probably feel more comfortable with biologists' explanations for observed events. While the outdoor recreation literature provides a well-grounded peer-reviewed basis for a deductive research approach to understanding the human dimensions of fisheries, these benefits are probably not appreciated to any great extent by managers with little or no social science background.

If managers are to reverse the decline in fishing participation with effective socialization efforts, be more responsive to angler needs and wants, and manage fishery resources and clientele on a scientific and sustainable basis, they will need a much greater understanding of and appreciation for the role of human dimensions research in fishery management. Doing human dimensions research is one thing; applying it appropriately to management decision-making is quite another.

Where Do We Go From Here?

Human dimensions of fisheries research is at a crossroads in fisheries management. If managers are to make greater use of the human dimensions literature, they must first acquire a comprehensive view of fisheries management. If they fail to appreciate the social components of resource management, believe that biology and ecology provide all of the answers, or do not value research from outside of the traditional fishery science field, they are not likely to put much stock in the existing human dimensions literature provided by social scientists.

Concurrently, there is an alarming trend of human dimensions research conducted by biologists that have little or no social science training. This research is mostly inductive in orientation and is not likely to withstand rigorous peer review by social scientists. Much of this research could qualify as *junk science* in that there are often faulty data and analyses and an underlying agenda whereby fishery resource concerns outweigh human concerns. As human dimensions researchers seek to produce the best scientific information available, their research will increasingly be subjected to independent peer review, where the only peers are social scientists. Greater communication and outreach efforts between human dimensions researchers and the fishery management community are required to resolve these issues.

References

Aas, O., Haider, W., & Hunt, L. (2000). Angler responses to harvest regulations in Engerdal, Norway: A conjoint based choice modeling approach. *North American Journal of Fisheries Management*, 20, 940 - 950.

Babbie, E. (1998). *The practice of social research*. Eighth edition. Belmont, CA: Wadsworth Publishing Company.

Bryan, H. (1977). Leisure value systems and recreational specialization: The case of trout fishermen. *Journal of Leisure Research*, 9, 174 – 187.

Bryan, R. C. (1974). *The dimensions of a saltwater sport fishing trip, or what do people look for in a fishing trip besides fish?* Vancouver, BC: Environment Canada, Fisheries and Marine Service, Southern Operations Branch.

Burch, W. R. (1969). The social circles of leisure. *Journal of Leisure Research*, 1, 125-148.

Dann, S. L., & Peyton, R. B. (1996). Facing realities in recruiting, retaining, and training consumptive fish and wildlife users. *Transactions of the North American Wildlife and Natural Resources Conference*, 61, 315 – 323.

Ditton, R.B. (1996). Human dimensions in fisheries. In A. Ewert (Ed.), *Natural resource management: The human dimension* (pp. 73 – 90). Boulder, CO: Westview Press.

Ditton, R. B., Loomis, D. K., & Choi, S. (1992). Recreation specialization: Reconceptualization from a social worlds perspective. *Journal of Leisure Research*, 24, 35 –51.

Driver, B. L. (1985). Specifying what is produced by management of wildlife by public agencies. *Leisure Sciences*, 7, 281 – 296.

Driver, B. L., & Knopf, R. C. (1976). Temporary escape: One product of sport fisheries management. *Fisheries*, 1(2), 21 – 29.

Fedler, A. J., & Ditton, R. B. (1994). Understanding angler motivations in fisheries management. *Fisheries*, 19(4), 6 –12.

Gillis, K. S., & Ditton, R. B. (2002). A conjoint analysis of the U.S. Atlantic billfish fishery management alternatives. *North American Journal of Fisheries Management*, 22, 1218 -1228.

Henderson, K. A. (1994). Broadening an understanding of women, gender, and leisure. *Journal of Leisure Research*, 26, 1 – 7.

Hunt, L., Haider, W., & Armstrong, K. (2002). Understanding the fish harvesting decisions by anglers. *Human Dimensions of Wildlife*, 7, 75 – 89.

Kelly, J. R. (1974). Socialization toward leisure: A developmental approach. *Journal of Leisure Research*, 6, 181 –193.

Knopf, R. C., Driver, B. L., & Bassett, J. R. (1973). Motivations for fishing. *Transactions of the North American Wildlife and Natural Resources Conference*, 38, 191- 204.

Kuentzel, W. F., & McDonald, C. D. (1992). Differential effects of past experience, commitment, and lifestyle dimensions of river use specialization. *Journal of Leisure Research*, 24, 269 – 28.

Louviere, J. J., & Timmermans, H. (1990). Stated preference and choice models applied to recreation research: A review. *Leisure Sciences*, 12, 9 – 32.

McGuire, F. A., Dottavio, F. D., & O'Leary, J. T. (1987). The relationship of early life experiences to later life leisure involvement. *Leisure Sciences*, 9, 251-257.

Murdock, S.H., Loomis, D. K., Ditton, R.B., & Hoque, M. N. (1996). The implications of demographic change for recreational fisheries management in the United States. *Human Dimensions of Wildlife*, 1, 14-37.

Roehl, W. S., Ditton, R. B., Holland, S.M., & Perdue, R. R. (1993). Developing new tourism products: Sportfishing in the southeast United States. *Tourism Management*, 14, 279 - 288.

Salz, R. J., Loomis, D. K., & Finn, K. L. (2001). Development and validation of a specialization index and testing of specialization theory. *Human Dimensions of Wildlife*, 6, 239 – 258.

Scott, D., & Shafer, C. S. (2001). Recreational specialization: A critical look at the construct. *Journal of Leisure Research*, 33, 319- 343.

Siemer, W. F., Brown, T. L., & Decker, D. J. (1989). *An exploratory study of Lake Ontario's boating salmonid anglers: Implications for research on fishing involvement* (HDRU Series No. 89-4). Ithaca, NY: Cornell University, Department of Natural Resources, Human Dimensions Research Unit.

U. S. Fish and Wildlife Service. (2002). *National survey of fishing, hunting, and wildlife-associated recreation*. Washington, DC: U. S. Fish and Wildlife Service.

Voiland, M. P., & Duttweiler, M. W. (1984). Where's the humanity? A challenge and opportunity for the fisheries community. *Fisheries*, 9(4), 10 –12.

19

Conflict in Natural Resource Recreation

Alan R. Graefe

Brijesh Thapa

Rapid growth in outdoor recreation following the Second World War led to competition over land and water resources, and subsequently conflict ensued between participants engaged in various recreation activities (Owens, 1985). Early research conceptualized recreation conflict as simply competition over the same resources by several competing activity groups (Devall & Harry, 1981), and/or incompatibilities between activities, groups or their respective goals (Bury, Holland & McEwen, 1983; Noe, Wellman & Buhyoff, 1982). Common findings in this research were that conflict seemed likely between users and non-users of mechanized recreation, and that conflict was often one-way, or asymmetrical. For example, cross-country skiers disliked their encounters with snowmobilers, but snowmobilers did not mind cross-country skiers (Jackson & Wong, 1982). Likewise, motorboaters held positive attitudes towards paddling canoeists, but paddling canoeists disliked the motorboaters (Adelman, Heberlein & Bonnicksen, 1982).

More recent research has also documented examples of conflict between participants of non-motorized activities. For example, an asymmetric antipathy existed between hikers and stock users whereby hikers disliked stock users and reported that encounters with stock users were undesirable (Watson, Niccolucci & Williams, 1994). To date, recreation conflict research has examined numerous combinations of activities that include cross-country skiers and snowmobilers (Jackson & Wong, 1982; Jackson, Haider & Elliot, 2002); motorized versus non-motorized rafters (Nielsen & Shelby, 1977; Shelby, 1980); water skiers and fishermen (Gramann & Burdge, 1981); off-road vehicles (ORV) users and bathers (Noe et al., 1982); hikers and mountain bike riders (Carothers, Vaske & Donnelly, 2001; Ramthun, 1995; Watson, Williams & Daigle, 1991); canoeists and motorboaters (Adelman et al., 1982); skiers and snowboarders (Baird, 1993; Thapa, 1996; Thapa & Graefe, 1999, 2003, in press; Vaske,

Carothers, Donnelly & Baird, 2000; Vaske, Dyar & Timmons, in press; Williams, Dossa & Fulton, 1994); hikers and stock users (Watson et al., 1994); helicopter skiers and backcountry users (Gibbons & Rudell, 1995); hikers, stock users and llama packers (Blahna, Smith & Anderson, 1995); hunters and non-hunters (Vaske, Donnelly, Wittman & Laidlaw, 1995); walkers, runners, in-line skaters, and bicyclists (Moore, Scott & Graefe, 1998); and walkers and mountain bikers (Cessford, 2002).

In spite of the extensive body of research on recreation conflict, accumulation of knowledge has been limited by inconsistent measurement and other methodological issues. For example, conflict has been operationalized based on whether participants found their encounters with others to be desirable or undesirable (Jackson & Wong, 1982; Watson et al., 1994), or whether encounters with other participants interfered with or affected one's goals or enjoyment (Moore et al., 1998; Thapa, 1996; Watson et al., 1991). Conflict has also been viewed from a normative perspective rather than based on goal interference theory (Carothers et al., 2001; Vaske et al., 1995). In light of these methodological issues, the purpose of this chapter is three-fold: first, to describe the dominant goal interference model as well as alternative approaches to studying recreation conflict; second, to provide a critical review of the various ways conflict has been measured; and third, to dispel several myths about recreation conflict.

Models of Recreation Conflict

Goal Interference Model

Jacob and Schreyer (1980) defined recreation conflict as "goal interference attributed to another's behavior" (p. 369). This definition has been widely accepted and has received some support in empirical research. According to this model, for conflict to occur, there must be social contact, direct or indirect. Direct contact refers to face-to-face encounters with another group, such as a cross-country skier encountering a snowmobiler. Indirect contact refers to the presence or evidence of certain behaviors, as in a cross-country skier seeing a snowmobiler's tracks. While research based on this model typically focuses on conflicts between different activities, certain non-activity based behaviors such as littering, drunkenness, noise, and rowdiness have also been reported as sources of serious conflict, and fall under the purview of the goal interference model (Jackson & Wong, 1982; Jackson, et. al., 2002; Rudell & Gramann, 1994; Todd, 1987). Gibbons and Ruddell (1995) further point out that goal interference does not necessarily imply goal incompatibility, as various groups may share the same goals but pursue incompatible ways of achieving those goals.

Jacob and Schreyer (1980) identified four major factors that contribute to conflict. A single factor alone may be sufficient to cause conflict but, in most circumstances, a combination of factors will occur. The first factor, *activity style*, denotes that individuals who are intensely involved in an activity have specific objectives, expectations, well-defined goals, high experience and skill levels, and are consequently more likely to experience conflict. The second factor, *resource specificity*, relates to attachment to a recreation resource. Recreationists who are possessive and consider the qualities of the recreation site to be exceptional when compared to other sites are more likely to experience conflict than those recreationists who lack attachment to the specific resource. The third factor, *mode of experience*, refers to ways of perceiving and experiencing the environment. Participants may be engaged in the "focused" or "unfocused" mode. Focused mode participants are very sensitive toward the particular details of the environment and are more likely to experience conflict when encountered with unfocused participants, as their recreational goals are different. The final factor, *tolerance for lifestyle diversity*, refers to the "tendency to accept or reject lifestyles different from one's own" (p. 370). Participants who are unwilling to share resources and are intolerant towards different lifestyles are more likely to experience conflict. Also, individuals are more likely to be tolerant of others who they perceive as similar to themselves.

Subsequent researchers have added support to the effects of Jacob and Schreyer's (1980) factors affecting conflict. In support of the resource specificity factor, Gibbons and Ruddell (1995) found a positive relationship between place attachment and conflicts among backcountry winter recreationists. Thapa (1996) elaborated on the role of tolerance in conflict perceptions. Other authors have suggested additional factors that might influence conflict perceptions. Among demographic variables, Thapa and Graefe (1999) found that perceptions of conflict and tolerance among skiers and snowboarders were related to age and gender. In this case, much of the effect was indirect in the sense that age and gender influenced the choice of activity, which in turn affected the participants' tolerance and perceived conflict. Gibbons and Ruddell (1995) also found a positive association between goal orientation and conflict; goal interference was greater for goals that were more important.

Social Values Conflict

Vaske et al. (1995) introduced the theoretical distinction between interpersonal and social values conflict. They noted that interpersonal conflicts between hunters and non-hunters on Mt. Evans, Colorado have been minimized by natural visual barriers and agency regulations that reduce encounters between the two activity groups. They suggest that conflicts that do exist between these groups stem from differences in social values held by hunters and non-hunters. Such conflicts can occur independently of actual contact between the two groups. Identification of interpersonal conflict and social value conflict was accomplished through a series of questions about potential conflicting behaviors. The behaviors included both hunting (e.g., seeing hunters, hearing shots, seeing an animal being shot) and non-hunting (e.g., seeing people feed wildlife, people harassing wildlife, dogs chasing wildlife) behaviors. Respondents were asked how often they had seen each of these behaviors during their visits to Mt. Evans and the extent to which they perceived each behavior to be a problem.

Combining these variables produced a conflict typology. Individuals who did not consider the behavior to be a problem were classified in the *no conflict* group, regardless of whether they had seen the behavior or not. Those who had seen a behavior and considered it a problem were assigned to the *interpersonal conflict* group. Those who had never observed the behavior but still considered it to be a problem were interpreted to be reporting a conflict in *social values*. Not surprisingly, the likelihood of observing the conflicting events increased with increasing rates of visitation. Both hunters and non-hunters judged the non-hunting behaviors as more problematic than the hunting events, largely reflecting the fact that these behaviors were more commonly seen.

In a subsequent study, Carothers et al. (2001) examined social values versus interpersonal conflict among hikers and mountain bikers. This study built on earlier social values research by comparing conflict perceptions of not only hikers and mountain bikers, but also of those who participate in both activities (the majority of respondents). In this case, conflict was expected to result from interpersonal behavior more than from differing social values because of the overlapping participation and similarity of the activities. Conflict was measured in the same way as in the Vaske et al. (1995) study. Respondents reported the incidence and acceptability of four hiking-related and six mountain biking-related behaviors selected from the most commonly reported complaints in the area. As expected, all three groups reported more interpersonal conflict than social values conflict. For all three groups, less conflict was reported for hiking than for mountain biking. Generally, the perceptions of dual-sport participants fell in between those of the two exclusive activity groups. Overall, results differed from those of the Mt. Evans hunter/non-hunter study, in which social values conflict was more evident. Further research is needed to explain when and where social values conflicts are more likely to occur.

Other Approaches to Conflict

Some researchers have suggested thinking about recreation conflict in terms of a process. Ramthun (1995), for example, attempted to build on the goal interference model by incorporating sensitivity to interference as a new element in the conflict perception process. Rather than tolerance leading to perceptions of conflict, however, he suggested it is more realistic to assume a reciprocal relationship between sensitivity to interference and attributions of conflict.

Schneider and Hammitt (1995) viewed conflict more as a process than an event, and focused on both the perceptions of and responses to conflict situations. They used the psychological concept of stress to define conflict, and theorized that conflict can result from stress induced by any type of obstruction between recreationists and their goals. In understanding how people respond to conflict situations, Schneider and Hammitt (1995) suggested various appraisal and coping mechanisms. Schuster (2000) followed with further research on the coping processes individuals use to respond to situations that are appraised as stressful. Two basic types of coping strategies are recognized: 1) emotion-focused coping and 2) problem-solving coping (Lazarus & Folkman, 1984).

In the crowding literature, emotion-focused coping behaviors (Hammitt & Patterson, 1991) such as product shift, rationalization, and displacement have been empirically documented, with displacement being the most common coping mechanism investigated (Shelby & Heberlein, 1986; Shelby, Bregenzer & Johnson, 1988). In a study of visitor response to stress in Glacier National Park, Miller (1997) found that visitors who encountered levels of interaction that exceeded their expectations perceived higher levels of stress than those who encountered what they had expected. Higher levels of stress are believed to lead to behavioral coping mechanisms like displacement, while lower stress levels are more likely dealt with through cognitive coping strategies. In a recent study, Schneider (2000) found that visitors to two urban-proximate recreation areas in the southwestern U.S. most often used emotion-focused coping responses (e.g., distancing themselves) to conflict. However, nearly 20 percent of the visitors that did experience conflict were displaced from the areas.

Measuring Recreation Conflict

A limiting factor in the literature on recreation conflict is the lack of consensus about its operationalization. Unlike related research areas such as recreational crowding, where measurement instruments have been replicated in many areas, almost every study of conflict has used its own measurement tools.

In reviewing previous research, it is immediately apparent that there is little consistency across studies. One notable finding is that virtually none of the measures have actually used the term *conflict*. Rather, they focus on respondents' likes and dislikes, problems encountered, reactions to various types of encounters, or other attitudinal ratings. Numerous researchers have tried to operationalize Jacob and Schreyer's (1980) definition of conflict by focusing on goal interference. However, few have measured conflict in agreement with that definition (Watson, 1995). Some have assumed that goal interference had occurred or considered only certain aspects or causes of goal interference. For example, Devall and Harry (1981) asked recreationists about activities that might interfere with their enjoyment of recreation, but did not ascertain whether the interference resulted from lack of attainment of goals, or whether it was due to behavior of other recreationists. Watson et al. (1991) asked a more specific question about behavior of others interfering with enjoyment, and then assumed any interference with enjoyment was a result of goal interference. Only Todd (1987) fully implemented Jacob and Schreyer's (1980) definition of goal interference due to the behavior of others. He asked river users a series of questions beginning with identification of the importance of a list of goals, interference with any goals that had any importance, and reasons for the goal interference. Todd's approach was cumbersome, but allowed for separation of goal interference that could be considered conflict (i.e., caused by others' behavior) versus goal interference due to other reasons. The open-ended reasons for interference also allowed examination of conflict resulting from within one's own activity, as well as the more typical conflict between different activities.

Given the complexity of measuring conflict, it is no surprise that many researchers have used multiple approaches within a single conflict study. Some have developed a conflict index based on ratings of various problems encountered, along with a more direct question about the extent to which other visitors' presence or behavior affected one's enjoyment (Moore et al., 1998; Thapa, 1996). Others have used as many as three different approaches to assess potential conflict situations (Adelman et al., 1982; Watson et al., 1991; Watson et al., 1994). While alternative measures offer validation and further insight into conflict, divergent results for different measures raise questions about whether the sources of conflict are real or merely an artifact of measurement.

Studies of conflict resulting from differing social values are not immune to measurement problems either. As in the goal interference model, measures of social values conflict require a complex sequence of questions. First, it is necessary to

213

Table 1. Summary Of Conflict Measures

Conflict Approach	Activities Examined	Conflict Measure	Citation(s)
Goal Interference	Multiple activities	"One of the problems in many recreation areas is activities which interfere with a person's own enjoyment. Below you will find a list of activities which might interfere with your enjoyment of recreation. Please indicate how you feel about each activity by marking an 'X' for degree of interference."	Devall & Harry (1981)
Goal Interference	Water skiers and fisherman	Based on recreational goals and behavior. Perceived conflict was a result of incompatible goals and behavior.	Gramann & Burdge (1981)
Goal Interference	Off-road vehicle users (ORV), non ORV users (pedestrians)	Attitudinal ratings toward the operation of vehicles and their effects, non ORV users' effects, and control of use. Considered a more general attitude toward the potential conflict group.	Noe, Wellman & Buhyoff (1982)
Like/Dislike	Cross-country skiers and snowmobilers	Three complementary sets of indicators of perceived conflict were used. These were views about encountering the other group, likes and dislikes of the other group using the same area, and statements about understanding the other group.	Jackson & Wong (1982)
Like/Dislike	Canoeists and motorcraft users	Three measures based on 1. competition for resources 2. expressed reactions to other user visitors 3. Actual encounters (disliked, neutral, enjoyed).	Adelman, Heberlein & Bonnicksen (1982)
Goal Interference	Canoeists, kayakers, rafters, anglers	Series of questions focusing on goal interference: 1. Rate importance of a series of goals (5-point scale), 2. Rate degree of interference with goals 3. Obtain reasons for goal interference	Todd (1987)

Goal Interference, Like/Dislike	Mountain bikers and hikers	Three conflict measures: 1. Feelings of enjoyment, dislike, or neutrality toward encounters with various types of groups on trails ("dislike" responses were considered conflict). 2. Has the behavior of any individual or group interfered with enjoyment of visits to the area. "Yes" responses (interpreted as goal interference) were followed with questions to identify the type of group that interfered. 3. Respondents were asked to rate the extent of potential problems encountered during their visit/s to the site (5-point scale, *small problem* to *big problem*).	Watson, Williams & Daigle (1991)
Goal Interference	Canoeists and motorboaters	Multiple-item scale (5-point Likert scale format): Encounters with motorboats decreased the enjoyment of my trip; My contact with people in motorboats interfered with the quality of my experience; Encounters with canoes decreased the enjoyment of my trip; My contact with people in canoes interfered with the quality of my experience.	Ivy, Stewart & Lue (1992)
Goal Interference	Winter visitors to Padre Island National Seashore (windsurfers, anglers, tent campers, RV campers, waders, picnickers, snorkelers, motorboaters)	Noise-induced conflict measured by visitor ratings of amount of interference with their recreation activity that would be caused by (5-point scale, *never interfere* to *interfere very much*). Activity-based versus non-activity-based conflict measured by ratings of how much 19 different behaviors would interfere with experiences they identified in a series of goal-importance questions (5-point scale, *never interfere* to *interfere very much*).	Ruddell & Gramann, (1994)

215

Table 1. Summary Of Conflict Measures (continued)

Goal Interference, Like/Dislike, Desirable/Undesirable	Hikers and recreation stock users	Three conflict measures used: 1. Feelings of enjoyment, dislike, or neutrality toward encounters with various types of groups. 2. Ratings (*very desirable* to *very undesirable*) to encountering other groups. 3. Ratings of whether the behavior of any group interfered with enjoyment of past visits to the wilderness.	Watson, Niccolucci & Williams (1994)
Goal Interference, Like/Dislike	Llama packers and other backcountry visitors (hikers and horseback riders)	Three conflict measures used: 1. Evaluations of encounters. Response format included *enjoyed meeting them, did not mind meeting them, disliked meeting them, or did not meet any.* 2. Extent to which meeting different user groups interfered with enjoyment of the visit. Response format was a *little, somewhat, or a lot.* 3. Ratings of 18 problems in the study area, four dealing with impacts of llamas, four with impacts of horses, and the rest with other resource management problems like crowding, litter, etc. (5-point scale).	Blahna, Smith & Anderson (1995)
Goal Interference	Hikers and mountain bikers	Two conflict measures used: 1. Sensitivity to interfering behaviors: "If you encountered the following behaviors on the Big Water Trail, how much would they interfere with . . . important experiences" (response to 24 common trail behaviors, scale = never interfere to interfere very much). 2. Conflict attribution: "On your last visit to the Big Water Trail did any of the above behaviors actually cause you problems?" (Yes/No).	Ramthun (1995)
Goal Interference	Helicopter skiers and non-motorized backcountry users	Goal interference conflict was measured by asking respondents to rate a set of interferences they experienced and attributed to helicopter skiing and discourteous behavior. Interferences were rated on a 5-point scale.	Gibbons & Rudell (1995)

Social Values	Hunters and non-hunters	Perceived conflict was operationalized though combination of responses from two sets of questions: 1. Responses related to observation of the frequency of occurrence of six events during their visit to the site. 2. Based on the responses to the events, respondents reported whether certain events were a problem (slight, moderate, or extreme problem)	Vaske, Donnelly, Wittmann & Laidlaw (1995)
Goal Interference Interpersonal Behavior	Alpine skiers, and snowboarders	Two measures of conflict: 1. *"How did the presence or behavior of any [snowboarders/skiers] you might have seen affect your enjoyment of the trails?"* (7-point scale) 2. Index based on ratings of a list of potential problems representing forms of goal interference due to another's behavior (7-point scale)	Thapa (1996)
Goal Interference Interpersonal Behavior	Walkers, runners, in-line skaters and bicyclists	Two measures of conflict: 1. *"How did the presence or behavior of any (walkers, runners, in-line skaters and bicyclists) you might have seen affect the quality of your trail experience?"* (7-point scale) 2. Index based on ratings of a list of potential problems representing forms of goal interference due to another's behavior (7-point scale)	Moore, Scott & Graefe (1998)
Coping with Stress	Visitors at an urban-proximate wilderness and developed area	Conflict perception (dichotomous yes/no measure)	Schneider (2000)

Table 1. Summary Of Conflict Measures (continued)

Goal Interference Interpersonal Behavior	Alpine skiers and snowboarders	A multiple item index to measure observed unacceptable behaviors between skiers and snowboarders. Six specific items listed for both groups categorized in a 5-point Likert scale (rarely, sometimes, frequently and almost always).	Vaske, Carothers, Donnelly & Baird (2000)
Social Values Interpersonal Behavior	Hikers and mountain bikers	Perceived conflict was operationalized though a combination of responses from two sets of questions: 1. Responses related to the observation of ten events that were commonly reported complaints received from hikers and mountain bikers. 2. Based on the responses to the events, respondents reported whether certain events were unacceptable.	Carothers, Vaske & Donnelly (2001)
Goal Interference Interpersonal Behavior	Walkers and mountain bikers	Two conflict measures used: 1. Respondents were asked if seeing [walkers/bikers] had, or would have, affected their enjoyment of the track. 2. Items based on ratings of a list of potential problems representing forms of goal interference due to bikers' behavior (3-point scale).	Cessford (2002)
Goal Interference Interpersonal Behavior	Skiing, snowmobiling and other winter sports	Two conflict measures used: 1. Respondents were asked the relative importance of their motivations to participate using 26 items (REP motivation scales), and then to report if these motivational goals were achieved. 2. Visitor perception of potential problem items – those related to inter-group conflict included noise associated with motorized or non-motorized users, and activities of motorized or non-motorized users."	Jackson, Haider & Elliot (2002)

identify how often certain problematic events occurred, and then how much they were considered a problem. Some difficulties of interpretation remain even with these two questions, as it is difficult to attribute the source of conflict for those who have both seen an event and considered it a problem (Vaske et al., 1995). Furthermore, the report of social values conflict may be a reflection of one's own values and philosophies rather than a level of conflict at the area in question. Their responses might be considered a measure of potential conflict, since they are speculating about behaviors that they believe exist even though they have not experienced them.

Inconsistent measurement of recreation conflict has limited theory development and accumulation of knowledge about its incidence, causes and consequences. Why have researchers failed to reach consensus on this issue, and why don't they just ask recreationists how much conflict they have experienced? To be sure, few recreationists have read Jacob and Schreyer's (1980) article, or any paper about conflict for that matter. But can't we still ask them about conflict even if we are not sure they understand the technical definition of conflict in the recreation literature? This is precisely what we have done in crowding studies, where we routinely ask visitors how crowded they feel in various situations. However, knowing how crowded people feel tells us little about how the quality of their experience was affected by the density of visitors. It is necessary, but not sufficient, to ask recreationists how much crowding or conflict they have experienced. We must follow this question with questions assessing how the quality of their experience was impacted (positively or negatively) by the conditions that they have experienced. In addition, from a managerial perspective, it is also important to understand visitors' responses and coping behaviors, as conflict intensity may be associated with aggressive behaviors and/or reduced frequency of visitation to the site (Schneider, 2000).

Myths About Recreation Conflict

Review of previous research on recreation conflict suggests that there are several myths or misconceptions that need further consideration. Some of these myths are based in truth but have become overgeneralizations, while others represent discrepancies between commonly held perceptions and research findings.

Myth 1: Conflict is high and growing. Based on the fact that participation in various outdoor recreation activities has increased significantly over the past decades, many papers begin with a statement to the effect that conflict between some particular activities is rampant and likely to grow in the future. Hence, with growth in participation, innovation in new activities, and increased accessibility, the potential for recreation conflict is considered to be high.

Empirical studies, however, have generally found low rates of conflict. Blahna et al. (1995) found few conflicts or problems related to the introduction of a non-traditional user group (e.g., llama users) in two wilderness areas. Both Vaske et al. (2000) and Thapa and Graefe (in press) found low levels of conflict between skiers and snowboarders. As noted above, the amount of conflict found depends on how the conflict was measured. Some of the conflicts reported could more accurately be called *general attitudes* or *predispositions* toward conflict. In addition, conflict is often lower than expected because recreationists use coping behaviors and similar mechanisms to reduce or eliminate conflict (Schneider, 2000; Schneider & Hammitt, 1995; Schuster, 2000).

Myth 2: Conflict is caused by mechanized and motorized activities. While this notion was the impetus for much early conflict research, more recent studies show that conflict is more complicated than that. The underlying causes of conflict, both interpersonal and social values-related, cut across all types of recreation activities. Many recent studies have focused on different non-mechanized activities that share a common resource base, such as ski areas or hiking trails.

Myth 3: Conflict is between different activities. Conflict can be as great or greater within the same activity as it is between different activities. While earlier studies were generally limited to conflicts caused by other activities, some researchers have included both in-group and out-group comparisons in their assessments. Thapa (1996) found that skiers were as likely to attribute conflict to other skiers as they were to snowboarders. Todd (1987) found that conflict among Delaware River canoeists was more likely to be caused by other canoeists than other water-based recreationists like motorboaters, tubers or rafters. Additionally, the intra-activity conflicts among river users were more likely to result from other members of one's own group (intra-group conflict) than from other canoeists (inter-group conflict).

Some conflict is not activity-based, but rather, based on undesirable behaviors that may be exhibited by participants in any activity. Gibbons and Ruddell (1995) found more goal interference attributed to discourteous behavior than to encounters with helicopter skiers. Todd (1987) also found that some conflicts perceived by canoeists resulted from non-activity based behaviors such as littering, noise, and drunken/rowdy behavior.

Myth 4: Conflict is asymmetrical. While this has been true in some instances, it is not necessarily the case. An asymmetrical antipathy was found between hikers and stock users whereby hikers disliked the stock users and reported that encounters with stock users were undesirable (Watson et al., 1994). Asymmetrical conflicts have also been documented between hikers and trail bikers (Ramthun, 1995; Watson et al., 1991), and water skiers and fishermen (Gramann & Burdge, 1981). Such one-way conflict relationships may be due to stereotyping and may lead to managerial actions such as limiting use by the outgroups.

Several studies have found resentment and dislike in both directions, however (Thapa, 1996; Vaske et. al., 2000). The symmetry of conflict relationships becomes more complicated when more than two activities occur in a given setting. For example, Blahna et al. (1995) found that hikers experienced more negative encounters with llama users than with horse users. The issue of symmetry should not be assumed, but should be examined in detail in every potential conflict situation.

Myth 5: More experienced recreationists are more sensitive to conflict. Level of experience with an activity is embedded in Jacob & Schreyer's (1980) activity style factor of recreation conflict. Experienced recreationists are expected to have better skills, be more focused and have more defined goals than less experienced recreationists. These characteristics should make experienced users less tolerant than beginners of goal interference due to others' behavior. While some research has supported this relationship, other studies have found different results. Ramthun (1995) found years of experience to be a significant predictor of sensitivity to conflict among hikers and mountain bikers, but in the opposite direction of what was hypothesized. Instead of more experienced hikers and bikers being more sensitive to the behaviors of the other group, the more experienced users tended to be less sensitive. Ramthun theorized that the unexpected finding might have resulted from more clear expectations on the part of more experienced recreationists, or user displacement.

Conclusion

We have come a long way since the initial views of conflict as simply competition or incompatibility between different activities occurring in the same setting. Over time, various theoretical approaches to recreation conflict have been proposed and tested. Research applications have expanded beyond traditional backcountry settings and now include urban areas as well as the built environment. Yet, we still cannot answer the very basic question, "How much conflict is out there?" It seems like the answer depends on several variables, including the type of conflict and the particular types of recreationists who may be in conflict with each other. Recreation researchers should try to build on the existing database and develop more consistent measures of conflict in the future. Better and more consistent measurement will allow us to effectively answer questions such as, "How much conflict exists in a given situation?", "How do levels of conflict in different areas compare with each other?", and "How can resource managers best manage recreation areas to minimize user conflict and maximize the quality of the visitor experience?"

References

Adelman, B. J., Heberlein, T. A., & Bonnicksen. T. M. (1982). Social psychological explanations for the persistence of a conflict between paddling canoeists and motorcraft users in the Boundary Waters Canoe Area. *Leisure Sciences,* 5, 45-61.

Baird, B. (1993). *Recreation conflict between skiers and snowboarders.* Unpublished master's thesis, Colorado State University, Fort Collins, CO.

Blahna, J. D., Smith, S. K., & Anderson, A. J. (1995). Backcountry llama packing: Visitor perceptions of acceptability and conflict. *Leisure Sciences,* 17, 185-204.

Bury, R.L., Holland, S. M., & McEwen, D. N. (1983). Analyzing recreational conflict: Understanding why conflict occurs in requisite to managing that conflict. *Journal of Soil and Water Conservation,* 3(5), 401-403.

Carothers, P., Vaske, J. J., & Donnelly, M. P. (2001). Social values versus interpersonal conflict among hikers and mountain bikers. *Leisure Sciences,* 23, 47-61.

Cessford, G. (2002). Perception and reality of conflict: Walkers and mountain bikes on Queen Charlotte track in New Zealand. In A. Arnberger, C. Brandenburg., & A. Muhar, A. (Eds.), *Proceedings of the monitoring and management of visitor flows in recreational and protected areas,* (pp. 102-108). Vienna, Austria: Bodenkultur University.

Cordell, H. K. (1999). *Outdoor recreation in American life: A national assessment of demand and supply trends.* Champaign, IL: Sagamore Publishing Inc.

Devall, B., & Harry, J. (1981). Who hates whom in the great outdoors: The impact of recreational specialization and technologies of play. *Leisure Sciences*, 4, 399-418.

Gibbons, S., & Rudell, J. E. (1995). The effect of goal orientation and place dependence on select goal interferences among winter backcountry users. *Leisure Sciences*, 17, 171-181.

Gramann, J. H., & Burdge, R. J. (1981). The effect of recreation goals on conflict perception: The case of water skiers and fishermen. *Journal of Leisure Research*, 13, 15-27.

Hammitt, W. E., & Patterson, M. E. (1991). Coping behavior to avoid visitor encounters: Its relationship to wildland privacy. *Journal of Leisure Research*, 24 (4), 638-646.

Ivy, M. I., Stewart, W., & Chi-Chuan, L. (1992). Exploring the role of tolerance in recreational conflict. *Journal of Leisure Research*, 24, 348-360.

Jackson, E. L., & Wong, R. A. (1982). Perceived conflict between urban cross-county skiers and snowmobilers in Alberta. *Journal of Leisure Research*, 14, 47-62.

Jackson, S., Haider, W., & Elliot, T. (2002). Resolving inter-group conflict in winter recreation: Chilkoot Trail National Historic Site, British Columbia. In A. Arnberger, C. Brandenburg, & A. Muhar, (Eds.), *Proceedings of the monitoring and management of visitor flows in recreational and protected areas*, (pp. 109-114). Vienna, Austria: Bodenkultur University.

Jacob, G. R., & Schreyer, R. (1980). Conflict in outdoor recreation: A theoretical perspective. *Journal of Leisure Research*, 12, 368-380.

Lazarus, R. S. & Folkman, S. (1984). *Stress, appraisal and coping*. New York: Springer Publishing.

Miller, T. A. (1997). *Coping behaviors in recreational settings: Substitution, displacement, and cognitive adjustments as a response to stress.* Unpublished doctoral dissertation, University of Montana, Missoula.

Moore, R. L., Scott, D., & Graefe, A. R. (1998). The effects of activity differences on recreation experiences along a suburban greenway trail. *Journal of Park and Recreation Administration*, 16(2), 35-53.

Noe, F. P., Wellman, J. D., & Buhyoff, G. (1982). Perception of conflict between off-road and non off-road vehicle users in a leisure setting. *Journal of Environmental Systems*, 11(3), 223-233.

Owens, P.L. (1985). Conflict as a social interaction process in environment and behavior research: The example of leisure and recreation research. *Journal of Environmental Psychology*, 5, 243-259

Ramthun, R. (1995). Factors in user group conflict between hikers and mountain bikers. *Leisure Sciences*, 17(3), 159-169.

Ruddell, E. J., & Gramann, J. H. (1994). Goal orientation, norms, and norm-induced conflict among recreation area users. *Leisure Sciences*, 16, 93-104.

Schneider, I. E. (2000). Responses to conflict in urban-proximate areas. *Journal of Park and Recreation Administration*, 18(2), 37-53.

Schneider, I. E. & Hammitt, W. E. (1995). Visitor response to on-site recreation conflict. *Journal of Applied Recreation Research*, 20 (4), 249-268.

Schuster, R. (2000). *Coping with stressful situations and hassles during outdoor recreation experiences in wilderness environments.* Unpublished doctoral dissertation, Clemson University, Clemson, SC.

Shelby, B., & Heberlein, T. (1986). *Carrying capacity in recreation settings.* Corvallis, OR: Oregon State University Press.

Shelby, B., Bregenzer, H., & Johnson, R. (1988). Displacement and product shift: Empirical evidence from two Oregon rivers. *Journal of Leisure Research*, 20, 274-288.

Thapa. B. (1996). *The role of tolerance in recreational conflict: The case of adult skiers and snowboarders.* Unpublished master's thesis, The Pennsylvania State University, University Park, PA.

Thapa, B., & Graefe, A.R. (1999). Gender and age group differences in recreational conflict and tolerance among adult skiers and snowboarders. In H.G. Vogelsang, (Ed.), *Proceedings of the 1998 Northeastern recreation research symposium* (General Technical Report NE-241, pp. 219-226). Radnor, PA: USDA Forest Service, Northeastern Forest Experiment Station.

Thapa, B. & Graefe, A. R. (2003). Level of skill and its relationship to recreation conflict and tolerance among adult skiers and snowboarders. *World Leisure*, 45(1), 15-27.

Thapa, B. & Graefe, A. R. (in press). Recreation conflict and tolerance among skiers and snowboarders. *Journal of Park and Recreation Administration.*

Todd, S. L. (1987). *Level of experience and perception of conflict among canoeists on the Delaware River.* Unpublished master's thesis, The Pennsylvania State University, University Park, PA.

Vaske, J. J., Carothers, P., Donnelly, M. P., & Baird, B. (2000). Recreation conflict among skiers and snowboarders. *Leisure Sciences*, 22, 297-313.

Vaske, J. J., Donnelly, M. P., Wittman, K., & Laidlaw, S. (1995). Interpersonal versus social value conflict. *Leisure Sciences*, 17, 205-222.

Vaske, J. J., Dyar, R., & Timmons, N. (in press). Skill level and recreation conflict among skiers and snowboarders. *Leisure Sciences.*

Watson, A. E. (1995). An analysis of recent progress in recreation conflict research and perceptions of future challenges and opportunities. *Leisure Sciences*, 17, 235-238.

Watson, A. E., Niccolucci, M. J., & Williams, D. R. (1994). The nature of conflict between hikers and recreational stock users in the John Muir Wilderness. *Journal of Leisure Research*, 26, 372-385.

Watson, A. E., Williams, D. R., & Daigle, J.J. (1991). Sources of conflict between hikers and mountain bike riders in the Rattlesnake NRA. *Journal of Park and Recreational Administration*, 9(3), 59-71.

Williams, P. W., Dossa, K. B., & Fulton, A. (1994). Tension on the slopes: Managing conflict between skiers and snowboarders. *Journal of Applied Recreation Research*, 19(3), 191-213.

20

A Synthesis of Tourism Research Topics

Joseph T. O'Leary

Xinran You Lehto

Chia-Kuen Cheng

Yoon-Jung Oh

Tourism has grown into an important and coherent field of academic research in the second half of the 20th century (Meyer-Arendt & Justice, 2002). Researchers acknowledge that tourism is a multi-faceted phenomenon. This is a reflection of the complexity of the tourism experience, the domain of human activity where a wide scope of organizations and business services join together to cater to the needs of travelers while managing the impact of this activity on the host communities. Disciplinary inputs to the tourism field come from many disciplines including psychology, anthropology, sociology, economics, geography and management. While many established social science disciplines provided the conceptual and methodological foundations for tourism research and education, there seems to be an increasing orientation towards a business administration and management emphasis (Dann and Phillips, 2000). With tourism identified as the leading economic activity in the world and the shifting business patterns brought upon by the changes in technology affecting the distribution of information and delivery of tourism products and services, these changes and shifts in research attention come as no surprise.

Changes in research attention raise questions about important areas of investigation in tourism research. The purpose of this chapter is to provide an overview of the recent research trends in tourism and identify leading areas of investigation.

Synthesis of Findings

Trends are different from predictions. Predictions are educated guesses of future events, but trends are based on historic precedents. In order to understand tourism research trends, it is necessary to review recent tourism research. Therefore, this chapter synthesizes trends based on a cataloging process where recent tourism publications were viewed and categorized. The cataloging framework suggested by Jafari (1977) and Jafari and Ritchie (1981) was employed with some modest modifications. The topic reviews were based on an examination of almost 50 years of dissertation topics and publications in the past five years in three of the major tourism journals: *Annals of Tourism Research (ATR), Tourism Management (TM),* and the *Journal of Travel Research (JTR).* A total of 723 journal papers were reviewed and indexed using titles, keywords and abstracts (see Table 1).

The number of articles about a given theme (e.g., *tourism marketing, host-guest* relationships) certainly serves as one indicator of the importance and influence of a particular tourism topic. In this review, many topics emerged based on a measure of how often they appeared in the literature. This measure, in addition to quality indicators provided by processes such as the Social Science Citation Index, help identify the trends and topics that are most important and salient to natural resource and tourism practitioners, and researchers, today.

From 1999 to 2003, the most popular tourism topics in the three journals included marketing, planning and development, host-guest relationships, tourism management, and travel motivation. More than half of the reviewed papers were related to one of these five categories. Marketing, planning and development, and host-guest relationships were especially prevalent: They collectively accounted for about one-fifth of the 723 papers. From the popularity of papers, strong interest was expressed in sustainable development and "how to" promotion of tourism destinations.

However, while most tourism journals acknowledge the multi-disciplinary nature of the field, each has its own its focus. For instance, in the past five years the *Annals of Tourism* has demonstrated a tendency toward publishing conceptual and theoretical development, including an emphasis on social psychological and anthropological analyses of tourism. *Tourism Management* and *Journal of Travel Research* have a decidedly more practical bent. They are clearly more focused towards empirical applications of theories and models, and their practical implications for tourism organizations.

Host-guest Relationships

One key agenda in tourism research is analysis of host-guest relationships through social psychological and anthropological analysis. In fact, host-guest relationships appear to be one of the most dominant themes across all publications. The focal points of these discussions are the authenticity of the tourism experience and the social impact of tourism on the host community.

With the emergence of heritage and/or culture-based tourism in recent years, challenges as to how academics conceptualize authenticity have been presented in numerous discussions. Such theoretical debate has implications for the tourism industry regarding how to measure the perceived authenticity of tourism experiences (Waitt, 2003). Research concerning the authenticity of tourism experience adopts the guest approach: the concern about the authenticity from the tourist's perspective. When a tourism product involves the representation of another or the past -- especially in ethnic, history, heritage or culture tourism -- authenticity becomes a concern.

Wang's (1999) article is a critical piece on the issue of authenticity. Further advancing the two conventional definitions of authenticity (i.e., *objective* and

Category	1999	2000	2001	2002	2003	Total
Marketing of Tourism	27	35	31	37	22	152
Tourism Planning and Development	22	25	16	22	8	93
Host-Guest Relationship	27	13	14	22	14	90
Management of Tourism Organizations	12	12	21	5	13	63
Motivation	6	15	16	19	6	62
Design with Nature	8	7	10	16	6	47
Research Methodology	22	6	11	5	1	45
Economic Implications	9	10	12	8	2	41
Sociology of Tourism	9	5	8	7	4	33
Role of Hospitality in Tourism	5	6	2	4	3	20
Tourism Education	3	5	1	5	5	19
World Without Border (Political)	3	3	5	2	3	16
Recreation Management	2	1	2	3	4	12
Rural Tourism	2	2	3	4		11
Tourism Laws	3	2	2		2	9
Fundamental of Transportation	1	1	3	1	1	7
Geography of Tourism		1			2	3
Total	161	149	157	160	96	723

Table1. Research Papers by Topic of Three Major Tourism Journals (1999-2003)

constructive), Wang proposes a third dimension: *existential*. He suggested that both objective and constructive authenticity are object-related notions, whereas existential authenticity more effectively explains activity-related tourism experiences, such as shopping or visiting friends and relatives. Existential authenticity is further classified into two different dimensions: intra-personal and inter-personal. This article has been cited frequently and contributes significantly to the body of knowledge in tourism host-guest relationships.

A second theme frequently addressed is the social impact of tourism on the host community. This is a "host" approach: the issue about preserving the authenticity and tradition of the host community. Although discussion on development of cultural and heritage tourism and its benefits has been center stage, more attention has been paid to whether the development contributes to or depreciates the very existence of the local cultural and heritage resources. For example, Palmer (1999) argues that heritage tourism contributes positively to the construction and maintenance of national identity. A step further, Tucker (2001), suggested that host communities are in a position to negotiate both their own traditional identity in the presence of tourists, and their personal quests and experiences as a result of their close interactions with tourists. The article challenges the assumptions that host communities must remain authentically traditional to meet the expectations of the tourists.

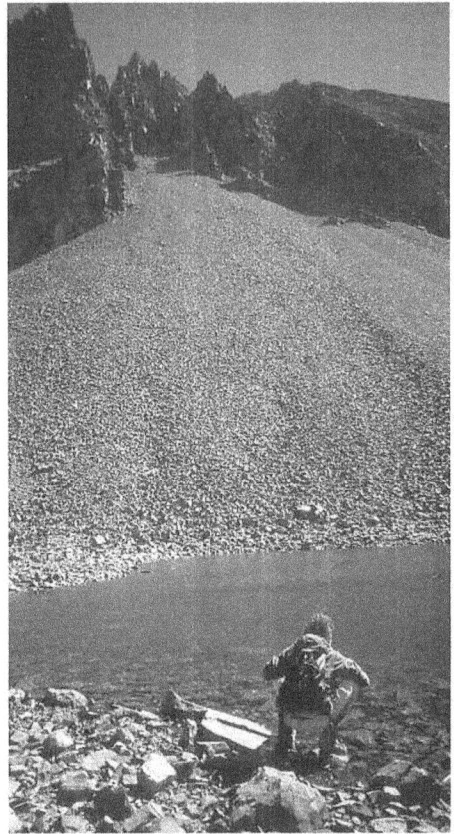

BRENT ERB

Tourism Product Planning and Development

Tourism product planning and development, especially in that of cultural and heritage attractions as well as regional development, has had high visibility in recent research. Involving stakeholders in the planning and development process has been a much discussed issue. For instance, Ritchie (1999) argued that optimum destination planning requires that a destination have a value-driven vision, one that includes the values and perspectives of the stakeholders, rather than a market-driven vision.

The concept of participatory development has been frequently discussed in the literature. Public participation in tourism in both the decision-making process and in the benefits of tourism development has been viewed as a paradigm to healthy and sustainable tourism development. Participatory development has also been explored and applied in the context of developing countries, with discussion about the constraints that exist within such countries for its successful implementation (Timothy, 1999). The main constraints were identified as: a) cultural and political traditions, b) poor economic conditions, c) lack of expertise, and d) lack of understanding by residents.

Various models have been proposed to actively and effectively involve stakeholders. Tourism development and planning tends to involve entities both from the public and private sectors. As a result, inter-organizational collaboration and partnerships in destinations have been considered as an effective planning framework. Bramwell and Sharman (1999) revisit the issue of collaboration among stakeholders in the process of destination development, and further enhance this model by presenting an analytical framework to assess whether local collaborative arrangements are inclusive and involve collective learning and consensus-building.

Another prominent topic is the issue of sustainability, related to the relationship and balance between conservation and use. Garrod and Fyall (2000) argue that there is a close association between the fundamental elements of the heritage mission and the widely acknowledged principles of sustainable development. Their study investigates the major constraints and imperatives relating to the long-term management of built heritage attractions. One major constraint is that heritage establishment tends to place more emphasis on conservation and education, and less on contemporary use and local community. As a result, heritage managers tend to reject the practice of applying the so-called "user pays principle" and, as a result, frequently lack financial resources for the development of sustainable products.

Tourism Marketing

Tourism marketing themes are very persistent in virtually all three journals. The most prominent issues appear to be destination image, internet marketing and market segmentation. An emphasis for the journals is often to publish significant theoretical pieces that outline a theme or direction for subsequent research. One example is Woodside and Dubelaar's (2002) article that discussed a conceptual framework for thoughts, decisions, activities and behaviors in a before, after and during trip timeframe. Other examples include Botha, Crompton and Kim's (1999) competitive positioning models; Bonn, Furr and Susskind's (1999) model of internet user segmentation; and Buhalis' (2000) model of marketing the competitive destination of the future.

Among all marketing issues, *destination image* appeared to receive the most attention. Image has emerged as a crucial marketing concept in the tourism industry, and its research has reflected several different perspectives. These include the relationship of image to destination choice, the image formation process, image modification and change, and image measurement (Baloglu & Shoemaker, 2001; Kim & Richardson, 2003; Murphy, Pritchard & Smith, 2000; Prentice & Andersen, 2003; Uysal, Chen & Williams, 2000).

Baloglu and McCleary's (1999) article is frequently cited within destination image literature. Their research suggested a model of the important determinants of destination image formation and empirically tested the framework. The authors found that travel motivations and travelers' characteristics appear to play a key role in image formation, in addition to stimulus factors such as cognitive perception of destination attributes, information sources and affective factors.

Image modification due to incidental factors are also explored extensively in previous research. For instance, the effect of a festival on destination image modification is examined by Prentice and Andersen (2003). The authors study the effect of Edinburg's festival positioning and its impact on the overall image modification of Scotland. The study revealed that the festival is judged successful in its international arts positioning in terms of the core of serious repeat tourists it attracts, but much less so in modifying the image of Scotland as a landscape and tradition destination.

The impact of organic information sources such as motion pictures and similar coverage has also been addressed extensively. Kim and Richardson (2003) examined the powerful role of autonomous image formation agents such as news coverage and popular culture (e.g., films, television programs, literature) and discovered that motion pictures increase the awareness of the places they depict, and have strong tourist-inducing effects.

Technology and Tourism

Another key topic in the literature and research is the issue of technology, especially the Internet and its profound impact on tourism organizations and travelers. Frew (2000) indicated that the number of research articles on this topic increased tenfold from 1988 to 1999. Since information is viewed as the lifeblood of the tourism industry, the technological revolution brought upon by the Internet has driven a process of business re-engineering. While researchers are tackling the issue from many perspectives, three major research trends can be identified.

The first area that has received increasing research attention centers around applications of information technology (IT) in tourism organizations, online business models and business strategies. There are a number of forces encouraging the tourism industry to adopt different business models and develop different markets in response to IT. Connell and Reynolds (1999) focused on IT implications on tourist information centers; Siguaw, Enz and Namasivayam (2000) examined the utilization of IT in hotel sectors; and Yuan, Gretzel, and Fesenmaier (2002) identified the key factors influencing the adoption of IT by conventions and visitors bureaus.

A number of articles have focused on propositions of business models for electronic tourism markets and strategies for their development. For instance, Buhalis and Licata (2002) discussed the evolution and adaptation model of the traditional global distribution systems that supported travel agents to the new concept of Internet-based eMediaries. According to the research, the Internet created the conditions for emergence of new eMediaries based on three ePlatforms: 1) Internet, 2) interactive digital television, and 3) mobile devices. The new eMediaries include a variety of organizations including suppliers (e.g., airlines, hotels) selling direct on the Internet, web-based travel agents, Internet portals and vortals, and auction sites. The expected proliferation of digital television and eCommerce will gradually intensify competition further. As a result, traditional eMediaries must re-engineer their business processes in order to remain competitive.

The integration of the online virtual community strategies within the overall business strategy has also been a focal point. The growing online travel consumers market and online communities have also contributed to a growing market environment that demands research attention. Wang, Yu and Fesenmaier (2002) proposed a theoretical foundation based upon the core characteristics of a virtual community and the fundamental needs of community members. Perspectives of how one can define and interpret virtual communities within the tourism industry are discussed and issues related to the functions of virtual communities are explored from members' viewpoints.

Tourism website performance evaluation appears as another much discussed area, especially in regards to quality of information. With the dramatic expansion of online information, information overload and online trust are common discussion points in recent research. Different methodologies and criteria have been developed and used to evaluate the performance of websites of different industry sectors

(Doolin, Burgess & Cooper, 2002; Tierney, 2000; Wan, 2002).

Other researchers propose and empirically test models that profile and compare travelers who are engaged in online travel-related activities such as information searching and online reservation booking. For instance, adoption and diffusion models have been frequently proposed and tested in an attempt to better understand online travel behaviors (Bonn, Furr & Susskind, 1999; Susskind, Bonn & Dev, 2002; Weber & Roehl, 1999). Researchers have indicated that information technology will be one of the important trends for tourism industry (Butler & Jones, 2001; Cetron, 2001; Gartner & Lime, 2000). While research is tackling the issue, the technology is developing with amazing speed. As a result, research gaps still exist and there is ever stronger demand in researching the IT arena.

Implications and Conclusions

As a global phenomenon, tourism has become a leading economic activity in almost 70 percent of the states in the U.S., and represents a very important economic contributor in many nations of the world. As observed from this research effort, a major focus of much of the tourism research is the heavy emphasis on *application*. The goal clearly seems to be making a difference in the way in which public and private organizations manage, plan or develop policies and strategies. The emphasis on application is probably tied to sources of funding and expectations for deliverables. It is also likely that the research will have implications for both rural and urban areas, and public and private agencies, particularly in terms of issues such as social and economic impacts, development, markets, infrastructure and stakeholder involvement. Tourism research will also have to be examined in light of its relationship to the longstanding research done in recreation, with the obvious linkage to activities, or products.

From the review of the three major tourism journals, there are several areas of scholarship that overlap, as previously identified. It is likely that in the short term, the leading research areas identified at the outset in this review will continue to lead the topic list. Behavioral studies that include attention to items such as demographics, experiences, product development, attitudes, motivation and satisfaction continue to grow, as is attention to the role, use and adoption of IT. The presentation of a number of theoretical models also suggests many opportunities for conceptual development and testing.

Tourism organizations are faced with unparalleled challenges and opportunities. To survive and thrive, organizations should respond by investing in research that will assist in developing innovative models of doing business and new ways of making and delivering products and services. For example, IT has contributed to the birth of new communities and cultures that cross the boundaries of geographic regions and nations. These new cultures in the virtual space will inevitably shape strong forces that will lead businesses into new ways of operating, learning and governing themselves in the dynamic commercial forefront. They also change at rates much faster than what has been experienced previously. In addition, experience marketing is likely to emerge in the research, following Pine and Gilmore's (1999) book *The Experience Economy*. Certainly in the natural resource and recreation arena, the experience area has been prominent in frameworks such as the Recreation Opportunity Spectrum.

Overall, new knowledge and information through research will be imperative for tourism businesses to successfully adapt, react and take advantage of these forces in order to stay competitive, enhance conservation and sustainability, and develop a strong vision for their future success.

References

Baloglu, S., & McCleary, K. W. (1999). A model of destination image formation. *Annals of Tourism Research*, 26(4), 868-897.

Baloglu, S., & Shoemaker, S. (2001). Prediction of senior travelers' motorcoach use from demographic, psychological, and psychographic characteristics. *Journal of Travel Research*, 40(August), 12-18.

Bonn, M. A., Furr, H. L., & Susskind, A. M. (1999). Predicting a behavioral profile for pleasure travelers on the basis of Internet use segmentation. *Journal of Travel Research*, 37(May), 333-340.

Botha, C., Crompton, J. L., & Kim, S. S. (1999). Developing a revised competitive position for Sun/Lost City, South Africa. *Journal of Travel Research*, 37(May), 341-352.

Bramwell, B., & Sharman, A. (1999). Collaboration in local tourism policymaking. *Annals of Tourism Research*, 26(2), 392-415.

Buhalis, D. (2000). Marketing the competitive destination of the future. *Tourism Management*, 21(1), 97-116.

Buhalis, D., & Licata, M. C. (2002). The future eTourism intermediaries. *Tourism Management*, 23(3), 207-220.

Butler, R., & Jones, P. (2001). Conclusions- problems, challenges and solutions. In A. Lockwood & S. Medlik (Eds.), *Tourism and hospitality in the 21st century* (pp. 296-309). Oxford, England: Butterworth-Heinemann.

Cetron, M. (2001). The world of today and tomorrow: The global view. In A. Lockwood & S. Medlik (Eds.), *Tourism and hospitality in the 21st century* (pp. 18-28). Oxford, England: Butterworth-Heinemann.

Connell, J., & Reynolds, P. (1999). The implications of technological developments on tourist information centres. *Tourism Management*, 20(4), 501-509.

Dann, G., & Philips J. (2000). Qualitative tourism research in the late twentieth century and beyond. In B. Faulkner, G. Moscardo and E. Laws (Eds.), *Tourism in the 21st Century*, (pp. 247-265). New York: Continuum.

Doolin, B., Burgess, L., & Cooper, J. (2002). Evaluating the use of the Web for tourism marketing: A case study from New Zealand. *Tourism Management*, 23(5), 557-561.

Frew, A. J. (2000). Information and communications technology research in the travel and tourism domain: Perspective and direction. *Journal of Travel Research*, 39(November), 136-145.

Garrod, B., & Fyall, A. (2000). Managing heritage tourism. *Annals of Tourism Research*, 27(3), 682-708.

Gartner, W. C., & Lime, D. W. (2000). So what? Implications of trends for management, public policy, marketing and planning. In W. C. Gartner & D. W. Lime (Eds.), *Trends in Outdoor Recreation, Leisure and Tourism* (pp. 403-413). New York: CABI Publishing.

Jafari, J. (1977). Editor's page. *Annals of Tourism Research*, 5 (Sp. No.), 6-11.

Jafari, J., & Ritchie, J. R. B. (1981). Toward a framework for tourism education: Problems and prospects. *Annals of Tourism Research*, 8(1), 13-34.

Kim, H., & Richardson, S. L. (2003). Motion picture impacts on destination images. *Annals of Tourism Research*, 30(1), 216-237.

Meyer-Arendt, K. J., & Justice, C. (2002). Tourism as the subject of North American doctoral dissertations, 1987-2000. *Annals of Tourism Research*, 29(4), 1171-1174.

Murphy, P., Pritchard, M. P., & Smith, B. (2000). The destination product and its impact on traveler perceptions. *Tourism Management*, 21(1), 43-52.

Palmer, C. (1999). Tourism and the symbols of identity. *Tourism Management*, 20(3), 313-321.

Pine, B. J., & Gilmore, J. H. (1999). *The experience economy*. Boston: Harvard Business School Press.

Prentice, R., & Andersen, V. (2003). Festival as creative destination. *Annals of Tourism Research*, 30(1), 7-30.

Ritchie, J. R. B. (1999). Crafting a value-driven vision for a national tourism treasure. *Tourism Management*, 20(3), 273-381.

Siguaw, J. A., Enz, C. A., & Namasivayam, K. (2000). Adoption of information technology in U.S. hotels: Strategically driven objectives. *Journal of Travel Research*, 39(2), 192-201.

Susskind, A. M., Bonn, M. A., & Dev, C. S. (2002). To look or book: An examination of consumers' apprehensiveness toward Internet use. *Journal of Travel Research*, 41(3), 256-264.

Tierney, P. (2000). Internet-based evaluation of tourism Web site effectiveness: Methodological issues and survey results. *Journal of Travel Research*, 39(2), 212-219.

Timothy, D. J. (1999). Participatory planning: A view of tourism in Indonesia. *Annals of Tourism Research*, 26(2), 371-391.

Tucker, H. (2001). Tourists and troglodytes: Negotiating for sustainability. *Annals of Tourism Research*, 28(4), 868-891.

Uysal, M., Chen, J. S., & Williams, D. R. (2000). Increasing state market share through a regional positioning. *Tourism Management*, 21(1), 89-96.

Waitt, G. (2003). Social impacts of the Sydney Olympics. *Annals of Tourism Research*, 30(1), 194-215.

Wan, C. S. (2002). The web sites of international tourist hotels and tour wholesalers in Taiwan. *Tourism Management*, 23(2), 155-160.

Wang, N. (1999). Rethinking authenticity in tourism experience. *Annals of Tourism Research*, 26(2), 349-370.

Wang, Y. C., Yu, Q., & Fesenmaier, D. R. (2002). Defining the virtual tourist community: Implications for tourism marketing. *Tourism Management*, 23(4), 407-417.

Weber, K., & Roehl, W. S. (1999). Profiling people searching for and purchasing travel products on the World Wide Web. *Journal of Travel Research*, 37(3), 291-298.

Woodside, A. G., & Dubelaar, C. (2002). A general theory of tourism consumption systems: A conceptual framework and an empirical exploration. *Journal of Travel Research*, 41(November), 120-132.

Yuan, Y., Gretzel, U., & Fesenmaier, D. R. (2002). Internet technology use by American convention and visitors bureaus. *Journal of Travel Research*, 41(3), 240-255.

21

Environmental and Natural Resource Sociologies

Understanding and Synthesizing Fundamental Research Traditions

Frederick H. Buttel

Donald R. Field

As University of Wisconsin colleagues who have served as co-editors of *Society and Natural Resources*, we have been deeply involved in the emerging fields of environmental sociology and sociology of natural resources for most of our respective careers. We have recognized for some time, however, that our styles of work and our patterns of collegial interaction varied enormously even though, by the standards of the larger discipline, we were essentially doing the same thing, namely examining society and environment connections. Over the years, these two patterns of study and research programs have been displayed at and nurtured by the International Symposium on Society and Resource Management (ISSRM) and in the *Society and Natural Resources (SNR)* journal. Intrigued by this pattern and paradox, we agreed to co-organize two sessions on the issue at the 2000 ISSRM in Bellingham, Washington. The March 2002 special issue of *SNR* on *Environmental Sociology and the Sociology of Natural Resources*, which was based on the papers presented at Bellingham, was the first instance in which the distinction between these two subdisciplines or research programs was candidly discussed in the context of a major refereed social science journal. Our key aim that led to the Bellingham sessions and the subsequent *SNR* special issue was to come to terms with the fact that, for nearly three decades and nine previous ISSRM symposia, there had existed two quite distinct styles of theory and research on the relationships between society and the biophysical environment. We were persuaded that a great deal could be gained by exploring the origins of these diverse research programs and that these understandings could make possible new routes to synthesis and cross-fertilization. As we indicated in our introduction to the special issue (Buttel & Field, 2002), the symposium at Bellingham on which the special issue was based attracted more interest and stimulated more intense debate than expected. A lively—and, we think, productive—dialogue has ensued.

The dialogue on the environmental sociology/natural resources sociology distinction initiated at Bellingham and institutionalized in the special issue of *SNR* proved to be more contested and emotive than we anticipated. We expected that the main axis of debate would revolve around whether environmental sociology or the sociology of natural resources was the more efficacious, productive, or innovative subdiscipline or research program. The Bellingham papers involved very little dialogue along these lines, however. The key debate, a surprisingly fervent one, had to do with whether the distinction exists or ought to exist at all. We grant that those who take the position opposed to our own (especially Freudenburg, 2002; Rosa & Machlis, 2002) have made some valuable points about why the distinction should not be exaggerated and how reinforcing the distinction may have negative implications for natural resource and environmental social science. Nonetheless, there is utility to making such a distinction.

The field is reasonably well served on account of the fact that the two research programs and research communities exist at all. Both of the fields are better off if they recognize and deal with the distinction than if they are blissfully unaware. The Bellingham sessions and SNR special issue accomplished our goal of increasing awareness of the distinction and its implications for scholarship.

While the opening up of the dialogue between practitioners of environmental sociology and the sociology of natural resources has been productive, we would be the first to agree that the distinction between the two research programs not be exaggerated, and that neither approach should be declared to be the superior subdiscipline or scholarly discourse. This chapter is premised on the notion that, to a substantial degree, the pattern depicted in the articles in the SNR special issue does exist and that there are understandable—and functional, if not sound— reasons why it does exist. This chapter is aimed at furthering the recognition of the point while also setting forth some notes on ways to develop closer channels of communication between the approaches and more commonality among concepts. The bulk of the present chapter will be devoted to developing a set of concepts that can help build bridges between environmental sociology and the sociology of natural resources. The fact of the matter is that there are a good many productive bridges that can be built between the two styles of environment-society research, but even if these avenues are pursued there will continue to be an environmental sociology/sociology of natural resources divide, at least for the foreseeable future, for reasons that will be discussed.

Environmental Sociology & Sociology of Natural Resources: Related but Distinct Research Programs

Table 1, which was originally reported in Buttel (2001), was revised for the 2002 special issue of SNR (Buttel, 2002) and has been revised and expanded once more, summarizes the major differences of theory and approach in the two subdisciplines or research programs. Of the dozen dimensions of difference between environmental sociology and the sociology of natural resources outlined in Table 1, three of these dimensions—the audience, spatial focus, and the conception of environment and sustainability—represent the most fundamental distinctions between the two research programs. Environmental sociology's main audience tends to be other

Dimension	Environmental Sociology	Sociology of Natural Resources
Origins	Grew out of the environmental movement, extension of certain lines of sociological interest (e.g., social movements, population studies)	Longstanding emphasis among rural sociologists, leisure/outdoor recreation researchers, and social scientists in resource agencies
Definition of Environment	"Singular," encompassing, cumulative disruption of environment	Local and regional parameters of ecosystems and landscape
Main Features of the Environment Stressed (Biophysical Dependent Variables)	Pollution, resource scarcity, global environment, ecological footprints	Conservation, stewardship (local) carrying capacity, crowding
Signature Environmentally Related Processes	Industrial and transport-related pollution	Extraction; conservation of of resources, habitats, and species
Definition of Sustainability	Reduce of aggregate levels of pollution and raw materials usage	Long-term sustained yields of natural resources, social equity in allocation and use of resources, reduction of social conflict over natural resources, planning and management of multiple use of resources
Predominant Cadre of Practitioners	Liberal arts sociologists	Natural resource agency staff; college of agriculture/natural resources staff; rural sociologists
Audience for Research	Academic community, other sociologists and environmental sociologists	Natural resource agencies and management decision-makers
Unit of Analysis	Nation-state	Community or region
Spatial Scope or Scale of Analysis	Metropolitan focus	Nonmetropolitan focus
Overarching Problematics	Explaining environmental degradation, understanding mechanisms of environmental reform	Improving public policy, minimizing environmental impacts and conflicts, improving resource management, organizational sociology of resource agencies, occupational sociology of resource professionals
Theoretical Commitments	Relatively theoretical, and often metatheoretical	Deemphasis on social theory
Multi- and Interdisciplinary Commitments	Relatively modest	Relatively strong

Table 1. Tendencies Within Environmental Sociology and the Sociology of Natural Resources

sociologists, its spatial focus is mainly metropolitan, and its conception of the nature of biophysical dependent variables is that of highly aggregated or omnibus measures of environmental quality such as the "ecological footprint" (York, Rosa & Dietz, 2003). By contrast, sociology of natural resources practitioners tend to see natural resource managers, planners, and agencies as the key audience for research, to focus on non-metropolitan phenomena, and to stress regionally-specific biological or biosocial parameters or indicators of landscape and environmental quality. Sociology of natural resources scholarship is considerably more likely to be applied research than is the case with environmental sociology scholarship.

It should be noted that Table 1 includes a number of other dimensions along which environmental sociology and the sociology of natural resources approaches tend to differ. One such example is that of the relative theoretical elegance or emphasis of the two research programs. Table 1 suggests that there is a tendency for environmental sociologists to be more theoretically oriented and to be more preoccupied with theory—if not metatheory—than are resource sociologists. We are inclined, however, to see this and several other dimensions of difference between the two styles of research noted in Table 1 as being less fundamental than those of audience, biophysical dependent variables, and spatial focus. The greater theoretical emphasis of environmental sociology arguably derives mainly from its emphasis on sociological audiences, while the emphasis on manager, planner, or agency audiences leads natural resource sociology practitioners to place less stress on theoretical elegance.

The fact that audience, biophysical dependent variables, and spatial focus are the fundamental dimensions of difference suggests two provisional conclusions drawn from previous work (Buttel, 2001, 2002; Buttel & Field, 2002; Field, Luloff & Krannich, 2002). The first of these conclusions is that while there is in some ultimate sense only one environment and only one underlying set of social processes, there are very understandable and enduring reasons that some sociologists will stress academic audiences, metropolitan phenomena, and highly aggregated units of analysis, while others are interested in addressing the managerial audiences, non-metropolitan phenomena, and less aggregated biophysical dependent variables. This pattern of quite variegated sociological emphases on different scopes or scales of phenomena is no more and no less legitimate than the fact that some ecologists stress the micro-unit of "patches" while other ecologists are interested in global environmental change. Both groups of ecologists, quite obviously, are aiming to undertake research on and understand the same biophysical environment, but the scopes and scales of their work are so different that the patch ecology and global environment research programs involve quite different styles of research. In ecology, the fact that the research programs of ecologists who study patch structures and dynamics and of those who study global environmental change differ quite considerably does not mean there are lacking avenues for conceptual and theoretical cross-fertilization. Thus, population and landscape ecology can be useful perspectives for bridging patch and global environment research. Much the same is the case with regard to environmental sociology and sociology of natural resources.

Concepts for Bridging and Enriching the Divide

Town-Country Division of Labor: Industry-Extraction Linkages, Generative Sectors, and Commodity Chains

As noted by many observers, rural sociologists have played pivotal roles in both environmental sociology and the sociology of natural resources (see, respectively, Humphrey, Lewis & Buttel, 2002; Field & Burch, 1988). The key concept underlying rural sociology is that of town-country division of labor and its synonyms or cognates (e.g., the metropolitan / non-metropolitan dichotomy, center-periphery structure, rural-urban continuum). The most elementary component of the town-country division of labor is that of the complementarities between industrial transformation, which has traditionally occurred largely in metropolitan spaces, and raw material extraction, which has characteristically occurred in non-metropolitan spaces. One could arguably say that both environmental sociology and the sociology of natural resources have tended to focus on one of these features (metropolitan industrialization and non-metropolitan extraction, respectively) to the (relative) exclusion of the other. Environmental sociology researchers' theories and research approaches lead them to stress metropolitan industrial systems, pollution, and aggregate transboundary environmental degradation, and to see that the environmental phenomena that tend to occur in rural or peripheral space are largely deducible from the logic of urban-led industrialization or modernization. Sociologists of natural resources are much more likely to stress the dynamics in extractive peripheries and non-metropolitan protected areas, recreational environments, and amenity zones. Natural resource sociologists are more likely to see these peripheral resource phenomena as being either substantially shaped by rural social structures or by nonindustrial aspects of metropolitan systems (such as the leisure and recreation styles of metropolitan people). Neither approach has been highly adept at recognizing the complexity and density of the connections between industrial and extractive social systems, although both scientific communities are beginning to address the continuous and interactive nature of society-environment relations from the city to remote countryside

Interestingly, much of the content of rural sociology over the past several decades has revolved around understanding the many processes (e.g., de-industrialization, rural industrialization, urban sprawl, exurbanization, amenity-driven service sector growth in rural regions, rural economic diversification, industrialization of agriculture, and globalization) that have led to a substantial diminution of the historically more straightforward town-country division of labor (e.g., Brown & Swanson, 2003). It is crucial to recognize, however, that despite the attenuation of the pronounced pattern of town-country division of labor (which characterized most Western societies at the time of the establishment of American rural sociology), this configuration remains important to this day. To be sure, some analysts have posited that there is a global dematerialization process that is well underway and that dematerialization has led to a decreased importance of extractive activities (Wernick, Herman, Govind & Ausubel, 1996). Likewise, it is apparent that only a minority of non-metropolitan counties in the U.S. exhibit a predominance of extractive industry, while many rural regions in the U.S are becoming transformed into recreational-service-providing and retirement regions.

However, the evidence (e.g., Bunker, 1996; York & Rosa, 2003) points to three conclusions contrary to the dematerialization position: 1) large-scale industrialization presupposes the extraction of raw materials; 2) industrial production is expanding more rapidly than resource conversion efficiencies are being made, and thus dematerialization is not occurring rapidly enough to sever the linkage between growth and raw materials consumption, and; 3) in this contemporary world of increasingly more capital-intensive industrialization (and of the consumptive infrastructures that accompany this pattern), the trend is, if anything, toward an increasingly more crucial role being played by extraction and extractive peripheries (Bunker, 1996; York et al., 2003; York & Rosa, 2003). These crucial extractive peripheries are increasingly concentrated in the developing countries, but non-metropolitan extractive economies in the industrial countries continue to be strongly related to industrial production and mass consumption, even as rural social and economic systems on the whole have become more diversified. It should also be stressed, however, that if the Bush Administration and Congress are able to restructure energy and public lands policies in the ways they prefer, there will be a renewed emphasis on resource extraction in many regions of the U.S.

Bunker and Ciccantell's (2003) work on generative sectors suggests another important dimension of the town-country division of labor and of the connections between primary resource extraction and industrial production. Their notion of generative sectors refers to the fact that established or rising industrial powers, such as the U.S. at the turn of the twentieth century and Japan from the 1950s through the 1980s, can be characterized in terms of a handful of fundamental or foundational industrial sectors that undergird economic growth and world-economic ascent. Generative sectors are characterized by a dynamic manufacturing structure (typically consisting of two or three foundational industrial sectors) and by a definite spatial pattern of primary raw materials provision. Thus, in Japan's (transitory) post-World War II world-economic ascent, its two key generative sectors were steel manufacturing and shipbuilding. Given Japan's lack of key natural resources these two generative sectors were provisioned through links to coal, iron ore, and bauxite mining in the rural peripheries of the ABC countries (Australia, Brazil, and Canada). The construction of deep-water ports and development of a large, efficient merchant fleet enabled steel and ship production to be amply provisioned with raw materials from the ABC countries.

Generative sectors are not necessarily those that appear to be the most profitable, dynamic, or modern industrial sectors; indeed, autos and electronics were seemingly the leading sectors in Japan in the 1960s through the 1980s. Bunker and Ciccantell (2003) demonstrate, however, that steel production and shipbuilding were the ultimate foundations for the auto and electronics sectors as well as for the other key components of the Japanese economy, such as its chemical industry. Even the real estate and international finance sectors in Japan had major connections to these two generative sectors.

The usefulness of the Bunker-Ciccantell analysis of generative sectors lies in its recognition that the links between extraction and industrial production are invariably crucial to any social economy, but that their foundational character may not be entirely apparent, either to environmental sociologists who tend to ignore the extractive lineages of industrial production or to sociologists of natural resources who tend not to follow rural-resource commodity chains once they enter metropolitan space. Rural extractive peripheries, which comprise much of the focus of the sociology of natural resources, are a crucial phenomenon in and of themselves, but particularly so in relation to the widespread industrial transformation that characterizes modern developed societies. The societies of the world today continue to exhibit multiple complex links between peripheral extraction, industrial production, and auxiliary processes. And we might note parenthetically that while the industrial ecology community may exaggerate the potentials of dematerialization and eco-efficiency (Bunker, 1996), this research tradition has considerable value in its development of a systems perspective that incorporates not only the production process, but the entire linkage from extraction through transportation, processing, production, distribution and consumption . As Graedel and Allenby (2003) have noted: "industrial ecologists seek to optimize the total materials cycle from virgin material to finished material, to component, to product to obsolete product to ultimate disposal" (p. 18). In their models, resources, energy, and capital are tracked in order to understand how more sustainable production systems can be developed. Environmental sociologists and natural resource sociologists each have an abundance of knowledge and parallel systems models to examine the human system from the rural remote production streams to global systems of production through distribution and consumption. Here is one place that the cross-fertilization of these two research programs can make a contribution.

Distanciation

Distanciation (also referred to as *distance* or *distancing*) is the degree to which there is "severing of ecological and social feedback as decision points along [a commodity] chain are increasingly separated along the dimensions of geography, culture, agency, and power . . . . [T]he concept of distancing highlights the increasingly isolated character of consumption choices as decision makes at individual nodes are cut off from a contextualized understanding of the ramifications of their choices, both upstream and downstream" (Princen, Maniates, Conca, 2002, p. 16). Developments in the means of transport, new production practices (e.g., subcontracting, outsourcing), and new patterns in the world trading system have given rise to a tendency for social groups to be spatially and socially removed from the areas in which their production and consumption activities interact with the biophysical environment. As Princen (2002) noted, geography or space is the principal, but not the only, dimension of distanciation.

Geographic distanciation refers to the degree to which the sites of decision-making about extraction and production and consumption are far removed spatially. All things being equal, to the degree to which there is high spatial distanciation of extraction and production-consumption, primary resource producers have less awareness of and knowledge about the conditions under which these materials become extracted, valuated, transported, and converted into industrial goods. Geographic distanciation thus tends to be accompanied by differences in bargaining power between extractive producers and industrial producers. Geographic distanciation also tends to be associated with lack of ecological feedback on important natural resource management issues at the site of extraction. Extractive producers tend to be unaware of the social and environmental conditions of *industrial transformation*, while industrial firms tend to be unaware (or face less of an imperative to become aware) of the social and environmental conditions of extraction.

Cultural distanciation pertains to the cognitive or social distance between extraction on one hand, and production and consumption on the other. It involves actors at the production pole, and especially at the consumption end, of commodity chains being unaware of the conditions of extraction. Cultural distanciation not only involves blockage of information flow, but it also reinforces the tendency of industrial producers and consumers to be indifferent about the ecological and social conditions within extractive regions. Finally, distanciation may involve a "multiple agency" or "multiple agents" dimension, in which raw materials tend to flow through many intermediaries, or involve pronounced competition among multiple raw materials suppliers. Multiple agency (e.g., networks of processors, wholesalers, and retailers that lie between a cow-calf rancher in Colorado and a chain restaurant) involves a complexity of social relations that exacerbates asymmetries of power and information flow.

Frontier Economies and Externalization

In Thomas Princen's (Princen, 2002; Princen et al., 2002) analyses of the structures of extraction, production, and consumption he has observed that "for a business firm, the ideal economy is a frontier economy" (p. 104). A frontier economy is one in which because there is a vacuum of state jurisdictional authority, industrial producers and other firms are best able to externalize costs. The three main processes of externalization of costs are provision of free or under-priced resources, provision of free or unregulated waste sinks, and the ability to be mobile and move to another periphery if a particular region no longer lends itself to cost externalization (related points are made by Dunlap and Catton, 2002, in the SNR special issue). To be sure, the trend during the 20th century has been for the jurisdictional authority of central or national states to be extended increasingly further into peripheral space, often forcefully so, as was the case in the American West (McCarthy, 2002; Walker, 2003). In the U.S., for example, a very substantial public domain—the vast bulk of it non-metropolitan—was consolidated, and laws and regulations governing rural resource use and extraction were promulgated (e.g., Reclamation Act, Endangered Species Act, National Environmental Policy Act, Coastal Zone Management Act). National resource and regulatory agencies such as U.S. Department of Agriculture, Department of Interior, the Environmental Protection Agency, and so on, now have considerable jurisdictional authority for regulating decision-making by private sector firms, subnational governments, and private individuals. The upshot has been that vacuums of state jurisdictional authority in the American periphery have progressively declined, creating a renewed search for (de)regulatory frontiers by natural resource firms.

There are limits to the uniform imposition of state jurisdictional authority, however. Frontiers and opportunities for externalization of costs are relative. Even in the U.S. context, where the regulatory and surveillance capacity of federal and subnational governments is considerable even in remote areas, there exist variations in "frontierness" that lend themselves to being exploited. State surveillance capacity with which to enforce laws and regulations is generally less in more sparsely populated peripheral regions than it is in more densely settled metropolitan contexts. Competition among regions for investments may create incentives for local governments to help create or maintain these relative vacuums of jurisdictional authority (a "pro-business" environment; Freudenburg, 1991) so that locales will be attractive to investors. Finally, as we will note below, social groups in peripheral regions may actively resist the extension of state jurisdictional authority to (and of associated systems such as retention of the public domain in) peripheral regions (McCarthy, 2002).

The Cultural Sociology & Symbolization of Landscape: Symbolization, Gentrification, and Conflict

One of the most well-developed and promising commonalities between environmental sociology and the sociology of natural resources is that of cultural approaches to the symbolization of space and nature. Both environmental sociologists and sociologists of natural resources have long been interested in environmentalism and the processes according to which individuals and groups mobilize in instrumental pursuit of preserving particular environmental features or in more abstract pursuit of the ideal of environmental protection and conservation. Much of the expansion of environmental sociology across the globe has corresponded with the growing fascination with environmental features and phenomena as cultural objects. In the U.S., for example, the connections between 1) outdoor recreation, leisure pursuits, and interests and 2) environmental movement membership have been recognized for decades (see Burch, Cheek & Taylor, 1972). Many European sociologists are concerned with accounting for the rise of new social movements, such as Europe's radical ecology movements and green parties (Norton, 2003), while sociological studies of tourism, habitus, and distinction have continued their impressive growth (Hopkins, 1998). In parallel fashion there has continued to be a vibrant line of socioculturally-oriented (and associated anthropological and ethnographic) research in natural resources on the meanings associated with environments, landscapes, and other biophysical objects. The enormous human dimensions tradition in the sociology of natural resources has been largely concerned with matters of social perception, symbolization, and the mobilization and expression of interests and orientations toward non-metropolitan landscapes, habitats, species, and other biophysical referents. The political ecology approach in geography and sociology has likewise stressed the importance of local histories, meanings, and micropolitics in struggles over resource use, access, and property rights (Belsky, 2002).

In the contemporary world, including but not limited to the United States, one of the key processes relating to natural resources and the environment is the symbolization and "amentization" of a growing range of environments, especially non-metropolitan and exurban environments. Here we construe symbolization broadly to include aesthetic and expressive, as well as cultural-symbolic, meanings.

Sociologists of natural resources know particularly well that the growing symbolization of peripheral spaces as tourism, recreation, and amenity habitats is playing an extraordinarily important social role. Major amenity zones, such as the Greater Yellowstone ecosystem, are not only witnessing increased utilization of resources for recreational purposes; in addition, this "amenitization" of the Greater Yellowstone area has led to a profound elaboration of the financial, legal, health, and other services in the gateway areas of the national park. Exurbanization and gentrification of territory represent powerful trends across much of non-metropolitan and well as metropolitan space in the advanced industrial countries (Walker, 2003).

Social Movements & Social Resistance to Resource Governance Regimes

Both environmental sociologists and sociologists of natural resources have devoted increasing attention to social movements and social resistance. The most common focus in this area, of course, has been on environmental movements and non-governmental organizations, and on conflicts among environmental groups, rural primary producers, local government officials, and resource management agencies.

However, environmental movements as conventionally understood by no means exhaust the range of resource-related social resistance. As an example of the broad relevance of the phenomenon, it is interesting to quote the introductory paragraph of a recent article about social resistance in a natural resource context:

> Imagine a movement composed of members of rural communities, whose livelihoods have long depended on a wide variety of uses of the lands and natural resources surrounding their homes. The movement's central complaint is that community members are losing access to and control over these lands and resources because of ever more vigorous pursuit of environmental goals by the resource conservation branches of central government—a trend spurred on largely by the interventions of distant, highly bureaucratic, and professionalized environmental groups, virtually none of whose staff or members has ever been to the particular lands in question. Attempting to defend their access to and control over these lands, members of the protest movement resist increasingly environmentally oriented management through a variety of tactics: they set forest fires, encroach on and take resources from protected lands, pressure government employees in the area to overlook violations, and support through silence community members who break conservation laws deemed unjust by local standards. To national and international audiences who will listen, they proclaim their superior knowledge and understanding of local environments, assets the historical precedence and legitimacy of their uses, and argue that local users should have greater rights than nonlocal claimants. Finally, they suggest that conservation is merely a cover for increased state control and the assertion of class privilege in the region (McCarthy, 2002, p. 1281).

This quote is aimed at conjuring up images of research results, such as those by Peluso (1992, 1993) on the developing world of indigenous movements among peasants and forest dwellers. McCarthy's referent, however, is to the American Wise Use movement. In the Wise Use movement, social resistance grows out of the real and perceived marginality of many rural primary commodity producers, landowners and users (McCarthy, 2002). In turn, such groups increasingly become affiliated with the conservative anti-environmental movement which is contesting environmental regulation and the legitimacy of the claims of environmental movements and non-governmental organizations. Each of the processes referred to in the foregoing—the continuing relevance of primary extraction, distanciation, externalization, extension of state jurisdictional authority, and symbolization-amentization—provide important bases for increasingly more variegated forms of social resistance.

Conclusion

There exists two relatively distinct sociological research traditions in environment-society analysis. We thus believe that one can take the universe of articles in a journal such as *Society and Natural Resources* and readily assign most of them to one category or the other. Within each category there would tend to be relatively little citation of works in the other category. While there are some scholars who work in both areas, only a minority does, and not surprisingly these scholars (e.g., Belsky, 2002; Freudenburg, 2002; Rosa & Machlis, 2002) are among the most likely to believe that the divide is imaginary. To a considerable degree, however, environmental sociologists and sociologists of natural resources have different audiences for their research, and stress different units of analysis and different concepts of the nature of the biophysical environment. This separateness of the two research programs has been reasonably functional, especially when one considers that the current pattern of specialization enables their relatively distinct audiences to be well served. At the same time, we do endorse several of the views of the critics of our position on the distinction between the two research programs. First, we agree that the further reinforcement of the division is not a desirable direction to go, and we recognize that since there is only one biophysical environment and one human species, there ultimately ought to be the possibility of developing a single sociology (or social science) of the natural world. We also recognize that the distinction is a social product in that it occurs largely in countries where there is a significant audience for applied non-metropolitan social science research on the environment.

In this chapter we have strived to develop a set of concepts that have potential to build linkages between the two research programs and nudge the two toward a more common purpose. This said, we doubt that even if these concepts—or others that our colleagues identify help to fill the interstitial academic space—are embraced, we will witness a decade or two hence the disappearance of the distinction between environmental and resource sociology research programs that have been depicted here.

References

Brown, D. L., & Swanson., L. (Eds.) (2003). *Challenges for rural America in the 21st century.* University Park: Pennsylvania State University Press.

Belsky, J. M. (2002). Beyond the natural resource and environmental sociology divide: Insights from a transdisciplinary perspective. *Society and Natural Resources*, 15, 205-211.

Bunker, S. G. (1996). Raw material scarcity and the global economy: Insights and distortions in industrial ecology. *Society and Natural Resources*, 9, 419-429.

Bunker, S. G., & Ciccantell, P. (2003). Generative sectors and the new historical materialism: Economic ascent and the cumulatively sequential restructuring of the world economy. *Studies in Comparative International Development*, 37, 3-30.

Burch, Jr., W. R., Cheek, Jr., N.H, & Taylor, L. (Eds.) (1972). *Social behavior, natural resources, and the environment.* New York: Harper & Row.

Buttel, F. H. (2002). The sociology of natural resources and environmental sociology: Their institutional histories and intellectual legacies. *Society and Natural Resources*, 15, 205-211.

Buttel, F. H. (2001). Environmental sociology and the sociology of natural resources: Strategies for synthesis and cross fertilization. In G. Lawrence, V. Higgins, and S. Lockie (Eds.), *Environment, society, and natural resource management* (pp. 19-37). Cheltenham, UK: Edward Elgar.

Buttel, F. H., & Field, D. R. (2002). Environmental and Resource Sociology: Introducing a Debate and Dialog. *Society and Natural Resources*, 15, 201-203.

Dunlap, R. E., & Catton, Jr., W. R. (2002). Which function(s) of the environment do we study? A comparison of environmental sociology and natural resource sociology. *Society and Natural Resources*, 15, 239-249.

Field, D. R., & Burch, W. R. (1988). *Rural sociology and the environment.* Westport, CT: Greenwood Press.

Field, D. R., Luloff, A. E., & Krannich, R. S. (2002). Revisiting the origins of and distinctions between natural resource sociology and environmental sociology. *Society and Natural Resources*, 15, 213-227.

Freudenburg, W. R. (1991). A 'good business climate' as bad economic news? *Society and Natural Resources*, 3, 313-331.

Freudenburg, W. R. (2002). Naval warfare? The best of minds, the worst of minds, and the dangers of misplaced concreteness. *Society and Natural Resources*, 15, 229-237.

Graedel, T.E. & Allenby, B. R., (2003). *Industrial ecology, 2nd edition.* Englewood Cliffs, NJ: Prentice Hall-Pearson Education Inc.

Hopkins, J. (1998). Signs of the post-rural: Marketing myths of a symbolic countryside. *Geografiska Annaler*, 8065-81.

Humphrey, C. R., Lewis, T., & Buttel, F. H. (2002). *Environment, energy, and society: A new synthesis.* Belmont, CA: Wadsworth.

McCarthy, J. (2002). First world political ecology: Lessons form the wise use movement. *Environment and Planning*, A 34, 1281-1302.

Norton, P. (2003). A critique of generative class theories of environmentalism and of the labour-environmentalist relationship. *Environmental Politics*, 12, 96-119.

Peluso, N. (1992). *Rich forests, poor people.* Berkeley, CA: University of California Press.

Peluso, N. (1993). "Forcing conservation? The politics of state resource control. *Global Environmental Change*, 3, 199-217.

Princen, T. (2002). Distancing: Consumption and the severing of feedback. In T. Princen, M. Maniates, & K. Conca (Eds.), *Confronting consumption* (pp. 103-131). Cambridge, MA: MIT Press.

Princen, T., Maniates, M., & Conca, K. (2002). Confronting consumption. In T. Princen, M. Maniates, & K. Conca (Eds.) *Confronting consumption* (pp. 1-20). Cambridge, MA: MIT Press.

Rosa, E. A., & Machlis, E. (2002). It's a bad thing to make one thing into two: Disciplinary distinctions as trained incapacities. *Society and Natural Resources*, 15, 251-261.

Walker, P. A. (2003). Reconsidering 'regional' political ecologies: Toward a political ecology of the rural American West. *Progress in Human Geography*, 27, 7-24.

Wernick, I. K., Herman, R., Govind, S., & Ausubel, J. H. (1996). Materialization and dematerialization: Measures and trends. *Daedalus*, 125, 171-198.

York, R., & Rosa, E. A. (2003). Key challenges to ecological modernization theory: Institutional efficacy, case study evidence, units of analysis, and the pace of eco-efficiency. *Organization & Environment*, 16, 273-288.

York, R., Rosa, E. A., & Dietz, T. (2003). Footprints on the earth: The environmental consequences of modernity. *American Sociological Review*, 68, 279-300.

22

The Use of Community in Natural Resource Management

A.E. Luloff

Richard S. Krannich

Gene L. Theodori

Carla Koons Trentelman

Tracy Williams

This chapter examines the use of *community* in research papers and articles that address a range of natural resource themes. A review from books of abstracts from previous International Symposia on Society and Resource Management (ISSRM) and the *Society and Natural Resources* (SNR) journal confirms that the use of *community* in natural resource management is complex and widespread. Similar to others who have conducted such assessments (e.g., Jakes & Anderson, 2000), we find that *community* remains an elusive concept. It has been used to frame units and levels of analysis, as both a central and peripheral concept, and as an independent and dependent variable. Moreover, uses and applications of the term *community* have changed over time.

In this chapter we review some of the more critical issues related to the use of *community* in natural resource management. First, we provide an overview of the uses of the term. We then focus on a differentiation between use of the concept as either a unit or level of analysis, examine use of the concept in the context of several key content domains, and identify the implications of the patterns and trends observed in the literature for future community-related work in natural resources.

Overview

Social science approaches to the study of community and related phenomena have always been multi-faceted, with only limited agreement regarding the core elements of the concept (Hillery, 1955). It comes as no surprise, then, that there is considerable diffuseness in the *SNR* articles and ISSRM papers as they incorporate some focus on the community concept, suggest that the term has some innate plasticity, and enable researchers to shape and mold it to their own particular needs and purposes.

This review begins with the first ISSRM in 1986. Eighteen of the presented papers reflected the general nature of community-related work at that particular time. These papers explored social impacts (Manring, West & Bidol, 1986; Milburn, 1986), policy (Hoogland, 1986), and forest stability (Weeks, 1986) through the use of case study approaches (Fortmann & Starrs, 1986), key informant interviews (Fore, 1986; Hooper & Branch, 1986), and survey data (Blahna, 1986; Jobes, 1986). Most importantly, these papers more or less served as harbingers for material presented at future meetings and or published in *SNR*. Nearly all of this work was characterized by the use of a *systems* or *human ecological* perspective, a pattern that remained in place throughout much of the first decade of ISSRM activity (see Kersey & Machlis, 1986; Muth, 1986; Salazar, 1986).

A similar pattern was observed for the next several symposia. However, with rapidly increasing attendance at ISSRM, many more papers on community appeared, and a greater diversity of subject matter, theoretical perspectives, and frameworks was observed. Despite this growth, the early work on natural resource-based communities, community-based resource management efforts, and case studies, remained a major focus of researchers. And, importantly, while there was a tremendous increase in the number of people presenting papers at the meetings, those involved earliest in community-related research remained active, presenting papers at later meetings as well.

Ten years after the inaugural ISSRM, nearly 50 community-related papers were presented at the 1996 symposium. Many were part of sessions that emphasized place meanings and attachment, tourism-related research (e.g., natural resource tourism, ecotourism, heritage tourism), citizen involvement in natural resource decisions, land use policy, and natural resource issues at the rural-urban interface (e.g., Austin, 1996; Burr, 1996; Mendez & Carroll, 1996; Stedman, 1996; Winter, 1996).

At the 2002 symposium, the number of community papers presented was roughly equivalent to that observed in 1996. However, the diversity of subjects expanded, including several papers that addressed community agency and interaction, collaboration, and participation (in addition to the broad categories present at earlier conferences). These newer subjects reflected a continued broadening of frameworks, including social construction and field-theoretical perspectives (Higgins, 2002; Moore, 2002; Steele & Luloff, 2002). In addition, many papers focused on disaster and risk-related research associated with the occurrence of serious forest fires in the American West. As with earlier proceedings, the level of interest in the work of natural resource scientists on community-related studies was expansive, with papers in a wide range of thematic sessions.

A similar pattern of expansion in both numbers of papers and areas of focus is evident over time in the content of SNR, though increased numbers are attributable in part to expansion from four issues per year to six, then eight, and eventually ten. Published work on community was relatively sparse in the first year of SNR, with articles focusing on communities as the object of study either in a comparative context (Seyfrit & Sadler-Hammer, 1988) or as a case study (Carroll, 1988). Ten years later, the journal published considerably more community-related research. Included were articles on community-based natural resource management (Brosius, Tsing & Zerner, 1998), forest dependency (Pendleton, 1998), and communities as the object of study, including comparative community responses to environmental and resource conditions (Beckley, 1998; Krannich & Smith, 1998; Spies, Murdock & White, 1998), community participation (Thwaites, De Lacy, Li & Liu, 1998), and community impacts (Richards & Womersley, 1998; Steelman & Carmin, 1998). In 2003, nineteen articles with a community context were published in SNR. These included several that focused on community as the context of study (Eser & Luloff, 2003; Field, Voss, Kuczenski, Hammer & Radeloff, 2003; Parisi, Taquino, Grice & Gill, 2003), community participation (Mclean & Straede, 2003; Stem, Lassoie, Lee, Deshler & Schelhas, 2003), natural resource dependence (Allison & McBride, 2003; Smith, Jacob, Jepson & Israel, 2003), and community-based forestry and other such analyses (Gupte, 2003; Schusler, Deceker & Pfeffer, 2003; Taylor, 2003; Virtanen, 2003).

As the foregoing overview reveals, work with a focus on some aspect of community has become increasingly evident over time in both ISSRM papers and SNR articles. However, while significant for its contributions to our understanding of specific issues, this admixture of work has not been terribly efficient at advancing our knowledge. Part of this problem is traceable to confusion between units and levels of analysis.

Units and Levels of Analysis

The review of ISSRM and SNR abstracts revealed that most of the community-related research could be sorted into one of two types of studies: studies *in* community or studies *of* community. Here, what is meant by each type of study is explained and illustrations of how community has been used in both are offered. First, however, it is important to differentiate *level* of analysis from the more vernacular *unit* of analysis, though both are important when framing and conducting community research.

At a minimum, two questions can be asked about any research paper, community-related or otherwise: 1) what is the unit of analysis?, and 2) what is the level of analysis? The former refers to whom or what is being studied and generally refers to an individual, social grouping (e.g., household, organization, community) or material objects (e.g., books, paintings, automobiles) and social interactions (e.g., weddings, divorces, friendship choices). This is contrasted to the level of analysis which refers to where the study is being conducted. All too often, researchers studying community and/or community-related topics ignore the level of analysis, confuse the unit of analysis with the level of analysis, or commit an aggregation fallacy of some form.

Confusion concerning levels of analysis has impeded the development of a coherent body of literature about community. Despite numerous warnings, community researchers continue to employ data that have been collected at and/or aggregated to a real level that differs from their level of interest (Luloff & Greenwood, 1980; Robinson, 1950). Unfortunately, such practices cause confusion in the levels of analysis. While neighborhood-, place-, county- and regional-level investigations are worthy, they become problematic when the findings from them are generalized to the community level (see Beckley, 1998).

In addition, it is important to differentiate between studies *in* community and studies *of* community. Studies in community are distinguished by their use of the community as the setting in which investigators conducted their work. A large number of investigators have examined perceptions, knowledge, attitudes, experience, behaviors, and behavioral intentions of community residents with respect to environmental and/or natural resource-related issues (e.g., Connelly & Knuth, 2002; Hooper & Branch, 1986; Spies et al., 1998). Often, in these studies, community was the *level* of analysis and the individual was the *unit* of analysis. However, in some studies the level of analysis was the county (Fore, 1986; Simmons & Wall, 1990) or region (Bright, Barro & Burtz, 2002; Colvin, 2002) and in some, the unit of analysis was the family, the household, groups of individuals, or citizen advisory committees (Busenberg, 1998; McDermott, 1994; Weeks, 1986).

The second distinguishable stream of research is labeled studies *of* community. Here, investigators deal explicitly with the relationship between environmental/natural resource and community. Community is not the backdrop for the study. Instead, community is the object of the study (Parisi et al., 2003; Seshan & Luloff, 1996). The community is incorporated as both the *unit* and *level* of analysis in this literature.

Key Content Domains

Even though applications of the concept of community have been highly variable, a review reveals several key content domains that collectively encompass a substantial majority of such applications. One of the overarching themes involves a focus on resource dependent communities. This content area is, in itself, quite heterogeneous. A major area of emphasis involves efforts to document and account for the natural resource, economic, political and social conditions that contribute to and cause variability in resource dependency (e.g., Becker & Harris, 2002; Beckley, 1998; Force & Machlis, 1996).

A second thematic focus involves the consequences of resource dependency for individual and collective well-being, including numerous analyses focusing on dependency-poverty links, employment and economic opportunity, community autonomy and viability, and patterns of social change (e.g., Bailey & Pomeroy, 1996; Machlis & Force, 1994; Nadeau, Shindler & Bouthiller, 1998; Overdest & Green, 1995; Russell & Harris, 2001). With some exception, a majority of these examinations of resource-dependent communities have focused on North American contexts.

A third area of emphasis that is apparent in both ISSRM and *SNR* pertains to community impacts of various types of environmental and natural resource utilization, development and management actions. A major focus within this area of emphasis involves the effects of decline or closure of resource-based economic activities for communities and residents (e.g., Kusel, Kocher, London, Buttolph & Schuster, 2000; Smith et al., 2003; Weeks, 1986). A second focal area involves the effects of resource-based extraction and commodity-oriented activities such as mining, energy and water resource developments (e.g., Corkran, 1996; Cortese, 2003; Kruger, Lee & Zientek, 1990). Studies of social impacts of exposure to or the siting of hazardous and noxious facilities, including radioactive waste disposal, toxic spills and exposure episodes, industrial emissions of toxic chemicals, and other undesirable land use events, represent a third major area of concentration (e.g., Kleiner, Rikoon & Seipel, 2000; Richards & Womersley, 1998; Wulfhorst & Krannich, 1999).

Finally, there have been numerous analyses of the community impacts associated with tourism and recreational visitation, park designation and management, and amenity-based growth and development (e.g., Allen &

Grumbling, 1990; Clendenning & Field, 2002; Dawson & Blahna, 1992; Lindberg & Johnson, 1994). Interestingly, this area of emphasis is far more evident in ISSRM papers than in *SNR* articles. Also interesting is that most of the presented and published papers in these community impact areas have been dominated by a focus on North American situations. This suggests either that much of the social impact assessment work focusing on international settings is presented at and published in other venues, or that relatively little such written work is produced internationally.

One of the most prominent areas of emphasis evident in ISSRM and SNR involves studies examining aspects of what can generally be described as *community-based resource management*. This includes examinations of community forestry, community-based fisheries management and community-based wildlife management. Dozens of such manuscripts and articles have appeared in both venues, with major expansion in the number of such pieces evident during the past five years (e.g., Brosius et al., 1998; Krogman & Beckley, 2002; Luloff & Finley, 2000; Taylor, 2003; Zanetell & Knuth, 2003). Unlike the areas examined above, this domain is characterized by a preponderance of analyses focusing on international contexts, particularly portions of southern Asia and Africa. Examination of *community-based resource management* in North American settings has become increasingly evident over time, likely reflecting paradigm shifts in the policies and practices adopted by various natural resource management agencies during the past decade.

Implications

Community remains an omnibus term, used in a variety of manners and purposes. While clear congruencies exist among certain uses, there is limited possibility of deriving mutually exclusive and totally exhaustive categories to adequately summarize the focus of all of these studies. In short, the concept is not a theme around which a coherent and cumulative body of knowledge and application has evolved, although researchers and managers appear to be increasingly cognizant of community-resource linkages. However, approaches used to analyze and understand such linkages remain highly divergent. Variations in theoretical orientations, in the units of analysis examined, and in levels of analysis contribute to a rich, but also complex and at times murky literature base addressing the community-resource interface.

In addition, a great deal of overlap exists across the key content domains reflecting application of the community concept to resource management. This is especially the case for the increasingly popular focus on community-based resource management and similar emphases that examine the ways in which communities are engaged in resource utilization and management decision processes. This includes the variety of public participation activities, community-based collaborative planning strategies, and episodes of community action and agency. These latter categories provide much fertile ground for concretizing the central concept under study. That is, by focusing on the community as both a unit and level of analysis, and including the roles of individuals and organizations in locality-relevant actions, researchers are more likely to identify central characteristics of community vital to natural resource issues.

Conclusion

The evidence clearly indicates an expansion in both the number and scope of analyses applying the concept of community to natural resource management topics over the time since ISSRM and *SNR* were founded. Such applications will likely remain highly prevalent in both ISSRM papers and *SNR* articles in the coming years, for several reasons.

First, expanded implementation of various community-based management processes has generated broadened public expectations regarding the legitimacy of community engagement and agency as a component of resource management decision-making. Once established, such expectations for civic involvement in resource management will not be easily extinguished. As a result, studies of such processes are likely to become increasingly common in future years. Second, there is increased interest in the ways in which natural resource conditions may contribute to or detract from individual and collective well-being, and there is a strong theoretical connection between notions of well-being and the concept of community (see Wilkinson, 1991). Finally, there can be little doubt that one important facet of resource management involves understanding how people living in specific places make use of, develop meanings and attachments to, and are affected by, the conditions of spatially proximate natural environments. Even in the face of global environmental processes and expanding resource use by geographically dispersed populations, the actions and fates of people living in localized communities are inextricably linked to the conditions of surrounding landscapes and resources.

As Wilkinson (1991) observed, community well-being and ecological well-being are closely intertwined. Because there is much about these linkages that remains unexplored and unexplained, there is considerable need for more and better community-oriented research addressing natural resource conditions and natural resource management issues.

References

Allen, J., & Grumbling, V. (1990). *A community's response to natural resource stressors created by accelerated population growth: A study of Wells, Maine.* Presented at the Third International Symposium on Society and Resource Management, College Station, Texas.

Allison, E., & McBride, R. (2003). Educational reform for improved natural resource management: Fisheries and aquaculture in Bangladeshi universities. *Society and Natural Resources, 16,* 249-264.

Austin, M. (1996). *Examining the success of a nonprofit, urban tree planting program.* Presented at the Sixth International Symposium on Society and Resource Management, University Park, Pennsylvania.

Bailey, C., & Pomeroy, C. (1996). Resource dependency and development options in coastal Southeast Asia. *Society and Natural Resources, 9,* 191-199.

Becker, D., & Harris, C. (2002). *Amenity or commodity-based rural economies? Diversity of resource-based industries in inland Northwest towns.* Presented at the Ninth International Symposium on Society and Resource Management, Bloomington, Indiana.

Beckley, T. (1998). The nestedness of forest dependence: A conceptual framework and empirical exploration. *Society and Natural Resources,* 11, 101-120.

Blahna, D. (1986). *Social bases for forest resource conflicts in areas of reverse migration.* Presented at the First International Symposium on Society and Resource Management, Corvallis, Oregon.

Bright, A. D., Barro, S. C., & Burtz, R. T. (2002). Public attitudes toward ecological restoration in the Chicago Metropolitan Region. *Society and Natural Resources,* 15, 763-785.

Brosius, J. P., Tsing, A., & Zerner, C. (1998). Representing communities: Histories and politics of community-based natural resource management. *Society and Natural Resources,* 11, 157-168.

Burr, S. (1996). *A conceptual process for facilitating rural tourism development based on a comparison of tourism planning and development processes in four rural Pennsylvania counties.* Presented at the Sixth International Symposium on Society and Resource Management, University Park, Pennsylvania.

Busenberg, G. (1998). *Social context and community participation in the environmental management of the marine oil trade.* Presented at the Seventh International Symposium on Society and Resource Management, Columbia, Missouri.

Carroll, M. (1988). A tale of two rivers: Comparing NPS-local interactions in two areas. *Society and Natural Resources,* 1, 317-333.

Clendenning, G., & Field, D. R. (2002). *Amenity-led development and culture clash in the Pine Barrens of Wisconsin.* Presented at the Ninth International Symposium on Society and Resource Management, Bloomington, Indiana.

Colvin, R.A. (2002). Community-based environment protection, citizen participation, and the Albany Pine Bush Preserve. *Society and Natural Resources,* 15, 447-454.

Connelly, N. A., & Knuth, B. A. (2002). Using the coorientation model to compare community leaders' and local residents' views about Hudson River ecosystem restoration. *Society and Natural Resources,* 15, 933-948.

Corkran, R. (1996). Quality of life, mining, and economic analysis in a Yellowstone gateway community. *Society and Natural Resources,* 9, 143-158.

Cortese, C. (2003). Conflicting uses of the river: Anticipated threats to the resource. *Society and Natural Resources,* 16, 1-18.

Dawson, S., & Blahna, D. (1992). *The economic and community impact of the creation of Great Basin National Park.* Presented at the Fourth International Symposium on Society and Resource Management, Madison, Wisconsin.

Eser, S., & Luloff, A. E. (2003). Community controversy over a proposed limestone quarry. *Society and Natural Resources*, 16, 1-14.

Field, D., Voss, P., Kuczenski, T., Hammer, R., & Radeloff, V. (2003). Reaffirming social landscape analysis in landscape ecology: A conceptual framework. *Society and Natural Resources*, 16, 349-361.

Force, J. E., & Machlis, G. (1996). *Alternative engines of change in resource-dependent communities: Additional analyses.* Presented at the Sixth International Symposium on Society and Resource Management, University Park, Pennsylvania.

Fore, R. (1986). *Community attitudes and impacts associated with the Mount Baker Wilderness.* Presented at the First International Symposium on Society and Resource Management, Corvallis, Oregon.

Fortmann, L., & Starrs, P. (1986). *Burning issues: How two California communities responded to proposed wood-fired power plants.* Presented at the First International Symposium on Society and Resource Management, Corvallis, Oregon.

Gupte, M. (2003). Reexamining participatory environmental policy: Social stratification and the gender dimension. *Society and Natural Resources*, 16, 327-334.

Higgins, L. (2002). *Network and community theory.* Presented at the Ninth International Symposium on Society and Resource Management, Bloomington, Indiana.

Hillery, G. (1955). Definitions of community: Areas of agreement. *Rural Sociology*, 20, 111-123.

Hoogland, J. (1986). *Legislative and policy responses to communities in National Park system areas.* Presented at the First International Symposium on Society and Resource Management, Corvallis, Oregon.

Hooper, D., & Branch, K. (1986). *Decision-making in rural rapid growth communities: A garbage can model of community choice.* Presented at the First International Symposium on Society and Resource Management, Corvallis, Oregon.

Jakes, P. J., & Anderson, D. (2000). Introduction: Diverse perspectives on community. *Society and Natural Resources*, 13, 395-397.

Jobes, P. (1986). *The changing importance of wilderness to residents in a high natural amenity area.* Presented at the First International Symposium on Society and Resource Management, Corvallis, Oregon.

Kersey, B., & Machlis, G. (1986). *Forestry stability in a Northern Quebec Village.* Presented at the First International Symposium on Society and Resource Management, Corvallis, Oregon.

Kleiner, A., Rikoon, S., & Seipel, M. (1998). *Pigs and proximity: Health and behavioral impacts of proximity to large-scale swine operations in northern Missouri communities.* Presented at the Seventh International Symposium on Society and Resource Management, Columbia, Missouri.

Krannich, R., & Smith, M. (1998). Local perceptions of public lands natural resource management in the rural West: Toward improved understanding of the 'Revolt in the West.' *Society and Natural Resources*, 11, 677-695.

Krogman, N., & Beckley, T. (2002). Corporate 'bail outs' and local 'buyouts': Pathways to community forestry? *Society and Natural Resources*, 15, 109-127.

Kruger, L., Lee, R., & Zientek, J. (1990). *Off-shore oil and gas development: Does a community's sense of place play a role in risk assessment?* Presented at the Third International Symposium on Society and Resource Management, College Station, Texas.

Kusel, J., Kocher, S., London, J., Buttolph, L., & Schuster, E. (2000). Effects of displacement and outsourcing on woods workers and their families. *Society and Natural Resources*, 13, 115-134.

Lindberg, K., & Johnson, R. (1994). *Evaluating the social impacts of tourism development and economic transition.* Presented at the Fifth International Symposium on Society and Resource Management, Ft. Collins, Colorado.

Luloff, A. E., & Finley, J. (2000). *Rediscovering community-based forestry.* Presented at the Eighth International Symposium on Society and Resource Management, Bellingham, Washington.

Luloff, A. E., & Greenwood, P. H. (1980). *Definitions of community: An illustration of aggregation bias.* Station Bulletin 516. New Hampshire Agricultural Experiment Station. Durham, NH: University of New Hampshire.

Machlis, G., & Force, J. E. (1994). *Understanding social change in resource-dependent communities: Part I.* Presented at the Fifth International Symposium on Society and Resource Management, Ft. Collins, Colorado.

Manring, N., West, P., & Bidol, P. (1986). *Social Impact Assessment and environmental conflict management: The potential for integration and applications in forest dependent communities.* Presented at the First International Symposium on Society and Resource Management, Corvallis, Oregon.

McDermott, C.L. (1994). *Local participation: What does it take? A case study of an environmental NGO and a farmers' wood industry cooperative in Costa Rica.* Presented at the Fifth International Symposium on Society and Resource Management, Ft. Collins, Colorado.

McLean, J, & Straede, S. (2003). Conservation, relocation, and the paradigms of park and people management: A case study of Padampur Villages and the Royal Chitwan National Park, Nepal. *Society and Natural Resources*, 16, 509-528.

Mendez, S., & Carroll, M. (1996). *Smoke on the hill: A comparative study of wildfire and two forest communities.* Presented at the Sixth International Symposium on Society and Resource Management, University Park, Pennsylvania.

Milburn, L. (1986). *The energy impact scenario: A conceptualization of events preceding and following a rural community's experience with mining activities.* Presented at the First International Symposium on Society and Resource Management, Corvallis, Oregon.

Moore, S. (2002). *Building community capacity: Is it important for biodiversity conservation?* Presented at the Ninth International Symposium on Society and Resource Management, Bloomington, Indiana.

Muth, R. (1986). *Community stability as social structure: The role of subsistence uses of natural resources in Southeast Alaska.* Presented at the First International Symposium on Society and Resource Management, Corvallis, Oregon.

Nadeau, S., Shindler, B., & Bouthiller, L. (1998). *Characterizing the viability of forest-dependent communities in the Haut-St-Maurice region.* Presented at the Seventh International Symposium on Society and Resource Management, Columbia, Missouri.

Overdest, C., & Green, G. (1995). Forest dependence and community well-being: A segmented market approach. *Society and Natural Resources*, 8, 111-131.

Parisi, D., Taquino, M., Grice, S., & Gill, D. (2003). Promoting environmental democracy using GIS as a means to integrate community into the EPA-BASINS approach. *Society and Natural Resources*, 16, 205-219.

Pendleton, M. (1998). Taking the forest: The shared meaning of tree theft. *Society and Natural Resources*, 11, 39-50.

Richards, R., & M. Womersley. (1998). Toxic contamination, community health, and the attribution of blame: The Dunsmuir metam sodium spill. *Society and Natural Resources*, 11, 817-828.

Robinson, W.S. (1950). Ecological correlations and the behavior of individuals. *American Sociological Review*, 15, 351-357.

Russell, K., & Harris, C. (2001). Dimensions of community autonomy in timber towns in the inland Northwest. *Society and Natural Resources*, 14, 21-38.

Salazar, D. (1986). *Counties, states, and regulation of forest practices.* Presented at the First International Symposium on Society and Resource Management, Corvallis, Oregon.

Schusler, T. M., Decker, D. J., & Pfeffer, M. J. (2003). Social learning for collaborative natural resource management. *Society and Natural Resources*, 16, 309-326.

Seshan, S., & Luloff, A. E. (1996). *Community agency and the evolution of environmental protest.* Presented at the Sixth International Symposium on Society and Resource Management, University Park, Pennsylvania.

Seyfrit, C., & Sadler-Hammer, N. (1988). Social impact of rapid energy development on rural youth: A statewide comparison. *Society and Natural Resources*, 1, 57-67.

Simmons, D., & Wall, G. (1990). *Local input into destination planning.* Presented at the Third International Symposium on Society and Resource Management, College Station, Texas.

Smith, S., Jacob, S., Jepson, M. & Israel, G. (2003). After the Florida net ban: The impacts on commercial fishing families. *Society and Natural Resources,* 16, 39-59.

Spies, S., Murdock, S., & White, S. (1998). Waste facility experience and perceptions of waste related health and safety risks. *Society and Natural Resources,* 11, 719-741.

Stedman, R. (1996). *Sense of place through hunting: A constructivist approach to landscape identity.* Presented at the Sixth International Symposium on Society and Resource Management, University Park, Pennsylvania.

Steele, J., & Luloff, A. E. (2002). *Community perspectives on the use of land use tools in rural Pennsylvania localities.* Presented at the Ninth International Symposium on Society and Resource Management, Bloomington, Indiana.

Steeleman, T., & Carmin, J. (1998). Common property, collective interests, and community opposition to locally unwanted land uses. *Society and Natural Resources,* 11, 485-504.

Stem, C., Lassoie, J., Lee, D., Deshler, D., & Schelhas, J. (2003). Community participation in ecotourism benefits: The link to conservation practices and perspectives. *Society and Natural Resources,* 16, 387-413.

Taylor, P. (2003). Reorganization or division? New strategies of community forestry in Durango, Mexico. *Society and Natural Resources,* 16, 1-19.

Thwaites, R., De Lacy, T., Li, Y. H., & Liu, X. H. (1998). Property rights, social change, and grassland degradation in Xilingol Biosphere Reserve, Inner Mongolia, China. *Society and Natural Resources,* 11, 319-338.

Virtanen, P. (2003). Local management of global values: Community-based wildlife management in Zimbabwe and Zambia. *Society and Natural Resources,* 16, 179-190.

Weeks, E. (1986). *Mill closures in the Pacific Northwest: The consequence of economic decline in rural industrial communities.* Presented at the First International Symposium on Society and Resource Management, Corvallis, Oregon.

Wilkinson, K.P. (1991). *The community in rural America.* Middleton, WI: Social Ecology Press.

Winter, P. (1996). *Environmental concern and environmental action: How do recreationists fare?* Presented at the Sixth International Symposium on Society and Resource Management, University Park, Pennsylvania.

Wulfhorst, J. D., & Krannich, R. (1999). Effects on collective morale from technological risk. *Society and Natural Resources,* 12, 1-18.

Zanetell, B., & Knuth, B. (2002). Knowledge partnerships: Rapid rural appraisal's role in catalyzing community-based management in Venezuela. *Society and Natural Resources,* 15, 805-825.

23

Whither Human Ecology?

Jonathan G. Taylor

Suzanne N. Taylor

Man is in the world,
And his ecology is the nature of that "Inness."
                                                        —Paul Shepard (1969, p. 1)

Human ecology is the scientific study of the interdependent relationship between humans and the environments. It is closely linked to the science of humans relationships with natural resources as well as to human dimensions in natural resources research. These fields are differentiated by their respective non-human focus of the interaction equation: human ecology focusing on ecosystems while society and natural resources focuses more on environment-as-resource. Dunlap and Catton (2002) clarify this differentiation when defining, for sociology, three primary functions of environment for human use: "supply depot, waste repository, and living space" (p. 243). They describe natural resource sociology as focusing primarily on environment-as-supply, while environmental sociology spreads across all three functions.

   Professionals in human ecology, society and natural resources, and human dimensions research are all studying the relationships between human groups and ecosystems, humans and the natural world, and the adaptation of society to ecosystems. The need for progress in these fields is so pressing that the similarity and potential for cross fertilization among them are far more important than the distinctions one might make. This chapter provides a brief history of human ecology's origins, offers a conceptual organization to this broad trans-disciplinary field, and suggests directions for future research.

Definition and History
Human ecology is eclectic, encompassing such a broad array of studies and interests, that a precise definition remains elusive. It draws from many disciplines: ecology, sociology, geography, anthropology, among

others. In describing the state of human ecology in western Europe, Luc Hens (1996) stated:

> There exist almost as many definitions of human ecology as there are training programs, research institutions, and eminent human ecologists working in this field. This situation imparts some vagueness to the field (p. 161).

The field can be viewed as a special focus of autecology (i.e., single-species ecology) with the species of focus being *Homo sapiens*. However, so much is modified by social organization, technology and self-awareness of this species that development of the field has occurred in several social sciences, and interconnected with biological ecology. It is the influence of mind and of ideas becoming a force that can shape the Earth (Bates, 1962) that sets humankind apart from other species. This overarching influence of mind was given the term *noosphere* by Teilhard de Chardin (1956). Overall, human ecology draws from many disciplines.

A central intellectual organizer and historian of human ecology, Gerald L. Young (1983), describes a sociological origin of human ecology in the United States as coming from the *Chicago School*, starting with Park and Burgess' (1921) book, *Introduction to the Science of Sociology*. Human ecology in sociology evolved from Amos Hawley's (1950) school of *community structure* and was later challenged by Catton (e.g., 1994) and others who created the branch of *environmental sociology*.

Ecological approaches can be traced back much further in geography. Young (1983) refers to the German geographer Alexander von Humboldt who, in 1807, wrote of the interconnectedness of all things as an example of early attention to man in environment. But geography has had an erratic association with ecology over the decades, at one time getting embroiled in a geographic debate over determinism: Does environment determine the possible forms of human adaptation?

Consideration of the ecological context of culture has been of central importance to anthropology, in ethnographic studies in particular, since the 1930s (e.g., Taylor, 1934; Kroeber, 1939). This focus was termed *cultural ecology* by Steward (1955). However, this line of inquiry was somewhat separated from other scholarship in human ecology due to the ethnographic concentration on cultures that were influenced least by modern technology and material artifacts. Cultural ecology has changed seriously (Kottak, 1999) with development of a new subfield, ecological anthropology, incorporating systems theory and addressing itself to modern and technologically-developed nations.

Psychology began a human ecological focus in the 1940s and 1950s (Barker & Wright, 1955). The field has progressed into present concentrations in environmental psychology, including theoretical treatises on humans and environment on the individual scale (e.g., Ittelson, 1973), and studies of perception of environment (Daniel & Boster, 1976; Daniel & Vining, 1983; Zube, Sell & Taylor, 1982). The ecosystem connection in economics was first developed by Kenneth Boulding (1950, 1958), but held little influence until the more recent focus on green economics (Schütz, 1997/98).

Political science had only a few researchers interested in an ecological context at the time of Young's synthesis, though this focus has grown in the ensuing two decades. Some researchers (e.g., Rudel, 2002) believe that several subfields (e.g., development sociology, anthropology, and geography; natural resource sociology; and cultural anthropology) converged into *political ecology* in the 1990s.

As these several foci have evolved, unfortunately they have not merged into a coherent, coordinated science of human ecology. Rather, the ecosystem connection has tended to hitch-hike as a marginal consideration or a *non-field* (Young, 1983) within each of the several social science disciplines. What is interesting is how multiple disciplines within the social sciences have tried to reach out to incorporate concepts of biological ecology, while generally failing to search each other for common, synergistic or complementary threads (Boardman, 2002). Not surprisingly, perhaps, as an interdisciplinary field or *trans-discipline*, human ecology has failed to become more defined over the ensuing decades.

An Alternative Organizational Approach

The definition of human ecology might be alternatively approached from a perspective that looks not at disciplines, but at functions based on what aspects of human~ecosystem interaction are being researched and applied in human ecology (Taylor & Taylor, in press). From this perspective, we can focus on what kind of research is being done in human ecology, rather than on the divisions arising between. Six themes, which transcend the boundaries of academic disciplines, appear to cover the topics of research articles in human ecology: 1) conceptual/theoretical issues, 2) environmental management, 3) social systems, 4) environmental health, 5) environmental philosophy and ethics, and 6) human ecology in the arts.

Human ecologists have been establishing theoretical foundations for the field from the beginning. *Conceptual / Theoretical issues* in human ecology include studies in the development of human ecological theory, as well as the application of theory from other disciplines (e.g., geography, sociology, psychology) to human ecology. The importance of developing new methods in social science using interdisciplinary research techniques is emphasized by Richerson and Boyd (1997/98) who discuss the development of a general theoretical model encompassing technological changes, environmental deterioration, and human populations. McLaughlin (2001) combines insights from several sociological traditions to create an "ecology of social action" (p. 12).

The next theme, *environmental or ecosystem management,* can be divided into several sub-themes including environmental impact, sustainable development and urban studies/landscape architecture/land use studies. Lackey (1997/98) defines several core principles of ecosystem management. He contends that this approach will "protect the environment, maintain healthy ecosystems, preserve biological diversity and ensure sustainable development" (p. 107). Other topics studied by scholars in this area include conservation, natural resources management, adaptive management, bioregulation and community resources management. Cottingham (2002) takes case studies from aquatic ecosystems to illustrate the key components of biocomplexity research projects that utilize a collaborative and interdisciplinary approach to understanding the complexity of biological systems.

Environmental impact studies include topics related to climate change, impact modeling, pollution of air and water and deforestation, to name a few. Energy supplies, limits to growth, population control and agricultural systems are additional issues of concern. As the impacts of humankind's activities on the natural environment become more evident, a number of scholars are examining ways to achieve sustainability. The final sub-theme within environmental management includes urban studies: relationships between the natural, social and built environments, and; land use management (e.g., Steiner, 2002).

The study of *social systems* is one of the largest themes in human ecology and incorporates a range of topics dealing with political systems, economics, culture, and society and environment. Decision-making studies fit into this category and include research about environmental issue analysis, integration of collaborative/participatory methods with an ecosystem approach, and public participation in environmental policy. For example, Dietz (1994) explores the ways that adopting a human ecological approach to collective decision-making can lead to better public policy decisions.

Environmental economics addresses topics such as consumption and human livelihood, economic structures and the use of natural resources, ecotourism, and patterns of world consumption of natural resources. An example of research in this area is an article by Simpson and Rapone (2000) who examine a fair trade model for a Mexican coffee-producing cooperative.

Culture and environment studies examine such topics as ethnobotany, traditional ecological knowledge, international and cross-cultural research, the extinction of traditional communities, and indigenous peoples. Nabhan (1989) relates stories about agriculture from local groups of Native Americans as examples of how indigenous knowledge can provide important insights about agricultural practices.

Society and environment includes studies of world systems analysis, nature/society relations, the role of society in environmental issues, and the evolutionary sources of human behavior. Quality of life and public perceptions research are central to this sub-theme. Environmental psychology research (e.g., Vining & Tyler, 1999), demonstrates the role of beliefs, attitudes, values and emotions in natural resource planning and management.

The final three themes are less emphasized in the literature. Studies in *environmental health* examine such areas as community health, diet, environmental medicine, epidemiology, health intervention strategies, and health and risk safety. Areas of interest to human ecologists studying *philosophy and ethics* are ecological ethics (e.g., Merchant, 1997), genomic and social values, green ecology, eco-feminism, deep ecology, environmental justice (e.g. Arler, 1995), and the philosophy of nature. *Human ecology and the arts* is perhaps the area with the least amount of research, but it is still visible in the literature. It includes studies in environmental or ecological aesthetics and literature (e.g., Slovic, 1999).

Current and Future Integration
Human ecology and similar fields suffer from limitations that stem from traditional disciplinary intellectual history and institutional structure, both in academe and applied institutions. Interdisciplinary programs dealing with human~environment interaction, adaptation and integration are simultaneously being constructed and dismantled. For example, in Australia, geography has been a pace-setter in cross-disciplinary linkages, creating multi-disciplinary departments. However, this trend is

proving short-lived, as a disciplinary reflux is spreading rapidly across the country driven by powerful budgetary squeezes (Holmes, 2002). Harvey, Forster and Bourman (2002) point out that merging of geography with environmental studies in Australia during the 1990s was a veneer masking financial opportunism, internal university politics and changes in personnel.

The constructive thrust comes from the near-universal recognition that it is not sufficient to be studying just the parts in isolation; a careful examination of how parts interrelate is critically needed (Odum, 1953). Impetus to dismantle inter-disciplinary programs comes from entrenched disciplines refusing to relinquish their control over the organization and flow of capital, reward and reputation. Many institutions have used the cutting edge of growth to create interdisciplinary programs, but the

BRENT ERB

danger inherent in this strategy appears when growth falters and the support for it disappears. To an extent, the trans-disciplinary community itself inhibits institutional reform, recognizing that disciplinary foundations are essential for inter-disciplinary work to proceed (Boardman, 2002). One cannot work on how parts interrelate without dedicated colleagues first defining and refining the parts.

The American Association for the Advancement of Science reported (Jasonoff et al., 1997) that critical issues facing science and society are: environmental change, population growth, public health, food and energy, and equitable distribution and education throughout the world. Functionally, these real-world problems demand an immense disruption of a true paradigm change in science, as elucidated by Kuhn (1962). Young (1990) pointed out, "the problems human ecology addresses, some of its concepts and the answers it seeks, challenge orthodox procedures. In the eyes of orthodoxy, this makes human ecology heretical" (Shephard & McKinley, 1969, p. 11).

Stern (1993) called for "a second environmental science – one focused on human environment interactions – to complement the science of environmental processes" (p. 1897). This science would focus on three principal fields: 1) the human causes of environmental change, 2) the effects of environmental change on things and systems that humans value, and 3) the feedback loops between humans and environment. Machlis, Force and Burch (1997) developed the Human Ecosystem Model linking critical resources with human social systems. Both constructs are intrinsically human ecology but neither employed that term.

265

Elements required for a new approach toward understanding, evaluating and guiding the interrelationships of humans, human groups and ecosystems are suggested by many involved professionals. Human ecology must be interdisciplinary, integrating advances from several social sciences (e.g., sociology, social-psychology, psychology, anthropology, economics, political science, human geography). The independent and interdisciplinary tracks of research in human-environment interrelations that have developed in these several sciences must set aside issue capturing, and critically examine what synergism may be gained by collaboration.

Human ecology specifically must be interdisciplinary in reaching out to connect and correlate the social and biological sciences, with special emphasis on ecology. In this socio-biological connection, it will be critical to carefully assess the meanings of terms and principles and to evaluate critically their trans-disciplinary application. Catton (1994) calls for clarification of the ecosystem concept as central to the social sciences -- sociology in particular -- for a truly incisive human ecology, one that can comprehend what is happening in modern society and why it matters so much.

Human ecology, especially as applied in such fields as ecosystem management and sustainable development, must be able to accept knowledge, variables and understanding that come from sources other than science. For example, locally evolved knowledge of and adaptation to ecosystem conditions are ignored at scientists' peril. Anthropological literature is replete with anecdotal descriptions of the great steps backward that can result from implementing improvements, while ignoring local ecosystem adaptations that are already in place, although not always couched as adaptations in local folk wisdom. The development field now is increasingly focused on finding adaptive strategies that have strong and diverse foundations in both scientific and local knowledge.

A corollary to sources of knowledge, in making environmental management and development decisions, is the necessity to involve parties of the public-at-interest or at-risk in those decisions. Many practitioners (e.g., Webler & Tuler, 2001; Johnson, Poulin, & Graham, 2003) are researching collaborative partnerships with broadly-based socio-political constituencies, and that jointly seek adaptive strategies. Ultimately, concomitant and sustainable human ecosystems are the goal of applied human ecology.

The extraordinary complexity of human-ecological systems requires incorporation of complex systems conceptualization and modeling (Young, 1999): in particular, systems ecology. Some practitioners from the systems modeling tradition are addressing energy flows as a central organizing function within human ecology. Goerner (2000), in discussing self-organizing systems, states this core function quite specifically: "As far as we know, energy flow is the source of all organization on earth" (p. 93).

New Developments

True interdisciplinary advancement of human ecology may require a paradigm shift. Given the need for such fundamental change, it is difficult to predict the way for human ecology. But the crises of human maladaptation to ecosystems and the continuing illusiveness of adaptive strategies that lead a society to true and long term sustainability certainly suggest that a paradigm shift is essential. But without a roadmap to unconventional, radically different science, are there any glimmers that suggest new paradigm directions?

Goerner (2000), espousing *dynamic evolution* for human ecology, suggests that human thought must progress from a clockwork to a web weltanschauung. She couches her arguments for human ecology in terms of self-organizing systems, all of which are energy-based in order to be functioning dynamic systems. In human organizing systems, she suggests we have run the model of hierarchical systems to exhaustion, their persistence now dependent upon coercion since they lack the intricacy to respond to current rates and amounts of change. A human ecological network of energy flows would focus on sustaining flows, not on antagonistic survival. Fitness would be defined by the ability to play a coherent role in the web of processes. Such a networked web would allow flow through which synergy and support could reach all parts of the human ecosystem.

Young (1998) has discussed the concept of *holism* proffered, rejected and embraced in biological ecology and a wealth of other fields, and applied that understanding to human ecology. He cites Hofstadter's (1979) response to the reductionism/ holism conflict of evoking the Zen Buddhist term mu, which "unasks the question" by rejecting the premise of dichotomous choice. It is the *individual in relation* that marks both the study of ecology and human ecology (Freese, 1997).

From this perspective, Young (1999) goes further, suggesting that part-whole relations are the fundamental problem to be investigated in human ecology. He proposes that the part (i.e., the individual human being) has changed very little in modern times, but the whole has changed drastically. He believes that understanding these complexities of human interactions is both the challenge and the promise of human ecology.

Two things seem clear regarding future directions in human ecology. First, we must reach far beyond our own disciplines, sometimes into quite unfamiliar territory, to advance ecological comprehension of our own species. And second, interdisciplinary fields, especially those grounded in the social sciences, must cooperate and learn from each other, if such advancements are to be made.

References

Arler, F. (1995). Justice in the air energy policy, greenhouse effect, and the question of global justice. *Human Ecology Review*, 2(1), 40-61.

Barker, R. G., & Wright, H. F. (1955). *The Midwest and its children*. Evanston, IL: Row Peterson.

Bates, G. (1962). *The human environment.* Berkeley, CA: School of Forestry, University of California, Berkeley.

Boardman, R. (2002). Fragmentation and integration in environmental research: The social sciences revisited. *Environmental Studies*, 59(2), 173-183.

Boulding, K. E. (1950). *A reconstruction of economics.* New York: John Wiley & Sons.

Boulding, K. E. (1958). *Principles of economic policy*. Englewood Cliffs, NJ: Prentice-Hall.

Catton, W.R. (1994). Foundations of human ecology. *Sociological Perspectives*, 37(1), 75-95.

Cottingham, K. L. (2002). Tackling biocomplexity: The role of people, tools, and scale. *BioScience*, 52(9), 793-799.

Daniel, T.C., & Boster, R. S. (1976). Measuring landscape esthetics: The scenic beauty estimation method [Research Paper RM-167]. Fort Collins, CO: USDA Forest Service, Rocky Mountain Forest and Range Experiment Station.

Daniel, T.C., & Vining, J. (1983). Methodological issues in the assessment of landscape quality. In I. Altman, & J. F. Wohlwill, (Eds.). *Behavior and the natural environment* (pp. 39-84). New York: Plenum Press.

Dietz, T. (1994). What should we do? Human ecology and collective decision making. *Human Ecology Review*, 1(2), 301-309.

Dunlap, R.E., & Catton, W. R. Jr. (2002). Which function(s) of the environment do we study? A comparison of environment and natural resource sociology. *Society and Natural Resources*, 15, 239-249.

Freese, L. (1997). *Environmental connections*. Greenwich, CT: JI Press.

Goerner, S. (2000). Dynamic evolution: Rules for building a solid human ecology. *World Futures*, 55, 91-103.

Harvey, N., Forster, C., & Bourman, R. P. (2002). Geography and environmental studies in Australia: Symbiosis for survival in the 21st century? Australian Geographical Studies, 40(1), 21-32.

Hawley, A.H. (1950). *Human ecology: A theory of community structure*. New York: Ronald Press Co.

Hens, L. (1990). International networking strategies in human ecology in Europe: The Brussels experience. In M. S. Sontag, S. D. Wright, & G. L. Young (Eds.), *Human ecology: Strategies for the future: Selected papers from the Fourth Conference of the Society for Human Ecology*, (pp. 255-264). Fort Collins, CO: Society for Human Ecology.

Hofstadter, D.R. (1979). *Godel, Escher, Bach: An eternal gold braid*. New York: Vintage Books.

Holmes, J.H. (2002). Geography's emerging cross-disciplinary links: Process, causes, outcomes and challenges. *Australian Geographical Studies*, 40(1), 2-20.

Ittelson, W. (1973). *Environment and cognition*. New York: Seminar Press.

Jasonoff, S.R., Cotwell, R., Dresselhaus, M. S., Goldman, R. D., Greenwood, M.R.,C., Huang, A. S., et al. (1997). Conversations with the community: AAAS at the millennium. *Science*, 278, 2066-2067.

Johnson M. C., Poulin, M., & Graham, M. (2003). Toward an integrated approach to the conservation and sustainable use of biodiversity: Leisure learned from the Rideau River Biodiversity Project. *Human Ecology Review*, 10(1), 40-55.

Kottak, C.P. (1999). The new ecological anthropology. *American Anthropologist,* 101(1), 23-35.

Kroeber, A. L. (1939). *Cultural and natural areas of native North America.* Berkeley, CA: University of California Press.

Kuhn, T.S. (1962). *The Structure of scientific revolutions.* Chicago: University of Chicago Press.

Lackey, R. T. (1997/98). Ecosystem management: In search of the elusive paradigm. *Human Ecology Review,* 4(2), 107-113.

Machlis, G.E., Force, J. E., & Burch, W. R. (1997). The human ecosystem, part 1: The human ecosystem as an organizing concept in ecosystem management. *Society & Natural Resources,* 10, 347-367.

McLaughlin, P. (2001). Toward an ecology of social action: Merging the ecological and constructivist traditions. *Human Ecology Review,* 8(2), 12-28.

McNeill, J. R. (2002). Earth, wind, water and fire: Resource exploitation in the twentieth century. *Global Dialogue,* 4(1), 11-19.

Merchant, C. (1997). Fish first!: The changing ethics of ecosystem management. *Human Ecology Review,* 4(1), 25-30.

Nabham, G. P. (1989). *Enduring seeds: Native American agriculture and wild plant conservation.* San Francisco: North Point Press.

Odum, E. P. (1953). *Fundamentals of ecology.* Philadelphia, PA: Saunders.

Park, R. E., & Burgess, E. W. (1921). *Introduction to the science of sociology.* Chicago: University of Chicago Press.

Richerson, P., & Boyd, R. (1997/98). Homage to Malthus, Ricardo, and Boserup: Toward a general theory of population, economic growth, environmental deterioration, wealth, and poverty. *Human Ecology Review,* 4(2), 85-90.

Rudel, T. K. (2002). Sociologists in the service of sustainable development? NGOs and environment-society studies in the developing world. *Society & Natural Resources,* 15(3), 263-268.

Schütz, J. (1997/98). Dreamtime economics 101. *Human Ecology Review,* 4(2), 75-83.

Shephard, P., & McKinley, D. (1969). *The subversive science: Essays toward an ecology of man.* New York: Houghton Mifflin.

Slovic, S. (1999). Giving expression to nature: Voices of environmental literature. *Environment,* 41(2), 7-32.

Steiner, F. (2002). *Human ecology: Following nature's lead.* Washington, DC : Island Press.

Stern, P.C. (1993). A second environmental science: Human-environment interaction. *Science,* 260, 1897-1899.

Steward, J. H. (1955). *Theory of culture change: The methodology of multilinear evolution.* Urbana, IL: University of Illinois Press.

Taylor, G. (1934). The ecological basis of anthropology. *Ecology*, 15, 223-242.

Taylor, S.N., & Taylor, J. G. (in press). Wayfinding in human ecology. In C. Delfino (Ed.), *Global challenges of parks and protected areas management: Proceedings of Regional ISSRM Symposia, La Maddalena, Sardinia, Italy, October* 10-13, 2002. Sassari, Sardinia, Italy.

Teilhard de Chardin, P. (1956). The antiquity and world expansion of human culture. In W. L. Thomas (Ed.), *Man's role in changing the face of the earth.* (pp.103-112). Chicago: University of Chicago Press.

Vining, J., & Tyler, E. (1999). Values, emotions and desired outcomes reflected in public responses to forest management plans. *Human Ecology Review*, 6(1), 21-34.

Webler, T., & Tuler, S. (2001). Public participation in watershed management planning: Views on process from people in the field. *Human Ecology Review*, 8(2), 29-39.

Young, G. L. (1983). Human ecology as an interdisciplinary concept: A critical inquiry. In G. L. Young (Ed.), *Origins of human ecology: Benchmark papers in ecology / 12.* (pp.355-399). Stroudsburg, PA: Hutchinson Ross.

Young, G. L. (1990). Minor heresies in human ecology. In S. Sontag, S. Wright, & G. Young (Eds.), *Human ecology: Strategies for the future.* Fort Collins, CO: Society for Human Ecology.

Young, G. L. (1998). Holism: Writ & reposte in ecology and human ecology. In L. Freese (Ed.), *Advances in human ecology, Volume 7.* (pp. 313-366). Stamford, CT: JAI Press.

Young, G. L. (1999). A piece of the main: Parts and wholes in ecology and human ecology. In L. Freese (Ed.), *Advances in Human Ecology, Volume 8.* (pp. 1-31). Stamford, CT: JAI Press.

Zube, E.H., Sell, J.L., & Taylor, J.G. (1982). Landscape perception: Research, application and theory. *Landscape Planning*, 9, 1-33.

24

Application of the Concepts of Values and Attitudes in Human Dimensions of Natural Resources Research

Michael J. Manfredo

Tara L. Teel

Alan D. Bright

This chapter provides a broad overview of research in human dimensions of natural resources (HDNR) that has employed or advanced the topics of *attitudes* and *values*. It deals only with sociological and social psychological definitions of these concepts, and draws primarily from presentations at previous International Symposia on Society and Resource Management (ISSRM) and from literature in selected journals that publish HDNR articles. Secondarily, and selectively, this chapter draws from the mainstream literature in sociology and social psychology. The review of relevant literature was limited to research articles and notes and did not include policy and thought pieces that have addressed attitudes, values or related concepts.

Attitudes

In 1935, Allport proclaimed that "the concept of attitude is probably the most distinctive and indispensable concept in contemporary American social psychology" (p. 198). In 1993, Eagly and Chaiken concluded that Allport's claim still applied. Recognizing there are numerous definitions of the attitude concept, the authors adopted Eagly and Chaiken's description that an attitude is an individual's evaluation of an entity. In the review of HDNR literature, concepts like perceptions, expectations, evaluations, satisfaction, beliefs and opinions were considered relevant in the context of this definition.

Attitudes are a particularly important concept because they are theorized to help predict human behavior (Ajzen & Fishbein, 1980; Homer & Kahle, 1988). Theory suggests that 1) if attitudinal positions are known, behavioral prediction (e.g., participation in recreation, voting on ballot initiatives, obeying regulations) is possible, and 2) by understanding attitudes and their bases, it is possible to change them and consequently affect human behavior (e.g., develop information that will change behaviors such as littering, regulatory violations and park visitation).

A review of the literature would suggest that, at a minimum, attitudes are one of the most frequently examined topics in HDNR. In fact, since its inception, about 20 percent of the research articles and notes in *Society and Natural Resources* and nearly 40 percent of those in *Human Dimensions of Wildlife* have dealt with attitudes in some capacity. In addition, HDNR ranks as the prominent approach to social science research reported in biologically-focused natural resource journals such as the *Wildlife Society Bulletin* where HDNR comprises approximately one-third of all social science research reported.

In addition to their many direct applications, attitudes (i.e., evaluations) are building blocks of many other concepts commonly applied in HDNR. For example, recreation conflict arises from a negative *evaluation* of others due to events that inhibit an individual's goal attainment (Jacob & Schreyer, 1980). Vaske, Donnelly, Wittmann and Laidlaw (1995) proposed the notion of value conflict which occurs when people form negative *evaluations* of others due to differences in social values. Crowding is defined as a negative *evaluation* of a certain density or number of encounters (Shelby & Heberlein, 1986). Trip satisfaction is a positive or negative *evaluation* of a recreational engagement (Manning, 1999). Wildlife acceptance capacity is based on an *evaluation* of the impacts associated with varying levels of wildlife populations in an area (Decker & Purdy, 1988). Willingness to pay might be considered *evaluations* of various price levels for a particular good (Ajzen & Peterson, 1988). Attitudes form the basis for each and every one of these evaluation constructs. In short, the attitude concept permeates many if not most areas of HDNR research.

Focus of Attitude Research
In examining the broad base of HDNR literature for this chapter, attitudinal studies were categorized into one of two groups: *descriptive* and *conceptual*. While categorization of research into these two groups was not mutually exclusive (a few studies fit appropriately into either), it provided a convenient and logical framework for examining the nature of attitude research. This classification is similar to the "policy" versus "theoretical" distinction used by Dunlap and Jones (2003) to categorize studies that measure environmental attitudes.

Descriptive attitude research. This category includes strictly descriptive studies that measure attitudes for the purpose of providing information about groups or subgroups of people. Approximately two-thirds of the attitude research reviewed for this chapter can be categorized as descriptive. Such studies are typically topic- or issue- driven with a purpose of providing information useful to natural resource mangers in decision-making. These studies often do not define attitudes, ground themselves in a specific attitude theory, or use methods that are linked to a particular theoretical position.

The methodological approach taken in descriptive studies varies from the use of single-item indicators (such as might be used in polling) to the use of item clusters to reveal attitudinal dimensions. Taking the latter approach, researchers develop a set of survey items that might address the wide spectrum of thoughts about an issue, administer the instrument, and factor or cluster analyze results to form item groupings that reveal the dimensions of a particular attitude. As an example, in a study of attitudes toward fire management, researchers might be interested in certain dimensions of thought including perceptions about the effectiveness of fire

TARA TEEL

management strategies in preventing wildfires, the effect of fire management strategies on the natural ecosystem, the ability of land management agencies to effectively manage for fire, and the appropriateness of techniques such as mechanical thinning and prescribed burning.

There is no doubt that descriptive studies yield useful insights about a specific public of interest. However, in an early commentary on HDNR attitude research, Heberlein (1973) noted that such studies have limited practical utility. Given the variable conclusions drawn from research that tests attitude-behavior relationships, the findings obtained outside established theoretical and methodological structures cannot be assumed to have predictive validity.

Conceptual attitude research. The second group of studies consists of concept-driven studies that, in addition to the functions described with descriptive research, also 1) attempt to predict behavior, attain a deeper understanding of why attitudes are held, or suggest ways of affecting attitudes, 2) clearly identify a theoretical orientation, and 3) test a theoretical or methodological model. These studies are far fewer in number (conceptual research comprised approximately one-third of the attitude research reviewed) but, due to their theoretical orientation, offer the most broadly generalizable conclusions.

A review of the conceptual attitude research reveals a number of observations. Of the attitudinal theories introduced in social psychological literature, only a handful have been applied in HDNR, and even fewer have been applied on a sustained basis. The most prevalent among these is Fishbein and Ajzen's (1975) Theory of Reasoned Action (TRA) and, to a lesser degree, Ajzen's (1991) revision of

TRA, the Theory of Planned Behavior (TPB).

The introduction of TRA marked an important turning point in the development of attitude theory. Prior to that, researchers focused their debate on whether or not attitudes were related to behavior. Researchers no longer question whether attitudes influence behavior, but instead, focus on why the relationship is particularly strong or weak in given scenarios (Chaiken & Stangor, 1987).

TRA was developed specifically to help resolve the debate over attitude-behavior prediction. It made at least three key contributions: First, TRA revealed the relationship between beliefs (and their associated evaluations), subjective norms, attitudes, behavioral intention and behavior (TPB added the concept of *perceived behavioral control* as a predictor of behavioral intention and behavior). Fishbein and Ajzen (1975) prescribed a specific methodology that allowed practitioners to easily apply the TRA and TPB models.

Second, Fishbein and Ajzen (1975) emphasized the importance of corresponding levels of specificity between attitude and behavioral measures. Characteristics of these measures must correspond on *the target* toward which the attitude and behavior focus, the specific action that is being considered, and the context and time within which the action is to take place. Without correspondence between these four factors, attitudes cannot be expected to predict behavior.

The third contribution of TRA is its emphasis on the importance of belief salience in understanding the basis of attitudes. This suggests that people's attitudes will be influenced primarily by those beliefs that are readily accessed in memory (i.e., those that are salient). Therefore, it is important to use techniques that assess beliefs that are salient to the specific group of interest.

In addition to descriptive applications of TRA and TPB (e.g., Manfredo, Fishbein, Watson & Haas, 1990), researchers in HDNR have tested their predictive validity (Daigle, Hrubes & Ajzen, 2002; Young & Kent, 1985), examined the importance of salience (Barro, Manfredo & Wells, 1994) and specificity (Heberlein & Black, 1976), and demonstrated the mediating effect of belief strength on the attitude-behavior relationship (Bright, Barro & Burtz, 2002). These areas of investigation will continue to be important if HDNR scientists are to expand the utility of attitudinal research.

Concepts similar to the Fishbein and Ajzen's TRA (1975) model, but different in their specific formulation, have received ongoing attention in the literature, particularly in the 1970s and 1980s under the heading of multi-attribute models. Used frequently in marketing and tourism, these models assume that each individual has objectives that he or she is trying to achieve in choosing a particular product or service (Woodside & Clokey, 1974). Based on these objectives, the individual assigns weights to attributes associated with the product. If the sum of the perceived values of the attributes is greater than that for alternative products, the product will evoke a positive attitude which will in turn lead to an intention to purchase that product.

Values

Researchers have regularly applied the values concept in HDNR literature, though not to the extent of attitudes. Similar to attitude studies, values research is complicated by the multiple and varied meanings that have been used and implied by the term *values*. Brown (1984) distinguished between *assigned* values (the process of evaluating) and *held* values, which are ideals or goals in life. In this respect, assigned values are consistent with the concept of attitudes, and resemble Rokeach's (1973) definition of values as basic, evaluative beliefs about appropriate modes of conduct and desired end states.

Values are of interest to HDNR researchers because they reveal the fundamental basis of an individual's thoughts, attitudes and opinions. Values reflect the enduring characteristics of a person that guide important life decisions, give direction to patterns of attitudinal positions, and hence, direct individual behavior. Values develop early in life and are shaped primarily by family, peers, and other significant groups. Once in place they are thought to change very slowly, if at all.

Understanding values has been useful in responsibilities related to natural resource planning and policy-setting where it is important to recognize the diversity of stakeholders and their respective ideals. Tourism marketers have also found values useful in identifying consumer lifestyle segments to target in marketing efforts.

From social psychology, the values research of Rokeach (1973) and Schwartz (1992) has attained widespread recognition among HDNR researchers. Each of these approaches offers a typology of values and item scale instrumentation for assessing value priorities. Rokeach's approach proposes 18 terminal values (i.e., desired end states) and 18 instrumental values (i.e., desired modes of conduct), while Schwartz's model consists of 10 values separated into two dimensions: 1) self-enhancement/ self-transcendence and 2) openness to change/conservation. Interestingly, both of these approaches purport to offer a comprehensive array of values, yet neither approach suggests environmentalism, affinity for the natural environment or a similar concept on their respective lists of values.

Not surprisingly, the emphasis of a significant amount of research in HDNR has been to develop natural resource value typologies. Research has been conducted to identify wildlife values (Kellert, 1980, 1987; Steinhoff, 1980), forest values (Steel, List & Schindler, 1994), and general environmental values orientations (Dunlap & Van Liere, 1978; Weigel & Weigel, 1978). The primary emphasis of these investigations has been to develop instrumentation that describes people's thoughts about a natural resource topic. This typically proceeds with qualitative interviews, development of survey items, data collection and item grouping analysis, labeling of item groupings, and using item grouping scores to describe values toward the natural resource topic of interest.

While these studies have certainly been useful, they are somewhat unclear with respect to how the concept they claim to measure (i.e., values) matches the measurement instrument. For example, Kellert (1980, 1981, 1987) created an item bank intended to measure nine different domains of thought about wildlife. Somewhat interchangeably, he suggested the items measure both wildlife values and wildlife attitudes. More recently, in an edited volume about biophilia, Kellert (1993) suggested that the responses tapped by these scales reflect inherited dispositions toward wildlife.

Similarly, Dunlap and Van Liere (1978) proposed the widespread adoption of a *new environmental paradigm* (NEP) worldview. The researchers suggested that a new and favorable environmental worldview would be revealed in an individual's beliefs, values and attitudes. The NEP instrumentation is widely used and intended to measure environmental attitudes, yet authors clearly use the instrument to make inferences about adoption of an NEP worldview, which includes values. Dunlap and Jones (2003) more recently reported that more than 1,000 articles on environmental attitudes and values have been published over the years. Consistent with Heberlein's (1981) observation, however, the authors noted that the multitude of studies on this topic have employed a diversity of techniques, leading to an inconsistent and somewhat disorganized literature base. Overall, a need remains for greater clarification of what is meant by the terms *environmental attitudes* and *environmental values*.

Greater conceptual clarity would enhance the utility of the HDNR research about attitudes and values. For example, given the transitional nature of attitudes and the stable nature of values, it is important to be clear about these concepts in addressing basic issues such as how natural resource values are formed, whether or not they can be changed, and identifying the institutional and societal factors that shape values.

The Connection Between Values and Attitudes

In the 1980s and 1990s, research in social psychology began emphasizing the causal link between broad-based concepts (e.g., values and personality characteristics), intermediate concepts (e.g., personal strivings and attitudes), and behavior. This hierarchical approach was tested in a study by Homer and Kahle (1988) and became a methodological prototype for later investigations. Researchers used structural equation modeling to test the relationships among values, attitudes toward natural foods, and consumption behavior.

Homer and Kahle's (1988) approach, known as the value-attitude-behavior (VAB) model, has been applied in a number of areas in HDNR. For example, Stern, Dietz, Kalof and Guagnano (1995) found significant relationships between a dimension of Schwartz's (1992) value typology, environmental attitudes, and environmentally-related behaviors. Shields, Martin, Martin, Wade and Haefele (2002) used the VAB framework to examine relationships among socially responsible values; ecological and personal accessibility goals; preservation attitudes; and motorized, non-motorized and commodity use behaviors on national forest lands. Vaske and Donnelly (1999) found that a biocentric/anthropocentric value orientation continuum predicted attitudes toward the preservation of wildlands, which in turn predicted intention to vote to preserve wildlands.

Building upon the VAB model, Fulton, Manfredo and Lipscomb (1996) proposed a definition for the notion of value orientations. Value orientations (e.g., a wildlife *utilitarian* orientation versus a wildlife *protection* orientation) are revealed in basic evaluative beliefs that give individual meaning to one's central value structures. However, one individual's *respect life* value might suggest one should never take an animal's life, while another individual's respect life value could suggest that hunting should only employ specific types of more humane methods. Fulton et al. (1996) found that these wildlife value orientations were predictive of behavior; specifically that a wildlife *appreciation* orientation predicted wildlife viewing participation, and a *utilitarian* orientation predicted hunting participation.

In more recent work, researchers expanded the VAB model to explore the link between micro (e.g., individual behavior) and macro (e.g., broader societal and cultural) forces. This research suggests that urbanization, affluence, residential stability and gender may all have an important influence on the development of wildlife value orientations (Deruiter & Donnelly, 2002; Manfredo, Teel & Bright, 2003).

Value and Attitude Shift

As the HDNR research matures and attracts more involvement from the broader social sciences, it is beginning to address a much broader array of questions related to the dynamic nature of attitudes and values. Due to the relative youth of the social science disciplines in natural resources and the relative recent interest in environmental topics, there are few databased studies that reveal trends in attitude or value shifts. Yet, research is beginning to document the nature of such trends and lend itself to further exploration. For example, polling data shows a rapid increase in pro-environmental attitudes in North America from the mid-1960s to the early 1970s, a decline in the 1980s, and renewed growth in the 1990s through to the present time (Dunlap, 2002; Dunlap & Mertig, 1992). Furthermore, content analysis of news stories between 1982 and 1993 suggests a shift from utilitarian forest values to spiritual and ecological values (Bengston, 1994). Other studies suggest a trend toward the adoption of pro-environmental beliefs are part of a global shift occurring in post-industrialized nations (Inglehart & Baker, 2000).

A number of theoretical positions have emerged to explain the shift of environmental attitudes and values. They address questions of if, how, and why attitudes and values toward the environment have been changing in post-industrialized society (Inglehart, 1997), how current environmental values can be contrasted with those held by previous cultures (Smith & Wishnie, 2000), how the growth of environmentalism occurred as a new social movement in post-industrialized societies (Buttell, 1992), the global growth of environmentalism (Dietz & Rosa, 2002; Hironaka, Frank & Schofer, 2000), and factors that will influence environmental attitudes and values in the future (Fisher & Freudenburg, 2001; Inglehart & Baker, 2000; O'Conner, 1998).

Theories that address value and attitude shift can be categorized into two groups. The first group is based on a social constructionist approach. This approach views values as *constructed knowledge* developed primarily as a result of societal conditions (Buttel & Humphrey, 2002). As noted by Milton (1996), the application of this notion to environmental values suggests they are "determined not by what exists in the 'real' world, but by the form of social organization they [people in a culture] are required to sustain" (p. 98). For example, Douglas and Wildavsky (1982) suggest the growth of environmental concern is related to the growth in sectarian forms of social organization in societies. Sectarian organization is founded on choice (e.g., *voluntary* versus *forced* group membership) and characterized by commitment to strong communal interest. It typically develops in opposition to existing institutions and promotes environmental values as a mechanism for questioning the assumptions upon which traditional forms of organization are based (e.g., supremacy of science and technology). Certain factors such as increasing access to higher education and loss of faith in government (as a result, in part, of events such as the Vietnam War and Watergate) fostered the development of this form of organization in the United States in the 1960s and 1970s (Douglas & Wildavsky, 1982)

A second group of theories to explain value and attitude shift focuses on the interaction between environments and key components of cultural systems, in particular, technology and economy. In this approach, values are an adaptation to this interaction and a source of innovation (Harris, 1999). For example, Bell (1973) discussed the importance of changing technology, its effect on day-to-day challenges in life (e.g., shifts from "games against nature" to "games against fabricated nature" to "games against other people"), and the growth of post-industrialized society.

As another example, O'Conner (1998) adapted the philosophies and theories of Karl Marx, and suggested that environmental neglect is the *second fallacy* of capitalism. Similarly, Schnaiberg (1980) proposed an acceleration of environmental degradation due to the *treadmill of production* inherent in capitalism. Conversely, Spaargaren and Mol (1992) introduced the concept of *ecological modernization* which suggests that capitalism and its technological innovations offer the only realistic solution to the expanding ecological crisis.

The theoretical approach with the most extensive empirical support is Inglehart's (1990, 1997) theory of Materialist/Post-Materialist value shift. He proposes that materialist values—with a focus on economic well-being, safety and security—emerged from industrial lifestyles, but that with increased affluence, values in post-industrialized nations have shifted toward emphasis on quality of life, environmental protection and self expression, or what he terms *post-materialist* values. Data from Inglehart's (1990) World Values Survey, conducted in 65 societies representing more than 75 percent of the world's population and spanning several decades, tend to support Inglehart's proposition. A recent application of this theory in examining variation in the proportion of "traditionalists" (i.e., those possessing both Materialist values and utilitarian wildlife value orientations) across six western U.S. states also lends support to Inglehart's proposition (Manfredo et al., 2003).

Future Research Needs

In some ways, current research needs are little different than they were in 1986, at the meeting of the first ISSRM. Attitudinal studies are theorized to offer information that will allow description, prediction, understanding and control. However, the majority of current approaches offer little more than description. To advance beyond this point, researchers will need to be more attentive to theoretical issues and design research to test and advance theory. Beyond HDNR's past emphasis on the attitude-behavior relationship, a number of theoretical issues about attitudes have emerged in the social psychology literature that have interesting implications. For example, recent research has focused on the functions of attitudes, the implications of attitude extremity, the influence of attitude accessibility, and the effect of social groups on attitude formation. Researchers might adapt those theoretical issues to the evaluative concepts used in HDNR. Moreover, it would benefit the application of attitude research to explore more than and beyond the handful of theories applied to date.

Given that the primary emphasis of prior research is descriptive, it is somewhat ironic that the second recommendation provided here is that researchers work with managers to improve the applicability of attitudinal research. Managers oftentimes express uncertainty about how to use results of attitudinal and other HDNR research. This reveals not only a lack of understanding of social science concepts and methods, but also differences in the basic philosophy of natural resource management (i.e., managers have strong opposition of "management by polling"). This points to the need for researchers to devote more attention to the needs of management, communicating results more effectively and working with management in the application of information in decision-making processes.

A third need for future research is to reach beyond the one-shot descriptive study and assemble more broadly generalizable findings. That would be accomplished in part by employing a theoretical approach to investigations. However, there is also a need to develop efforts that allow broad geographic and temporal comparisons. Further, there is a strong need to conduct cross-cultural studies, particularly to begin to understand the factors that affect attitude and value change. A significant challenge is the development of methods that would allow cross-cultural comparisons.

Finally, as noted by Dietz and Rosa (2002), there is a need to advance research that links macro and micro approaches to understanding natural resource value shifts in society, such as approaches that link the attitudes and values held by individuals to the broad societal factors that shape culture. While the separation of these methodological paradigms occurs along disciplinary lines, the benefits from more holistic approaches will be substantial. It is likely that attitudes and values will continue to be central to HDNR research. To meet the promise of these concepts, researchers will need to invest more in the concepts themselves, and address the challenges that constrain current applications.

References

Ajzen, I. (1991). The theory of planned behavior. *Organizational Behavior and Human Decision Processes*, 50, 179-211.

Ajzen, I., & Fishbein, M. (1980). *Understanding attitudes and predicting social behavior*. Englewood Cliffs, NJ: Prentice-Hall.

Ajzen, I., & Peterson, G. L. (1988). Contingent value measurement: The price of everything and the value of nothing? In G.L. Peterson, B.L. Driver, & R. Gregory (Eds.), *Amenity resource valuation* (pp. 65-76). State College, PA: Venture Publishing.

Allport, G. W. (1935). Attitudes. In C. Murchison (Ed.), *Handbook of Social Psychology* (pp. 798-844). Worcester, MA: Clark University Press.

Barro, S., Manfredo, M., & Wells, M. (1994). Cueing as a method effect in studies on recreation choice. *Leisure Sciences*, 16, 61-71.

Bell, D. (1973). *The coming of post-industrial society*. New York: Basic Books.

Bengston, D. (1994). Changing forest values and ecosystem management. *Society and Natural Resources*, 7, 515-533.

Bright, A. D., Barro, S. C., & Burtz, R. T. (2002). Public attitudes toward ecological restoration in the Chicago metropolitan region. *Society & Natural Resources*, 15(9), 763-785.

Brown, T. C. (1984). The concept of value in resource allocation. *Land Economics*, 60(3), 231-246.

Buttell, F. H. (1992). Environmentalization: Origins, processes, and implications for rural social change. Rural Sociology, 57(1), 1-27.

Buttel, F. H., & Humphrey, C. R. (2002). Sociological theory and the natural environment. In R.E. Dunlap, & W. Michaelson (Eds.), Handbook of Environmental Sociology (pp. 33-69). Westport, CT: Greenwood Press.

Chaiken, S., & Stangor, C. (1987). Attitudes and attitude change. Annual Review of Psychology, 38, 575-630.

Daigle, J. J., Hrubes, D., & Ajzen, I. (2002). A comparative study of beliefs, attitudes, and values among hunters, wildlife viewers, and other outdoor recreationists. Human Dimensions of Wildlife, 7(1), 1-19.

Decker D. J., & Purdy, K. G. (1988). Toward a concept of wildlife acceptance capacity in wildlife management. Wildlife Society Bulletin, 16, 53-57.

DeRuiter, D., & Donnelly, M. P. (2002). A qualitative approach to measuring determinants of wildlife value orientations. Human Dimensions of Wildlife, 7, 251-271.

Dietz, T., & Rosa, E. A. (2002). Human dimensions of global environmental change. In R.E. Dunlap, & W. Michaelson (Eds.), Handbook of Environmental Sociology (pp. 370-406). Westport, CT: Greenwood Press.

Douglas, M., & Wildavsky, A. (1982). Risk and culture: An essay on the selection of technical and environmental dangers. Berkley, CA: University of California Press.

Dunlap, R. E. (2002). An enduring concern: Light stays green for environmental protection. Public Perspective, 13, 10-14.

Dunlap, R. E., & Jones, R. E. (2003). Environmental attitudes and values. In R. Fernandez-Ballesteros (Ed.), Encyclopedia of psychological assessment, vol. 1 (pp. 364-369). London: Sage.

Dunlap, R.E., & Mertig, A. G. (1992). American environmentalism: The U.S. environmental movement 1970-1990. London: Taylor and Francis.

Dunlap, R.E., & Van Liere, K. D. (1978). The new environmental paradigm. Journal of Environmental Education, 9(4), 10-19.

Eagly, A. H., & Chaiken, S. (1993). The psychology of attitudes. New York: Harcourt Brace Jovanovich, Inc.

Fishbein, M., & Ajzen, I. (1975). Belief, attitude, intention, and behavior: An introduction to theory and research. Reading, MA: Addison-Wesley.

Fisher, D. R., & Freudenburg, W. R. (2001). Ecological modernization and its critics: Assessing the past and looking to the future. Society & Natural Resources, 14, 701-709.

Fulton, D., Manfredo, M., & Lipscomb, J. (1996). Wildlife value orientations: A conceptual and measurement approach. Human Dimensions of Wildlife, 1(2), 24-47.

Harris, M. (1999). *Theories of culture in postmodern times*. Walnut Creek, CA: Altamira Press.

Heberlein, T.A. (1973). Social psychological assumptions of user attitude surveys: The case of the wildernism scale. *Journal of Leisure Research*, 5(3), 18-33.

Heberlein, T. A. (1981). Environmental attitudes. *Zeitschrift fur Umweltpolitik*, 2, 241-270.

Heberlein, T.A., & Black, J. S. (1976). Attitudinal specificity and the prediction of behavior in a field setting. *Journal of Personality and Social Psychology*, 33, 474-479.

Hironaka, A., Frank, D. A., & Schofer, E. (2000). The nation-state and natural environment over the twentieth century. *American Sociological Review*, 65, 96-116.

Homer, P. M., & Kahle, L. R. (1988). A structural equation test of the value-attitude-behavior hierarchy. *Journal of Personality and Social Psychology*, 54, 638-646.

Inglehart, R. (1990). *Culture shift in advanced industrial societies*. Princeton, NJ: Princeton University Press.

Inglehart, R. (1997). Modernization and postmodernization. Princeton, NJ: Princeton University Press.

Inglehart, R., & Baker, W. E. (2000). Modernization, cultural change, and the persistence of traditional values. *American Sociological Review*, 65, 19-51.

Jacob, R., & Schreyer, R. (1980). Conflict in outdoor recreation: A theoretical perspective. *Journal of Leisure Research*, 12, 368-380

Kellert, S. R. (1980). Contemporary values of wildlife in American society. In W. W. Shaw, & E. H. Zube (Eds.), *Wildlife values* (pp. 31-60). Tucson, AZ: Center for Assessment of Noncommodity Natural Resource Values, University of Arizona.

Kellert, S. R. (1981). *Activities of the American public relating to animals*. Washington, DC: U.S. Government Printing Office.

Kellert, S. R. (1987). Attitudes, knowledge, and behaviors toward wildlife as affected by gender. *Wildlife Society Bulletin*, 15, 363-371.

Kellert, S. R. (1993). The biological basis for human values of nature. In S. R. Kellert, & E. O. Wilson (Eds.), *The biophilia hypothesis* (pp. 42-69). Washington, DC: Island Press.

Manfredo, M. J., Fishbein, M., Watson, A., & Haas, G. (1990). A national survey of public attitudes toward prescribed fire policy. *Journal of Forestry*, 88(7), 19-23.

Manfredo, M. J., Teel, T. L., & Bright, A. D. (2003). Why are public values toward wildlife changing? *Human Dimensions of Wildlife*, 8(4), 285-304.

Manning, R. E. (1999). Studies in outdoor recreation: Search and research for satisfaction (2nd ed.). Corvallis, OR: Oregon State University Press.

Milton, K. (1996). *Environmentalism and cultural theory*. London: Routledge.

O'Conner, J. (1998). *Natural causes: Essays in ecological Marxism*. New York: The Guilford Press.

Rokeach, M. (1973). *The nature of human values*. New York: The Free Press.

Schnaiberg, A. (1980). *The environment: From surplus to scarcity*. New York: Oxford University Press.

Schwartz, S. H. (1992). Universals in the content and structure of values: Theoretical advances and empirical tests in 20 countries. *Advances in Experimental Social Psychology*, 25, 1-65.

Shelby, B., & Heberlein, T. A. (1986). *Carrying capacity in recreational settings*. Corvallis, OR: Oregon State University Press.

Shields, D., Martin, J., Martin, I. M., Wade, E., & Haefele, M. (2002). Survey results of the American public's values, objectives, beliefs and attitudes regarding forests and grasslands: A technical document supporting the 2000 USDA Forest Service RPA Assessment (General Technical Rep. RMRS-GTR-95). Fort Collins, CO: Rocky Mountain Research Station, U.S. Forest Service.

Smith, E. A., & Wishnie, M. (2000). Conservation in small-scale societies. *Annual Review of Anthropology*, 29, 493-524.

Spaargaren, G. and Mol, A. P. J. (1992). Sociology, environment and modernity: Ecological modernization as a theory of social change. *Society & Natural Resources*, 5, 323-344.

Steel, B. S., List, P., & Schindler, B. (1994). Conflicting values about forests: A comparison of national and Oregon publics. *Society & Natural Resources*, 7, 137-153.

Steinhoff, H. W. (1980). Analysis of conceptual systems for understanding and measuring wildlife values. In W. W. Shaw, & E. H. Zube (Eds.), *Wildlife values* (pp. 11-21). Tucson, AZ: Center for Assessment of Noncommodity Natural Resource Values, University of Arizona.

Stern, P. C., Dietz, T., Kalof, L., & Guagnano, G. A. (1995). Values, beliefs, and pro-environmental action: Attitude formation toward emergent attitude objects. *Journal of Applied Social Psychology*, 25(18), 1611-1636

Vaske, J. J., & Donnelly, M. P. (1999). A value-attitude-behavior model predicting wildland preservation voting intentions. *Society & Natural Resources*, 12, 523-537.

Vaske, J. J., Donnelly, M. P., Wittmann, K., & Laidlaw, S. (1995). Interpersonal versus social value conflict. *Leisure Sciences*, 17, 205-222.

Weigel, R. H., & Weigel, J. (1978). Environmental concern: The development of a measure. *Environment and Behavior*, 10, 3-16.

Woodside, A.G., & Clokey, J. D. (1974). Multi-attribute/Multi-brand models. *Journal of Advertising Research*, 14(5), 33-40.

Young, R., & Kent, A. T. (1985). Using theory of reasoned action to improve the understanding of recreation behavior. *Journal of Leisure Research*, 17(2), 90-106.

25

Normative Approaches to Natural Resources

Jerry J. Vaske
Doug Whittaker

The debate started as soon as the two backpackers reached the campsite on a small alpine lake, 15 miles into the wilderness. It was a classic Rocky Mountain outfitter camp, well-used by horsepackers, with a neat stack of cut wood next to a fire ring three feet in diameter that was filled with ashes and visible traces of melted aluminum cans. One backpacker was disgusted with the scene, her purist values offended. The other was looking for a match, anticipating the warmth and crackle of an open fire: a link to memories of childhood camping trips with her grandfather. There was agreement on some points (the inappropriateness of litter, the need for enforcement, the unacceptable size of the fire ring, that people should collect their own wood), but less agreement on others (Should fires be tolerated or banned? Should fire rings be at least dismantled after use?). Arguments were built on both sides, with appeals to personal responsibility and concerns about cumulative impacts facing off against demonstrable aesthetic benefits and traditions. But not much was resolved. As the purist steadfastly dismantled the fire ring and dispersed the cooled ashes the next morning, both were still muttering about the right thing to do and the right way to think.

To understand and explain the issues underlying such debates, social scientists have turned to the concept of *norms*. Norms can refer to what most people are doing (i.e., a descriptive norm) or to what people *should* or *ought* to do (i.e., an injunctive norm) in a given situation (Cialdini, Kallgren & Reno, 1991). *Social norms* are standards shared by members of a group (Vaske, Shelby, Graefe & Heberlein, 1986), while *personal norms* are an individual's own expectations learned from shared expectations (Schwartz, 1977).

In many definitions, norms are also intimately tied to the concept of sanctions: punishment for people who break norms or rewards for compliance with norms (Grasmick, Blackwell, Bursik & Mitchell, 1993; Heywood,

2002). Norms that are widely shared by most members of society (e.g., not littering) often become legal mandates complete with formal sanctions for noncompliance (e.g., fines). Such norms are also likely to be internalized, becoming "... part of the individual's motivational system in the sense that he is committed to it as being right, legitimate, and hence obligatory" (Blake & Davis, 1964, p. 478). When there is less agreement or the norms are emerging, informal sanctions may be used to encourage acceptable behavior or conditions. Wilderness visitors, for example, are not obligated to camp a specific distance from others. Those who fail to comply with this privacy norm are not formally sanctioned. Rather, informal sanctions such as "dirty looks" serve to communicate and enforce the norm (Heberlein & Dunwiddie, 1979; Shelby, Vaske & Donnelly, 1996). If individuals internalize a norm, external sanctions are less likely to be necessary.

Many of these norm concepts are evident in the fire ring example. Both backpackers expressed standards for acceptable behaviors and conditions, and they discussed formal sanctions for different behaviors. The purist tried informal sanctions as a way to prevent her friend from having the fire, and sanctioned herself for allowing the fire by cleaning it up the next morning, even though no societal sanction would have otherwise occurred.

Norms can help explain why people (either individually or collectively) often act in regular ways, as well as aid our understanding of *irregular* human behavior (Baron, Kerr & Miller, 1993; Heywood, 1996a). Anti-litter norms, for example, are strong and widely held (Heywood & Murdock, 2002); yet litter is often present, even in wilderness. Norms are interesting precisely because they vary by the proportion of people who hold them, their strength in an individual or group, the level of agreement about them, their influence on behavior, and their wider enforcement of social regularities. If norms were unbreakable rules for behavior, they would be indistinguishable from descriptions of behavior itself. Norms, like attitudes, however, are not static within or across people, or across situations. In a given social context, some people may have a well-formed norm that dominates their behavior or evaluation, while others may have only an emerging norm that barely influences what individuals do or think (Heywood, 1996b). Still others may be unaware of a norm and become bewildered when sanctions are brought against them for breaking it. Even well-formed norms may fail to influence behavior because of competing norms, attitudes, or motivations. The wilderness purist, for example, apparently valued her friendship more than her anti-fire norm, but then compensated for the guilt from having a fire by cleaning up the fire ring.

Norms are a multi-faceted concept that are defined and used differently within the social sciences and in their applications to natural resource issues. One conceptual tradition, for example, examines the relationships between norms that are *focused* (Cialdini et al., 1991) or become activated (Bratt, 1999; Schwartz, 1977), and the resulting behavior. A second tradition hypothesizes that norms exert social pressure to influence behavior (Ajzen & Fishbein, 1980; Fishbein & Ajzen, 1975). Under this paradigm, *subjective norms* (i.e., what you think others would want you to do) are similar to attitudes (i.e., whether you think the behavior is good or bad) in directing behavioral intentions and behavior. A third tradition is more descriptive, emphasizing the *structural characteristics* of norms (e.g., prevalence, range of tolerable conditions, intensity, crystallization), which provide a framework for evaluating behaviors (or conditions stemming from those behaviors) in a social setting (Donnelly, Vaske, Whittaker & Shelby, 2000; Shelby et al., 1996; Vaske & Donnelly, 2002).

Although these three traditions may appear competitive, they are best viewed as complementary. All three share the notion that norms are constructs in an individual's mind that can be aggregated to explain larger social regularities. Each paradigm provides information about when a norm exists and is likely to direct behavior. The successful use of the paradigms, however, requires clarity about what each provides and the research question at hand. Each paradigm does some things better than the others. For example, norm focus / activation models may be more appropriate for understanding the factors that influence responsible environmental behavior (e.g., not littering, recycling newspapers), while structural approaches may be a better choice for determining standards for acceptable recreation use impacts.

In this chapter, we review these three social psychological norm paradigms (norm focus / activation theories, theory of reasoned action [subjective norms], and structural characteristics of norms), suggest the natural resources applications where they excel, and discuss how the different perspectives help inform each other. The chapter concludes with a summary of the conceptual distinctions between the traditions and concepts.

Norm Focus and Activation Models

Norm focus theory (Cialdini et al., 1991; Cialdini, Reno & Kallgren, 1990) suggests that norms only affect behavior when they are salient or in focus. In an elegant series of experiments about littering, the researchers found strong support for the model. The experiments set up situations where people were given a piece of paper, no place to dispose of it, and varied environmental cues that emphasized either descriptive social norms (a lot versus a little litter), injunctive social norms (messages *not to litter* versus no messages at all), or both. They also surveyed people's personal norms after the situation. The experiments demonstrated that norms against littering had powerful and systematic effects on littering behavior, but only if the norm was *in focus.*

Schwartz' norm activation model (1968, 1973, 1977) also explored the conditions under which norms affect behavior, focusing specifically on altruistic acts caused by beliefs of what is morally correct. Conceived as an internal norm, enforced by an internal sense of obligation to others, Schwartz (1977) suggested that norms are activated only when certain conditions are met. First, individuals need to be aware of the consequences (AC) their behavior has on others. Second, individuals must ascribe responsibility (AR) for their actions to themselves. AC and AR are predicted to influence how situations are evaluated, the extent of norm activation, and whether behavior will change.

Although the norm activation model was initially used to explain norm-behavior consistency in helping behaviors (Schwartz, 1973, 1977), its applicability to environmental behavior is well demonstrated. Heberlein (1972) has argued that decisions regarding the environment have become a moral issue, and that the collective effect of individual behaviors is important. Increasing concern over greenhouse effects, for example, illustrates how heightened awareness of, and personal responsibility for, global warming consequences (e.g., flooding of coastal areas due to rising sea levels, increased skin disease) has stimulated efforts to reduce potentially harmful emissions.

Research has documented the utility of the AC and AR constructs in predicting behavioral changes or evaluations of those behaviors. Specific issues have included recycling (Hopper & Nielsen, 1991), littering, the purchase of lead-free gasoline, and other energy conserving behavior (Heberlein, 1971); environmental conservation behavior (Black, 1978); support for environmental laws and regulations with links to moral judgments about government and industry responsibilities (Stern, Dietz & Black, 1986); yard waste burning (Van Liere & Dunlap, 1978); and water pollution related to human waste dumped by boaters (Cottrell & Graefe, 1997).

Norm activation concepts were also evident in the introductory fire ring example. The purist's arguments emphasized the negative consequences of having a fire, while suggesting that personal decisions mattered ("What if everyone had a fire?"). If her pro-fire friend had agreed with these points, an anti-fire norm might have been activated. For natural resource issues concerned with environmental behavior and particularly the control of it (e.g., Cialdini, 1996), norm focus and activation models are likely to prove useful.

Theory of Reasoned Action (TRA)
In the fire ring example, the fire-building hiker may have agreed about the consequences of, or her personal contribution to, the impacts, but still disagree about the *right* behavior (if other attitudes or norms trumped the anti-fire norm). The Theory of Reasoned Action (TRA) offers a possible explanation for how these competing attitudes and norms direct behavior. This model suggests that volitional behavior is directed by intentions to behave, which are directed by both norms and attitudes (Ajzen & Fishbein, 1980; Fishbein & Ajzen, 1975). Under this paradigm, however, subjective norms identify what an individual believes others think s/he should do, while the individual's attitudes clarify the person's beliefs and evaluations about an object (e.g., person, situation, context). In contrast to other norm theories, TRA researchers measure perceived social norms, and assume that the personal norm is implicitly reflected in the individual's beliefs and evaluations (i.e., the attitude variable).

Natural resource applications of TRA models have shown that subjective norms predict camping participation (Young & Kent, 1985) and support for natural resource management (Bright, Manfredo, Fishbein & Bath, 1993). Young and Kent (1985) found that intentions to go camping were influenced by beliefs about whether important others, especially family, think they ought to go camping. Because camping is a group activity, other people may be important influences on participation. Bright et al. (1993) also showed that support for controlled burns in U.S. National Parks was influenced by individuals' beliefs about what other people think they should believe. This influence may be particularly important for people who are uninformed about an issue. Talking to others was one of the top sources of information for Colorado residents voting on a proposed trapping ban in 1996, an issue about which many voters appeared unsure (Manfredo, Fulton & Pierce, 1997).

Bratt (1999) blended norm concepts from both Fishbein and Ajzen (1975) and Schwartz (1977) in a study on recycling behavior (Figure 1). The subjective social norm was measured by asking respondents whether they believed that a) their spouse and b) their children thought they should recycle paper products.

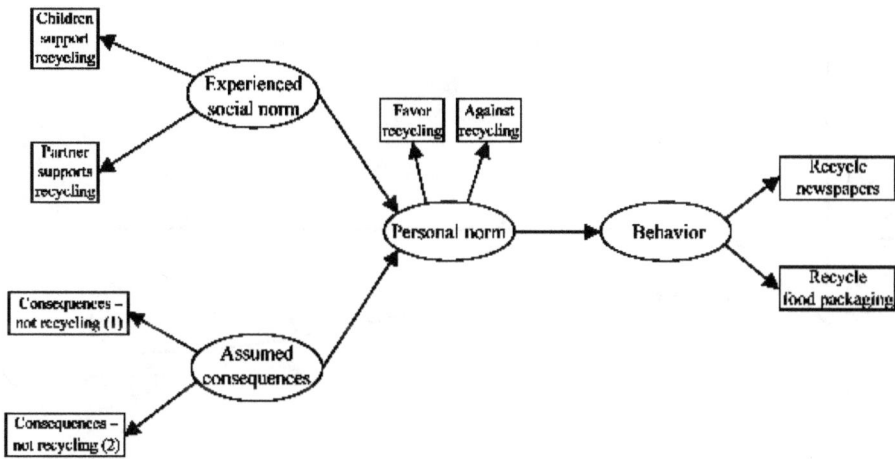

Figure 1. Combining Fishbein & Ajzen's subjective norms with Schwartz's norm activation model. Adapted from Bratt (1999).

Assumed consequences were measured with two variables that reflected beliefs about the collective and individual consequences of not recycling on the environment. Results showed that individuals who experienced the social norm (i.e., believed that their children and spouse thought they should recycle) and who had assumed the consequences of their actions were more likely to have a pro-recycling norm and recycle.

Overall, TRA norm concepts are useful for measuring perceived social pressure and the influence of norms and attitudes on behavior. Such concepts can facilitate the design of persuasion campaigns intended to modify impact behavior (e.g., "leave no trace" efforts). For anti-litter campaigns, Grasmick, Bursik and Kinsey (1991) suggest appealing to individual's conscience (i.e., internal norms of guilt or shame) and / or their community spirit (i.e., informal sanction of embarrassment). Many low impact behaviors involve the diffusion of innovative practices that were initially adopted by guides or experienced trip leaders (e.g., human waste disposal systems). TRA paradigms offer an explanation of how these innovations are diffused in a larger population through the influence of others (i.e., subjective norms).

Structural Characteristics Models
A third social psychology tradition focuses on the characteristics of social norms through use of a graphic device that Jackson (1965) initially described as the return potential model (now more generally known as *impact acceptability curves*). Applied to environmental conditions, impacts are displayed on a horizontal axis while evaluation (i.e., acceptability) is displayed on the vertical axis (Figure 2). The curves

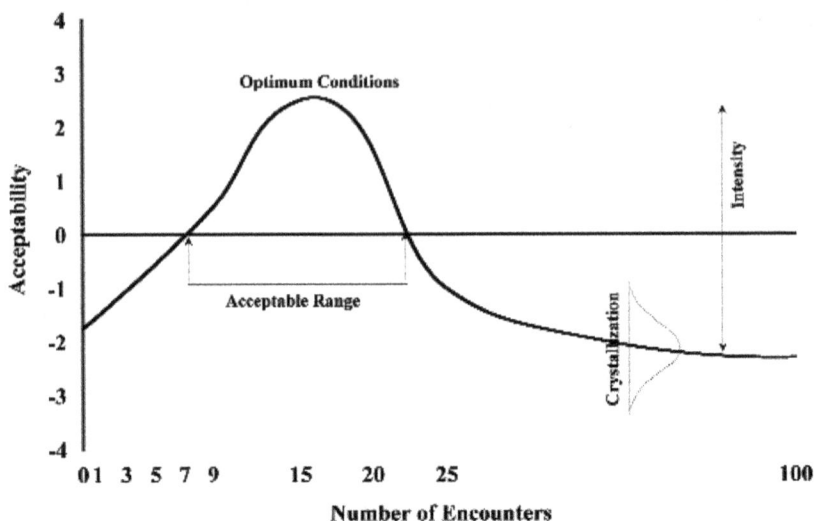

Figure 2. The structural characteristics of norms.

describe social norms as aggregate averages of personal norms, but they can also describe evaluations for an individual.

The curve can be analyzed for various structural characteristics. The high point of the curve shows the optimum or best situation. The range of impacts where evaluations are above the neutral line defines the *range of tolerable conditions*. The amplitude of the curve describes the intensity of the norm (one measure of strength), while variation among evaluations at each impact level shows the amount of agreement or *crystallization* (a second measure of strength). Evaluative standards for backpacking in a wilderness setting (Figure 3), for example, often have an optimum of zero encounters, a low range of tolerable contacts, high intensity and high crystallization. Norms for hiking in a developed recreation area tend to show a greater tolerable range, lower intensity, and less agreement (Shelby et al., 1996). For deer hunting, too few and too many people can be evaluated negatively; hunters want enough people to move deer, but not so many that crowding or competition problems emerge.

Jackson's model has been extensively applied to natural resources, often with respect to encounter norms that describe how many people are too many in a recreation setting (see Donnelly et al., 2000; Manning, Lawson, Newman, Laven, & Valliere, 2002; Shelby et al., 1996; Vaske & Donnelly, 2002). Other applications have extended the structural approach to interaction impact issues such as campsite or attraction site sharing (Heberlein & Dunwiddie, 1979; Shelby, 1981), the number of people in sight at attraction areas (Manning, Lime, Freimund & Pitt, 1996), fishing competition (Martinson & Shelby, 1992; Whittaker & Shelby, 1993), discourteous behavior incidents (Whittaker & Shelby, 1988, 1993; Whittaker, Vaske & Williams, 2000), capacities on wildlife viewing platforms (Whittaker, 1997), or other resource

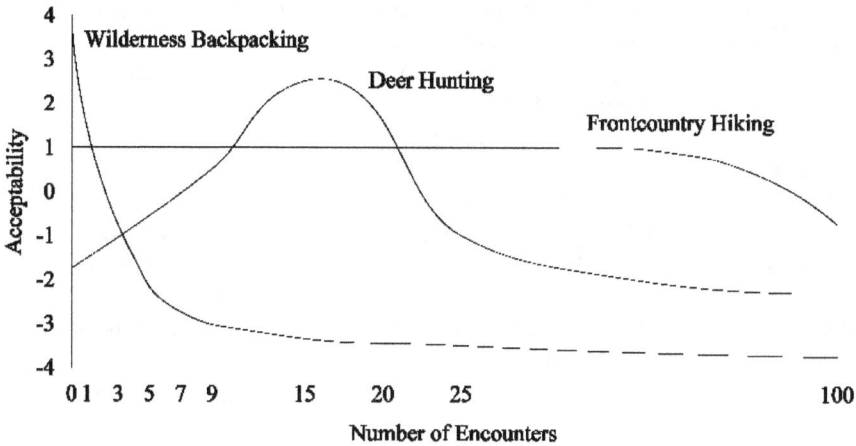

Figure 3. Hypothetical norm curves for three activities.

issues such as instream flow requirements for different river recreation activities (Whittaker & Shelby, 2002), the amount of bare ground and size of fire rings in campgrounds (Shelby, Vaske & Harris, 1988), the acceptability of wildlife management practices (Wittmann, Vaske, Manfredo & Zinn, 1998; Zinn, Manfredo, Vaske & Wittmann, 1998), and wildfire policies (Kneeshaw, Vaske, Bright & Absher, 2003). In all of these applications, researchers have explored either acceptable behaviors or acceptable conditions caused by behavior.

This approach is powerful because it facilitates the development of standards for acceptable social and physical conditions that are central to planning frameworks such as Limits of Acceptable Change, Visitor Impact Management, or Visitor Experience and Resource Protection (Shelby & Vaske, 1991). While acknowledging the management utility, some natural resource researchers have critiqued the extension to conditions, noting that conditions cannot be sanctioned and that norms need to have an explicit obligation dimension (Heywood, 1996a; Heywood & Murdock, 2002). The issues in this debate are beyond the scope of this paper (see Roggenbuck, Williams, Bange & Dean, 1991; Shelby & Vaske, 1991), but the extension is important because it links natural resource problems to the *Tragedy of the Commons*. As described by Hardin (1968), this idea suggests that collective rather than individual behavior can significantly harm a resource (as each minor individual act is cumulative). For an individual, a behavior may be rational because the marginal benefit is greater than the marginal cost. For the collective, however, marginal costs can exceed marginal benefits. Accordingly, norms that constrain individual behavior (e.g., mutually agreed upon obligations and sanctions) are necessary to protect the commons. In applying Jackson's approach to natural resource problems, researchers have shifted the focus to the question of "How much is too much collective impact?" (a condition evaluation), which has implications for managing agencies. Institutions have a sense of obligation and institutional behaviors that allow unacceptable conditions have clear normative elements (Baland & Platteau, 1996; Vaske, Donnelly & Whittaker, 2000).

Conclusions

Different social psychologists define and use the concept of norms differently. Some concentrate on the variables that serve to focus (Cialdini et al., 1990, 1991) or activate a norm (e.g., Bratt, 1999; Schwartz, 1977), while others address how social pressure can influence behavior or aid in the diffusion of ideas (Ajzen & Fishbein, 1980; Fishbein & Ajzen, 1975). Still others emphasize the structural characteristics of norms (Shelby et al., 1996; Vaske et al., 1986) to help evaluate appropriate behavior or conditions. Knowing how different researchers use the same basic concept of norms clarifies what theoretical approach is most appropriate for examining a given situation or problem.

The theories also differ in how they measure the concept of norms. Norm focus / activation theories and the structural norm approach measure norms at the individual level (i.e., personal norms) and then aggregate the data to derive social norms. TRA, in contrast, focuses primarily on perceived social norms (i.e., subjective norms) and does not directly address the concept of a personal norm (which is subsumed within a person's attitude).

Norms can be linked to attitudes in other ways as well, and are often construed as a parallel construct. Like attitudes, norms have both cognitive and affective components, as well as the ability to influence behavior (Heywood, 2002). Some attitudes and norms are more global than others, and the specificity of each is critical for determining whether the attitude or norm will accurately predict behavior. Norms are different from attitudes, however, because of the added dimension of obligation. Attitude measures focus on positive or negative evaluations, while norm variables examine acceptability evaluations (i.e., what a person, group or institution should do). Beliefs about internal or external sanctions are additional components without parallels in attitude models.

To illustrate the attitude-norm distinction, consider the fire ring example. "I dislike seeing fire rings in wilderness" may be the attitude, but the norm is proscriptive: "Fire rings are unacceptable." The norm rises from the attitude, but with additional elements implicit, including: "People should not build them," "I will sanction people who build them," "I expect people to sanction me if I build one," "I will feel guilty if I build one," and "I expect government agencies to do something about people who build them."

A fundamental issue with either norms or attitudes involves norm (or attitude) strength. The ability of a norm to predict individual or group behavior is influenced by how strongly a norm is held in that individual or group. Norm strength (like attitude strength), however, is poorly defined in social psychology (Krosnick, Boniger, Chuang, Berent & Carnot, 1993). Jackson's (1965) norm intensity and crystallization tap two dimensions of the concept, as might Rossi and Berk's (1985) classes of consensus. Schwartz' (1968) concept of moral norms (with presumably greater strength) may relate to a third, and seems consistent with Heywood's (1996a) notion that some norms have more *shouldness* or obligation than others. Miller and Prentice's (1996) discussion of a few global and many more situational norms also reflects norm strength issues (the former has great strength and applies across situations, the latter does not and works situationally).

A possible integrating concept is the notion of a normative continuum (Heywood, 1996b). A norm does not simply exist or not exist. As a construct in a person's mind, a norm may be weakly held, difficult to access, without much sense of obligation, with no connection to moral values, and may be associated with low expectations of trivial external sanctions. As such, one would not expect the norm to have much effect on behavior. However, if the converse were true (the norm is strong, has a sense of obligation attached, brings expectations of sanctions), the norm should influence a person's response. The research challenge is to measure a variety of information about normative concepts in people or across groups, and then relate that to behavior.

Norms, like attitudes, are not tangible things, but latent constructs researchers use to describe how cognitions and affective responses are represented in an individual. As with attitude research, norm research measures dimensions of these latent constructs, with implicit understanding that they will be related to each other and the behavior we are trying to understand, predict and possibly control. The multiplicity of dimensions provides more alternatives for understanding when a norm is activated, salient and relevant. As with attitude work, no theory of norms is likely to effectively encompass all of the ways the concept may be used to understand how people think or act in social situations. However, with continued work in the field, it is likely that the paradigms in use will increasingly inform each other and provide a more coherent view.

References

Ajzen, I., & Fishbein, M. (1980). *Understanding attitudes and predicting social behavior.* Englewood Cliffs, NJ: Prentice-Hall.

Baland, J. E., & Platteau, J. P. (1996). *Halting degradation of natural resources: Is there a role for rural communities.* Oxford, UK: Oxford University Press.

Baron, R. S., Kerr, N. L., & Miller, N. (1993). *Group process, group decision, group action.* Pacific Grove, CA: Brooks/Cole Publishing.

Black, J. S. (1978). Attitudinal, normative, and economic factors in early response to an energy-use field experiment. Unpublished doctoral dissertation. The University of Wisconsin, Madison.

Blake, J., & Davis, K. (1964). Norms, values and sanctions. In R. E. L. Harris (Ed.), *Handbook of modern sociology* (pp. 456-484). Chicago: Rand McNally.

Bratt, C. (1999). The impact of norms and assumed consequences on recycling behavior. *Environment and Behavior,* 31, 630-656.

Bright, A. D., Manfredo, M. J., Fishbein., M., & Bath, A. (1993). Application of the theory of reasoned action to the National Park Service's controlled burn policy. *Journal of Leisure Research,* 25(3), 263 – 280.

Cialdini, R. B. (1996). Activating and aligning two kinds of norms in persuasive communications. *Journal of Interpretation Research,* 1(1), 3-10.

Cialdini, R. B., Kallgren, C. A., & Reno, R. R. (1991). A focus theory of normative conduct: A theoretical refinement and reevaluation of the role of norms in human behavior. *Advances in Experimental Social Psychology*, 24, 201-234.

Cialdini, R. B., Reno, R. R., & Kallgren, C. A. (1990). A focus theory of normative conduct: Recycling the concept of norms to reduce littering in public places. *Journal of Personality and Social Psychology*, 58, 1015-1026.

Cottrell, S. P., & Graefe, A. R. (1997). Testing a conceptual framework of responsible environmental behavior. *Journal of Environmental Education*, 29 (1), 17-27.

Donnelly, M. P., Vaske, J. J., Whittaker, D., & Shelby, B. (2000). Toward an understanding of norm prevalence: A comparative analysis of 20 years of research. *Environmental Management*, 25(4), 403-414.

Fishbein, M., & Ajzen, I. (1975). *Belief, attitude, intention and behavior: An introduction to theory and research*. Reading, MA: Addison-Wesley.

Grasmick, H. G., Blackwell, B. S., Bursik, R. J., Jr., & Mitchell, S. (1993). Changes in perceived threats of shame, embarrassment, and legal sanctions for interpersonal violence, 1982-1992. *Violence and Victims*, 8, 313-325.

Grasmick, H.G., Bursik, R.J., Jr., & Kinsey, K.A. (1991). Shame and embarrassment as deterrents to noncompliance with the law: The case of an antilittering campaign. *Environment and Behavior*, 23, 233-251.

Hardin, G. (1968). The tragedy of the commons. *Science*, 78, 20-27.

Heberlein, T. A. (1971). Moral norms, threatened sanctions, and littering behavior. *Dissertation Abstracts International*, 32, 5906A. (UMI No. 72-2639).

Heberlein, T. A. (1972). The land ethic realized: Some social psychological explanations for changing environmental attitudes. *Journal of Social Issues*, 28, 79-87.

Heberlein, T. A., & Dunwiddie, P. (1979). Systematic observations of use levels, campsite selection and visitor characteristics at a high mountain lake. *Journal of Leisure Research*, 11, 307-316.

Heywood, J. L. (1996a). Social regularities in outdoor recreation. *Leisure Sciences*, 18, 23-38.

Heywood, J. L. (1996b). Conventions, emerging norms, and norms in outdoor recreation. *Leisure Sciences*, 18, 355-364.

Heywood, J. L. (2002). The cognitive and emotional components of behavior norms in outdoor recreation. *Leisure Sciences*, 24, 271-281

Heywood, J. L., & Murdock, W. E. (2002). Social norms in outdoor recreation: Searching for the behavior-condition link. *Leisure Sciences*, 24, 283-295.

Hopper, J. R., & Nielsen, J. (1991). Recycling as altruistic behavior: Normative and behavioral strategies to expand participation in a community recycling program. *Environment and Behavior*, 23, 195-220.

Jackson, J. M. (1965). Structural characteristics of norms. In I. D. Steiner & M. F. Fishbein (Eds.), *Current studies in social psychology* (pp. 301-309). New York: Holt, Rinehart & Winston.

Kneeshaw, K., Vaske, J. J., Bright, A. D., & Absher, J. D. (2003). *Acceptability norms toward fire management in three national forests.* Manuscript submitted for publication.

Krosnick, J. A., Boniger, D. S., Chuang, Y. C., Berent, M. K., & Carnot, C. G. (1993). Attitude strength: One construct or many related constructs? *Journal of Personality and Social Psychology, 65,* 1132-1151.

Manfredo, M. J., Fulton, D. C., & Pierce, C. L. (1997). Understanding voter behavior on wildlife ballot initiatives: Colorado's trapping amendment. *Human Dimensions of Wildlife, 2,* 22-39.

Manning, R., Lawson, S., Newman, P., Laven, D., & Valliere, W. (2002). Methodological issues in measuring crowding – related norms in outdoor recreation. *Leisure Sciences, 24,* 339-348.

Manning, R., Lime, D., Freimund, W., & Pitt, D. (1996). Crowding norms at frontcountry sites: A visual approach to setting standards of quality. *Leisure Sciences, 18,* 39-59.

Martinson, K. S., & Shelby, B. (1992). Encounter and proximity norms for salmon anglers in California and New Zealand. *North American Journal of Fisheries Management, 12,* 559-567.

Miller, D. T., & Prentice, D. A. (1996). The construction of social norms and standards. In E. T. Higgins & A. W. Kruglanski (Eds.), *Social psychology: Handbook of basic principles.* New York: Guilford.

Roggenbuck, J. W., Williams, D. R., Bange, S. P., & Dean, D. J. (1991). River float trip encounter norms: Questioning the use of the social norms concept. *Journal of Leisure Research, 23,* 133-153.

Rossi, P. H., & Berk, R. A. (1985). Varieties of normative consensus. *American Sociological Review, 50,* 333-347.

Schwartz, S. H. (1968). Awareness of consequences and the influence of moral norms on interpersonal behavior. *Sociometry, 31,* 355-369.

Schwartz, S. H. (1973). Normative explanations of helping behavior: A critique, proposal, and empirical test. *Journal of Experimental and Social Psychology, 9,* 349-364.

Schwartz, S. H. (1977). Normative influences on altruism. In L. Berkowitz (Ed.), *Advances in experimental social psychology* (Vol. 10, pp. 221-279). New York: Academic Press.

Shelby, B. (1981). Encounter norms in backcountry settings: Studies of three rivers. *Journal of Leisure Research, 13,* 129-138.

Shelby, B., & Vaske, J. J. (1991). Using normative data to develop evaluative standards for resource management: A comment on three recent papers. *Journal of Leisure Research*, 23, 173-187.

Shelby, B., Vaske, J. J., & Donnelly, M. P. (1996). Norms, standards, and natural resources. *Leisure Sciences*, 18, 103-123.

Shelby, B., Vaske, J. J., & Harris, R. (1988). User standards for ecological impacts at wilderness campsites. *Journal of Leisure Research*, 20, 245-256.

Stern, P. C., Dietz, T., & Black, J. S. (1986). Support for environmental protection: The role of moral norms. *Population and Environment*, 8, 204-222.

Van Liere, K. D., & Dunlap, R. E. (1978). Moral norms and environmental behavior: An application of Schwartz's norm-activation model to yard burning. *Journal of Applied Psychology*, 8, 174-188.

Vaske, J. J., & Donnelly, M. P. (2002). Generalizing the encounter – norm – crowding relationship. *Leisure Sciences*, 24, 255-269.

Vaske, J. J., Donnelly, M. P., & Whittaker, D. (2000). Tourism, national parks and impact management. In R. Butler & S. Boyd (Eds.), *Tourism and National Parks: Issues and Implications* (pp. 203 – 222). New York: John Wiley and Sons.

Vaske, J. J., Shelby, B. B., Graefe, A. R., & Heberlein, T. A. (1986). Backcountry encounter norms: Theory, method and empirical evidence. *Journal of Leisure Research*, 18, 137- 153.

Whittaker, D. (1997). Capacity norms on bear viewing platforms. *Human Dimensions of Wildlife*, 2, 37-49.

Whittaker, D., & Shelby, B. (1988). Types of norms for recreation impacts: Extending the social norms concept. *Journal of Leisure Research*, 20, 261-273.

Whittaker, D., & Shelby, B. (1993). *Kenai River carrying capacity study: Findings and implications for management* (RTCA Report, Alaska State Parks). Anchorage, AK: Alaska Department of Natural Resources.

Whittaker, D., & Shelby, B. (2002). Evaluating instream flows for recreation: Applying the structural norm approach. *Leisure Sciences*, 24, 363-374.

Whittaker, D., Vaske, J. J., & Williams, T. V. (2000). *Gulkana River 1999 on-river user survey.* (Project Rep. No. 45). Fort Collins, Colorado: Colorado State University, Human Dimensions in Natural Resources Unit.

Wittmann, K., Vaske, J. J., Manfredo, M. J., & Zinn, H. C. (1998). Standards for lethal response to problem urban wildlife. *Human Dimensions of Wildlife*, 3, 29-48.

Young, R. A., & Kent, A. (1985). Using the theory of reasoned action to improve the understanding of recreation behavior. *Journal of Leisure Research*, 17, 90-106.

Zinn, H. C., Manfredo, M. J., Vaske, J. J., & Wittmann, K. (1998). Using normative beliefs to determine the acceptability of wildlife management actions. *Society and Natural Resources*, 11(7), 649-662.

26

The Role of Economics in Managing Natural Resources for Society

John Loomis

At its core, economics is a social science that attempts to predict and explain human behavior. In terms of natural resources, the last several decades has seen the economic approach broadened from emphasis on commodity extraction (Hotelling, 1931) to studying recreation consumption decisions (Clawson & Knetsch, 1964) and preservation of natural environments (Krutilla, 1967). Economics are often central to these issues; gains and losses are consistently raised in arguments over whether to protect roadless areas as wilderness, phase out snowmobiles from national parks or dam free-flowing rivers for water storage. However, economic arguments are often misused and confused with financial accounting in these debates. Understanding what is and is not a legitimate economic benefit or impact is critical to putting economics in its proper perspective along with other public policy criteria in natural resource decision-making. This chapter will describe how economic principles and techniques have followed this evolution, with emphasis on natural resource recreation and preservation of natural environments.

Definition

Economics is a study of how people choose between competing wants and desires for allocation of scarce resources, including: labor; constructed capital; and natural resources such as land, forests, wildlife and water. The traditional focus of natural resource economics was on marketed commodities such as timber, commercial fisheries and mining. The original distinguishing characteristic of natural resource economics compared with standard microeconomics was the emphasis of the former on the linkage of one period's harvesting decision on the next. Given a finite amount of non-renewable resources such as oil, or a slow growing resource such as forests, extraction today reduced the opportunities for extraction tomorrow. Thus harvesting decisions in one period influenced the amount available for harvesting in future periods.

In the 1960s, growing incomes, widespread ownership of automobiles and other factors shifted the focus on forests from timber management to recreation, such as hunting and fishing. Natural resource-based recreation is not a marketed commodity in most states, and thus traditional natural resource economic models were not useful for determining optimum management of forests for recreation instead of timber. But the basic consumer economic theory of demand and the recognition by Hotelling (1947) that travel costs involved in visiting recreation areas created a spatial market resulted in the genesis of a travel cost method for estimating recreation demand.

Many of the first applications of recreation demand models and valuation were to hunting (Davis, 1963) and fishing (Brown, Singh & Castle, 1964). Since the 1960s, the tourism industry has also eclipsed traditional extractive industry in many rural areas of the world. In many areas, nature-based tourism has become the renewable resource industry that provides jobs and attracts residents to an area.

While studies continue today on the recreational value of hunting and fishing, these activities have declined in popularity relative to non-consumptive uses of natural resources (e.g., wildlife viewing, hiking). Recreation demand models for valuation of both consumptive and non-consumptive activities are now quite common.

As recreational use of natural resources has grown and the economy expanded, maintaining the quality of natural resources for recreation and tourism has been difficult. Resource extraction and commercial development has often adversely affected the suitability of natural resources for recreation. This has shifted the focus in recreation economic analysis from simply estimating the value of existing recreation, to measuring how the value of recreation would change with adverse environmental changes, such as that often brought forth by development. On a proactive note, the same recreation demand models have been applied to estimate the benefits that would result from protecting (or restoring) natural resources for the purpose of recreation.

The growing popularity of recreation has resulted in excess demand and the need to replace worn-out recreation facilities. As a result, agencies have begun to increase recreation fees from nominal amounts to levels that will ration use as a means to raise revenue. Research into the economic efficiency and equity of entrance fees has emerged over the past two decades as an area of interest primarily to economists (Loomis, 1980; Rosenthal, Loomis & Peterson, 1984). This work has greater relevance now as the U.S. Congress has given agencies the authority to use entrance fees as a recreation management tool (Luloff, Field & Krannich, 2000; Taylor, Vaske, Shelby, Donnelly & Browne-Nunez, 2002).

In the 1960s economists began to recognize that non-visitors also obtained benefits from protection of natural resources. The initial discussion of the benefits received by people from just knowing a resource will continue to exist in a natural state was put forward by Krutilla (1967). This was followed by a series of articles that have quantified the economic benefits individuals receive from the existence of wilderness (Walsh, Loomis & Gillman, 1984), free flowing rivers (Sanders, Walsh & Loomis, 1990) and wildlife (Loomis & White, 1996). This value has been formally recognized by U.S. federal courts and resource management agencies such as the U.S. Department of Interior.

Economic Valuation versus Economic Impacts

One of the first challenges in demonstrating the relevance of economics to natural resource management and communicating with other disciplines was to make clear the distinction between *financial analysis, tourism impact analysis* and *economic benefits*. *Financial analysis* concerns only the cash flow received by agencies or companies, and ignores the benefits to the tourism-based communities or visitors themselves. *Tourism impact analysis* focuses primarily on the jobs and income provided to tourist-related workers by visitor spending. The actual *economics benefits* of recreation are reflected in visitors' willingness to pay in excess of actual cost or spending (Loomis & Walsh, 1997).

Concern about the application of economic principles to recreation management was often attributable to misunderstandings of these three types of analyses. For example, public agency concerns that recreation benefits would be undervalued by economists stemmed from the mistaken notion that the value of recreation was just the entrance or license fees paid (i.e., financial analysis), or just the amount of money actually spent by the visitor (i.e., impact analysis). While fees are a financial cash flow of revenue, and visitor expenditures create economic impacts such as jobs, neither of these measures reflects the visitors' maximum willingness-to-pay (WTP) of the visitor. The WTP (or consumer surplus) is the correct concept of benefits that can be compared to the agency's costs, or the opportunity costs of using natural resources for recreation versus in commodity production.

Non-market Valuation Methods for Recreation

Contingent Valuation Method

One of the two most frequently used methods to estimate visitors net WTP is the contingent valuation method (CVM). This method uses direct questioning of visitors regarding how much more they would pay for a recreation experience beyond current trip costs. As a survey technique it is subject to many methodological concerns, and thus has been the subject of investigation by a range of social scientists.

The CVM method has been improved by collaboration between economists and other social scientists. Bishop & Heberlein (1990) were one of the first to address the core concern of CVM: whether statements of WTP are valid measures of actual behavior. They tested validity by comparing expressed WTP to actual cash WTP for hunting permits. Since that time, validity testing has been a major research focus in CVM, giving rise to numerous comparisons of WTP (Carson, Flores, Martin & Wright, 1996).

Similarly, concerns regarding the reliability of CVM methods and results are an issue. Reliability and temporal stability of CVM responses received significant research since the appearance of Loomis' (1989) original research on this topic (Bowker, Betz, Cordell & Super, 1994; Jorgensen, Syme, Smith & Bishop, 1998). Unlike most of the literature which used identical individuals in a test-retest approach, and found high reliability and temporal stability (Loomis, 1989; Reiling, Boyle, Philips & Anderson, 1990), Bowker et al. (1994) tested temporal reliability using different samples of visitors to the same seven U.S. National Forests. They found that there was considerable variation in WTP values across the two time periods, suggesting that test-retest methods of the same sample are perhaps a more reliable method for CVM research. However, using different samples of individuals at the same site over several time periods enables CVM-WTP to detect differences in visitor sample composition, or changes in resource conditions from year to year. This second result, that CVM can measure changes in values when changes occur, is the other condition necessary for a reliable measure (Bailey, 1994).

Another important area of CVM research has been testing whether CVM-WTP estimates are sensitive to the scale of the resource protection program offered. Sensitivity to scale became a concern when a panel chaired by two Nobel laureates suggested that sensitivity to scope would be an indicator of a reliable CVM instrument (Arrow, Solow, Portney, Leamer, Radner & Schuman, 1993). However, demonstrating scope has proven difficult because it is not always clear what the salient units of "more" are for natural resource programs. Errors in defining the scale can lead to erroneous rejection of scope.

One of the most thorough investigations regarding scope in CVM is by Heberlein, Wilson, Bishop & Schaeffer (2000). By comparing scope tests for resources ranging from water quality (unambiguously a perceived good) to wolves (more is good to some, but bad to others) and conducting post survey interviews, they were able to investigate why CVM passed a scope test for water quality but not for wolves. The researchers went as far as to conclude that scope tests may not be a good test for evaluating the validity of CVM responses.

In part due to concerns about the sensitivity of CVM results to WTP question format and difficulty in finding sensitivity of WTP estimates of the scope of resources being offered, there was interest in developing alternatives to CVM to estimate the value of recreation and natural resources. Two of the most prominent efforts are the Values Jury (Brown & Peterson, 1995) and the method of paired comparison (Peterson & Brown, 1998). The Values Jury is modeled after a courtroom jury process of hearing the facts of a case before rendering a verdict. In this method, a citizen panel is given in-depth information about particular natural resources in order to elicit informed value judgments about the relative worth of these resources.

Paired comparison uses a series of dichotomous choices between different pairs of natural resources and monetary amounts to infer a valuation for the natural resource. Paired comparison is particularly useful at eliciting Willingness to Accept, something that CVM has greater difficulty in addressing.

Travel Cost Method (TCM)
The TCM for estimating recreation demand and net WTP has also been used for several decades since the appearance of Clawson and Knetsch's (1964) book. This method uses variations in travel costs as proxies for trip prices, and number of trips taken as a measure of quantity, to elicit a demand curve for recreation. From the demand curve, the net WTP or consumer surplus is calculated. For the first two decades a zonal TCM was popular. This was due to the fact that this variant of TCM could be used with secondary data on visitor origin, and be grouped into zones. Extensive use and refinement of zonal TCM occurred during the last several decades (Bowes & Loomis, 1980; Hellerstein, 1991).

With the design and implementation of recreation demand surveys, the individual observation and random utility model TCM's have become the norm in recreation demand modeling since the 1990s (Hanley, Shaw & Wright, 2003; Herriges & Kling, 1999). TCM allows each person's reported annual trips to a site to be related to their own reported travel cost, as well as a host of personal demographic variables. This allows for a richer understanding of the factors influencing an individual's demand for a particular recreation site. The random utility model involves a sophisticated econometric model of how individuals choose among competing substitute sites on the basis of not only the sites relative travel cost, but also the relative quality of the competing sites.

Determining how Recreation Values Change with Natural Resource Quality
Early non-market valuation was primarily concerned with refining methods so they would yield accurate measures of existing recreation use values. In recent decades the research focus has shifted to more management relevant issues of how changes in natural resource management affect recreation benefits. Research in this area includes how recreation use and benefits are affected by changes in in-stream flows (Loomis & Gonzalez-Caban, 1997) and reservoir levels (Cameron, Shaw, Ragland, Callaway & Keefe, 1996). More recently, with the growing prevalence of forest fires, research has focused on the effect of fire on recreation (Gonzalez-Caban, Loomis & Englin, 2002; Hesseln, Loomis & Gonzalez-Caban, 2002). The overall results from this research suggest that the natural resource quality at a site has a statistically significant effect on the number of trips an individual takes and on the net WTP per day. However, these models find that there is diminishing marginal effect of increased quality, as each additional increase results in a smaller and smaller increase in visitation.

Promoting Economic Efficiency in Recreation Management Through Fees
With growing recreation use but declining budgets, U.S. public agencies and Congress have authorized increased fees. Early research suggested that fees could be more than a revenue device; they could be used for recreation management by adopting peak load pricing and differential site pricing (Bamford, Manning, Forcier & Koenemann, 1988; Harris & Driver, 1987; Loomis, 1980; Rosenthal et al., 1984). With Congressional passage of the Fee Demonstration Program in 1996, federal agencies raised existing fees substantially (50-100 percent) and began charging fees in areas that were previously free. This program resulted in a great deal of research to monitor the effect of fees on visitor use. Fees were increased substantially at many National Parks and thus they were the focus of a majority of research (Krannich, Luloff & Field, 2002; Leahy & Johnson, 2000; Luloff et al., 2000; Thompson, Lime, Lundgren, Warzecha & Leffel, 2000). Research on the acceptability of the introduction of fees at previously free National Forests and National Wildlife Refuges were also commonly undertaken (e.g., Taylor et al., 2000; Graefe & Burns, 2002).

Findings from the fee demonstration research showed that National Park visitors generally supported park fees, with this support increasing over the time periods of study. Part of the reason for this strong support may be due to the fact that with the *fee demonstration program*, 80 percent of the revenue is retained at the park where it is collected. Taylor et al's (2002) evaluation of 14 National Wildlife Refuges found on average that about 9 percent (with a range of 0-23 percent) of visitors would be displaced by the fees. While income had a statistically significant effect, the magnitude of the influence of income on visitor displacement was quite low.

Use of fees in game management and less developed countries was also an active area of research. Fish and game agencies began to see fees as a way to manage user numbers and maintain revenues. Fee studies included Loomis, Pierce and Manfredo (2000), and Sutton, Ditton and Stoll (2000). Findings from their research suggested that while visitor use decreases with increased fees, the reduction in use is less than proportionate to the increase in fee. That is, within the current range of hunting and fishing license fees, the demand is *price inelastic*. For example, a 20 percent increase in fishing license fee causes a 10 percent reduction in use (Sutton et al., 2000). This elasticity is similar to that of nature tourism in Costa Rica (Lindberg & Aylward, 2000). The common finding here of price inelastic demand is likely related to the fact that the current level of license or entrance fees is a small part of the total trip cost. This price inelastic response allows agencies to reduce use levels, while increasing revenues, at least for small increases to the current fees.

Quantifying Economic Impacts of Tourism

Even more prevalent than managerial interest in valuation of recreation has been the interest in quantifying local tourism employment and income from visitor spending. These studies date back to the 1960s and have been conducted for individual recreation areas, as well as entire states (Loomis & Walsh, 1997). These studies involve not only reporting the direct effect of visitor spending, but also the ripple or multiplier effects that arise from the re-spending of money in the local economy. The multiplier effects range from 1.5 to 2.5 (Loomis & Walsh, 1997), meaning that each dollar of visitor spending eventually generates $1.50 to $2.50 in total spending in the local economy. Tourism economics has blossomed into a distinct field within economics, with its own journal (i.e., *Tourism Economics*) and several books (e.g., Sinclair & Stabler, 1997).

The techniques to calculate economic effects of tourism and multipliers have become more standardized during the last decade. The preferred approach, and one commonly used, is an input-output model called IMPLAN (Minnesota Implan Group, 1997). The term *input-output model* refers to the model reflecting how the direct effect of initial spending requires additional inputs from the economy, which stimulates the demand for more outputs, which then further stimulates the demand for more inputs, etc. The net effect of these rounds of spending and re-spending is quantified as the multiplier.

Significance of Non-market Valuation Results

How has this body of research affected recreation resource management? Two areas have seen direct application of the valuation techniques to recreation resource management issues: 1) hydropower versus in-stream recreation at sites ranging from small streams under the Federal Energy Regulatory Commission (FERC) re-licensing to re-regulation of large dams such as Glen Canyon Dam and the Colorado River through Grand Canyon, and 2) Natural Resource Damage Assessments (NRDA) ranging from the Exxon Valdez oil spill to mine drainage adversely affecting fishing in Montana. In the first case, economic values of river recreation that were comparable to power generation values have helped to increase in-stream flows in rivers in Arizona (i.e., the Colorado River in the Grand Canyon), California (e.g., North Fork of the Feather River), Idaho and Montana. In NRDA cases, economic valuation has resulted in millions of dollars in fines that have been spent on environmental restoration. Public land management agencies have used economic valuation analyses in endangered species critical habitat determinations and fire management/fire restoration efforts, as well.

Issues for the Future
One of the major areas for future research will be greater emphasis on ecosystem valuation of landscape characteristics using CVM (Walsh et al., 1984), conjoint analysis and choice experiments (Boxall, 1996). If economics is to have relevance in ecosystem management, we must move toward valuation of landscapes (e.g., acres of wetlands, old growth forests) and the attributes of ecosystems. The value of preserving ecosystems will also involve more emphasis on measuring existence values since the value of self-regulating ecosystems is more than just recreational (Walsh et al., 1984). Finally, a new frontier in valuation techniques is to combine TCM and CVM data into a single econometric model (Cameron et al., 1996; Loomis, Gonzalez-Caban & Englin, 2001). This provides the strengths of both actual behavior-based TCM with the flexibility of CVM to value potential management changes.

Conclusions
Economics has made progress in valuing broad dimensions of human uses of natural resources. Its theory has broadened from considering only the extractive uses of natural resources to the values of recreation, and now valuing existence values to the public. In this way, economic theory reflects the public's changing values of natural resources. Along with the broadening of theory has been the corresponding expansion in ability to measure the monetary value of natural resources. At the heart of this has been the extension of the CVM from valuing recreation to measuring the existence value of natural resources to citizens who have neither ever visited an area, nor intend to do so. This success at the conceptual and empirical level has led to significant infusion of non-market valuation into natural resource policy decisions. If non-market valuation can make the next great leap into ecosystem service valuation, it will continue to have policy relevance in natural resource management for years to come.

References
Arrow, K., Solow, R., Portney, P, Leamer, E., Radner R., & Schuman, H. (1993). *Report of the NOAA Panel on contingent caluation*. (Federal Register 58). Washington DC: U.S. Department of Commerce.

Bailey, K. (1994). *Methods of social research, 4th edition*. New York: Macmillian.

Bamford, T., Manning, R., Forcier, L., & Koenemann, E. (1988). Differential campsite pricing: An experiment. *Journal of Leisure Research*, 20, 324-342.

Bishop, R., & Heberlein, T. (1990). The contingent valuation method. In R. Johnson & G. Johnson (Eds.) *Economic valuation of natural resources: Issues, theory and application*. Boulder, CO: Westview Press.

Bowes, M., & Loomis, J. (1980). A note on the use of travel cost models with unequal zonal populations. *Land Economics*, 56, 465-470.

Bowker, J., Betz, C., Cordell, K., & Super, G. (1994). *Temporal stability of dichotomous choice contingent valuation: An examination with management implications.* Paper presented at the meeting of the International Symposium on Society and Resource Management, Fort Collins, CO.

Boxall, P. (1996). A comparison of stated preference methods for environmental valuation. *Ecological Economics*, 18, 243-53.

Brown, W., Singh, A., & Castle, E. (1964). *An economic evaluation of the Oregon salmon and steelhead sport fisheries.* (Technical Bulletin 78). Corvallis, OR: Oregon Agricultural Experiment Station, Oregon State University.

Brown, T., & Peterson, G. (1995). The values jury to aid natural resource decisions. *Land Economics*, 71, 250-260.

Cameron, T., Shaw, W., Ragland, S., Callaway, J., & Keefe, S. (1996). Using actual and contingent behavior data with differing levels of time aggregation to model recreation demand. *Journal of Agricultural and Resource Economics*, 21, 130-149.

Carson, R., Flores, N., Martin, K., & Wright, J. (1996). Contingent valuation and revealed preference methodologies: Comparing estimates for quasi-public goods. *Land Economics*, 72, 80-99.

Clawson, M., & Knetsch, J. (1964). *The economics of outdoor recreation.* Washington DC: Resources for the Future.

Davis, R. K. (1963). *The value of outdoor recreation: An economic analysis of the Maine Woods.* Unpublished doctoral dissertation, Harvard University, Cambridge, MA.

Gonzalez-Caban, A., Loomis, J., & Englin, J. (2002). *Do forest fires affect the demand and benefits of recreationists differently: Hiking and mountainbiking.* Paper presented at the meeting of the International Symposium on Society and Resource Management, Sardina, Italy.

Graefe, A., & Burns, R.. (2002). *Outdoor recreation fees in Pacific Northwest forests: Perceptions of Oregon and Washington residents.* Paper presented at the meeting of the International Symposium on Society and Resource Management, Sardina, Italy.

Hanley, N., Shaw, D., & Wright, R. (2003). *The new economics of outdoor recreation.* Northampton, MA: Edward Elgar.

Harris, C., & Driver, B. L. (1987). Recreation user fees: Pros and cons. *Journal of Forestry*, 84, 25-29.

Heberlein, T., Wilson, M., Bishop. R., & Schaeffer, N. (2000). *Rethinking the scope "problem" in contingent valuation.* Paper presented at the meeting of the International Symposium on Society and Resource Management, Portland, OR.

Hellerstein, D. (1991). Using count data models with aggregate data. *American Journal of Agricultural Economics*, 73, 860-867.

Herriges, J., & Kling, C. (1999). *Valuing recreation and the environment.* Northampton, MA: Edward Elgar.

Hesseln, H., Loomis, J., & Gonzalez-Caban, A. (2002). *The economic effects of wildfire on recreation in Montana.* Paper presented at the meeting of the International Symposium on Society and Resource Management, Sardina, Italy.

Hotelling, H. (1931). The economics of exhaustible resources. *Journal of Political Economy,* 39, 137-175.

Hotelling, H. (1947). *The economics of public recreation.* Washington DC: U.S. National Park Service.

Jorgensen, B., Syme, G., Smith, L., & Bishop, B. (1998). *The reliability of contingent values.* Paper presented at the meeting of the International Symposium on Society and Resource Management, Columbia, MO.

Krannich, R., Luloff, A., & Field, D. (2002). *The effects of recreational fees at United States National Park Service sites: Perspectives of Park Managers.* Paper presented at the meeting of the International Symposium on Society and Resource Management, Sardina, Italy.

Krutilla, J. (1967). Conservation reconsidered. *American Economic Review,* 57, 787-796.

Leahy, J., & Johnson, R. (2000). *Displacement of backcountry users due to fees at Grand Canyon and Everglades National Parks.* Paper presented at the meeting of the International Symposium on Society and Resource Management, Portland, OR.

Lindberg, K., & Aylward, B. (2000). *Pricing and price responsiveness in developing country nature tourism: Review and Costa Rican case study.* Paper presented at the meeting of the International Symposium on Society and Resource Management, Portland, OR.

Loomis, J. (1980). Monetizing benefits under alternative river recreation use allocation systems. *Water Resources Research,* 16, 28-32.

Loomis. J. (1989). Test re-test reliability of the contingent valuation method: A comparison of general population and visitor responses. *American Journal of Agricultural Economics,* 71, 76-84.

Loomis, J., & Gonzalez-Caban, A. (1997). How certain are visitors of their economic values of river recreation. *Water Resources Research,* 33, 1187-1193.

Loomis, J., Gonzalez-Caban, A., & Englin, J. (2001). Testing differential effects of forest fires on hiking and mountain biking demand and benefits. *Journal of Agricultural and Resource Economics,* 26, 508-522.

Loomis, J., Pierce, C., & Manfredo, M. (2000). Using the demand for hunting licenses to evaluate contingent valuation estimates of willingness to pay. *Applied Economic Letters,* 7, 435-438.

Loomis, J., & Walsh, R. (1997). *Recreation economic decisions: Comparing benefits and costs,* 2nd Ed. State College, PA: Venture Publishing.

Loomis, J., & White, D. (1996). Economic benefits of rare and endangered species: Summary and meta analysis. *Ecological Economics*, 18, 197-206.

Luloff, A., Field, D., & Krannich, R. (2000). *Assessing the National Park Service recreational fee demonstration program.* Paper presented at the meeting of the International Symposium on Society and Resource Management, Portland, OR.

Minnesota Implan Group. (1997). *IMPLAN Pro: User's guide, analysis guide and data guide.* Stillwater, MN: Implan Group.

Peterson, G., & Brown, T. (1998). Economic valuation by the method of paired comparison, with emphasis on evaluation of the transitivity axiom. *Land Economics*, 74, 240-61.

Reiling, S., Boyle, K., Phillips, M., & Anderson, M. (1990). Temporal reliability of contingent values. *Land Economics*, 66, 128-134.

Rosenthal, D., Loomis, J., & Peterson, G. (1984). Pricing for efficiency and revenue in public recreation areas. *Journal of Leisure Research*, 16, 195-208.

Sanders, L., Walsh, R., & Loomis, J. (1990). Toward empirical estimation of the total value of protecting rivers. *Water Resources Research*, 26, 1345-1357.

Sinclair, T., & Stabler, M. (1997). *The economics of tourism.* New York, NY: Routledge.

Sutton, S., Ditton, R., & Stoll, J. (2000). *Predicting angler response to fishing license fee increases: Insights from contingent valuation analysis.* Paper presented at the meeting of the International Symposium on Society and Resource Management, Portland, OR.

Taylor, J., Vaske, J., & Donnelly, M. (2000). *Visitor displacement response to demonstration fees at National Wildlife Refuges.* Paper presented at the meeting of the International Symposium on Society and Resource Management, Portland, OR.

Taylor, J., Vaske, J., Shelby, L., Donnelly, M., & Browne-Nunez, C. (2002). *Visitor response to demonstration fees at National Wildlife Refuges.* Wildlife Society Bulletin, 39, 1238-1244.

Thompson, J., Lime, D., Lundgren, A., Warzecha, C., & Leffel, M. (2000). *Monitoring visitor reactions to recreational fee demonstration program.* Paper presented at the meeting of the International Symposium on Society and Resource Management, Portland, OR.

Walsh, R., Loomis, J., & Gillman, R. (1984). Valuing option, existence and bequest demands for wilderness. *Land Economics*, 60, 14-29.

27

Managing Depreciative Behavior in Natural Settings

A Review of Research and Implications for Management

Richard C. Knopf

Kathleen L. Andereck

Depreciative behavior is an increasingly pervasive challenge for natural resource managers. It results in the irreversible loss of cultural and historical artifacts that define the human legacy (Neary, 1991), unquantifiable impact on the sustainability of natural ecosystems (Cole, Hammond & McCool, 1997), eroded visitor experiences (Christensen, Johnson & Brooks, 1992), and hundreds of millions of dollars in damage to parklands and natural environments annually in the United States alone (Winter, Sagarin, Rhoads, Barrett & Cialdini, 2000). The USDA Forest Service contends with nearly 300,000 reports of crime and violence annually, increasing an average of 15 to 20 percent each year (Chavez & Tynon, 2000). Acts of domestic terrorism have crept into the backcountry (Eagan, 1996), and reports of violence or intimidation toward federal natural resource managers have now reached 100 per year (Tynon, Chavez & Kakoyannis, 2001). The popular media have exacerbated the challenge; parks and natural environments have been characterized as "dangerous" and "crime plagued" (Pendleton, 1998).

During the past two decades, science has responded to such sobering statistics vigorously and productively. The revelations have been both encouraging and informative. As managers and policy-makers, the literature is teaching us that many of the solutions to the challenges we face are well within our grasp. Most importantly, it is causing us to re-think our paradigm. We have long held the belief that our clients are the source of negative tendencies and that our role as natural resource managers was to control, confine and otherwise thwart whatever intentions they might have. We have long saddled the blame on the perpetrators, when in fact much of the blame—according to the literature—might better be placed upon ourselves. It raises the very real possibility that much of the depreciative behavior confronting us has emerged because we have not managed our resources in the most informed manner possible.

The purpose of this chapter is to highlight what scientists have taught us about the thorny challenge of depreciative behavior in natural settings. It begins with a summary of what we knew when the first International Symposium on Society and Resource Management (ISSRM) was convened in 1986. Then, it tracks progress made since that time. It describes what we know about the forces that cause depreciative behavior, and outlines twelve principles for ameliorating it. It concludes with a statement of what challenges remain ahead if scientific inquiry is to catapult us into the next level of understanding about depreciative behavior and its remedial forces.

Historical Tracings

During the era of the first ISSRM, the state of inquiry was appropriately described as absent of empirically-based evaluation research capable of directing management response and action (Christensen, 1983). This reality notwithstanding, it was not as if there was a void of attention given to the topic. Indeed, the multi-disciplinary review by Knopf and Dustin (1992) concluded that the early recreation and parks literature "seemed to carry more review and synthesis publications on vandalism and depreciative behavior than any other field" (p. 222).

One might suggest that the early 1970s work of Clark, Burgess and Hendee (1972) represented a defining moment in the origins of inquiry. At one level, it represented the first fruits of a substantial new wave of investment by public land management agencies in the emerging social challenges in the backcountry. At another level, it modeled the application of theoretical perspective from the social sciences (e.g., stimulus-reward, norm manipulation) to specific management challenges in park and recreation management (e.g., littering). Essentially, the publication served as a beacon to illuminate the potential of public investment (largely driven by federal dollars) in the social science enterprise for purposes of better mitigating the impacts emerging from burgeoning levels of backcountry use.

With this pioneering work setting the tone and expectation, a dramatic increase of studies, pilot projects and theoretical treatises on depreciative behavior in wildland settings emerged. The increase was fueled by continued public land management agencies in field-driven research, and an emerging wave of public policy-oriented scientists with heritage in interdisciplinary studies. This escalated activity continued throughout the fourteen year period leading up to the first ISSRM. In 1976, a major symposium on vandalism and outdoor recreation generated 40 specific strategies for mitigating depreciative behavior in recreation areas (Alfano & Magill, 1976). In addition to these resources, a number of management handbooks, rather exhaustive in scope, outlined strategies for ameliorating the expression of depreciative behavior in park and wildland settings (e.g., Christensen, 1983; Dopkeen, 1978).

All of these efforts notwithstanding, the field entered the era of the first ISSRM with a sense of conceptual incoherency. Indeed, such sentiment was so pervasive that it continued to be expressed some ten years after the first ISSRM (Johnson & Vande Kamp, 1996). Yet, the field of inquiry was beginning to jell. Spurred along by the thirst for theoretical rigor and synthesis, a fascination with discovery from other disciplines, and a quest to anchor science in application, the relevancy and cohesion of inquiry ultimately solidified. The remainder of this chapter focuses on capturing these changes, which have been informed not only through efforts of individual investigators, but also through two decades of conversations at ISSRM meetings.

A Step Forward

The beginnings of conceptual deepening and synthesis were best articulated by the comprehensive reviews of Vande Kamp, Johnson and Swearingen (1994), and Knopf and Dustin (1992). At about the same time, a second major symposium on vandalism and natural resources-based policy was held (Christensen, Johnson & Brookes, 1992). These contributions were highly reflective of the ambition of the era: to draw deeply from the conceptual perspectives of other disciplines, to explore the promise of qualitative research, and to implement experimental design methodologies with the capacity to more clearly account for confounding effects of intervening variables.

These synthesizing reviews have been followed in more recent years by a myriad of studies that reflect this new spirit. But in terms of numbers of studies, the production has waned, mirroring the trends for the whole of the environmental action research venue in general (Dwyer, Leeming, Cobern, Porter & Jackson, 1993). The waning appears to be linked more to the erosion of financial support for inquiry than any other factor. Yet, the studies which do appear tend to be of more tightly-controlled design, and of greater theoretical rigor (e.g., Cialdini, Reno & Kallgren, 1990; Pendleton, 1998; Swearington & Johnson, 1995).

So what general themes can be gleaned from these past two decades of inquiry? First, we have gained insight into the motives for depreciative behavior. Most helpful in this regard has been the taxonomy developed by Gramann and Vander Stoep (1987). The taxonomy frames six categories of normative violations in outdoor environments based upon underlying motivation: 1) *unintentional violations* (i.e., much depreciative behavior is inadvertent due to unawareness of the "rules," rather than willful or malicious intent), 2) *uninformed violations* (i.e., some depreciative behavior is embedded in lack of awareness of consequences), 3) *releasor-cue violations* (i.e., some depreciative behavior is precipitated by cues in the environment that could be eliminated), 4) *responsibility-denial violations* (i.e., some depreciative behavior occurs because the actor denies having a moral responsibility to conform), 5) *status-confirming violations* (i.e., some depreciative behavior is prompted by the desire to overtly confirm status as accepted members of groups with deviant norms), and 6) *willful violations* (i.e., committed by individuals motivated by financial gain, ideological protest, malice, revenge or the desire to inspire fear). The latter category in particular has focus of fruitful conceptual unpacking (Knopf & Dustin, 1992; Moser, 1992). Most of the concept-building centers on three themes: 1) the quest for equity (e.g., retaliation, alienation, rebellion, countering abuse of power, unfair enforcement of rules), 2) the quest for competence (e.g., control, expression of effectiveness, artistic expression, cultural transmission), and 3) the quest for arousal (e.g., curiosity, novelty, excitement, and countering boredom).

Second, we have learned that natural resource managers carry significant capacity to thwart the expression of depreciative behavior in outdoor environments (Vander Stoep & Gramann, 1987). Indeed, a study of U.S. National Park Service unit managers leads us to conclude that at least half of the potential expression of depreciative behavior is already being defused by the most modest of managerial intervention programs (Johnson & Vande Kamp, 1996). The literature reminds us that much can be done to counter these very real challenges without controlling or coercing the individual, but through very simple modifications of the environment, particularly with respect to site design (Knopf & Dustin, 1992; Vande Kamp, Johnson & Swearingen, 1994).

Third, we have learned that the particular *strategies* selected for intervention must be defined by the genre of *motives* that drive the targeted behavior. In general, intervention strategies range from subtle and unobtrusive (e.g., information and education campaigns) to direct and coercive (e.g., overt imposition of rules and subsequent enforcement, including incarceration for non-compliance). Over time, sophisticated typologies of possible action arrayed along this indirect/direct continuum have been developed (Manning, 1999). And, fueled by such typologies, conceptual models have been developed to specify the conditions under which certain treatments are more effective than others (Knopf & Dustin, 1992; Vander Stoep & Gramman, 1987).

One of the prevailing tenets of this body of literature is that indirect forms of intervention should be favored over direct forms of intervention whenever possible. At one level, this is true because natural resource managers seek to maximize perceived freedom for individuals engaged in backcountry recreation (Manning, 1999). At another level, this is true because indirect intervention techniques have been proven to be profoundly effective in deterring all but the most vindictive, predatory or spite-driven behaviors (Gramann, Christiansen & Vander Stoep, 1992). Yet, lurking in the gleeful promise that much can be done to dissipate unwanted depreciative behavior is the hard reality of the rapidly increasing prevalence (and social/financial impact) of intentional vandalism and crime (e.g., arson, domestic violence, sexual predation, murder, robbery, theft, gang violence, assault, terrorism). In this regard, the literature of the past two decades leaves us conceptually and operationally undernourished. But we can be heartened by newly emerging work in this arena which is developing insight into appropriate managerial and social policy responses to the most socially and environmentally destructive behaviors in natural settings (Eagan, 1996; Tynon, Chavez & Kakoyannis, 2001).

In sum, 20 years of inquiry has sharpened our appreciation for the reasons why depreciative behavior emerges in natural environments, the phenomenal capacity that resides within the immediate control of resource managers to ameliorate the expression of such behavior, and the desirability of favoring soft and indirect forms of intervention (e.g., information, education) over heavy-handed and direct forms of intervention (e.g., citations). We now turn to the question: What specific things have we learned about behavioral intervention that might be helpful to natural resource managers in the field?

Management Principles

Many helpful reviews of the research on depreciative behavior are available to field managers (Johnson & Vande Kamp, 1996; Knopf & Dustin, 1992; Manning, 1999; Vande Kamp et al., 1994). When combined with revelations from research of the past few years, these reviews provide insights on specific actions that field managers can take to minimize its expression. These insights are framed in twelve principles for effective intervention outlined below.

Principle 1: Focus on the causes of depreciative behavior, not the perpetrator. Gaining a more complete understanding of the reasons for depreciative behavior is necessary to controlling such behaviors. As managers, we are quick to focus on recreationists as the sources of the problem. Research is compelling us to think otherwise. It suggests that much of the negative phenomena are better understood as resulting from poorly-managed social and environmental systems. In a sweeping review of vandalism control strategies, Christensen and Clark (1979) posited nine arenas in which controls for vandalism should focus. None of these arenas referred to inherent problems within the recreationist. Christiansen (1986) identified 24 spheres of influence, also all external to the perpetrator. Research is suggesting that our instinctive impulses to judge, control and confine perpetrators of unwanted acts are unwarranted and ultimately ineffectual (Knopf & Dustin, 1992).

Principle 2: Eliminate environmental prompts. Environmental psychologists and recreation scientists alike have suggested that as much as 90 percent of depreciative behavior in outdoor recreation areas is prompted by poor environmental design and management (Christiansen, 1986; Knopf & Dustin, 1992). People respond to cues on how to behave. Thus, managers must eliminate the cues in the physical array that trigger depreciative behavior. The presence of litter triggers increased littering behavior, vandalism triggers increased vandalism, and off-tail impact triggers increased off-trail impact (Christiansen & Clark, 1979). Hardening the site to absorb and deflect cumulative signs of impact also provides effective deterrent to expression of depreciative behavior (Christiansen, 1986). In general, uncompromising adherence to high standards of environmental quality is one of the most potent forces to counter depreciative behavior (Manning, 1999).

Principle 3: Manage social norms. In similar fashion, people respond to cues in the social environment on how to behave. Thus, managers should look for creative ways in which to facilitate the expression of social norms that encourage non-depreciative behavior. The strategies are many: teaching recreation group leaders to model desired behavior, having resource managers model desired behavior, breaking norms of non-involvement through by-stander intervention programs, promoting identification with groups possessing desired norms, limiting visitor exposure to non-compliant behavior, building ways for recreationists to identify with park staff, increasing authority and legitimacy of rule-makers, convincing recreationists that their needs and the needs of policy makers are mutual, producing evidence that most visitors follow rules, and communicating normative standards for activity groups with which the recreationist identifies (Knopf & Dustin, 1992; Vande Kamp et al., 1994).

Principle 4: Communicate rules clearly and coherently. One of the most consistent themes of the literature is that many recreationists engage in depreciative behavior simply because they are unaware of the rules that prohibit it (Vander Stoep & Gramann, 1987). In fact, research clearly demonstrates that simple communication of rules and desired behaviors to recreationists decreases their non-compliant behavior in substantial ways (Swearingen & Johnson, 1995). But the literature further suggests that information must be presented in a clear, cogent, understandable and simple fashion.

Principle 5: Provide information about consequences. Information about rules and expected norms will be more influential if it is accompanied by reasons why the rules and norms are important. Research has repeatedly shown that when the link between the actions of recreationists and environmental or social impact is made explicit, depreciative behavior declines (Oliver, Roggenbuck & Watson, 1985; Gramann & Vander Stoep, 1987). It has also shown that recreationists are more likely to accept restrictions on their behavior (e.g., use limits or resource closures) if the rationale for imposing them is communicated (Clark, 1976). Thus, intervention strategies are more likely to work if the negative consequences of status quo management are communicated, and the ultimate personal benefits to the target audience can be articulated.

Principle 6: Deflect the behavior into reasonable options. Behavioral controls are more likely to be successful if reasonable alternatives are offered for the needs underlying the undesired behaviors (Christiansen, 1986). Rather than being told "no," recreationists should be deflected into available options. Without substitutable options, they have little incentive to forego a preferred behavior simply out of moral obligation to comply (Roggenbuck & Berrier, 1982).

Principle 7: Use positive overtones rather than negative overtones. It is clear that recreationists are more responsive to suggestions about what they *should do* than to suggestions about what they *shouldn't do* (Johnson & Vande Kamp, 1996). In spite of this clear directive from research, much of the signage that populates recreational settings in natural areas is negative in disposition (Winter et al., 2000). A realignment of this signage, and the managerial disposition that precipitates it, would be one of the most immediately fruitful ways for managers to respond to the revelations of research on effective intervention.

Principle 8: Favor personal communication over impersonal communication. Face-to-face communication has been shown to be consistently more effective than impersonal media in managing depreciative behavior in recreation settings (Oliver et al., 1985). It is more effective because of its holding power, superior source credibility, ability to promote identification with agency goals, and ability to reduce the anonymity of recreationists as potential helpers (Gramann et al., 1992). However, face-to-face communication is also inherently the most costly alternative of communication.

Principle 9: Juxtapose communication with place and time of noncompliance. There is considerable evidence that messages to deter noncompliance are most effective when transmitted as closely as possible to the time and place in which noncompliance is likely (Vande Kamp et al., 1994; Johnson & Vande Kamp, 1996). In natural environments, signs are a particularly effective medium in this regard (Johnson & Vande Kamp, 1996).

Principle 10: Use uniformed personnel at high risk areas. The stationing of uniformed employees near areas of high rates of noncompliance has been proven to be a powerful deterrent (Swearingen & Johnson, 1995). It has been suggested that this intervention strategy is particularly effective in natural areas because it causes people to behave conservatively in what normally is an ambiguous situation (Gramann & Vander Stoep, 1987). It also reminds visitors of their own personal norms that are inconsistent with noncompliance. While some might suggest that the presence of uniformed officials may negatively impact the quality of visitor experience, studies have found that uniformed employees are perceived by the public as a neutral or positive attribute of their experiences (Swearingen & Johnson, 1995).

Principle 11: Institute appropriate reward structures. The use of reward mechanisms has been proven effective in dissipating depreciative behavior. Rewards can be either positive or negative, and in the form of financial gain, social gratification, or other opportunities for the gratification of blocked needs (Knopf & Dustin, 1992). The power of using positive rewards has been demonstrated most convincingly in littering research, where only modest awards have resulted in substantial changes in both littering behavior and litter pickup (Clark et al., 1972). Threatened punishments or negative rewards may induce behavioral change, but they may have adverse impacts on visitor enjoyment and may lead to negative reactions to the resource manager by the public (Roggenbuck & Berrier, 1982; Winter et al., 2000). The broadly held view is that positive rewards should be instituted when managerial costs are containable, and negative rewards should be instituted only when other initiatives fail (Winter et al., 2000).

Principle 12: Use direct coercion as a last, but effective, resort. Direct coercion or forced compliance should be implemented only in circumstances where the more indirect forms of intervention become ineffectual. To be effective, direct coercion must be anchored in five conditions (Knopf & Dustin, 1992). First, it must be clear to perpetrators which behaviors are subject to control and which are not. Second, the sanctions must be sufficiently severe to make the attraction of compliance shadow the attraction of noncompliance. Third, perpetrators must perceive that resource administrators can indeed impose what is threatened. Fourth, the perpetrators must perceive that administrators care about uniformity, and will use the sanctions consistently to bring about conformance. And fifth, perpetrators must believe that administrators will observe them if they commit the sanctioned behavior. While these five conditions hold merit, it seems clear that poorly organized internal communication systems within government agencies impede their expression (Tynon et al., 2001). But beyond these broad tenets, the literature offers little insight about the potential of direct coercion techniques in the management of depreciative behavior in natural settings. This arena is perhaps one of the most underdeveloped lines of inquiry in parks and natural environments research today.

Issues for Future Inquiry

This chapter began with a clear suggestion: We need to change our thinking about where the blame for depreciative behavior should be placed. It suggested that, as resource managers, we would have greater insight on how to change depreciative behavior if the blame were focused less on the individual and more on the systems which provide services to this individual. Twenty years of research has affirmed our necessity to do so. As resource managers, we have tremendous capacity to create change without operating under the assumption that individuals are inherently a problem and can only be shaped by confinement and direct coercion. Perhaps the greatest insight from research is that natural resource managers can solve many of their challenges through soft and positive intervention strategies.

This perspective sets the stage for defining pathways for future research. First, the broader systems of influence in shaping depreciative behavior need to be explored. The literature has posited a number of influential factors including the conditions of the physical environment; prevailing social norms, and; social, family and community systems in home environments (Knopf & Dustin, 1992). Many of the challenges expressed in natural environments may well be a direct reflection of poorly-delivered social and environmental systems in urban areas. One important role of research is to provide illumination on how natural resource managers might work in settings other than their own to solve the challenges they face. Second, research needs to broaden its focus to explore the impacts of various intervention strategies on the visitor experience. While we have done well in exploring impacts of intervention on behavior, we have been less productive in exploring impacts on the quality of experience. Third, research should examine the potential of interventions that develop commitment, employ positive modeling of appropriate behavior, and foster internal goal-setting processes that are in harmony with the quest for environmental protection and quality visitor experiences (Dwyer et al., 1993). This line of inquiry would bring focus back to the goal of fulfilling individual needs while simultaneously dissipating depreciative behavior.

In addition to these relatively novel and unprecedented forms of inquiry, the historical lines of inquiry need to expand and evolve. To echo the pleas of many other reviewers (Dwyer et al., 1993; Vande Kamp et al., 1994), experimental designs must be tightened, inferential processes must be less situational, and long term consequences of intervention must be monitored through time series studies. But all the while, research on depreciative behavior in natural settings has been wonderfully productive through all of its limitations. It has empowered us with the tools we need to increase the quality of human experiences in natural settings.

References

Alfano, S.S., & Magill, A.W. (Eds.). (1976). *Vandalism and outdoor recreation: Symposium proceedings* (USDA Forest Service General Technical Report PSW-17). Berkeley, CA: USDA Forest Service, Pacific Southwest Forest and Range Experiment Station.

Christensen, H. H. (1986). Vandalism and depreciative behavior. In *President's Commission on Americans Outdoors: Literature review* (pp.73-85). Washington, DC: U.S. Government Printing Office.

Christensen, M. L. (1983). *Vandalism control management for parks and recreation.* State College, PA: Venture Publications.

Christensen, H. H., & Clark, R.N. (1979). Understanding and controlling vandalism and other rule violations in urban areas. *Proceedings, National Urban Forestry Conference* (Environmental Sciences and Forestry Publication 80-003). Syracuse, NY: State University of New York, College of Environmental Sciences and Forestry.

Christensen, H.H., Johnson, D. R., & Brookes, M. H. (Eds.) (1992). *Vandalism: Research, prevention, and social policy* (USDA Forest Service General Technical Report PNW-GTR-293). Portland, OR: USDA Forest Service, Pacific Northwest Research Station.

Chavez, D. J., & Tynon, J. F. (2000). Triage law enforcement: Societal impacts on national forests in the west. *Journal of Environmental Management, 26,* 403-407.

Cialdini, R. B., Reno, R. R. & Kallgren, C. A. (1990). A focus theory of normative conduct. *Journal of Personality and Social Psychology*, 58, 1015-1026.

Clark, R. N., Burgess, R. L., & Hendee, J. C. (1972). The development of anti-litter behavior in a forest campground. *Journal of Leisure Research*, 3, 143-159.

Clark, R. N. (1976). Control of vandalism in recreation areas – fact, fiction or folklore? In S. S. Alfano & A.W. Magill (Eds.), *Vandalism and outdoor recreation: Symposium proceedings* (USDA Forest Service General Technical Report PSW-17). Berkeley, CA: USDA Forest Service, Pacific Southwest Forest and Range Experiment Station, 62-72.

Cole, D. N., Hammond, T. P., & McCool, S. F. 1997). Information quantity and communication effectiveness. *Leisure Sciences*, 19.

Dopkeen, J. C. (1978). *Managing vandalism: A guide to reducing damage in recreation areas.* Boston: City of Boston, Parkman Center for Urban Affairs.

Dwyer, W. O., Leeming, F. C., Cobern, M. E., Porter, B. E., & Jackson, J. M. (1993). Critical review of behavioral intentions to preserve the environment: Research since 1980. *Environment and Behavior*, 25, 275-321.

Eagan, S. P. (1996). From spikes to bombs: The rise of eco-terrorism. *Studies in Conflict and Terrorism*, 19, 1-18.

Gramann, J. H., & Vander Stoep, G. A. (1987). Prosocial behavior and natural resource protection. *Journal of Environmental Management*, 24, 247-257.

Gramann, J. H., Christiansen, H. H., & Vander Stoep, G. A. (1992). Indirect management to protect cultural and natural resources. In H. H. Christensen, D. R. Johnson & M. H. Brookes (Eds.), *Vandalism: Research, prevention, and social policy* (USDA Forest Service General Technical Report PNW-GTR-293). Portland, OR: USDA Forest Service, Pacific Northwest Research Station.

Johnson, D. R., & Vande Kamp, M. E. (1996). Extent and control of resource damage due to noncompliant visitor behavior: A case study from the U.S. National Parks. *Natural Areas Journal*, 16, 134-161.

Knopf, R.C., & Dustin, D. L. (1992). A multidisciplinary model for managing vandalism and depreciative behavior in recreation settings. In M. Manfredo (Ed.), *Influencing human behavior: Theory and applications in recreation, tourism, and natural resources management* (pp. 210-261). Champagne, IL: Sagamore Books

Manning, R. E. (1999). *Studies in outdoor recreation.* Corvallis, OR: Oregon State University Press.

Moser, G. (1992). What is vandalism? Toward a psycho-social definition and its implications. In H. H. Christensen, D. R. Johnsonn & M. H. Brookes (Eds.), *Vandalism: Research, prevention, and social policy* (USDA Forest Service General Technical Report PNW-GTR-293). Portland, OR: USDA Forest Service, Pacific Northwest Research Station.

Neary, J. (1991). Chaco Canyon under siege. *Archeology*, May/June, 50-68.

Oliver, S. S., Roggenbuck, J. W., & Watson, A.E. (1985). Education to reduce impacts in forest campgrounds. *Journal of Forestry*, 80, 343-346.

Pendleton, M. R. (1998). Policing the park: Understanding the soft environment. *Journal of Leisure Research*, 30, 552-571.

Roggenbuck, J. W., & Berrier, D. (1982). A comparison of the effectiveness of communication strategies in dispersing wilderness campers. *Journal of Leisure Research*, 14, 77-79.

Swearingen, T. C., & Johnson, D. R. (1995). Visitors' responses to uniformed park employees. *Journal of Park and Recreation Administration*, 13, 73-85.

Tynon, J. F., Chavez, D. J., & Kakoyannis, C. (2001). If you go to the woods today, you're sure of a surprise. *Women in Natural Resources*, 22, 6-16.

Vande Kamp, M. E., Johnson, D. R., & Swearingen, T. C. (1994). *Deterring minor acts of noncompliance* (U.S. National Park Service Technical Report NPS/PNRUM/NRTR-92/08). Seattle, WA: University of Washington, College of Forest Resources.

Vander Stoep, G. A., & Gramann, J. H. (1987). The effect of verbal appeals and incentives on depreciative behavior among youthful park visitors. *Journal of Leisure Research*, 19, 69-83.

Winter, P. L., Sagarin, B. J., Rhoads, K., Barrett, D. W., & Cialdini, R. B. (2000). Choosing to encourage or discourage: Perceived effectiveness of prescriptive versus proscriptive messages. *Environmental Management*, 26, 589-594.

28

Scenic Beauty Research in Society and Natural Resources

Terry C. Daniel

Scenic beauty research has a long and venerable history in the human-society and natural resources fields. A substantial scientific literature base has developed during the past 30 years. Surprisingly, however, scenic beauty has barely been represented at the International Symposia on Society and Resource Management (ISSRM); only three papers were presented at the ninth symposium, and there are only three relevant papers published in *Society and Natural Resources*, the associated journal. Thus, any review of scenic beauty research must rely mostly on studies published in other human/society and natural resources venues. Honoring the celebratory intent of this volume, however, the few relevant papers published in *Society and Natural Resources* will be featured as illustrations of issues that have been central to scenic beauty research.

Definition

Debate continues about the definition of scenic beauty and its appropriate place in environmental policy-making (e.g., Parsons & Daniel, 2002), but short of the development of a more general theory of human-environment relationships, it is unlikely ever to be fully and consensually defined. That said, scenic beauty has variously been taken to be a property of the landscape, a human perceptual-psychological response (i.e., the *eye of the beholder*), or some combination of both (Daniel & Boster, 1976; Zube, Sell & Taylor, 1982). It is generally agreed that scenic beauty pertains to the *aesthetic value* of the landscape, but there remains considerable ambiguity about what that means (Lothian, 1999). In some accounts scenic beauty is explicitly limited to the visual experience of landscape (Daniel, 2001), while others assert the importance of other senses, and even extra-sensory meanings and interpretations (Herzog, 1984; Herzog & Bosley, 1992; Kaplan, Kaplan & Brown, 1989). At one extreme, scenic beauty can be viewed as a superficial feature of the environment, as mere *decoration* with no substantive biological basis or natural resource value. Alternatively, scenic beauty may have a very deep biological base, derived from evolutionary forces of natural selection over millennia of human-environment interactions (Balling & Falk, 1982; Kaplan, 1987; Parsons, 1991). But, scenic beauty has also been charged as a negative force, obstructing public appreciation and support of proper ecological values in environmental management and policy (Carlson, 1977; Gobster, 1999).

In spite of the lack of a generally accepted definition, scenic beauty continues to be widely cited by the public as one of the most sought after and appreciated benefits of national forests, parks and other natural landscapes. Thus, one way or another, resource managers and the social scientists that seek to serve them must contend in the best way they can with identifying scenically beautiful landscapes and how alternative management policies might affect this resource.

Scenic Beauty: The Past

As a practical matter, *scenic beauty* became a declared concern for day-to-day natural resource management in the United States somewhere around the time of the Multiple-use Sustained Yield Act (1961) and the National Environmental Policy Act (1970). This was the multiple-use era, and scenic beauty was counted among the expanding number of resources that public land managers were pressed to consider. It was clear at the time that people enjoyed viewing the natural landscapes offered by national parks, forests and other public lands, and it was equally clear that they resented management actions that threatened what they perceived as natural scenic beauty. The problem for managers in this context was identifying this "resource" consistently, and to credibly incorporate it into management policies that were primarily conceived in bio-physical terms and evaluated in economic terms.

The predominant solution to scenic beauty management was to rely on experts. Much as one might send out a trained forester to locate, inventory and assess timber resources, trained landscape architects performed parallel tasks for scenic beauty, or as it was more often termed, *visual resources*. In the USDA Forest Service, the procedures were codified in the *Visual Management System* (United States Department of Agriculture [USDA], 1974). This approach was based on the notion that scenic beauty is a property of the landscape and thus can be assessed by individuals trained to identify and measure appropriate aesthetic features (e.g., form, color, texture, variety). Systematic evaluations challenged whether professional landscape assessments could achieve even minimal levels of reliability (e.g., Feimer, Smardon & Craik, 1981) and other disadvantages have been noted in other reviews (e.g., Zube et al., 1982). Still, the expert approach continued to be predominant in practical public land management.

Also during the multiple-use era, a number of scenic beauty pioneers operating in a research mode (more than a management mode) began developing a different approach based on human perception and judgment. That is, scenic beauty was defined and measured by the perceptual judgments of untrained *landscape consumers* (Buhyoff & Leushner, 1978; Daniel, Wheeler, Boster & Best, 1973; Daniel & Boster, 1976; Shafer, 1969; Shafer & Brush, 1977; Ulrich, 1977). This approach had intuitive appeal in a democratic society, and it is not without legitimate foundations in the philosophy of aesthetics (Lothian, 1999). However, there was controversy about the legitimacy of quantifying landscape scenic beauty on the basis of judgments by presumably ecologically and aesthetically unsophisticated publics (Carlson, 1977; Ribe, 1982). But the approach showed considerable promise. First, there was substantial consistency in scenic beauty scores within and between different groups of people (i.e., perceptual assessments showed internal reliability). Second, perceptual measures sensitively distinguished between different landscapes in ways that seemed reasonable, given conventional notions of what was and was not beautiful (i.e., they showed external validity). In addition, some important public landscapes (e.g., forests) were shown to be consistently related to the bio-physical features that land managers had traditionally monitored and manipulated (e.g., trees, vegetation). This feature of perception-based scenic beauty assessments offered the important possibility of trading off scenic beauty against other resources in quantitative decision schemes. Finally, the approach gained utility by the fact that assessments based on color photographs, which could conveniently be taken to relevant public audiences, were quite consistent with assessments made directly on-site (Arthur, Daniel & Boster, 1977; Ribe, 1989; Zube et al., 1982).

In the multiple-use era, scenic beauty was treated as just one of many considerations to balance in the management of public lands. In spite of a number of short-comings, the expert approach (i.e., the landscape architect representing visual resource interests) was the method of choice for most public land management applications. Public perception-based methods were rarely applied in specific land management contexts, though quantitative scenic beauty models were incorporated in a number of computer-implemented forest management decision systems. Most often, perception-based assessment methods were used for research which had less direct effects on management. The current USDA Forest Service *Scenery Management System* attempts to combine the expert and perception-based approaches, but it is not yet clear how either system fits into the post-multiple-use era of public land management.

Scenic Beauty: The Present

The multiple-use era in public land management has passed, and a new ecosystem management era has begun. What role should scenic beauty play in ecosystem management? There has long has been a concern that scenic beauty, as perceived by the general public, may not be ecologically sensitive, or worse, that it may be incompatible with good ecological management (Carlson, 1977). This concern was debated in the first volume of *Society and Natural Resources* (Daniel, 1988; Rolston, 1988) and it has found a new voice in land management debates under the banner of the ecological aesthetic (Gobster, 1999). The premise is that public landscape preferences should be consistent with ecological principles, such as *succession, biodiversity* and *sustainability*. What is assumed to be the prevailing scenic aesthetic is thought to be incongruent with ecological principles, and thus to be blocking public support for appropriate ecosystem management policies.

Whether public perceptions of scenic beauty *should be* consistent with principles of ecosystem management is a philosophical and ethical question. Whether public perceptions of scenic beauty *are* consistent with principles of ecosystem management is largely an empirical question. If the standard procedures for determining public perception of scenic beauty (e.g., people's ratings) are accepted, the only obstacle to answering the empirical question is some consistent determination of the relevant ecological qualities of landscapes with which to correlate. Of course, ecological quality probably cannot be determined for any given place at any given time, as the diversity, sustainability, resilience, naturalness and other often-cited properties of ecosystems are not static. That is, they are generally construed to depend upon patterns of environmental features and conditions that change over time. If instances of the appropriate temporal-spatial patterns could be specified for a given ecosystem, the challenge on the scenic beauty side of the equation would be to capture that changing pattern and effectively represent it to human observers to obtain reliable and valid judgements of scenic beauty. The few attempts at empirical tests suggest that public scenic beauty perceptions are more often consistent with ecological values than not (Anderson, Levi, Daniel & Dieterich, 1982; Brunson & Shelby, 1992; Ribe, Armstrong & Gobster, 2002; Taylor & Daniel, 1984), but the potential for aesthetic-ecological conflict in some contexts cannot be ruled out.

The current ecological aesthetic controversy raises several issues that have long been central to perceived scenic beauty research. *Representation* questions previously focused on the validity of photographs for representing static landscape scenes. Representations must now be extended to encompass ecologically relevant and dynamic spatial-temporal patterns of landscape features in a way that allows reliable and valid public judgments. This is an especially challenging task when ecological space and time parameters substantially exceed human scales (Daniel, 2001). Concerns about basing environmental management policies on the judgments of untrained publics are extended by the call to apply *ecological education* to bring public aesthetic preferences into line with ecosystem principles (Gobster, 1999). Parsons and Daniel (2002) offer reasons to be pessimistic about the effectiveness of any conventional education methods in this regard, but they also offer some reservations about the necessity or appropriateness of such efforts.

Finally, should conflicts between public scenic beauty preferences and ecosystem management principles prove unresolvable, which should determine public land management policy? The issue of the *worth* or *value* of scenic beauty has previously been addressed in an economic context (Brown, 1984), but arises more recently in terms of the relationship between scenic beauty and social acceptability in public

BRENT ERB

land management (Ribe, 2002; Shindler, Brunson & Stankey, 2002). In the following sections the issues of landscape representation, ecological education and scenic beauty valuation will be briefly discussed and illustrated by papers selected from *Society and Natural Resources*.

Representing Scenic Beauty

Photographic representations have long been used in scenic beauty research, and color photographs have repeatedly been shown to be valid for scenic beauty assessments of landscapes (Daniel & Boster, 1976; Shafer & Richards, 1974; Shuttleworth, 1980; Stamps, 1990). The effects of both spatial variations and temporal variations have been addressed in studies using photographic representations with some success. However, effective and valid representation of spatial and temporal variations at ecologically-relevant scales remains an unmet challenge. The combination of computer graphic and environmental simulation technologies has shown promise for creating ecologically and perceptually adequate landscape representations (Bergen, Ulbricht, Fridley & Ganter, 1995; Orland, 1994; Ribe et al., 2002; Thorn, Daniel, Orland & Brabyn, 1997). These methods continue to rapidly advance in capability and in economic feasibility (Orland, Budthimedhee & Uusitalo, 2001). Virtual reality technology has not yet lived up to its early promise. Nonetheless, high-resolution interactive computer systems are beginning to offer practical possibilities for realistic environmental representation, as well as expanding observer response options (Gimblett, Daniel, Cherry & Meitner, 2001;

Orland et al., 2001; Rohrmann & Bishop, 2002).

An obvious shortcoming of relying on pictorial landscape representations is that only visual experience is provided. Environmental experience is clearly multi-sensory, but it is less clear how non-visual sensations might affect scenic beauty. Several studies have investigated the effects of adding sound to landscape representations, with the general finding that sounds congruent with the visual features of the represented landscape do not significantly alter scenic beauty judgments (Anderson, Mulligan, Goodman & Regen, 1983). Hetherington, Daniel and Brown (1993) found that adding recordings of congruent moving water sounds to video-clips of wild and scenic river landscapes influenced one's assessment of scenic beauty. The relative rankings of river scenes were not changed, but adding sound increased the magnitude of the difference between the most-preferred moderate flow levels above the less-preferred lower and higher levels.

In a paper published in *Society and Natural Resources*, Mace, Bell and Loomis (1999) assessed the effects of incongruent sounds on judgments of photographically-represented wilderness and park scenery. They studied the effects of helicopter noise on ratings of the scenic beauty of Grand Canyon landscapes represented by digital color photographs. Observers also rated *naturalness, freedom, preference, annoyance, solitude* and *tranquility* for the same scene and sound combinations. Helicopter sound was represented by audio recordings at two levels, ranging from volumes similar to soft music to something like a freight train passing at 50 feet. A third sound condition presented nature sounds congruent with the landscape settings being assessed (e.g., wind, bird songs, natural quiet). Compared to the natural sounds, both levels of helicopter noise had negative effects on landscape ratings, with the louder noise having the most negative effect. The effect of noise on *scenic beauty* was statistically significant, but very small. These findings are consistent with an earlier verbal survey of over-flight effects on wilderness experience (Tarrant, Haas & Manfredo, 1995), where the strongest effects of verbally-cued recalled noise were on ratings of *annoyance*, followed closely by *tranquility* and *solitude*. No landscape scenes were presented and no ratings of scenic beauty were collected in the survey, but *enjoy scenic beauty* had the highest percentage of *extremely important* ratings for recreation motives; the scenic beauty motive was not significantly related to negative evaluations of recalled over-flights.

There has been relatively little research into the effects of other stimulation on judgments of landscape scenic beauty, with sound being by far the most studied. The studies reviewed above indicate that sounds that are congruent with the visually-represented landscape either have no effect or moderate impacts on scenic beauty evaluations, perhaps by making the sound-relevant features of the landscape more salient. Incongruent sounds, especially technological sounds in a pristine natural landscape, have been found to be substantially annoying and disruptive of efforts to find solitude and tranquility, but show only small effects on scenic beauty assessments. This pattern of findings is consistent with the view that scenic beauty is defined and predominantly determined by visual features of the landscape, and suggests that the addition of congruent or conflicting olfactory or tactile stimulation might be expected to produce similar effects.

Scenic Beauty and Education

Following from the notion that *beauty is in the eye of the beholder*, it is commonly believed that scenic beauty preferences will differ depending upon an individual's landscape experience, interests and knowledge. For example, a forest that is beautiful to a logger may not be expected to be similarly beautiful to a member of an environmental protection group. As noted above, this view underlies the recent call for ecological aesthetics, where scenic beauty judgments are expected to reflect the observer's level of understanding of ecological principles (Gobster, 1999). As intuitively appealing as this argument might be, there is little or no empirical evidence of such a relationship between experience/knowledge and scenic beauty preferences. Groups differing a priori in experience and knowledge have shown significant differences in ratings averaged over sets of relevant landscapes. However, to show differing scenic beauty preferences requires significant group differences in the pattern of preferences among the landscapes assessed (i.e., an interaction between landscapes and groups).

Several studies have assessed groups that were expected *a priori* to differ in environmental experience and interests. For example, McCool, Benson and Ashor (1986) sampled 18 different citizens groups in western Montana, ranging from the *Montana Loggers Association* to the *Missoula Sierra Club*. Individuals in all 18 groups were presented with the same 125 color slides sampled from Montana forests exhibiting forest conditions ranging from pristine to areas of recent and substantial modification by timber harvests. Groups expressing more favorable attitudes toward timber harvesting tended to rate all harvest-impacted scenes higher in scenic beauty than did those with less favorable attitudes toward timber harvesting. However, the rank order of scenic beauty across the range of scenes assessed was the same for every group. That is, these nominally different interest groups, with different expressed attitudes toward harvesting and scenic beauty, nonetheless agreed on the relative scenic beauty of the scenes presented. This pattern of results was recently replicated in a large study by Ribe (2002).

An alternative to the nominal group procedure is to directly manipulate the environmental information provided to observers (e.g., Anderson, 1981; Hodgson & Thayer, 1980). Taylor and Daniel (1984) presented illustrated brochures describing the ecological benefits of low intensity fires in ponderosa pine forests. Reading these brochures produced significant increases in *knowledge* of fire effects and more positive (tolerant) *attitudes* toward prescribed fire, compared to reading only general forest information brochures. At the same time, ratings of scenic beauty by specific and general information groups were highly correlated. A *Society and Natural Resources* paper by Kearney (2001) investigated the effects of ecological and forest management information on the acceptability of landscape scenes depicting clearcutting. The study did not collect direct ratings of scenic beauty. Rather, a mailed questionnaire presented landscape photographs (black and white) to be rated for "*how much you would like to see that scene*" in the forest. These acceptability ratings would be expected to correlate very highly with scenic beauty ratings (Ribe, 2002). Ecological information was presented in the form of short stories about the benefits of patch clearcuts (in paper birch forests) and the desirability of efforts to convert jack pine plantations to more natural areas by creating large areas of cut trees. Each participant rated 16 landscape photographs, showing relevant birch stands with and without patch cuts, and jack pine stands with and without clearcuts. Then, half of the respondents read the paper birch story and half read the jack pine story. All participants then rated another set of birch and jack pine landscape scenes, matched to the pre-intervention scenes. For the post-information ratings, each scene was accompanied by a verbal label that was directly relevant to the presented story (e.g., "birch patch-cut," "jack pine clearcut"). Compared to the pre-information ratings, the labeled birch patch-cut and jack pine clearcut scenes were rated less negatively than in the pre-information condition. However, undisturbed forest scenes were most preferred both before and after information and multiple regression analyses showed that pre-information ratings were the largest positive contributor to post-information ratings. This preference pattern is consistent with the findings reviewed above; ratings of the landscape were not affected by information provided.

Valuing Scenic Beauty

While no study has yet shown that public scenic beauty preferences are in substantial conflict with principles of ecosystem management, such a conflict could present a troubling dilemma for public land management. How much weight should be given to scenic beauty preferences? Such questions are common in environmental management where multiple goals must routinely be balanced. One approach to resolving tradeoffs is to relate both scenic beauty and ecological goals to a common value scale (e.g., dollars). However, this is proving to be a daunting, and from many perspectives, unpopular task for ecological goals (Daily et al., 1997), and there are few examples of efforts to relate economic values to scenic beauty. For one example, Daniel, Stewart, Brown, King and Richards (1989) studied the effects of forest characteristics on the perceived quality of forest campground settings. Visitors sampled from 11 different forest campgrounds were asked either to rate scenic beauty, rank overall quality of camping experience afforded or indicate their willingness-to-pay a camp fee in different forest settings represented by color photographs. Not surprisingly, scenic beauty ratings, camping quality rankings and willingness-to-pay for the represented settings were all strongly and positively correlated. The correlations between scenic beauty ratings and willingness-to-pay could, with appropriate economic adjustments, be used to assign a dollar value to units of scenic beauty.

A paper in *Society and Natural Resources* by Kim and Johnson (2002) provides a less direct, but perhaps more convincing, valuation of scenic beauty using a hedonic pricing method. They estimated the effect of visible clearcuts (a popular target for scenic beauty assessments) on the value of residential properties near forests. While perceived scenic beauty was not actually assessed, the design of the study assured that the scenic impact of the clearcuts studied was responsible for a major share of the observed negative effects on home values. Data on 752 homes near a research forest in the Pacific Northwest (U.S.) were subjected to multiple regression analyses to estimate the sales price contributions of *proximity to forest, type of forest* (as determined by management practices) and *presence or absence of a view of a recent clearcut.* The regression analyses effectively controlled for the multitude of non-environmental factors that affect home prices (e.g., lot size, house size, age, year of purchase). Thus, the results can be interpreted as an estimate of the contribution (in dollars) of the forest features to home price, holding all other important features equal. The finding most relevant to scenic beauty was the estimated effect of a visible clearcut. Using a case study analysis, the authors' hedonic pricing model estimated the cost of views of recent clear cuts at $724 per year per household in decreased property values (based on 1990-1995 prices).

If scenic beauty, ecosystem quality and other environmental values were all successfully translated into dollars, land management decisions could be made by simply adding up the dollar values associated with each alternative. Aside from the many technical obstacles to achieving such valuations, the unidimensional / commensurate value, efficient utility-maximization and other assumptions underlying the economic valuation model are not universally accepted as appropriate or sufficient for public environmental policy. Economic valuations of scenic beauty or ecological goals can best be viewed as contributors to, rather than a replacement for, the complex, multi-dimensional and highly political processes that characterize environmental policy-making. The fact that citizens still consistently list it among the most important benefits of public parks and wildlands assures that scenic beauty must continue to be considered in any responsible public land management process.

Conclusions

Scenic beauty has been and continues to be an important natural resource, and an important component of human/society and natural resource management research. Public perception-based scenic beauty assessments have met traditional standards of measurement reliability and validity, and have demonstrated potential for useful contributions to public land management and policy-making. The transition from multiple-use to ecosystem management paradigms poses new challenges for scenic beauty assessment in both practice and research. As discussed, questions related to representation, education and valuation are issues and challenges to address. Because landscape features consistently account for the greatest share of variance in scenic beauty assessments, how well relevant environmental variables are represented is of great concern. Photographs, videotapes, and more recently, computer-visualizations and virtual reality systems, have all been employed with some success. However, the challenge of achieving and confirming valid representations of ecologically relevant temporal and spatial variations in landscape patterns is yet to be fully met.

The potential for conflict between public scenic beauty preferences and ecosystem management goals has long been a concern, and is more recently being revisited in the context of calls for an ecological aesthetic. While the small body of relevant empirical research mostly indicates agreement between public scenic preferences and ecological goals, the prospect of conflict raises questions about whether and how public preferences might be altered. The research evidence offers little encouragement that conventional information and education manipulations would achieve any substantive change in public landscape preferences. This leaves the issue of what more potent persuasive techniques might provide. If conflicts between public scenic beauty preferences and ecosystem management goals were to exist and persist, economic valuation methods offer one way to represent and resolve value tradeoffs in environmental policy decisions. But, efforts to assign economic values to ecological goals are rather recent and controversial.

Natural resource management continues to move (albeit glacially) toward an ecosystem approach. It is not yet clear what this new natural resource management universe will be, or what philosophical, legal and methodological challenges it will present. For the vast areas of public lands in America, citizens' perception and appreciation of the scenic beauty of the landscape will undoubtedly continue to be an important consideration. The substantial historic base and the continuing progress in scenic beauty research support the optimistic prediction that these challenges will be met.

References

Anderson, L. M. (1981). Land use designations affect perceptions of scenic beauty in forest landscapes. *Forest Sciences*, 27, 392-400.

Anderson, L. M., Levi, D. J., Daniel, T. C., & Dieterich, J. H. (1982). *The esthetic effects of prescribed burning: A case study*. (Research note RM-413). Fort Collins, CO: USDA Rocky Mountain Forest and Range Experiment Station.

Anderson, L. M., Mulligan, B. E., Goodman, L. S., & Regen, H. Z. (1983). Effects of sounds on preferences for outdoor settings. *Environment and Behavior*, 15, 539-566.

Arthur, L. M., Daniel, T. C., & Boster, R. S. (1977). Scenic assessment: An overview. *Landscape Planning*, 4, 109-129.

Balling, J. D., & Falk, J. H. (1982). Development of visual preference for natural environments. *Environment & Behavior*, 14, 5-28.

Bergen, S. D., Ulbricht, C. A., Fridley, J. L., & Ganter, M. A. (1995). The validity of computer-generated graphic images of forest landscapes. *Journal of Environmental Psychology*, 15, 135-146.

Brown, T. C. (1984). The concept of value in resource allocation. *Land Economics*, 60, 231-246.

Brunson, M. W., & Shelby, B. (1992). Assessing recreational and scenic quality: How does "new forestry" rate? *Journal of Forestry*, 90, 37-41.

Buhyoff, G. J., & Leuschner, W. A. (1978). Estimating psychological disutility from damaged forest stands. *Forest Sciences*, 24, 424-432.

Carlson, A. A. (1977). On the possibility of quantifying scenic beauty. *Landscape Planning*, 4, 131-171.

Daily, G., Alexander, S., Ehrlich, P. R., Goulder, L., Lunchenko, J., Matson, P. A., Mooney, H. A., Postel, S., Schneider, S. H., Tilman, D., & Woodwell, G. M.(1997). Ecosystem services: Benefits supplied to human societies by natural ecosystems. *Issues in Ecology*, 2, 1-16.

Daniel, T. C. (1988). Human values and natural systems: A psychologist's response. *Society & Natural Resources*, 1, 285-290.

Daniel, T. C. (2001). Whither scenic beauty? Visual landscape quality assessment in the 21st century. *Landscape and Urban Planning*, 54(1-4), 267-281.

Daniel, T. C., & Boster, R. S. (1976). *Measuring landscape esthetics: The scenic beauty estimation method* (RM-66). Ft. Collins, CO: USDA Forest Service.

Daniel, T. C., Stewart, W. P., Brown, T. C., King, D. A., & Richards, M. T. (1989). Perceived scenic beauty and contingent valuation of forest campgrounds. *Forest Science*, 35(1), 76-90.

Daniel, T. C., Wheeler, L., Boster, R. S., & Best, P. (1973). Quantitative evaluation of landscapes: An application of signal detection analysis to forest management alterations. *Man-Environment Systems*, 3, 330-344.

Feimer, N. R., Smardon, R. C., & Craik, K. H. (1981). Evaluating the effectiveness of observer-based visual resource and impact assessment methods. *Landscape Research*, 6, 12-16.

Gimblett, R., Daniel, T., Cherry, S., & Meitner, M. J. (2001). The simulation and visualization of complex human-environment interactions. *Landscape and Urban Planning*, 54(1), 63-78.

Gobster, P. H. (1999). An ecological aesthetic for forest landscape management. *Landscape Journal*, 18, 54-64.

Herzog, T. R. (1984). A cognitive analysis of preference for field-and-forest environments. *Landscape Research*, 9, 10-16.

Herzog, T. R., & Bosley, P. J. (1992). Tranquility and preference as affective qualities of natural environments. *Journal of Environmental Psychology*, 12, 115-127.

Hetherington, J., Daniel, T. C., & Brown, T. C. 1993). Is motion more important than it sounds? The medium of presentation in environment perception research. *Journal of Environmental Psychology*, 13, 283-291.

Hodgson, R.W., & Thayer, Jr., R. L. (1980). Implied human influence reduces landscape beauty. *Landscape Planning*, 7, 171-179.

Johnson, R. L., Brunson, M. W., & Kimura, T. (1994). Using image-capture technology to assess scenic value at the urban-forest interface: A case study. *Journal of Environmental Management*, 40, 183-195.

Kaplan, R., Kaplan, S., & Brown, T. (1989). Environmental preference: A comparison of four domains of predictors. *Environment & Behavior*, 21(5), 509-530.

Kaplan, S. (1987). Aesthetics, affect and cognition: Environmental preference from an evolutionary perspective. *Environment & Behavior*, 19, 3-32.

Kearney, A. (2001). Effects of an informational intervention on public reactions to clear-cutting. *Society & Natural Resources*, 14(9), 777-790.

Kim, Y., & Johnson, R. L. (2002). The impact of forests and forest management on neighboring property values. *Society & Natural Resources*, 15, 887-901.

Lothian, A. (1999). Landscape and the philosophy of aesthetics: Is landscape quality inherent in the landscape or in the eye of the beholder? *Landscape and Urban Planning*, 44, 177-198.

Mace, B. L., Bell, P. A., & Loomis, R. J. (1999). Aesthetic, affective and cognitive effects of noise in natural landscape assessment. *Society and Natural Resources*, 12, 225-242.

McCool, S. F., Benson, R. E., & Ashor, J. L. (1986). How the public perceives the visual effects of timber harvesting: An evaluation of interest group preferences. *Environmental Management*, 10, 385-391.

Orland, B. (1994). Visualization techniques for incorporation in forest planning geographic information systems. *Landscape & Urban Planning*, 30(1-2), 83-97.

Orland, B., Budthimedhee, K., & Uusitalo, J. (2001). Considering virtual worlds as representations of landscape realities and as tools for landscape planning. *Landscape and Urban Planning*, 54(1-4), 139-148.

Parsons, R. (1991). The potential influences of environmental perception on human health. *Journal of Environmental Psychology*, 11, 11-23.

Parsons, R., & Daniel, T. C. (2002). Good looking: In defense of scenic landscape aesthetics. *Landscape and Urban Planning*, 60(1), 43-56.

Pukkala, T., Nuutinen, T., & Kangas, J. (1995). Integrating scenic and recreational amenities into numerical forest planning. *Landscape and Urban Planning*, 32(3), 185-195.

Ribe, R. G. (1982). On the possibility of quantifying scenic beauty - a response. *Landscape Planning*, 9(1), 61-75.

Ribe, R. G. (1989). The aesthetics of forestry: What has empirical preference research taught us? *Environmental Management*, 13(1), 55-74.

Ribe, R. G. (2002). Is scenic beauty a proxy for acceptable management? The influence of environmental attitudes on landscape perceptions. *Environment and Behavior*, 34(6), 757-780.

Ribe, R.G., Armstrong, E. T., & Gobster, P. H. (2002). Scenic vistas and the changing policy landscape: Visualizing and testing the role of visual resources in ecosystem management. *Landscape Journal*, 21, 42-66.

Rohrmann, B., & Bishop, I. D. (2002). Subjective responses to computer simulations of urban environments. *Journal of Environmental Psychology*, 22, 319-331.

Rolston, H. (1988). Human values and natural systems. *Society & Natural Resources*, 1, 271-284.

Shafer, E. L., & Brush, R. O. (1977). How to measure preferences for photographs of natural landscapes. *Landscape Planning*, 4, 237-256.

Shafer, E. L., & Richards, T. A. (1974). *A comparison of viewer reactions to outdoor scenes and photographs of those scenes* (Research Paper NE-302). Upper Darby, PA: USDA Forest Service

Shafer Jr., E. L. (1969). Perception of natural environment. *Environment and Behavior*, 1, 71-82.

Shindler, B., Brunson, M., & Stankey, G. H. (2002). *Social acceptability of forest conditions and management practices: A problem analysis* (USDA Forest Service General Technical Report 537). Washington DC: USDA Forest Service.

Shuttleworth, S. (1980). The use of photographs as an environmental presentation medium in landscape studies. *Journal of Environmental Management*, 11, 61-76.

Stamps, A. E., III (1990). Use of photographs to simulate environments: A meta-analysis. *Perceptual and Motor Skills*, 71, 907-913.

Tarrant, M. A., Haas, G. E., & Manfredo, M. J. (1995). Factors affecting visitor evaluations of aircraft overflights of wilderness areas. *Society & Natural Resources*, 8, 351-360.

Taylor, J. G., & Daniel, T. C. (1984). Prescribed fire: Public education and perception. *Journal of Forestry*, 82(6), 361-365.

Thorn, A. J., Daniel, T. C., Orland, B., & Brabyn, N. (1997). Managing forest aesthetics in production forests. *New Zealand Forestry*, 42, 21-29.

Ulrich, R. S. (1977). Visual landscape preference: A model and application. *Man-Environment Systems*, 7, 279-293.

United States Department of Agriculture (1974). *National forest landscape management, Vol. II: The visual management system*. Washington, DC: USDA Forest Service.

Zube, E. H., Sell, J. L., & Taylor, J. G. (1982). Landscape perception: Research, application and theory. *Landscape Planning*, 9(1), 1-33.

29

The Wildland-Urban Interface

Increasing
Significance,
Complexity and
Contribution

John F. Dwyer
Sarah M. McCaffrey

During the past two decades, presentations at International Symposia on Society and Resource Management (ISSRM) have covered an increasingly broad scope of topics on natural resource issues. The wildland-urban interface (WUI) was a key topic of discussion at the ninth ISSRM in 2002: a reflection of the response by social scientists to increasing residential development in wildland environments and fire management in the WUI. The dialogue included the causes, effects and policy implications of expanded residential development in wildland areas. This dialogue is certain to continue and become more dynamic, especially as ISSRM continues to evolve.

Although much of the WUI discussion at the 2002 ISSRM was related to fire policies, the implications of WUI management go well beyond wildfire. Historically, many WUI-related topics have been discussed at ISSRM (although not always in the specific context of the WUI), including: urban growth and influence, ecosystem health, restoration, wildfire, fragmentation, collaborative and adaptive management, communities, acquisition and management of public lands, and linkages across the landscape. Effectively addressing these and other important topics within the context of the WUI will call for the application of the full range of social sciences, as well as integration at multiple scales with the physical, biological, and ecological sciences. The landscape scale is an increasingly essential focus in efforts to address key policy issues concerning natural resource management and use. As with other subjects that have received significant attention at ISSRM, it is likely that discussion of the WUI will continue to evolve to include a widening range of significant management and policy issues, and areas of scientific inquiry.

After an initial focus on the definition, spatial configuration, and dynamics of the WUI, this chapter discusses several other key topics, with particular emphasis on WUI's evolution and possible changes in the future. It concludes with a discussion of future issues and implications, including how ISSRM can continue to address the needs of WUI research and management.

Changing Definitions

The term *wildland-urban interface* first appeared as a session title at the second ISSRM in 1990. Presentations in that session focused on managing interface lands on U.S. National Forests in southern California, with particular emphasis on outdoor recreation use by Hispanic Americans. The WUI next arose as a session topic in 1996 with a session on natural resource issues of the rural-urban interface. Other previous ISSRM paper topics with a similar or related focus include: urban-rural interface, residential-rural interface, urban-forest interface, peri-urban interface, urban-edge, urban-proximate, urban-forest fringe, residential forest, urbanizing landscape, urban sprawl, and rural-urban fringe. What these titles share is a focus on an interface or intermix environment involving residences and open or natural areas. Technically, the term *interface* refers to the edges of urban areas that are expanding into the wildland, while *intermix* refers to structures (e.g., residences) scattered throughout natural areas. Although the predominant term in current usage is *wildland-urban interface*, the term *wildland-urban intermix* is likely to increase; intermix areas are much more common than interface areas throughout the United States.

Interfaces and intermixes exist at many scales across the WUI. In these landscapes, the arrangement of natural resources, residences, and infrastructure has become increasingly important to critical management and policy issues. The spatial pattern of the area helps define the character of places where people want to live, visit, and recreate. Spatial factors also affect interactions between elements of the landscape and ecosystem functions, ultimately influencing landscape value and sustainability.

Although currently they are not generally perceived as part of the WUI, agricultural lands are likely to become an important part of the WUI discussion as residential development continues to expand into areas where agriculture is a dominant land use (Sullivan, 1992a, 1992b). Changes in management of crop and pasture lands, such as increasing use of trees and other perennial plants, tend to blur the distinctions between farms and natural areas. The addition of croplands and other non-wild lands to the discussion of residential interfaces and intermixes complicates the analysis of many landscape functions, and makes the spatial configuration of resources particularly critical. While the prospects for the spread of wildfires may be reduced by croplands and pasture in the landscape, issues such as animal habitats, exotic plants and animals, biodiversity, water quality, and plant and animal health may increase in importance and complexity.

Agricultural issues have received significant attention at ISSRM since the first meeting in 1986. Since that time, the range of agricultural issues addressed has broadened, and more recently included the sustainability of agriculture and how agriculture fits with other land uses at the landscape level. Sustainability of complex landscapes that include agriculture may well become a key dimension of future policy discussion for the WUI and beyond. It is likely that in many areas of the United States, the future will bring integrated management of natural areas, agricultural areas, and residential developments across the landscape. It is not clear what the resulting composite landscape will be called, as it goes beyond wildland cover; perhaps terms such as *residential open land intermix* will be useful to describe these lands.

Critical Issues in WUI

As changes in people, natural resources, and their interactions across the landscape accelerate, there is likely to be increasing interest in the dynamics of the spatial extent of the WUI. Building on presentations at the ninth ISSRM (Bengston, Fletcher & Nelson, 2002; Dwyer, 2002; Stewart, Hammer & Radeloff, 2002), future sessions are likely to focus on changing human migration and settlement patterns, changing patterns of housing growth, characteristics of residents and communities, and the associated implications for public policy. Remote imagery can be highly useful in tracking physical landscape changes; the Natural Land Cover Data has been particularly useful in this respect. Linking demographic and physical changes across the landscape can be particularly revealing to policy-makers and researchers in understanding the complex dynamics of the WUI.

Traditionally, most natural resource management discussion has focused on rural areas. However, in more recent times, increasing attention has been given to the influence of urban residents on natural resources, in both rural and urban areas. This has been reflected in several previous ISSRM: a paper on the social functions of urban open space at the first meeting in 1986, a workshop on urban forest management at the second ISSRM in 1988, and a substantial session devoted to urban forestry at the third symposium in 1990. The management of natural resources like parks and river corridors in urban areas has also received increased attention as it has become clear that these resources have a significant influence on urban environments and quality of life (Kaplan, Austin & Kaplan, 2002). The management of urban ecosystems, including their human dimensions, also is emerging as an important topic area (Grove & Burch, 2002; Wilson, Grove, Boumans & Burch, 2002).

As urban residents' use of resources on public and private lands has grown, their influence on the management of those resources has also increased. At the 1992 ISSRM, Ewert (1992) presented a paper entitled *Urban-proximate Wilderness: Managing for Difference*. This was followed by Stedman's (1994) presentation two years later, *Urban and Rural-based Hunters: An Exploration of the Culture of Hunting*. With expansion of residential areas into wildland settings, due in part to amenity and retirement migration and the establishment of seasonal homes, research on urban residents has expanded to include the WUI landscape (Constance, Denq & Kirkoon, 1998; McLeod, Kruse, Wolrhaye & Inman, 1998; Nelson & Kalmar, 1994; Stewart, Williams, VanPatten & Watson, 2000). This builds on previous research that focused on urban landowners and seasonal residents in rural areas, as well as the interactions between urban residents and the urban forest. Research on the interactions between urban residents and natural resources is beginning to focus more broadly on ecosystems, landscapes, and sustainability in the WUI and beyond.

Ecosystem Health

There has always been some attention given to ecosystem health at ISSRM, but the linkages with resource management issues, policies, and programs have not always

been explicit. Ecosystem health and sustainability are important WUI issues as many of the activities associated with expanding residential areas, such as house and infrastructure construction, can have a significant influence on ecosystem health. Important concerns include changes in drainage and stormwater flows, introduction of exotic plants and animals, and increased air and water pollution. Affected ecosystems can include a range of environments such as forests, savannas, wetlands, prairies, and (human) communities within the WUI. Water (quantity, quality, and timing) and biodiversity are likely to be critical policy issues, with exotic invasive plants and animals posing a significant threat. Fire and restoration also are key components of forest health and sustainability in the WUI that are discussed in more detail below. In addition, human health can be an important consideration; individuals may move to a WUI area seeking a more healthful environment, but significant health risks can emerge such as Lyme disease and West Nile Virus.

Restoration

Restoration is emerging as a significant natural resource management issue. It includes the rehabilitation of areas that were previously used for farming or commercial and industrial purposes, and the ecological renovation of areas damaged by invasive plants, animals and, in some cases, fire. Such damage tends to be accelerated in the WUI as widespread interactions between people and natural resources disrupt locally-evolved natural processes. As interest in the WUI increases, residential areas and other sites may be the focus of significant restoration activities, which may be a growing component of the creation of open-space residential subdivisions. In addition, as more residents and users are exposed to damaged or disrupted natural areas, they may demand substantial restoration work, as occurred in the Midewin National Tallgrass prairie southwest of Chicago (Stewart, Larkin & Liebert, 2002). In that area, the USDA Forest Service is working to restore native prairie to a 15,000 acre landscape that was significantly altered by agricultural and industrial use.

Fire

Fire is a major issue in the WUI; there are a number of critical issues to consider. Information is especially needed regarding the identification of high-risk fire areas, most effective ways to reduce fire risk and protect important values (e.g., houses, watershed), how to best allocate efforts to mitigate risk, and the best provision of protection and suppression capabilities. Other important concerns include the portion of fire management efforts, particularly fuels reduction, that should be allocated to the WUI; how fuels reduction in adjacent areas affects fire risk and damage; how to best engage residents in reducing risk; and characteristics of effective partnerships between communities and land management agencies for fire management. Although the second ISSRM in 1988 included a paper on controlled burning (McConnell, 1988), wildland fire is essentially a new topic at ISSRM with only a few papers prior to the sixteen presented at the ninth meeting. In some natural resource forums, fire has dominated the WUI issue to the exclusion of others. This has not happened at ISSRM, and is not likely to do so, given the symposia's breadth of approaches and issues.

Fragmentation

Fragmentation of land ownerships (e.g., parcelization) and natural resources often accompanies the development of residential areas in wildland environments. Residential structures and the supporting infrastructure, particularly roads and utilities, divide the landscape unnaturally. This has important implications for resource management and for the sustainability and diversity of the landscape. Timber harvesting, agriculture and outdoor recreation can often be difficult to undertake in small land tracts that often characterize WUI parcels. In addition, habitat fragmentation can pose major problems to the sustainability of animal and, to a lesser degree, plant species. Managing landscapes with increasingly fragmented natural areas and ownerships will necessitate adaptive and collaborative management approaches to respond to continuing changes and to the need to manage across ownerships (see the following section). At ISSRM, there have been a small but persistent number of papers on the management of non-industrial private forest lands, but not a great deal of attention to fragmentation of private ownerships in the WUI or the implications. A presentation by Kendra and Hull (2000) looking at the new owners of residential forests is a hopeful sign that ISSRM will begin to address fragmentation and the WUI.

Collaborative and Adaptive Management

To sustain dynamic and complex landscapes in the WUI, collaborative and adaptive management is important. Collaboration among managers is critical because of the many owners, partners, and interests involved with land management in the WUI, while adaptation of management is critical because of the significant changes over time that are continually occurring. Partnerships involving communities, non-profit groups, and landowners will become critical. Current collaborative efforts to develop comprehensive strategies to reduce wildfire losses and manage watersheds are likely to expand to manage additional resources and reduce negative ecological and social impacts.

Communities

ISSRM has a long tradition of research on communities and their interactions with resource managers that can help provide a foundation for future work on issues concerning the WUI. Early discussion focused on the impact of resource management, particularly timber production and outdoor recreation, on the growth, development and stability of nearby communities, often called *resource dependent communities*. Since then, more comprehensive analyses of communities as part of regional assessments have been done to guide the implementation of ecosystem management. In more recent times, particular attention has been given to the role of communities in natural resource management, including urban and ex-urban resources. Communities are critical in the WUI, particularly with respect to fire and residential development. A paper by Selin and Chavez (1992), *From Public Input to Public Participation: Developing a Collaborative Model of Natural Resource Decision-making*, captures some of the evolution of work with communities.

Acquisition and Management of Public Lands

The acquisition and management of public lands in WUI areas will become increasingly significant issues. Often public lands play a very important role of being the largest contiguous area of greenspace in the interface. Existing public lands in the WUI may experience new uses and influences from nearby residents, as well as increasing usage by people from more distant areas. The growth and development of the WUI can greatly complicate the management of these lands, but also enhance their values. Public agencies may purchase land to prevent development, or to provide social and ecological opportunities and functions not available on nearby private lands (e.g., outdoor recreation, habitat). Prioritization for public acquisition in the WUI can be complex, given both the multiple functions that these lands can play and rapidly rising property values. What is learned from the management of these lands can be useful for other areas that experience urban pressure in the years ahead.

Linkages Across the Landscape

The linkage between the WUI and management issues across the wider landscape is reflected in a number of previous ISSRM presentations. Over time, linkages between the interface / intermix environments and more distant parts of the landscape will become critical. For instance, growth of the interface environment can contribute to loss of population, economic activity, and development in the center of urban areas (Dwyer, 2002). Partnerships between social scientists and landscape ecologists will be critical to implementing a landscape approach to future resource analysis, with geographers and others skilled in geographic information systems and spatial analysis techniques providing important contributions. The movement towards increasing attention to landscape-level analysis will hopefully continue at ISSRM, with scientists participating in a dialogue on the WUI and its linkages with other areas of the landscape.

Summary and Conclusions

WUI emerged as a significant issue in the 2002 ISSRM and will most likely increase in significance in the years ahead. A number of issues addressed at previous symposia are significantly important. These areas include urban growth and influence, communities, and collaborative and adaptive management. Although ISSRM has given some attention to wildfire, ecosystem health (e.g., exotic-invasive species), linkages across the landscape, and ecological restoration, these issues are likely to increase in significance, in no small part due to their importance in the WUI. This will also continue a trend of integrating physical, biological, and social science work to better address significant policy issues, many of them at the landscape level. Collaboration with landscape ecologists and others who work from a landscape perspective will become increasingly critical. ISSRM is the ideal forum for developing comprehensive landscape approaches to major natural resource policy issues, and the WUI is a prime focus for such efforts. In turn, examining the WUI will help ISSRM to continue to expand the breadth and significance of natural resources issues that are presented, particularly landscape level policy issues.

References

Bengston, D. N., Fletcher, J. O., & Nelson, K. (2002). Public policy instruments for managing urban growth: An assessment of lessons learned (abstract). *Proceedings of the Ninth International Symposium on Society and Resource Management, USA,* 247.

Constance, D. H., Denq, F., & Kirkoon, J. D. (1998). Environmental protection and/or economic development: The views of urbans, rurals, and forest owners in Missouri (abstract). *Proceedings of the Seventh International Symposium on Society and Resource Management,* USA, 140.

Dwyer, J. F. (2002). Landscape change in the Midwest: Implications for natural resource management (abstract). *Proceedings of the Ninth International Symposium on Society and Resource Management,* USA, 10-11.

Ewert, A. (1992). Urban-proximate wilderness: Managing for difference (abstract). *Proceedings of the Fourth North American Symposium on Society and Resource Management,* USA, 248.

Grove, J. M., & Burch, W. R. (2002). A social patch approach to urban ecological systems (abstract). *Proceedings of the Ninth International Symposium on Society and Resource Management,* USA, 104.

Kaplan, R., Austin, M. E., & Kaplan, S. (2002). Nearby nature at the urban edge: Residents views and preferences (abstract). *Proceedings of the Ninth International Symposium on Society and Resource Management,* USA, 89.

Kendra, A., & Hull, IV, R. B. (2000). Understanding new forest owners: Market segmentation of motivations and behaviors in Virginia's residential forest (abstract). *Proceedings of the Eighth International Symposium on Society and Resource Management*, USA, 168-169.

McConnell, D. W. II. (1988). Controlled burning use by Alabama private, non-industrial forest owners: A study of diffusion and adoption (abstract). *Proceedings of the Second Symposium on Social Science in Resource Management*, USA, 15.

McLeod, D. M., Kruse, C., Wolrhaye, J., & Inman, K. (1998). Resident and non-resident preferences concerning land use in a high growth, amenity-rich county: A survey of Sublette County, Wyoming (abstract). *Proceedings of the Seventh International Symposium on Society and Resource Management*, USA, 59-60.

Nelson, L., & Kalmar, A. (1994). The constituency base for openspace protection in the metro-rural interface: A case study (abstract). *Proceedings of the Fifth International Symposium on Society and Resource Management*, USA, 275-276.

Selin, S., & Chavez, D. J. (1992). From public input to public participation: Developing a collaborative model of natural resource decision-making (abstract). *Proceedings of the Fourth North American Symposium on Society and Resource Management*, USA, 200-201.

Stedman, R. (1994). Urban and rural based hunters: An exploration of the culture of hunting (abstract). *Proceedings of the Fifth International Symposium on Society and Resource Management, USA*, 128.

Stewart, S. I., Hammer, R. B., & Radeloff, V. C. (2002). Characterizing housing density patterns across the Midwest: Growth hotspots in seven states (abstract). *Proceedings of the Ninth International Symposium on Society and Resource Management, USA*, 54.

Stewart, S. I., Williams, D. R., VanPatten, S. R., & Watson, A. (2000). Where does the land management debate reside? (abstract). *Proceedings of the Eighth International Symposium on Society and Resource Management, USA*, 303-304.

Stewart, W. P., Larkin, K. W., & Liebert, D. (2002). Protecting community identity amidst landscape change at Midewin prairie (abstract). *Proceedings of the Ninth International Symposium on Society and Resource Management, USA*, 207-208.

Sullivan, W. C. (1992a). Perceptions of the rural-urban fringe: Citizen preferences for natural and developed settings (abstract). *Proceedings of the Fourth North American Symposium on Society and Resource Management, USA*, 302-303.

Sullivan, W. C. (1992b). Preserving farmland through cluster housing: The search for adequate and satisfying places to live (abstract). *Proceedings of the Fourth North American Symposium on Society and Resource Management, USA*, 303-304.

Wilson, M. A., Grove, J. M., Boumans, R. M., & Burch, W. R. (2002). Exploring the role of social capital in urban revitalization and ecological restoration (abstract). *Proceedings of the Ninth International Symposium on Society and Resource Management, USA*, 28-29.

30

Environmental Psychology

Human Responses
and Relationships to
Natural Landscapes

Daniel R. Williams

The purpose of this chapter is to present a thorough assessment of environmental psychology as a way to understand relationships between people and natural landscapes, and to describe how this knowledge can be applied to natural resource management. Environmental psychology seeks to clarify how individuals perceive, experience and create meaning in the environment. In part, it constitutes a branch of social psychology that studies individual behavior embedded in its large-scale social and ecological context, as well as actively defining and giving shape to that context. In addition, environmental psychology encompasses an interdisciplinary field of environment and behavior research that includes human geography and the design and planning professions (e.g., architecture, landscape architecture, urban and regional planning). The field grew out of controversies within psychology over the external and ecological validity of laboratory experiments, and the simultaneous emergence of an environmental movement within social science and the design and planning professions. Beyond the emphasis on environmental matters, an important reason for focusing on environmental psychology in natural resource management is that it is a particularly integrative and eclectic area within environmental social science.

Conceptualizing Human-Environment Relationships

Environmental psychology is distinct from other fields of environmental social science in its emphasis on the individual as the unit of analysis and its focus on mental and behavioral responses to environmental stimuli as its subject matter. What distinguishes environmental psychology from many other psychologies (and makes it particularly relevant to natural resource management) is that it takes a broad approach to conceptualizing both the stimuli (i.e., to include large-scale environments) and subsequent response (i.e., from immediate affective and behavioral responses to more extensive and enduring understandings and relationships to places). This broader human-environment relationship is captured by the concept of environmental meaning or what is often understood as *perceptions, preferences, values, beliefs, attitudes* and so forth. Much of applied environmental psychology involves describing the range and diversity of meanings people associate with particular places and the factors that influence the formation of these meanings (Groat, 1995). This includes understanding how relatively tangible and objective properties of the environment shape and influence human responses, as well as identifying the emotional bonds and symbolic meanings people associate with specific landscapes or places.

Synthesis and Integration of Research

What follows is a presentation of research findings based on a framework presented at the 1994 International Symposium on Society and Resource Management (ISSRM) (see Williams & Patterson, 1996, 1999), based in part on Saegert and Winkel's (1990) review of environmental psychology. The framework identifies four paradigms for conceptualizing human-environment relationships: 1) adaptive, 2) goal-directed, 3) sociocultural, and 4) expressive. This section describes the basic features of each paradigm, how each has been or can be applied to natural resource management topics, and their respective strengths and weaknesses. The four paradigms are distinguished from one another based on how each conceptualizes environmental meaning. Building on Fournier's (1991) work, the paradigms vary in: a) the degree to which meaning is objective and verifiable through the senses (i.e., tangibility), b) the degree to which meanings are shared or highly individualized (i.e., commonality), and c) the degree to which meaning is associated with arousal, intensity, or depth of involvement (i.e., emotionality).

The Adaptive Paradigm

According to Saegert and Winkel (1990), the adaptive paradigm builds on the idea that biological and psychological survival motivates behavior. They describe the way psychological functioning has evolved to address three adaptive issues: 1) how organisms come to know the environment, 2) how organisms cope with stressful environments, and 3) how the environment functions as a restorative or therapeutic medium.

Two examples that address how organisms come to know the environment are Gibson's (1979) theory of ecological perception and the concept of cognitive mapping (Golledge, 1987). Accordingly, human perceptual mechanisms (e.g., sight, hearing) are adapted to facilitate functioning in an information or stimulus environment dominated by uncertainty. Understanding how individuals acquire information from the environment supports research on how the public responds to information in planning decisions, designing environments to enhance navigation and information acquisition, and environmental learning and interpretation (Kaplan & Kaplan, 1982).

The common approach in understanding how organisms cope with stressful environments is to look for direct *dose-response* linkages between specific environmental stimuli (i.e., the relationship between amount of exposure to environmental stimuli such as sound or temperature), and psychological functioning and well-being. For example, a dose-response model was used to explain the impact of aircraft noise on wilderness experiences (Tarrant, Haas & Manfredo, 1995).

The stress paradigm is also a dominant theme in the crowding, conflict, and social carrying-capacity literature, in which the stressor stimuli are other people and/or their behaviors (Miller & McCool, 2003; Vaske & Donnelly, 2002). From the stress perspective, outdoor recreation has been studied as both a context within which people find opportunities to cope with daily stressors (Wellman, 1979), as well as a context in which people must adapt to stressors in the outdoor recreation environment (Iwasaki & Schneider, 2003).

Where the concept of stress portrays "the person as struggling against the environment to maintain health and well-being" (Saegert & Winkel, 1990, p. 450), the third area of research within the adaptive paradigm involves the natural environment as having an intrinsic capacity to promote healing and mental restoration (Kaplan & Kaplan, 1989; Kellert & Wilson, 1993). Accordingly, human responses to the environment are better adapted to natural stimuli, and therefore exposure to nature promotes well-being and affords an opportunity to recover from stress (Hull & Michaels,1995).

Following the restoration thesis, the adaptive view has been very influential in modeling aesthetic preferences for landscape features. Much of the research on landscape preference is premised on innate biological explanations (Ulrich, 1993; Ulrich, Simons, Losito, Fiorito, Mile & Zelson, 1991). Aesthetic models appear to tap important meanings of the landscape with considerable reliability, sensitivity and commonality (Daniel & Vining, 1983). Research supports that aesthetic responses can be sufficiently isolated from other meanings of the landscape to warrant some attempt to inventory them. Further, aesthetic types of meanings are tangible (in that they can be mapped onto the landscape using formal, psychophysical and psychological theories of scenic beauty), emotionally potent, and provide a common and valued basis for natural resource decision-making.

Overall, the adaptive paradigm is particularly relevant because it focuses on highly valued outcomes such as health and well-being, an understanding of the compatibility of the environment with fundamental human needs, and the real and perceived control mechanisms for effective coping (Saegert & Winkel, 1990). However, by treating the person as a biological and psychological individual, and the environment as naturally given, studies following the adaptive paradigm fail to place their data in the larger context of political, social and economic factors that structure the environment and distribute power and control within society. It privileges biological reality while ignoring the social construction of that reality through active, interpretive and behavioral engagements with the environment.

The Opportunity Structure / Goal-Directed Paradigm
What Saegert and Winkel (1990) refer to as the *opportunity structure* or *goal-directed* paradigm is perhaps the most widely applied environmental psychology approach in natural resource management. It constitutes the psychological equivalent of the commodity paradigm that has historically guided resource management. In contrast to the adaptive paradigm, humans are viewed as rational decision-makers rather than respondents to biological imperatives. Emphasis is given to how people

process information in arriving at a decision, action or evaluation.

In natural resource management, the social science of goal-directed behavior is quite well-developed, drawing a great deal from social psychology and microeconomics (Manfredo, 1992; Manning, 1999; Peterson, Driver & Gregory, 1988). Consequently, psychological theories related to attitude formation, motivation, and decision-making are prominent within the opportunity structure paradigm. Examples can be seen in such natural resource applications as choice and behavioral modeling (Louvière & Timmermans, 1990), recreation motivation (Driver, Brown, & Peterson, 1991), recreation satisfaction (Williams, 1989), non-market economics (Peterson et al., 1988), and studies of environmental attitude-behavior relationships (Manfredo, 1992). In sum, this paradigm is popular within natural resource management because it is well-suited to the rational, instrumental and commodity-oriented traditions of resource planning.

The advantage of the goal-directed approach is that it supports psychological models of individual choice that can be integrated with non-market approaches to resource valuation (Peterson et al., 1988). Inherent in this paradigm is the notion that environmental settings are theoretically interchangeable (i.e., substitutable), even reproducible, given that the replacement provides a similar combination of goal-fulfilling attributes. Psychological responses (e.g., satisfaction of behavioral and economic needs) are understood as instrumentally dependent on specific properties of the environment. This amounts to thinking of resources as a means rather than an end (Gee, 1994), which works well for commodities and services (e.g., timber) that are relatively generic, homogeneous and substitutable.

At the same time, however, this approach makes tenuous assumptions of the rationality and volitionality of the individual, provides limited understanding of the socioeconomic and sociocultural (e.g., class, race) forces influencing opportunity structures and individual goal orientations, reduces environmental meanings to behavioral utilities, and generally ignores the symbolic environment. Ignored are the intangible meanings attached to a given landscape, which are not necessarily determined by the resource uses or activities that occur there. Over time, as people recognize that resources and landscapes become places filled with their own histories, they begin to assign unique meanings to them. Some meanings associated with an environment do not derive so much from how it can be used, but simply what it represents symbolically. *Meaning*, instrumentally defined, fails to adequately address the more emotional, symbolic, and spiritual benefits of values and how these are socially produced.

The Socio-cultural Paradigm

The *sociocultural* approach reflects a conceptual shift away from predominantly stimulus-based (i.e., adaptive) and intrapersonal (i.e., goal-directed) explanations of behavior toward those that view place and landscape meanings as socially-constructed within the cultural, historical and geographical contexts of day-to-day life (Greider & Garkovich, 1994; Williams & Carr, 1993; Williams & Patterson, 1996). Rather than viewing the person as an autonomous individual having survival needs or instrumental goals, the person is viewed as a social being who seeks out and creates meaning in the environment (Saegert & Winkel, 1990). Investigations of these social and symbolic environmental meanings have their origins in phenomenological studies of human-environment relations, including sense of place within human and cultural geography (Relph, 1997; Tuan, 1977), place attachment within psychology (Altman & Low, 1992), semiotic analysis within architecture and environmental design (Rapoport, 1982), and community identity (Cuba & Hummon, 1993) and politics (Kemmis, 1990) within sociology. From a sociocultural perspective, for example, the same forest landscape can symbolize ancestral ways of life, valued commodities, or essential livelihood to different groups of people (Greider & Garkovich, 1994). Thus, an environment acquires varied and competing social and political meaning through its association over time with particular activities and groups.

An early example of applying the sociocultural perspective to natural resources was Lee's (1972) examination of public parks as repositories of meanings that symbolized intergroup relationships. He found that neighborhood parks often constituted local territories defined by its users as belonging to them informally through familiarity and knowledge. In contrast, the meanings of regional parks and wildland settings were more often governed by formal rules of ownership and use; rules that were perceived by ethnic minorities as White, middle-class and exclusionary.

Similarly, Brandenburg and Carroll (1995) examined symbolic and expressive meanings of a popular river drainage and found that stakeholders from the most nearby community often exhibited strong attachment to the drainage and a desire to protect it regardless of their multiple use values. Stakeholders in more distant communities, who were rarely involved directly in the use of the drainage, valued it in terms that reflected the orientation (e.g., utilitarian, preservation) of their dominant social group. Moreover, locals who expressed personal affection for the place in private interviews exhibited quite different attitudes at public meetings when among members of their ostensibly more utilitarian-oriented neighbors.

The main advantage of the sociocultural paradigm is the recognition that environmental meanings extend well beyond biological imperatives and individual goal-oriented constructions, to include the ways in which meaning is socially structured. Though much of the research focuses on the social use of the environment to incorporate individuals into groups, American society is a multi-group mosaic. Recent work is beginning to explore social differences in access to the economic and political power necessary to create meaning and define the use of resources—the basis of much intergroup conflict (see Cheng, Kruger & Daniels, 2003; Stokowski, 2002; Williams, 2002).

Individual / Expressive Paradigm
Like the sociocultural approach, the individual expressive paradigm emphasizes a socially constructed and more voluntaristic view of reality. The study of expressive meaning, however, is even more deeply rooted in a subjectively oriented phenomenology (Altman & Low, 1992), emphasizing individual level processes and recognizing that individuals have the potential to assign intangible and relatively unique meaning to places and things. Unlike adaptive and goal-directed meanings, expressive meanings do not apply so much to abstract classes of environments or their separable features as they do to specific places. The significance of individual/expressive meanings is captured in the concept of *place-identity*. According to

Cuba and Hummon (1993), "place identity arises because places, as bounded locales imbued with personal, social, and cultural meanings, provide a significant framework in which identity is constructed, maintained, and transformed" (p. 112). With involvement and attachment to places, individuals actively construct and affirm a sense of self. Our affiliations with places helps to communicate our sense of identity to ourselves and others.

Interest in individually-held meanings has often focused on concepts of place attachment and identity as affective bonds to place (Giuliani & Feldman, 1993). Place attachment can be thought of as an emotional dimension of meaning (i.e., an indication of the intensity, depth or extent of meaning) with symbolic and spiritual meanings developed through interaction with a place over time. These attachments can be distinguished from other emotional processes (e.g., scenic beauty, subjective utility) by the emphasis on bonds, ties and connections. Within environmental psychology, studies of place attachment are often associated with home, neighborhood and community, but a growing number of studies have applied place attachment to natural or outdoor landscapes (Jorgensen & Stedman, 1999; Moore & Graefe, 1994; Williams, Patterson, Roggenbuck & Watson, 1992; Williams & Vaske, 2003).

Survey-based studies of resource users and community residents have demonstrated that the strength of place attachments can be quantified for multiple places and at multiple geographic scales (Williams & Vaske, 2003). Some have been directed at resource- and tourism-dependent communities (McCool & Martin, 1994), while others have attempted to relate place attachment to national parks, wilderness and other outdoor recreation settings (Moore & Graefe, 1994). Although survey research may not be able to probe detailed spatial patterns or the subtleties of meaning, it may be useful for providing broad mapping of the emotional intensity individuals and groups associate with various places.

Using a qualitative approach, Mitchell, Force, Carroll and McLaughlin (1993) conducted personal interviews with visitors to a river drainage to identify attachment-oriented users who assigned specific social meaning to the drainage. In the process they pointed out how several planning technologies and frameworks were amenable to incorporating both utilitarian and place perspectives. Similarly, Schroeder (1996) asked people to write essays about the meaning and experience of being in the Black River area to develop knowledge about places of special significance within the forest. The implication from this work is that an inventory at a *special places* level might be obtained through such methods for public land managers and others.

Expressive meanings may not provide a common basis for managing natural landscapes, but they demonstrate the importance of site-specific relationships and bonds. Individualized meanings of places both *enable* people to create individuation by distinguishing themselves from their primary social group or community and, at the same time, *embed* the individual in a larger social context as place meanings are transmitted from a social group to the individual (Brandenburg & Carroll, 1995). The importance of acknowledging individualized meaning is that people are likely to resist management actions that threaten their individual sense of self.

Managerial and Social Significance of Environmental Psychology
Within the resource management community, procedures for classifying and

mapping adaptive and goal-directed uses and meanings have evolved into relatively well-defined research programs (e.g., assessments of scenic quality, valuation or choice modeling). Moreover, because these approaches address relatively tangible environmental meanings that can be linked directly to the physical properties of the environment, they have been readily integrated into the utilitarian philosophy that has long guided resource management and planning. This ability to link meaning to physical attributes has facilitated inventory strategies that allow resource managers, in principle, to integrate various and competing aesthetic and instrumental meanings in prioritizing land management goals.

In contrast, the cultural and expressive forms of meaning (often the most intangible and contentious forms of environmental meaning) have received little attention. While they have been the subject of environment and behavior research, there has been little systematic effort to characterize these meanings within natural resource management, a prospect made more difficult by the lack of correspondence to on-the-ground features. Still, this emerging work suggests that a variety of methods, from surveys to various forms of public involvement, may be used to identify varying and competing landscape meanings (Eisenhaur, Krannich & Blahna, 2000; Kruger, 1998). The work suggests that the public can identify and classify land units that hold intangible meanings and values, and demonstrates that it is important to distinguish spatially *generalized values* regarding public lands policy from *place-specific values* (Brown, Reed & Harris, 2002). It also suggests that a mix of both personal and public judgments about the meaning of places is important.

Issues for the Future

Place, Context and Scale
In proposing the need for a synthesis of paradigms in environmental psychology, Saegert and Winkel (1990) note that previous research findings are largely products of specific historic or geographic contexts. They argue that the goal of finding general relationships continues to elude researchers, and further, that some investigators have suggested it might be more appropriate to view person-environment relationships as necessarily specific to particular historical and geographic contexts.

One implication is that the emphasis in environmental psychology should shift from seeking generalizable relationships to seeking geographically and historically specific ones (not unlike the shift in natural resources from the commodity to ecosystem paradigm). In other words, a more contextual and integrated understanding of resource management, in addition to benefitting from a broader view of environmental meaning, may profit from geographic theorizing on the concept of place in which human culture and history imbued a landscape with meaning (Sack, 1997).

Consideration of meaning in defining *place* complements the increasing focus in natural resource management on the spatial and temporal context of management decisions. Attending to larger scale processes (moving from typically *site* level to *landscape* or *ecosystem* level) presumably facilitates a more integrated view and understanding of the impacts of resource policies and management. Thus, social science suited to the needs of collaborative and adaptive management of complex social and biological systems involves not just a more inclusive understanding of the realm of meaning, but must also address the expanded spatial and temporal scales emphasized in ecosystem management. In particular, the concept of place draws attention to the processes by which resources and ecosystems are socially and politically constructed and contested.

Mapping and Constructing Socio-cultural Meanings and Relationships
Beyond more attention to scale and context, there is a need to address the lack of knowledge in cultural, symbolic, spiritual and expressive meanings of the landscape. This will require a long-term and continuous commitment by resource managers to nurture local knowledge of place and integrate that knowledge within larger regional and national values. This represents a continuous engagement in public discussion about the meaning of places.

Cultural and expressive meanings are not as stable in place, time and group as aesthetic and instrumental meanings. Consequently, management is not so much a matter of applying technology and technique, but of building trust, applying the principles of adaptive learning, and learning the art of participating in public dialogue and collaboration. This dialogue is a critical part of the process of creating and negotiating landscape meanings. Such ongoing discussion does not require any greater magnitude of effort than has been devoted to various forms of ecological analysis or resource inventory, but it does require an openness to diverse ways of knowing places and their meanings.

Post-positivist Approaches to Science
In addition to characterizing the nature of human responses and relationships, this openness to diverse ways of knowing requires critical pluralism in the practice of science (Patterson & Williams, 1998). For example, there are important ontological and epistemological assumptions behind each of the four paradigms of human-environment relationships. Ontologically, forms of human-nature responses and relationships can be differentiated in terms of whether human behavior is adapted to and/or determined by a reality composed of separable parts, or if it involves the actions of voluntary agents actively constructing a more holistic reality.

Epistemologically, the different research models describe how humans come to know reality, with contrasting points of view ranging from generalizable and objective knowledge, to contextual and subjective knowledge. Thus, to advance research on these various relationships we must broaden what counts as knowledge, how we conceptualize and value places and landscapes, and how we integrate this knowledge into theory and practice.

Conclusions

In addressing meanings and relationships as *responses* to the environment, environmental psychology is well-suited to bridging the paradigmatic shift in natural resources from utilitarian models, which emphasize tangible things that a resource can produce (Shanon, 1992), towards more holistic landscape or place perspectives. Whereas a response to a stimulus may be understood as something direct and largely unmediated, a meaning or relationship implies something more constructed, connected to the past, and embedded in a web of social affiliations and practices. In this latter view, the environment (e.g., ecosystems, places) to which people respond and relate is conceptualized as more than a resource of separately valued properties. The totality of any particular relationship to an environment that a researcher might want to describe is likely to involve an amalgamation of adaptive, goal-directed, socio-cultural and expressive meanings. Taken together, the different research paradigms within environmental psychology provide a framework for natural resource management to transcend its traditionally commodified view of nature, and adopt a view that emphasizes more holistic geographic units.

If we think of environmental psychology as a way to identify and map landscape meanings, then we need to move toward a wider conception of meaning. Metaphorically, if not literally, we need to expand our knowledge on how to map landscape meanings, and the natural and social processes that structure or distribute these meanings across spatial and temporal dimensions. Similarly, if modern society hopes to forge a more sustainable basis for human habitation of the planet, it will need to recognize the inherent assumptions underlying human-environment relations that guide environmental research and management, and endeavor to broaden and recreate new modes of thinking about its place and impact on the rest of the planet. An underlying theme of this chapter has been that the gaps in knowledge about human-environment relations are, in large part, a result of the dominance of certain guiding metaphors (e.g., commodity, production) used in natural resource management. The emergence of ecosystem management as a resource management philosophy is in many ways an effort to rethink these metaphors, and to chart new ways of viewing the world.

References

Altman, I., & Low, S. M. (Eds.). (1992). *Human behavior and environment: Advances in theory and research, Vol. 12.* New York: Plenum Press.

Brandenburg, A. M., & Carroll, M. S. (1995). Your place, or mine: The effect of place creation on environmental values and landscape meanings. *Society and Natural Resources,* 8, 381-398.

Brown, G. G., Reed, P., & Harris, C. C. (2002). Testing a place-based theory for environmental valuation: An Alaska case study. *Applied Geography,* 22(1), 49-76.

Cheng, A. S., Kruger, L. E., & Daniels, S. E. (2003). "Place" as an integrating concept in natural resource politics: Propositions for a social science research agenda. *Society and Natural Resources,* 16(2), 87-104.

Cuba, L., & Hummon, D. (1993). A place to call home: Identification with dwelling, community, and region. *Sociological Quarterly,* 34, 111-131.

Daniel T. C., & Vining, J. (1983). Methodological issues in the assessment of landscape quality. In I. Altman & J. Wohlwill (Eds.), *Human behavior and environment, Vol. 6* (pp. 39-84). New York: Plenum Press.

Driver, B. L, Brown, P. J., & Peterson, G. L. (Eds.). (1991). *Benefits of Leisure.* State College, PA: Venture Publishing, Inc.

Eisenhaur, B. W., Krannich, R. S., & Blahna, D. J. (2000). Attachment to special places on public lands: An analysis of activities, reasons, for attachments, and community connections. *Society and Natural Resources*, 13(5), 421-443.

Fournier, S. (1991). A meaning-based framework for the study of consumer-object relations. *Advances in Consumer Research*, 18, 736-742.

Gee, M. (1994). Questioning the concept of the 'user'. *Journal of Environmental Psychology*, 14, 113-124.

Gibson, J. J. (1979). *The ecological approach to visual perception*. Boston: Houghton Mifflin.

Giuliani, M. V., & Feldman, R. (1993). Place attachment in a developmental and cultural context. *Journal of Environmental Psychology*, 13, 267-274.

Golledge, R. (1987). Environmental cognition. In D. Stokols & I. Altman (Eds.), *Handbook of environmental psychology: Vol. 1.* (pp. 131-74). New York: Wiley.

Greider, T., & Garkovich, L. (1994). Landscapes: The social construction of nature and the environment. *Rural Sociology*, 59, 1-24.

Groat, L. (Ed.). (1995). *Giving places meaning: Readings in environmental psychology*. San Diego, CA: Academic Press.

Hull, R., & Michael, S. (1995). Nature-based recreation, mood change, and stress restoration. *Leisure Sciences*, 17, 1-14.

Iwasaki, Y., & Schneider, I. E. (2003). Leisure, stress, and coping: An evolving area of inquiry. *Leisure Sciences*, 25, 107-114.

Jorgensen, B. S., & Stedman, R. C. (1999). Sense of place as an attitude: Lakeshore owners attitudes toward their properties. *Journal of Environmental Psychology*, 21(3), 233-248.

Kaplan, R., & Kaplan, S. (1989). *The experience of nature: A psychological perspective*. New York: Cambridge University Press.

Kaplan, S., & Kaplan, R. (1982). *Cognition and the environment: Functioning in an uncertain world*. New York: Praeger.

Kellert, S. R., & Wilson, E. O. (Eds.). (1993). *The biophilia hypothesis*. Washington, D.C.: Island Press.

Kemmis, D. (1990). *Community and the politics of place*. Norman, OK: University of Oklahoma Press.

Kruger, L. (1998, May). *A civic science approach to social assessment and knowing place*. Paper presented at the Seventh International Symposium on Society and Natural Resource Management, Columbia, MO.

Lee, R. G. (1972). The social definition of recreation places. In W. Burch, Jr., N. Cheek, Jr., & L. Taylor (Eds.), *Social behavior, natural resources and the environment* (pp. 68-84). New York: Harper and Row.

Louvière, J., & Timmermans, H. (1990). Stated preference and choice models applied to recreation research: A review. *Leisure Sciences*, 12, 9-32.

Manfredo, M. (Ed.). (1992). *Influencing human behavior: Theory and application in recreation tourism and natural resource management*. Champaign, IL: Sagamore Publications.

Manning, R. (1999). *Studies in outdoor recreation: Search and research for satisfaction (2nd Ed.)*. Corvallis, OR: Oregon State University Press.

McCool, S. F., & Martin, S. R. (1994). Community attachment and attitudes toward tourism development. *Journal of Travel Research*, 22(3), 29-34.

Miller, T. A., & McCool, S. F. (2003). Coping with stress in outdoor recreational settings: An application of transactional stress theory. *Leisure Sciences*, 25, 257-276.

Mitchell, M. Y., Force, J. E., Carroll, M. S., & McLaughlin, W. J. (1993). Forest places of the heart: Incorporating special places into public management. *Journal of Forestry*, 91(4), 32-37.

Moore, R. L., & Graefe, A. R. (1994). Attachment to recreation settings: The case of rail-trail users. *Leisure Sciences*, 16, 17-31.

Patterson, M. E., & Williams, D. R. (1998). Paradigms and problems: The practice of social science on natural resource management. *Society and Natural Resources*, 11, 279-295.

Peterson, G. L., Driver, B. L., & Gregory, R. (Eds.). (1988). *Amenity resource valuation: Integrating economics with other disciplines*. University Park, PA: Venture Publishing, Inc.

Rapoport, A. (1982). *The meaning of the built environment*. Beverly Hills, CA: Sage Publications.

Relph, E. (1997). Sense of place. In S. Hanson (Ed.), *Ten geographic ideas that changed the world* (pp. 205-226). New Brunswick, NJ: Rutgers University Press.

Sack, R. D. (1997). *Homo geographicus: A framework for action, awareness, and moral concern*. Baltimore, MD: John Hopkins University Press.

Saegert, S., & Winkel, G. H. (1990). Environmental psychology. *Annual Review of Psychology*, 41, 441-477.

Schroeder, H. W. (1996). Ecology of the heart: Understanding how people experience natural environments. In A. Ewert (Ed.), *Natural resource management: The human dimension* (pp. 13-27). Boulder, CO: Westview Press.

Shannon, M. A. (1992). Foresters as strategic thinkers, facilitators, and citizens. *Journal of Forestry*, 90, 24-40.

Stokowski, P. A. (2002). Languages of place and discourses of power: Constructing new senses of place. *Journal of Leisure Research*, 34, 368-382.

Tarrant, M. A., Haas, G. E., & Manfredo, M. J. (1995). Factors affecting visitor evaluations of aircraft overflights of wilderness areas. *Society and Natural Resources*, 8, 351-360.

Tuan, Y. (1977). *Space and place: The perspective of experience.* Minneapolis, MN: University of Minnesota Press.

Ulrich, R. S. (1993). Biophilia, biophobia and natural landscapes. In S. Kellert & E. O. Wilson (Eds.), *The biophilia hypothesis* (pp. 73-137). Washington, DC: Island Press.

Ulrich, R. S., Simons, R. F., Losito, B. D., Fiorito, E., Mile, M. A., & Zelson, M. (1991). Stress recovery during exposure to natural and urban environments. *Journal of Environmental Psychology*, 11, 201-230.

Vaske, J. J., & Donnelly, M. P. (2002). Generalizing the encounter-norm-crowding relationship. *Leisure Sciences*, 24, 255-270.

Wellman, J. D. (1979). Recreational response to privacy stress: A validational study. *Journal of Leisure Research*, 11, 61-73.

Williams, D. R. (1989). Great expectations and the limits to satisfaction: A review of recreation and consumer satisfaction research. In A. Watson (Ed.), *Outdoor recreation benchmark 1988: Proceedings of the National Outdoor Recreation Forum* (pp. 422-438). Asheville, NC: USDA Forest Service, Southeastern Forest Experiment Station.

Williams, D. R. (2002). Leisure identities, globalization and the politics of place. *Journal of Leisure Research*, 34, 351-367.

Williams, D. R., & Carr, D. S. (1993). The sociocultural meanings of outdoor recreation places. In A. Ewert, D. Shavez, & A. Magill (Eds.), *Culture, conflict, and communication in the wildland-urban interface* (pp. 209-219). Boulder, CO: Westview Press.

Williams, D. R., & Patterson, M. E. (1996). Environmental meaning and ecosystem management: Perspectives from environmental psychology and human geography. *Society and Natural Resources*, 9, 507-521.

Williams, D. R., & Patterson, M. E. (1999). Environmental psychology: Mapping landscape meanings for ecosystem management. In H. K. Cordell & J. C. Bergstrom (Eds.), *Integrating social sciences and ecosystem management: Human dimensions in assessment, policy and management* (pp. 141-160). Champaign, IL: Sagamore Press.

Williams, D. R., Patterson, M. E., Roggenbuck, J. W., & Watson, A. E. (1992). Beyond the commodity metaphor: Examining emotional and symbolic attachment to place. *Leisure Sciences*, 14, 29-46.

Williams, D. R., & Vaske, J. J. (2003). The measurement of place attachment: Validity and generalizability of a psychometric approach. *Forest Science*, 49(6),

31

Dominant Socioeconomic Forces Shaping the Future of the United States

H. Ken Cordell

John C. Bergstrom

Carter J. Betz

Gary T. Green

This chapter is devoted to providing up-to-date summaries of a number of highly important social and economic trends that will play a role in the future of the United States and its natural resources. The topics covered include population growth, changing composition of the population, urban growth and sprawl, transition of rural lands, economic growth, consumer spending, and recreation demands. It is undertaken in part to meet data and information needs associated with the 2005 Update of the Renewable Resources Planning Act Assessment of Forest and Range Lands (RPA). More special is that it is also undertaken to celebrate the 2004 International Symposium on Society and Resource Management (ISSRM).

Population Trends

There are three fundamental indicators that determine trends in human population: birth rate, death rate and net migration. The difference between birth and death rates is natural population growth (of a resident population). Net migration to and from a country, added to (or subtracted from) its natural growth is total population growth (or, rarely, decline). Following are current statistics and projections of the population to 2100.

Natural Growth

At the beginning of the 1800s, birth rates were much higher than now, being around 55 births per every 1,000 population per year. By the early 1900s, birth rates had fallen to around 30 per 1000. At the time of the 2000 Census, the birth rate per 1000 was approximately 14.5. The death rate per 1000 population in 1900 was just over 17, with a spike around 1918 and 1919, due in part to casualties during the First World War. Since then, the death rate has fallen to under 10 per 1000, reaching 8.7 by the 2000 Census. The net difference between birth and death rates was approximately 5.8 per 1000

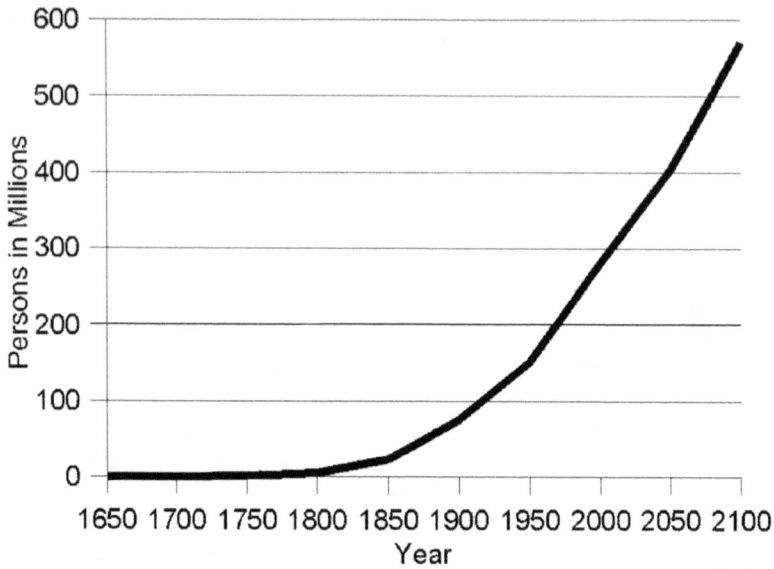

Figure 1. Historical and projected population in the U.S. (U.S. Bureau of Census, 2000a , 2002b).

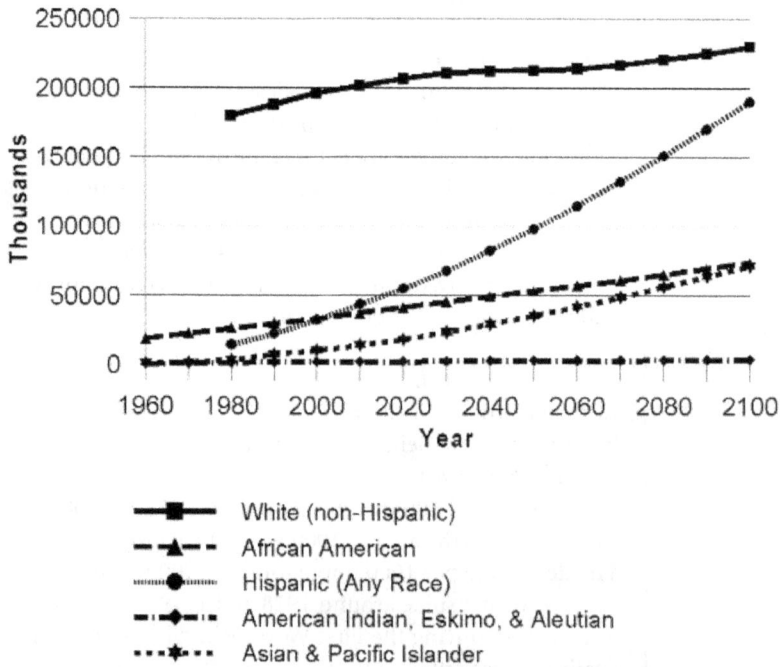

Figure 2. Historic and projected population by race or ethnicity from 1960-2100 (Gibson & Jung 2002; U.S. Bureau of Census, 2000c).

residents per year, or a natural growth estimated at 1.63 million for the year 2000 (U.S. Bureau of Census, 2002).

Longevity

A very significant factor in overall birth and death rates is life expectancy, or longevity. In 1900, the average life span expected for persons born that year was 46.4 years for males and almost 49 years for females. By 1950, life expectancy for males born that year was up to 65.6 years, and for females, to 71.1 years. In 2000, average life spans predicted was 73.7 for males and 79.4 for females. Bell and Miller (2003) predict an average life span of almost 83 years for males and 87 years for females born in 2100.

Net Migration

Each year hundreds of thousands of persons move to or from the United States. The net result has historically been to add population as more people move in than out (U.S. Bureau of Census, 2000a). In 1995, net migration to the U. S. was estimated at approximately +856,000. By 2000, net migration was up to +970,000 (U.S. Bureau of Census, 2000b) The Census Bureau predicts net migration will remain at about the level it was in 2000 through the year 2100, an average net growth of around +935,000 per year. At this rate, over the 100-year period from 2000 to 2100, a net of 93.5 million more people would be added to the U.S. population. Applying the prevailing birth and death rates to this added population would result in an approximate 36 percent growth from immigration alone during the 100 years between 2000 and 2100.

Population Growth

As of April 1, 1990 the country's population was just under 249 million. Based on birth rates, death rates and immigration, the Bureau of Census projected that population would grow to 274.6 million by 2000 (U.S. Bureau of Census, 2000b). However, the recent 2000 Census indicated those early projections were low. Population had grown to more than 281 million by 2000, a growth rate of 13.1 percent since 1990. Figure 1 indicates an expected total population by 2025 of around 337 million, around 403 million by 2050 and almost 570 million by 2100. Thus, a doubling of the population is projected in the United States in just 100 years.

Changing Composition of the Population

Race and Ethnicity

In 1900, 87.9 percent of the U. S. population was White, mostly non-Hispanic. Blacks (also mostly non-Hispanic) composed 11.6 percent of the population. The remaining half percent was mostly either American Indian or Asian Pacific Islander. By 1950, Whites composed almost 89.5 percent of the population and Blacks 10 percent. Very few then were of other races or ethnicity. By 1980, however, this had begun to change: Whites composed 83.1 percent, Blacks 11.7 percent and others the remaining 5.1 percent (see Figure 2). By 2000, non-Hispanic Whites were just 69.1 percent, a dramatically smaller proportion than in earlier decades. Hispanics were 12.5 percent,

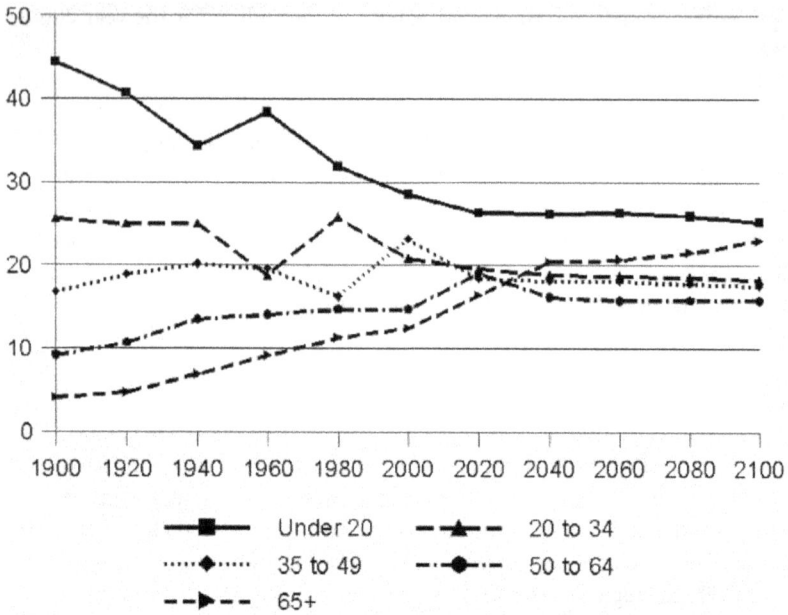

Figure 3. History and projected percent of population by age for the U.S., 1900-2100 (U.S. Bureau of Census, 2000a).

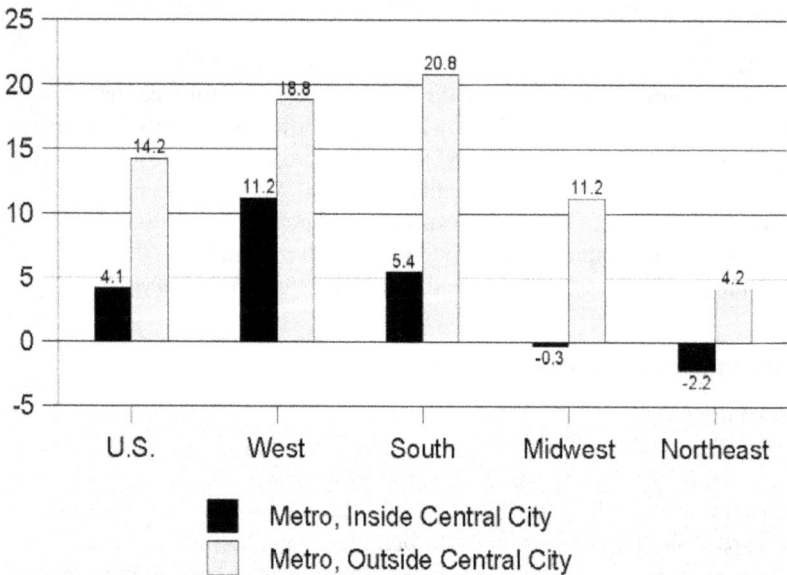

Figure 4. Percentage change in metropolitan population inside and outside of central cities: 1990-99 (Mackun & Wilson, 2000).

and for the first time in U.S. history, exceeded the percentage who were Black. Asians were 3.6 percent, while American Indians were just 0.7 percent in 2000.

Age

In 1900 Census estimates showed nearly 45 percent of the population was younger than 20 years of age (see Figure 3). Persons 20 to 34 made up almost 26 percent of the total population. Persons 65 or over were relatively few, under 5 percent. Over time, however, the distribution of the population among age groups has shifted dramatically. By 2000, less than 30 percent was younger than 20, over 44 percent was 20 to 49, and more than 12 percent was 65 or older. As we progress through the 21st Century, the proportion under 20 will likely continue to drop to around 27 percent by 2100, while the percentage 65 or older will rise to about 23 percent in that year. These two age groups will make up about 50 percent of the population by 2100.

Suburban Expansion

The post World War-II home building boom ushered in the Age of the Suburbs, an age that continues today and contributes to what is referred to as *sprawl*. Figure 4, which shows metropolitan population growth during the 1990s inside and outside of central cities, typifies the long-term trend of people moving out of the central city to the outlying suburbs. During the 1990s, over 80 percent of all new homes were built in the suburbs. As people have moved out of the urban core, so have commercial development and jobs. Massive suburban shopping malls, "big box" discount retail superstores, and franchise restaurants have produced long-term shifts in shopping patterns from downtown central business districts to suburban retail centers. The shift of people and their expenditures to the suburbs has caused the demise of many downtown areas across the U.S. In many metropolitan areas today, 85 to 90 percent of all jobs are in the suburbs, rather than in central cities (Hirschhorn, 2000).

Another dimension of urban sprawl is the increasing per capita development footprint needed to satisfy modern concepts of suburban lifestyles. This means more acres per person for residential, retail, school, road, recreational facility and other development. Data from the National Resources Inventory (NRI) indicate that in the U.S. since 1960, the rate of conversion of rural land to urban and other built-up uses has exceeded the rate of population growth, a trend that generally holds for all the major regions of the nation (Hirschhorn, 2000). Now, compared with former development patterns, home and lot sizes tend to be larger, and they are larger in the suburbs than in the city. This trend toward lower housing density is a hallmark of contemporary urban sprawl.

Rural Impacts of Sprawl and Other Land Use Conversions

The lower 48 states include a total of over 1.9 billion acres of land and water. The majority of this area, 74 percent (almost 1.4 billion acres) is non-federal rural land. These non-federal rural lands include rangeland, forest land, cropland, pastureland and other miscellaneous categories (USDA, 1997). Cropland and pasture together comprise 25.1 percent of non-federal rural area, while developed land is 5.5 percent. Non-federal natural lands, forest and range, are about equal in total area, at 20.9

Year	Cropland	CRP Land	Pasture-land	Rangeland	Forest Land	Other Rural Land	Developed Land	Water Areas
1982	420.4 ± 2.0	0 *	131.4 ± 1.3	414.5 ± 4.3	402.6 ± 2.3	48.3 ± 1.3	72.8 ± 0.7	48.6
1987	406.2 ± 2.0	13.8	127.2 ± 1.2	409.3 ± 4.3	404.4 ± 2.3	48.6 ± 1.3	79.0 ± 0.8	49.8
1992	381.6 ± 2.0	34.0	125.4 ± 1.2	405.9 ± 4.3	403.6 ± 2.3	49.8 ± 1.3	86.5 ± 0.8	49.4
1997	376.4 ± 2.0	32.7	119.5 ± 1.2	404.9 ± 4.3	404.7 ± 2.3	50.3 ± 1.3	97.6 ± 0.9	49.9
2001	369.6 ± 2.3	31.8	116.9 ± 1.7	404.7 ± 4.4	404.9 ± 2.5	51.4 ± 1.5	106.3 ± 1.1	50.3

Source: National Resources Inventory, USDA Natural Resources Conservation Service, Washington DC.

Table 1. Total surface area by land use/land cover and year in millions of acres, with margins of error

percent each. Federal land makes up almost 21 percent of the total area of the 48 lower states; water areas are about 2.6 percent.

Conversion of Rural Land

In Table 1, trends in the total land area by type of cover and use are listed for the years 1982 to 2001. As shown, forest land, water areas, and federal land have remained more or less constant in total acreage since 1982. Consequently, Conservation Reserve Program (CRP) land and developed land has increased (USDA, 1997). Decreasing have been cropland, pastureland, and, to a lesser extent, rangeland (USDA, 2003). In total, an estimated 33.5 million acres of non-federal rural land were developed between 1982 and 2001, a rate of almost 1.8 million acres per year nationally. Between 1997 and 2001, in just four years, the estimated annual rate of development of non-federal rural land was almost 2.2 million acres. As more of its land base is developed, the demise of the once dominant rural America is hastened.

States with Greatest Rural Land Conversion

By magnitude of rural area developed, nine of the top 20, six of the top 10, and all of the top three states are in the South. Texas tops the list with an annual rural-to-developed-land conversion between 1992 and 1997 of almost 179,000 acres per year. Georgia's conversion was almost as large for this period. Combined, Texas, Georgia and Florida, the top three states nationwide, saw more than 514,000 acres developed per year for the period 1992-97. The annual amount of development for the country for the five years of 1992-97 is more than 2.2 million acres.

Fewer Farms and Less Land in Farms

Two additional trends significantly influencing the rural land base during the past century have been increased mechanization and government price supports.

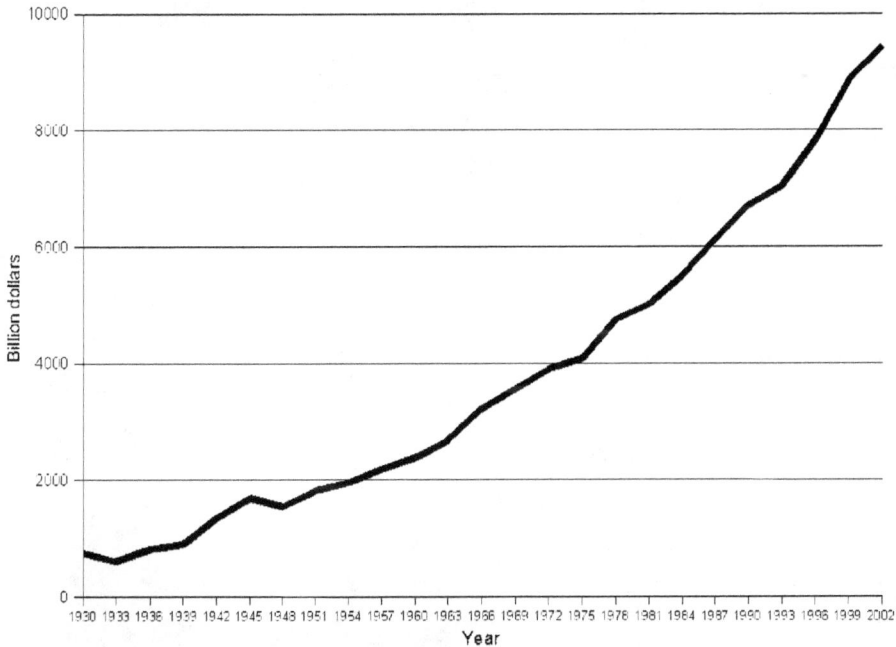

Figure 5. Real gross domestic product, 1930-2002 (U.S. Department of Commerce, 2003).

Together, these trends have encouraged farm owners to increase the size of individual farms, move toward greater crop specialization, and production of larger quantities of a more limited number of products. As a result of gains in efficiencies, fewer but larger farms are now needed to produce sufficient agricultural products to meet demand. Growing competition from non-agricultural land uses together with fewer, more specialized farms nationwide are the major factors behind the decline in overall farm acreage in the country.

Economic Trends
If judged by the size of Real Gross Domestic Product (GDP) and Real GDP per capita, the U.S. economy keeps growing and people keep getting wealthier, with or without recessions. This is one of the most important and far-reaching megatrends in the United States, and all signs point toward continued long-term growth.

Growth of the U. S. Economy
The GDP is the most comprehensive and widely used economic measure in the U.S. Since the Great Depression, the story of the U.S.' economic growth can be told by tracking GDP, which is defined as the market value of all goods and services produced in a given year. Real GDP is a more specific economic measure, and as a measure of growth it is more accurate, since it is adjusted to account for price changes over time (i.e., inflation or deflation). The Real GDP trend line in Figure 5

clearly shows that the size of the U.S. economy, in terms of the amount of material goods and services produced, has continued to increase over time. Relative to the rest of the world, the U. S. population is only 4.6 percent of world population, yet the U. S. economy represents almost one-third of global GDP (World Bank Group, 2003).

Consumer Spending Trends
The huge growth of the U.S. economy, both in terms of real GDP and real GDP per capita, reveals only a part of the U. S. economic story. GDP is composed of four major components: personal consumption expenditures (PCE), gross private domestic investment, net exports of goods and services, and government expenditures and gross investment. PCEs overwhelm the other three GDP components. But on what do Americans spend their incomes? Mostly, it is on material goods and services, and an

PONTUS OBERG

increasing share of this spending has been going to services such as medical, financial, and recreation services. Over the past 20 years, PCEs on services has outpaced nondurable and durable goods expenditures. As of 2002, Americans spent 59 percent of personal consumption expenditures on services, 29 percent on nondurable goods, and 12 percent on durable goods (U.S. Department of Commerce, 2003). Medical care has been the largest single services expenditure category, accounting in 2002 for 59 percent of all service expenditures. While Americans spend, one thing they do not do to any great extent is save. Since the end of World War II, gross savings as a percentage of GDP has been around 15-20 percent (U.S. Department of Commerce, 2003).

Outdoor Recreation
Outdoor recreation is a highly significant aspect of American's lifestyles. Our country began in earnest to evaluate the significance of outdoor recreation in the late 1950s and early 1960s. During that period, the U.S. Congress created and funded the Outdoor Recreation Resources Review Commission (ORRRC) to study demand and supply of outdoor opportunities for Americans. From that time, trends in outdoor recreation are tracked using the National Recreation Survey Series that was begun by ORRRC (Cordell et al., 1996). In this section, we examine long and

short-term trends in Americans' participation in outdoor recreation activities based on data from various applications of the National Recreation Survey.

Historic Trends

Since the first national recreation survey was conducted in 1960, the number of people legally living in this country has increased to more than 285 million. This is population growth of around 100 million in just 43 years. Obviously, population growth has been one of the dominant drivers of outdoor recreation participation growth. Other drivers include economic prosperity, improved personal equipment technology, and better information. Among outdoor activities growing fastest since 1960 were bicycling, camping, canoeing/kayaking and swimming. More recently, in the last 20 years, viewing or photographing birds has ranked as the fastest-growing activity in the United States. There are more than 50 million additional birding participants now than in the early 1980s. Following birding, other growth in the last 20 years include day hiking; backpacking; snowmobiling; attending outdoor concerts, plays and other events; walking for pleasure; camping in developed sites; canoeing or kayaking; running or jogging; downhill skiing; and; swimming in natural waters.

Current Trends, Since 1995

The most popular activities in 2000-01 (i.e., those having the most participants) included walking for pleasure, outdoor family gatherings, and visiting a beach. These are the same activities that were at the top of surveys in 1994-95. Of the overall 62 activities examined through the National Survey on Recreation and the Environment, many at the top of the list, when ranked by percentage growth from 1994-95 to 2000-01, are physically demanding. Highly physical and challenging sports, such as kayaking, snowboarding, backpacking, and mountain climbing, typically require specialized equipment and skills that not everyone possesses. Together with larger numbers of people participating in outdoor activities, this means very noticeable differences between what one would have witnessed at a typical outdoor area in earlier times, such as in 1960, versus now. While many of the activities at or near the top of this list do not represent large numbers of added people (e.g., kayaking), others not much further down the list have increased more substantially. Numbers viewing and photographing wildlife, for example, have risen by over 34 million. Over the years, however, regardless of activity or region of the country, outdoor recreation has grown steadily as a significant land use.

Implications for Natural Resources

The World and especially the United States are changing at a pace unprecedented in history. Population growth, changing composition of the population, urban growth and sprawl, development of rural lands, economic growth, rising consumer spending, and outdoor recreation participation together have and will continue to change this country. There are five areas where these trends collectively will likely have profound consequences.

A Smaller Rural Land Base

By the year 2025 the population of the United States is projected to grow to around 337 million. This is an additional 56 million persons in just 25 years. In large part due to this population growth, it is projected that the U. S. could lose an estimated 45± million acres of rural land to development between 2000 and 2025 (assuming continuation of the historical development rate). Thus, for each additional 1,000 people, there could be a corresponding loss to development of almost 804 acres of forest, range, pasture, cropland and other rural land. While this may seem small relative to the total land base of the United States, from another perspective, it is large. It is large because much of the rural land that is most subject to development often lies close to metropolitan areas, public lands, riparian areas, rivers, other water bodies, and prime agricultural land. Development is long-term, if not permanent, and future options for other uses are severely restricted. In addition, other rural land becomes more scarce and of higher market value, affordable usually to only a few of the highest bidders.

A More Fragmented Rural Land Base

As growing population and wealth drive development of rural land for residential and commercial purposes, there typically will be added rounds of development and land modification for highways, railroads, utility corridors, water and sewage treatment facilities, fences, and other infrastructure to support residential and commercial developments. Combined, residential, commercial and infrastructure development usually result in significant fragmentation of natural ecosystems and habitat, a consequence that has been identified as perhaps the dominant ecological issue in contemporary United States. Few would argue against a conclusion that development and its associated infrastructure result in less naturally functioning land to serve as habitat for wildlife and aquatic species, and to provide clean air and water. In all likelihood, fragmentation will remain a highly significant ecological issue in the future as development of rural lands continues. As well, few would argue that the aesthetic and scenic character of rural lands is not greatly compromised by roads and other construction activity.

Disproportionate Pressures on Public Lands for Recreation and Raw Materials

A natural and very predictable outcome of a shrinking and further fragmented private rural land base is greater pressure on public lands. In the 1990s, between 15 and 20 percent of rural private land had been open to the public for recreation. Recently, however, less of the private rural land base has been open for the public's use, shrinking to around 11 percent at the beginning of the 21st Century. Together with a shrinking overall rural land area, privately owned lands in the future are likely to play a smaller role in providing outdoor recreation and other land uses. As projections show continuing growth of outdoor recreation (Cordell et al., 1999), greater pressures are likely for the use of public lands, which are nearly constant in overall area and facility infrastructure over time.

In addition to outdoor recreation, there are growing demands for raw materials for manufacturing. Yet, rising numbers of rural land owners are more interested in protecting the natural character of their land than in commercial uses (Cordell et al., 1999). Public lands in some areas of the country may seem the only viable option for recreation, minerals, water, forage, timber, and other raw materials.

Greater Conflicts and Competition for Access

As the uses of public lands and other rural lands grow and diversify, there undoubtedly will be greater competition for the space, resources and facilities they afford. This will and has been leading to greater conflicts and more competition for access. Interests in oil drilling, mining, timber harvesting, motorized outdoor recreation, non-motorized outdoor recreation, preservation, water diversions, and many other interests will increasingly compete for access to the resources, space, and amenities on public lands. These conflicts will not be resolved easily and will require well developed policy, legislation and in all likelihood, improved legal mitigation processes. It is imperative that the values and features of public lands held in highest esteem by the general public,

BRETT BRUYERE

more so than local or special interests, be a significant part of these proceedings. For the most part, the public considers clean water, protection for future generations, wildlife habitat, and naturalness as the most highly valued purposes for public forests (Tarrant, Cordell & Green, 2003). In the eyes of the public, these uses are often at odds with motorized and resource extraction uses.

Less Connection between People and the Land

As population grows; as urban development expands; as more people live in urban surroundings; as people increasingly rely on air conditioning in the home, workplace or transportation; and as greater proportions of people work in service instead of farming or other on-the-land jobs, there is less and less connection between people and the land. Less "connectiveness" with forests, rangelands, watersheds or any other generally defined aspect of natural resources will mean less understanding of the relationships and dependency of human and all life on the natural world. In the United States, food, shelter, medicines, and other needs for most people are met by purchasing goods and services in grocery stores, pharmacies, and other commercial establishments. Not seen by the vast majority of people are the industrial croplands, pastures, forest operations, ranches, water diversion projects, and other operations from which the goods they purchase originate.

359

Without such consciousness, people are challenged to understand the relationship between their lifestyle choices, their consumption patterns, and the management and condition of natural lands.

Where might this disconnect lead? One can only speculate. But, it is clear that in recent years rising economic wealth and real purchasing power has led to greater and greater consumption, more intensive and extensive use of natural resources and greater amounts of waste. Rising economic status for a substantial and growing number of Americans has also led to migration to rural areas for home development, and for many, to greater use of large, heavy, fuel inefficient vehicles of many kinds. Ability to afford large homes, fuel-hungry vehicles and consumptive lifestyles in many different forms has led to greater extraction of raw materials and demand of non-renewable energy. These increased demands in turn mean greater drilling, greater amounts of mining, larger farm operations and many other forms of on-the-land production operations to produce gasoline, home heating fuels, electricity, steel, water for irrigating, feed for meat animals, food for humans, and many other forms of increased production and consumption. While there are many, many wonderful aspects and comforts to our modern, consumptive society, one wonders how sustainable it is.

References

Bell, F.C., & Miller, M.L. (2003). *Actuarial Study 116: Period life expectancies at selected ages by sex and calendar year.* Retrieved October 20, 2003, from http://www.ssa.gov/OACT/NOTES/as116/as116_Tbl_10.html#wp1098786 .

Cordell, H.K., Betz, C.J., Bowker, J.M., English, D.B.K., Mou, S.H., Bergstrom, J.C., et al. (1999). *Outdoor recreation in American life: A national assessment of demand and supply trends.* Champaign, IL: Sagamore.

Cordell, H.K., McDonald, B.L., Lewis, B., Miles, M., Martin, J., & Bason, J. (1996). United States of America. In G. Cushman, A. J. Veal, & J. Zuzanek (Eds.), *World leisure participation: Free time in the global village* (pp. 215-225). Oxon, UK: CAB International.

Gibson, C., & Jung, K. (2002). *United States—Race and Hispanic origin: 1790-1990.* Retrieved October 20, 2003 from http://www.census.gov/population/documentation/twps0056/tab01.pdf.

Hirschhorn, J.S. (2000). *Growing pains: Quality of life in the new economy.* Washington, DC: National Governors Association.

Mackun, P. J., & Wilson, S. R. (2000). *Population trends in metropolitan areas and central cities, 1990 to 1998.* Retrieved October 20, 2003 from http://www.census.gov/prod/2000pubs.pdf

Tarrant, M.A., Cordell, H.K., & Green, G.T. (2003). PVF: A scale to measure public values of forests. *Journal of Forestry, 101*(6), 24-30.

U.S. Bureau of Census (2000a). *Components for the total resident population.* Retrieved October 20, 2003, from http://www.census.gov/population/projections/nation/summary/np-t6-a.txt.

U.S. Bureau of Census (2000b). Population projections of total resident population. Retrieved October 20, 2003, from http://www.census.gov/population/projections/nation/summary/np-t2.txt.

U.S. Bureau of Census (2000c). Projections of the total resident population by 5-year age groups, race and Hispanic origin with special age categories. Retrieved October 20, 2003, from http://www.census.gov/population/projections/nation/summary/.

U.S. Bureau of Census (2002a). *Births, deaths, marriages and divorces: 1800 to 2000.* Retrieved October 20, 2003, from http://www.census.gov/prod/2003pubs/02statab/vitstat.pdf.

U.S. Bureau of Census (2002b). *Population and area: 1790 to 2000.* Retrieved October 20, 2003, from http://www.census.gov/2003pubs/02statab/pop.pdf

U.S. Department of Agriculture (1997). *Conservation Reserve Program, USDA Farm Service Agency fact sheet.* Retrieved October 20, 2003, from http://www.fsa.usda.gov/pas/publications/facts/crp1.pdf

U.S. Department of Agriculture (2003). *National resources inventory 2001: Land use report.* Retrieved October 20, 2003, from http://www.nrcs.usda.gov/technical/land/nri01/nri01lu.html

U.S. Department of Commerce, Bureau of Economic Analysis. (2003). *National income and product accounts.* Washington, DC: U.S. Department of Commerce, Bureau of Economic Analysis.

World Bank Group (2003). *Total GDP 2002.* Retrieved October 7, 2003, from http://www.worldbank.org/data/databytopic/GDP.pdf.

www.ingramcontent.com/pod-product-compliance
Lightning Source LLC
Chambersburg PA
CBHW070609030426
42337CB00020B/3720